SUBVERSIVE INTENT

SUBVERSIVE INTENT

Gender, Politics, and the Avant-Garde

SUSAN RUBIN SULEIMAN

HARVARD UNIVERSITY PRESS
Cambridge, Massachusetts, and London, England

Library of Congress Cataloging-in-Publication Data

Suleiman, Susan Rubin, 1939–
    Subversive intent: gender, politics, and the avant-garde /
    Susan Rubin Suleiman.
        p.   cm.
    Includes bibliographical references (p.   ).
    ISBN 0-674-85383-0 (alk. paper)
    1. French literature—20th century—History and criticism.
    2. Literature, Experimental—History and criticism.
    3. Feminism and literature—History—20th century.
    4. Women and literature—History—20th century.
    5. Erotic literature—History and criticism.
    6. Postmodernism (Literature).
    7. Sex role in literature.
    I. Title.
PQ307.E95S85   1990   89-27458
840.9′352042—dc20   CIP

Designed by Gwen Frankfeldt

To Michael and Daniel

ACKNOWLEDGMENTS

Many people have contributed to my thinking about this book: my students at Harvard, with whom I have spent several years discussing (and fruitfully arguing about) "women and the avant-garde" and related matters; scholars whose work has provided inspiration and occasion for dialogue, as I have tried to acknowledge throughout; and members of various study groups, especially the Cambridge "theory group" in 1983 and 1984 and the "mothers' group" in 1985 and 1986. In addition, this work benefited from the challenging discussions in the 1987 and 1989 Harvard Summer Institutes on the Study of Avant-Gardes, which I organized and codirected with Alice Jardine.

It is a special pleasure to thank the friends and colleagues who provided suggestions and criticisms for individual chapters, as well as intellectual sustenance over the years. I have benefited for a long time from my ongoing or recurrent conversations with Mieke Bal, Janet Bergstrom, Christine Brooke-Rose, Dorrit Cohn, Danielle Haase-Dubosc, Marianne Hirsch, Denis Hollier, Nancy Huston, Alice Jardine, Barbara Johnson, David Lodge, Nancy Miller, Thomas Pavel, Gerald Prince, Naomi Schor. Over the past few years, it has been a particular help to me to exchange ideas relating to this book with Patricia Boudoin, Svetlana Boym, Whitney Chadwick, Rikki Ducornet, Elinor Fuchs, Marjorie Garber, Bernard Gendron, Carol Gilligan, Heidi Gilpin, Ingeborg Hoesterey, Andreas Huyssen, Rosalind Krauss, Richard Martin, Ruth Perry, Régine Robin, Mary Russo, Ernst Van Alphen, Marina Warner, Patricia Yaeger. I am aware that such lists are inadequate, at once too long and incomplete. To those I may have neglected to mention, my apologies; to all, my warm thanks.

A year-long fellowship, in 1984, from the Rockefeller Foundation in the Humanities allowed me to think seriously about the shape of this book and to write some of the longer essays in it. A Guggenheim Fellowship in 1988–89 allowed me to bring the book to completion—partly in Belmont, Massachusetts, and partly in Paris, where—as I explain in Chapter 8—the atmosphere felt particularly "postmodern." I thank both foundations for their generous support.

Earlier versions of the Prologue and Chapters 1–6 appeared in the following journals or volumes (in order): *Novel*, Winter/Spring 1988; *Yale French Studies*, 75 (1988); *Studies in Twentieth-Century Literature*, 6, nos. 1–2 (1982); *Romanic Review*, 68, no. 1 (1977); *The Poetics of Gender*, ed. Nancy K. Miller (New York: Columbia University Press, 1986); *Discourse in Psychoanalysis and Literature*, ed. Shlomith Rimmon-Kenan (New York and London: Methuen, 1987); *The Female Body in Western Culture: Contemporary Perspectives*, ed. Susan Rubin Suleiman (Cambridge, Mass.: Harvard University Press, 1986).

My editor at Harvard University Press, Margaretta Fulton, provided hot lunches and heartwarming enthusiasm and, most important, excellent editorial advice and efficiency for which I am most grateful. Elizabeth Hurwit did a superb job as manuscript editor.

I thank Susan Fuerst for her efficient, always cheerful work as typist and "first reader." For their indispensable help as research assistants, I thank Clare Parsons and (at earlier stages) David McCarthy and Louise Wills.

My special thanks to Barbara Kruger for sending me generous samplings of her work, for patiently discussing its technical aspects, and for allowing its liberal use and reproduction in this book.

Finally, to my family, immediate and extended, I owe the sense of connectedness and hope for the future without which, I believe, no really sustained work can be accomplished. I am especially grateful to— and for—my sister, Eve Rubin Sprotzer, whose love and laughter have lightened many of my days. Thanks to my children, Michael and Daniel, I have known the "laugh of the mother" as a lived reality, not only as a myth.

Belmont, Massachusetts
August 1989

CONTENTS

ILLUSTRATIONS

INTRODUCTION

In December 1982, after more than twenty years of continuous presence on the international intellectual scene, the French avant-garde journal (as it had long characterized itself and been characterized by others) *Tel Quel* published its last issue. Without tears, without grandiose farewells—without the slightest indication that number 94 would not be followed by 95.

In truth, for a while already, *Tel Quel* had been preparing its demise. Or, if one prefers, its transfiguration—for the first issue of a new journal, *L'Infini,* with the same directeur (Philippe Sollers), the same kind of layout and cover (down to the typeface in which the titles were set), many of the same authors, but a different publisher (the venerable house of Gallimard, rather than the postwar upstart, Editions du Seuil) appeared in spring 1983, without missing a beat. This time, there was an opening editorial to explain the shift; it was in the form of a dialogue between two unidentified voices, those of a "typical" Parisian questioner and Sollers. "*Tel Quel* has stopped and *L'Infini* begun. What do you mean by that?" the questioner asks. Sollers replies it was not "we who stopped *Tel Quel.*" The old publisher would not release the title, insisted on keeping it. Now it was dead. But there is nothing to regret, he says two pages later: "*L'Infini* is a much better title than *Tel Quel.* Which was only a threshold [*seuil*—a belittling pun on the abandoned publisher], which in any case had had its day."[1]

Tel Quel had had more than a day. For well over a decade, starting with the heady days and months that preceded May 1968, its name not only had been synonymous with the radically new—new conceptions of writing, of language, of subjectivity, of history, promising to revolutionize the "human sciences," including philosophy and the study of literature, in France and elsewhere—but also had represented, for many people, the latest incarnation of the European avant-garde. Like its historical precursor, Surrealism, *Tel Quel* considered itself a collective movement with a doubly revolutionary program. "One cannot make an economic and social revolution without making at the same time, and on a different level, a symbolic revolution." This declaration by Sollers, speaking for *Tel Quel* in 1970, appeared like a distant echo of André

Breton's often-quoted statement, made in a speech in 1935: "'Transform the world,' said Marx; 'change life,' said Rimbaud: for us, these two watchwords are one."[2]

What, then, happened between the brave (if not altogether new) words of 1970 and the flippant self-dismissal of 1983? *Tel Quel* discovered, according to Sollers, that the dream of the avant-garde was a delusion. Looking back in 1981 on his own hopes of a decade earlier, Sollers told an interviewer: "I was in that utopia, which I no longer have at all now, that the revolution in language and the revolution in action are things that must absolutely go hand in hand. It is an idea that comes from the formalists and the surrealists in a certain way. It is the illusion of the European avant-gardes of the 20th century, which must be completely abandoned because it is an error to want everything to advance at the same speed."[3] And already a year earlier, he had stated in another interview: "I think that this history of the European avant-gardes is over too, because it is linked to a very specific period . . . It has become academic, the avant-garde, you understand. The avant-garde poet is perfectly foreseen on the checkerboard, he no longer has any subversive function, he is asked to do his little thing and not ask any questions, to be just a little bit hermetic, erotic, esoteric, formalist, but not to ask any embarrassing questions. That is why I no longer agree with this concept of the avant-garde."[4] In short, the "collective idea" was over.[5] *Tel Quel* was dead in more than its name.

Why begin this book with an ending? What does the ending, almost ten years ago, of a small Parisian journal—however influential or "avant-garde"—have to do with gender and politics? And what do those relations have to do with a present that seems to define itself primarily as an age of "post": postmodern, post-Marxist, post-Freudian, post-feminist, post–avant-garde, post-post?

To try and answer those questions directly now would be tantamount to summarizing everything that follows. And since what follows is no more than a series of partial answers, complicated by further questions and coming from multiple, not always obviously compatible directions and perspectives, such an attempt at a summary would necessarily fail. Which does not mean that I lack conviction or a point of view, or that I wish to exploit the by now no doubt wearisome deconstructive move that consists in refusing to state any thesis without immediately cutting the ground from under its feet. The fact is, I envisaged this book from the start as a set of overlapping essays, ranging over a certain historical and theoretical territory without attempting to "cover" it in systematic fashion. This decision may have been provoked, in part, by the tight construction of my previous book, which called for a reaction.[6] But it was prompted above all by the nature of the territory: shifting ground seems best dealt with by movement.

The essays in this book do not present a "theory of the avant-garde," although they engage in ongoing dialogue with a number of theories. Nor do they present a chronological account of twentieth-century avant-garde movements, although in their zigzagging way they move between the historical marking posts of Surrealism and postmodernism—and concurrently between France and the United States, with a few resting points in England. Common to them all is a concern with the political potential and implications of avant-garde artistic practices. This concern is itself the result of my understanding, which I share with a number of other theorists, that the hallmark of an avant-garde practice or project— or dream—is the attempt to effect radical change and innovation *both* in the symbolic field (including what has been called the aesthetic realm) *and* in the social and political field of everyday life. Where this book differs most sharply from other, often-cited general "theories of the avant-garde"—some of which I myself cite in Chapter 1—is that it introduces as major categories into the theoretical discussion gender and the politics of gender.

In Chapter 5 I remark that an essay by a critic I admire exists at the conjunction of three major moments or movements in recent French thought: the Lacanian psychoanalytic moment, with its emphasis on specularity and the problematics of self and Other; the deconstructive moment, with its emphasis on textual rhetoric and self-reflexiveness; and the feminist moment, with its political and theoretical emphasis on the exclusion of women from traditional discourse, including the discourse of psychoanalysis. The essays in this book can be situated at the same conjunction, to which I would, however, add a fourth moment: the postmodern, which I interpret as that moment of extreme (perhaps tragic, perhaps playful) self-consciousness when the present—our present—takes to reflecting on its relation to the past and to the future primarily as a problem of repetition. How does one create a future that will acknowledge and incorporate the past—a past that includes, in our very own century, some of the darkest moments in human history— without repeating it? How does one look at the past with understanding, yet critically, in the etymological sense of "critical" (from Greek *krinein*, to separate, choose), which has to do with discrimination and choice *in* the present? These, it seems to me, are the questions that provide the urgency, as well as the apparently inexhaustible energy, of the contemporary "debate on postmodernism."

Not coincidentally, they are also questions that have been central both to contemporary thinking about avant-gardes and to feminist literary theory and criticism. The question for the avant-garde, as Peter

Bürger and many others who have reflected on the history of European avant-garde movements have made clear, is how to avoid the impasse of recuperation, whereby "the avant-garde poet is perfectly foreseen on the checkerboard"—or, as Marcelin Pleynet put it in an early issue of *Tel Quel,* whereby "in our time, no more transgression, no more subversion, no more rupture," only "a parody of transgression, a parody of subversion, a simulacrum, repetition of rupture."[7] The question for feminist literary theory is how to read the works of the past (and of the present) critically, without simplifying them; without reducing every opposition to a qualitative difference between "masculine" and "feminine," for example; without reading (and writing) always the same story, no matter how edifying or ideologically "correct" it may appear.

In these essays, the question of reading is probably the one that recurs most often, in a number of guises. First, I am concerned not only with "how to read" certain problematic, exemplarily modern texts, visual or verbal, by men and women, and *as* men or women, but also with how to read theories that have been elaborated to account for and justify a given way of reading, or that underlie a reading without necessarily being formulated. Chapters 2, 3, and 4 are most explicitly devoted to these questions, which are present, with varying degrees of emphasis, in every other chapter as well.

The question of reading applies to more than texts, as our everyday language indicates: "Do you read me?" "How do you read where we're at?" To read is also to try and make sense of one's life; it is to interpret, as best one can at a given moment (hence, never definitively) the historical, cultural, and existential situations that have led to the present. Reading in this sense—which defines, of course, the project of psychoanalysis but a great many other projects as well—is never gratuitous, never "self-sufficient," never innocent. It is, inevitably, *motivated* (situated, to use the Sartrean word), and it is oriented toward a future. How we read Surrealism today, for example, is neither a purely textual question nor a purely historical one. It is both; and the questions we—or I—ask about Surrealist texts are determined both by Surrealism's history (itself "to be read") and by our (my) own.

Is it because of my history that I return so regularly, and with increasing emphasis throughout this book, to the figure—image, body, voice—of the mother? The mother denied or displaced, played with and over and on, the object of apparently endless inventions in the perverse games of transgressive sons; the mother repudiated by rebellious daughters, or else idealized. The mother finally moving, laughing and playing, a subject—my contribution, as a trope to live on or as an enabling myth (note that I say *a,* not *the*) to the "theory of the avant-garde."

The aesthetic as well as political implications of this trope or myth or figure will gather momentum as the book advances. Here, I want to suggest only one of them, more as speculation than as elaborated argument. An argument I do elaborate, in Chapter 7, concerns the relation between contemporary avant-garde women writers and artists and their male predecessors, notably their predecessors in the so-called historical European avant-gardes. Unlike some feminist critics, who tend to emphasize only the substantive (existential and ideological) differences and hostilities between women's work and men's, I argue for the recognition of both differences and joint allegiances between the male avant-gardes and contemporary feminists, as well as for the recognition of multiple differences between and among women artists. Specifically, I argue that a double allegiance characterizes much of the best contemporary work by women: on the one hand, an allegiance to the formal experiments and some of the cultural aspirations of the historical male avant-gardes; on the other hand, an allegiance to the feminist critique of dominant sexual ideologies, including the sexual ideology of those same avant-gardes.

In short, I argue for complication and fine distinctions over simple oppositions, for internal divisions and double allegiances, even at the expense of disorder and a certain clutter. Although I will not claim that mothers live most intimately with disorder and clutter, I do believe that a mother knows internal division and double allegiance as a daily experience; and if she has borne a child, she knows these as a bodily experience as well. If, in addition, she is a mother of sons (here I return to my own history), she may also, very likely, be unwilling to consider the other sex as always and only "other."

Speculation, as I say. Mothers, like other humans, have no exclusive or categorical claims to exemplariness.[8] Let me not be accused, therefore, of easy idealization or self-satisfied self-mythification. Consider this, merely, as an introductory indulgence.

Having been written over a period of several years, these essays could themselves trace a certain history, both personal and collective. However, rather than leave those that were previously published "as is," I have preferred to revise them in light of my present thinking, which is most fully represented in the last two essays, appearing here for the first time. (The only exception is Chapter 3, which I have left almost completely untouched and unretouched, for reasons I explain in the introductory note to that chapter.)

I have not arranged the essays chronologically, that is, either in the order in which they were written or in the order of the subjects they treat. Although in a general way the book moves from Surrealism to postmodernism, it does not do so in a single or simple line. Following the Prologue, whose subject is general (not to say "eternal"), Chapter 1 deals chiefly with the historical place of women in the Surrealist movement—after discussing the theoretical question of margins and their relation to both women and avant-gardes, however. The ending of Chapter 1 suggests that I will discuss in some detail (that is, read) works by women associated with the Surrealist movement and by women associated with the renewal of feminism, particularly in France, after 1968; which I do, but not until Chapter 5, and even there only in part. Chapters 2, 3, and 4, meanwhile, explore the question of reading, specifically as concerns those quintessentially problematic modern works (by, as it happens, male writers) that have been called "unreadable" or transgressive, the directions of this exploration being chiefly psychoanalytic and rhetorical.

In Chapter 5 I return to Surrealism, this time textually as well as historically. I discuss in some detail what is perhaps the best-known Surrealist text, Breton's *Nadja,* juxtaposing it with a woman's text from the 1960s and reading both in relation to the discourse of psychoanalysis from Charcot to Lacan, via Freud. Chapters 6 and 7 deliver the original promise about reading women's work, but necessarily inflected by all the intervening subjects, in every sense of that term. Chapter 8, finally, moves from specific readings-in-a-theoretical-perspective to the exclusively "meta" discourse of theory, indeed of theory about theory, meta-meta; ending with a "look to the future."

The future: is that not what the "collective idea" (or dream—but not to be dismissed as "only a dream") of the avant-garde has always been compellingly about?

PROLOGUE

Playing and Modernity

> It is clear that the world is parodic, which is to say that each thing
> one looks at is the parody of another, or else the same thing in a
> parodic form.
>
> —GEORGES BATAILLE

> What tedium. And I call that playing.
>
> —SAMUEL BECKETT

There is nothing quite like the idea of play to get us into a muddle.

Does all playing involve a game? Are all games playful? What's the difference between playing with and playing against? Playing at and playing on? Playing up and playing down, playing to and playing around? And what about "just playing"? Do all games have players? Does all play have players? Does the game stop if there is no one around to see it—or to play it?

Little wonder that, when trying to explain what he meant by a "concept with blurred edges," Wittgenstein chose the example of "game."[1] And that when Gregory Bateson, a playful man, was faced with such questions, he invented the metalogue. "A metalogue is a conversation about some problematic subject. This conversation should be such that not only do the participants discuss the problem but the structure of the conversation as a whole is also relevant to the same subject." And in case that sounds easy, Bateson adds: "Only some of the conservations here presented achieve this double format."[2]

In Bateson's metalogues, the speakers are anonymous (perhaps symbolic?) figures, identified only as the Father and the Daughter. The Daughter asks, "Daddy, why do things get in a muddle?" "Why do Frenchmen?" "Why a Swan?" "Daddy, are these conversations serious?" The Father replies, mostly, in one form or other, "What do you mean?" And then the conversation starts. The endings vary, but they never provide an answer. And the metalogue on games and being serious ends with the Father replying, to the Daughter's question, "Why do kittens and puppies play?" "I don't know—I don't know."

Why is playing modern? Why is the modern playful? I don't know, I don't know. But the rules of the game we are playing now require that I make a case for the connection between playing and modernity, coherently if at all possible, and not waste time playing games. Therefore, with a lingering *au revoir* to the Father and his Daughter (for I shall come back to them, you may be sure—and to the Mother too, if she is somewhere to be found), I turn my discourse down a more disciplined and clearly laid out path.

Pleasures of Theory

That modern art and literature, and modern writing about art and literature, are preoccupied with the question of play is a truism, which according to my dictionary is a statement so self-evident as scarcely to need to be stated. From Mallarmé's dice-throw (which appears to be an obligatory reference point, if not necessarily a point of origin, for any discourse about the modern) through Surrealist parlor games, Oulipian exercises, Joycean punnings, Steinian button games, Beckettian endgames, Cooverian baseball games, Robbe-Grilletian mirror games, Borgesian labyrinths, Bataillian rituals, Barthian funhouses, etcetera, etcetera—modern writing is rife with play. Any theory of modern writing must therefore be, at the same time, a theory of play. In its tidiest form, such a theory is descriptive and classificatory. (By calling it tidy I am in no way suggesting that it is valueless, merely that it has the values proper to it, no loose ends.) Bracketing the philosophical questions which might get it into a muddle, this theorizing starts with questions it can answer by working at them. For example: How are games and playing thematized, or otherwise inscribed in literary texts? What are some specifically modern modes of such inscription? By looking at a great many different texts, or choosing a single writer whose work offers a particularly rich field for investigation, one can arrive at potentially generalizable results.

Thus in the short essay "Games and Game Structures in Robbe-Grillet," published already some years ago, Bruce Morrissette suggested three different, mutually nonexclusive ways in which games are inscribed in Robbe-Grillet's fiction and films: the game as internal reduplication or *mise en abyme,* like the various games played by the characters in *L'Année dernière à Marienbad;* the game as an "inner principle of organization left unrevealed to the reader," like the tarot game which (together with the Oedipus myth) structures but is never explicitly mentioned in *Les Gommes (The Erasers);* and the game as a metaphor or allegory for the activity of writing, like the labyrinth pattern in *Dans le labyrinthe.*[3]

Although Morrissette did not attempt to generalize his observations or pursue them beyond the descriptive level (other than to say, in conclusion, "It would be possible to argue that since Raymond Roussel, the creation of novels on game premises has given rise to certain tendencies in fiction leading away from the 'serious' thematics . . . associated with the novel in the mind of the public"), I find his essay, even today, full of interesting implications. His three categories, for instance, can obviously be extended to works other than Robbe-Grillet's. In George Perec's great novel *La Vie mode d'emploi* (rendered, in David Bellos's prize-winning translation, as *Life: A User's Manual*), the jigsaw puzzle appears as both a *mise en abyme* (the main character, one Percival Bartlebooth, literally spends his life creating and unmaking puzzles) and as a metaphor for the kind of writing that Perec is practicing, as well as for one kind of reading that his novel solicits. In addition to the jigsaw puzzle, which is explicitly thematized and is accompanied by other thematized games such as riddles, crossword puzzles, and mathematical games of various kinds, *La Vie mode d'emploi* uses at least two systems of implicit formal constraints, modeled on an expanded chessboard and on a complicated mathemaical figure, the *bi-carré latin orthogonal d'ordre 10*. For details on all this, I refer you to Warren Motte's delightfully informative book on Perec, *The Poetics of Experiment*.[4] My point here is simply that Morrissette's categories are applicable to, and serve interestingly to order, many other texts besides Robbe-Grillet's.

Furthermore, these categories allow one to raise other theoretical questions. For example, what is the role of the unstated "inner principle of organization" in a reading of the text? Its role in the *writing* of the text is clear enough, for it functions like any other formal constraint: it sets a "task" for the writer's ingenuity to solve. Perec was notoriously fond of this kind of game and was diabolically clever at it; witness his "hypogrammatic" novel, *La Disparition*, which in over two hundred pages of intelligible narrative never once uses the most frequent vowel in the French language, the letter *e*. It is almost unbelievable (yet true) that some of *La Disparition*'s first readers didn't notice the disappearance in *The Disappearance*. Much more likely, however, is that most readers of *La Vie mode d'emploi* would never notice, without being told, the expanded chessboard structure and the *bi-carré latin orthogonal d'ordre 10*. In *La Disparition,* I believe, a great deal of the reader's pleasure consists in following—and admiring—as one reads the author's verbal resourcefulness, his veritable tour de force. Therefore, not to notice the absence of the *e* is to be deprived of an essential pleasure, and in fact no one nowadays reads that book who doesn't already know, and enjoy, the game. In *La Vie mode d'emploi,* however, I wonder whether a knowledge of the mathematical organizing principles adds much to the actual pleasure of reading? I tend to think not, although I may be wrong.

That is the kind of question we tidy theorists savor. Here are a few more to sink our teeth into: Is the game of pebbles in Beckett's *Molloy* a *mise en abyme* or a metaphor for writing, or both? Ditto for the bullfight and the obscene games with eggs and bull testicles that the narrator plays with his friend Simone in Bataille's *Story of the Eye*. Should we distinguish between "primary" games and "secondary" games (like the puzzle versus other represented games in *La Vie mode d'emploi*) in our thematic readings? Are there comic versus tragic thematizations of play? When Malone says, "Now it is a game, I am going to play," and soon after says, "It is playtime now," and not long after that says, "What tedium. And I call that playing,"[5] is that progression comic or tragic—or is the question itself badly put? Besides being a metaphor for writing, can play also be a metaphor for living? Perec's Bartlebooth (whose name is itself a game, calling other texts into play: Parsifal, Bartleby, Barnabooth) dies while working on his four hundred and thirty-ninth puzzle; Malone dies while spinning out his most ambitious piece of narrative invention, which is what he calls play; and so on.

Finally, can we define criteria for distinguishing the modern "playful" text and modern thematizations of play from earlier ones (for obviously, thematization of play in literature is not a new phenomenon, witness Rabelais and the Grands Rhétoriqueurs, as well as nineteenth-century realist fiction such as *The Gambler*)? Might we say that it is the over-determined *coexistence* of play as *mise en abyme*, as implicit organizing principle, and as metaphor for writing and living that is specific to modern texts? Or should we, in addition (or instead?) try to categorize and distinguish specifically modern kinds, or clusters of kinds, of games and playing: sado-erotic play (in which case our starting reference point would have to be not Mallarmé but the Marquis) and more generally playing as fantasy, or playing as free invention, as mastery, as mockery, as parody (which is a form of what Roger Caillois calls mimicry), as self-mutilation (which Bataille would call *le jeu majeur*), as transgression, as perversion, as *jouissance*, as "an absolutely de-centered game," as . . .

Hello, Mr. Bateson. I didn't expect to see you again so soon.

In other words, there is no such thing as a totally tidy theory of playing and modernity—or of anything else, probably. The very search for tidiness and attempt to eliminate loose ends, if carried far enough, leads to the recognition of blurred edges.

But if that's the case, then we might as well have fun. Or as Roland Barthes would have put it, we might as well take our pleasure wherever—and however—we can. I therefore offer this bit of conversation, in the spirit of Gregory Bateson doubled by that of (perhaps) Julia Kristeva.

Metapolylogue: On Playing and Modernity

FATHER (*reading aloud from a book*). "As has rightly been noted, girls' fantasy toys are meant to imitate local, domestic, realistic behavior, whereas those for boys evoke activities that are faraway, fantastical, inaccessible or even downright unreal."[6]

(*Enter* DAUGHTER.)

DAUGHTER. Daddy, when I play at being Mommy, am I serious?
FATHER. I don't know, dear. Are you?
DAUGHTER. It depends. If I'm telling my doll to do her homework or to wash her hands before dinner, then yes, I'm very serious. But if I'm tickling her to make her laugh, then I'm joking.
FATHER. I see. And what happens when I tell you to stop playing and come help me take the garbage out?
DAUGHTER. Daddy, don't be dumb. Then we're working.
FATHER. But don't we sometimes have fun—like when I bang the lids together and you go oompa—oompa—oompapa?
DAUGHTER. Yes, but then we're playing.
FATHER. Oh, I thought we were taking the garbage out.

(*Enter the* MOTHER, *disguised as Georges Bataille, bearing a plate of bull testicles.*)

"BATAILLE". "Reason is the opposite of play. It is the principle of a world which is the exact opposite of play: that of work."
DAUGHTER. Who is that?
FATHER. Why, I think it's your . . . It's a famous author, who is dead. You'll read him when you get older.
"BATAILLE". "An authentic game demands such an unleashing of violence that the aspect of play, which seduces, is not immediately visible in it: on the contrary, it is terrifying, and ravishes only in horror."

(*Exit* "BATAILLE.")

DAUGHTER. Daddy, I don't think I like that man. What was he carrying?
FATHER. Eggs. But where were we?
DAUGHTER. I forget. Daddy, what did he mean, that a real game is terrifying? Is it sort of like a roller coaster, when you're scared to death but still want to do it?

FATHER. Yes, sort of like that. Except he meant *real* death, I think, not just fooling.

Voice of "BATAILLE," *offstage.* "Frazer tells the story of a king of the province of Quilacare, in Southern India: 'This province is governed by a king, who, from one jubilee to the other, has only 12 years to live . . . At the end of the 12 years, an immense crowd assembles . . . The king has a platform built, covered with silken coverings . . . He mounts the platform, and before the assembled crowd takes sharp kives and starts to cut his nose, his ears, his lips, his members and as much flesh as he can . . . until finally he loses so much blood that he begins to faint. At that point, he cuts his throat.' I doubt that I can cite an example of a game played more sovereignly and more extremely."[7]

DAUGHTER. Daddy, I'm scared.

FATHER. Don't worry, dear. He was only talking. He died in his bed, like a good bourgeois.

DAUGHTER. What's a good bourgeois?

FATHER. Hm . . . let's see. It's somebody who takes himself very seriously.

DAUGHTER. You mean, he doesn't play?

FATHER. Well, he does—but only at certain times and in certain places. He wants to draw the lines very clearly, you see—everything in its place.

DAUGHTER. Oh, then he's tidy. Like me. I like things in their place.

FATHER. Yes, I guess you do. In a way, we all do. Why do you think that is?

DAUGHTER. I dunno. It's kind of . . . safe, you know ? I feel . . . all mixed up inside when I'm in a messy place, almost as if I didn't know who I was.

(*Enter* JACQUES DERRIDA *and the* MOTHER *disguised as D.W. Winnicott, riding bicycles.*)

"WINNICOTT". "The searching for the self can come only from desultory formless functioning, or perhaps from rudimentary playing, as if in a neutral zone. It is only here, in this unintegrated state of the personality, that that which we describe as creative can appear."[8]

DERRIDA. "There are thus two interpretations of interpretation, of structure, of sign, of play. The one seeks to decipher, dreams of deciphering, a truth or an origin which is free from play and from the order of the sign . . . The other, which is no longer turned toward the origin, affirms play and tries to pass beyond man and humanism, the name man being the name of that being who, throughout the history of metaphysics—in other words, through the history of all of his history—has dreamed of full presence, the reassuring foundation, the origin and the end of the game."[9]

(*Exit* DERRIDA *and* "WINNICOTT.")

DAUGHTER. What were they saying? They went by so fast I couldn't hear.

FATHER. Me neither. Something about a reassuring foundation and the end of the game.

DAUGHTER. Well, *I* never like to stop playing, even if it's my bedtime.

FATHER. Which it soon will be, I'd like to remind you.

DAUGHTER. I know, I know, but this is fun. Daddy, do you believe in God?

FATHER. Hm . . . Sometimes. Sometimes when something terrible happens, I say, "Dear God, please help me."

DAUGHTER. Yes, but that doesn't count. I mean, every day all day long. Did God create the world? Does he know what we're doing? Is he behind it all?

FATHER. You're asking very difficult questions today. To tell you the truth, I don't know. I rather doubt it, though.

DAUGHTER. If you believed in God, would you be more sure about things? I wish you wouldn't say "I don't know" so often!

FATHER. Aha, you want me to be strict and stern and lay down the law? Up to bed you go, then!

DAUGHTER. No. I like you just the way you are, Daddy. But sometimes I feel it would be nice to be sure of things—what's good and what's bad, what everything *means* when you really get down to it.

(*Enter* ALAIN ROBBE-GRILLET, *carrying a pack of what appear to be oversized playing cards.*)

ROBBE-GRILLET. "What is called serious, what is upheld by values (work, honor, discipline, etc.) belongs . . . to a vast code, situated and dated, outside of which the idea of depth loses all of its meaning; the serious supposes that there is something behind our gestures: a soul, a god, values, the bourgeois order . . . whereas behind the game, there is nothing. Playing affirms itself as pure gratuitousness."[10]

DAUGHTER. Could you say that again, sir? It sounds interesting.

ROBBE-GRILLET. Yes, my charming girl—I'll be happy to explain. You see, each one of us plays a game with the cards we've got—like these in my hand. "In themselves they have no meaning or value, but each player will give them meaning, his own, by arranging them in his hand and then throwing them on the table according to his own ordering, his own invention of the game being played."[11] That's what I call freedom.

(*He throws a card on the table: it is a still photograph from Robbe-Grillet's film* Glissements progressifs du plaisir, *showing a beautiful young girl tied eaglespread to a bed, naked, with blood running down her legs. The* DAUGHTER *looks at the picture, then jumps back in surprise and fright.*)

ROBBE-GRILLET. Don't be frightened, my dear. It's only make-believe—see, that's red paint we smeared on the legs of the actress. Remember, there's nothing behind this, it's only me playing.
FATHER (*steering him toward the door*). Monsieur, I admire your work. Someday I'll explain it to my daughter. For now, *au revoir.*

(*Exit* ROBBE-GRILLET.)

DAUGHTER. Daddy, you didn't have to make him go. I was scared at first, but then I saw it was just pretending. He was kind of nice, Monsieur Robbe-Grillet.
FATHER. Yes, He's charming.
DAUGHTER. Daddy, do you ever dream of tying girls to a bed?
FATHER. ———
DAUGHTER. You can tell me, I know you'd never do it for real.
FATHER. There are some things we'll talk about when you get older. Now it's time for you to go to bed, young lady. Off with you!
DAUGHTER. Goodnight, Daddy.

(*She kisses him and starts to leave the room. Just then, a soft knocking is heard at the door. The* FATHER *goes to open, and the* DAUGHTER *stops to see who is there. In the doorway stands the* MOTHER, *disguised as Roland Barthes.*)

"BARTHES". Good evening. May I come in?
FATHER. Monsieur! Why, of course. I am delighted to see you again. (*To* DAUGHTER): Come here, dear. I want you to meet an old teacher of mine, who was very important in my life. (*To* "BARTHES"): Monsieur, this is my daughter.
"BARTHES". I am pleased to meet you, my dear. (*To* FATHER): Forgive me for coming unannounced. I could not help overhearing your conversation with Robbe-Grillet. He and I were good friends, you know. I wrote about his very first books, back in the structuralist days. A very writerly writer.
FATHER. Yes, I remember.
"BARTHES". We did not see eye to eye on everything, of course. Especially about the body of the mother. I never understood why he

was so intent on attacking it—for you agree, do you not, that playing with the female body is always, in the end, playing with the body of the mother?

FATHER. Yes. But Monsieur, do you remember the famous sentence you wrote, which has so often been quoted—about the writer playing with his mother's body?

"BARTHES". Ah, yes. "No object is in a constant relationship with pleasure. For the writer, however, this object exists: it is the *mother tongue.*"

FATHER *(continuing the same text).* "The writer is someone who plays with the body of his mother: in order to glorify it, to embellish it, or to dismember it, to take it to the limit of what can be known about the body. I would go so far as to take *joissance* in a *disfiguration* of the . . ."[12]

"BARTHES". Hm . . . Yes, I did write that. But it was not my last word. As you know, I was very attached to my mother. Do you remember what I said in my inaugural lecture at the Collège de France? "I would therefore like the speaking and listening that will be woven here to resemble the comings and goings of a child who plays around his mother, leaving her and then returning to her to bring her a pebble, a piece of yarn, thus drawing around a peaceful center a whole area of play."[13]

FATHER. Yes, that was very beautiful. I was very touched by that image—the mother as peaceful center, a necessary still point around which the child weaves his play. But tell me, did you ever imagine the mother moving, joining in the play?

"BARTHES". Hm . . . to tell you the truth, that thought never occurred to me.

FATHER. As I recall, you said in that same lecture: "Only the son has fantasies. Only the son is alive." Of course you meant in opposition to the Father, who is always dead.

"BARTHES". Yes—the symbolic Father. The Father who stands for the Law.

FATHER. Yes, I know. I suppose you also meant that the daughter is alive, the daughter also plays.

"BARTHES". Yes—yes, of course. Now I really must be going.

(Exit "BARTHES.")

DAUGHTER. He didn't say goodbye to me. Daddy, is fantasy play? I have lots of fantasies!

FATHER. Yes, dear, I know you do. Monsieur Barthes didn't mean to exclude you—he just didn't think of it.

(In the meantime, the M O T H E R *has come in, still carrying her Roland Barthes mask.)*

M O T H E R . That's why we have to think of it for ourselves!

(The daughter sees her, understands the game, and starts to laugh. They are all laughing now; hugging each other, they start to dance around the room to the strains of the Blue Danube waltz. Offstage, a chorus of women's voices, including those of Luce Irigaray, Hélène Cixous, and Julia Kristeva, is heard chanting.)

C H O R U S . Revise, re-view
To see things anew
Teach the daughter to play
Imagine the mother playing.

ONE

A Double Margin:
Women Writers and the Avant-Garde
in France

Now you see us . . .
Now you don't.

—BARBARA KRUGER

To use the term "avant-garde" today is to risk falling into a conceptual and terminological quagmire. Is "avant-garde" synonymous with, or to be subtly distinguished from, the experimental, the bohemian, the modern, the modern*ist,* the postmodern? Is it a historical category or a transhistorical one? A purely aesthetic category or a philosophical/political/existential one? Is it still to be taken seriously or does it "conjure up comical associations of aging youth"?[1] In short, does the term have specific content or has it become so vague and general as to be virtually useless?

In particular, the relation between postmodernism (whatever one means, exactly, by that term) and "the avant-garde" (whatever one means by *that* term) has become a hotly debated issue among literary and cultural theorists. Some, like Peter Bürger, consider the genuine avant-garde as already historical—gone for good with Dada and Surrealism. Hence, postmodernism (which for Bürger would qualify at best as a "neoavant-garde") becomes merely an inauthentic repetition of the original avant-garde project: the challenging of art as an autonomous institution and the attempt to make it more a part of life, or what Bürger Germanically calls "the sublation of art into life." For Bürger, this project was necessarily radical, subverting both traditional notions of art and of life; the neoavant-garde, by contrast, "stages for a second time the avant-gardist break with tradition" and thereby "becomes a manifestation that is void of sense."[2]

Other left-wing theorists are more sanguine about postmodernism. Andreas Huyssen, for example, has argued that postmodernism is a significant attempt to renew with a radical avant-garde tradition that had been obscured by the quite different, generally conservative, and until recently dominant trend of "high modernism."[3] Still others, like Rosalind Krauss, place both modernism and the avant-garde on one side of a historical divide, with postmodernism figuring as a totally new—and on the whole positive—development.[4]

As it happens, this essay will not chiefly be concerned with such conceptual and terminological problems, interesting as they are. The relation that concerns me here is not the one between or among various manifestations of "the modern" (yet another term to throw into the fray, especially in French: *la modernité*), but the relation between any or all of these manifestations and women. For my purposes, then, "avant-garde" will designate the whole field—however messy and full of dividing lines it may be—in which modernism, postmodernism, and the historical avant-gardes can be said to occupy a place.

This would seem to locate me, as far as the avant-garde/postmodernism question is concerned, close to Charles Russell, who sees "avant-garde" as a general term that subsumes postmodernism; or close to Renato Poggioli, who died before the question of postmodernism came to the fore, but who considered the avant-garde as a general designation quasi synonymous with the modern.[5] Since I don't agree with many of Russell's and Poggioli's specific observations, however, I had probably better take full responsibility for my starting propositions, which are relatively simple.

Of Margins and Avant-Gardes

Although avant-garde movements in modern Western art and thought can be traced at least as far back as Romanticism (as Poggioli has shown), they came fully into their own in the early years of this century and found what was perhaps their fullest elaboration in the Surrealist movement between 1924 and 1939. Focusing on the area I know best, France, I would say that the Situationists, who in many ways modeled themselves on Surrealism, the *Tel Quel* group and its allies of the 1960s and early 1970s, and the various feminist groups after 1968 associated with specific journals and theoretical positions regarding women and "the feminine" also constituted genuine artistic and cultural avant-gardes (*pace* Peter Bürger). The hallmark of these movements was a collective project (more or less explicitly defined and often shifting over time) that linked artistic experimentation and a critique of outmoded artistic practices with an ideological critique of bourgeois thought and a desire for social change, so that the activity of writing could also be seen as a genuine intervention in the social, cultural, and political arena.

Finally, although most of the participants in the later movements are still alive and writing in France today, the movements themselves are now dispersed and have not been replaced.[6]

To be sure, qualifications and additions are possible: should the *nouveaux romanciers* be considered an avant-garde movement, and if not, why not? The same question can be asked about the *Temps Modernes* group, led by Sartre and Beauvoir, during its heyday in the 1950s and early 1960s. The point I wish to make is that there has existed, at least since Surrealism, a strong and almost continuous current in French literary and artistic practice and thought, based on the double exigency to "be absolutely modern" (Rimbaud) and to change, if not the world (Marx), at least—as a first step—the way we think about the world. Furthermore, this recurrent tendency has expressed itself with remarkable consistency, privileging certain concepts (heterogeneity, play, marginality, transgression, the unconscious, eroticism, excess) and mounting heavy attacks on others (representation, the unitary subject, stable meaning, linear narrative, paternal authority, Truth with a capital *T*).

Alice Jardine has argued that perhaps the most important thread of continuity, subtending all of the above oppositions, has been the "putting into discourse of 'woman'": "We might say that what is generally referred to as modernity is precisely . . . the perhaps historically unprecedented exploration of the female, differently maternal body."[7] One has but to think of the Surrealists' celebration of *amour fou* (or, in the case of Bataille, *amour obscène*) in poetry and narrative, and their obsessive preoccupation with the female body in painting and photography; of the recurrent "pin-up" photos, with no discernible relation to the text, in early issues of the Situationist journal *Internationale Situationniste;* of Alain Robbe-Grillet's and other *nouveaux romanciers'* combination of a thematics of erotic violence with a poetics of antirealist transgression; of Phillippe Sollers's attempts to wed Joycean wordplay to erotic exhibitionism (especially in *Paradis,* his last work of the *Tel Quel* period); of Julia Kristeva's theory of the maternal/semiotic and Jacques Derrida's concept of "invagination"; and of contemporary women writers' exploration/inscription of the female body, whether as maternal *jouissance* or as the *jouissance* of female lovers, to assent to Jardine's daring generalization.

One question is whether the "putting into discourse of 'woman'" by a woman writer is comparable, in its meaning and effects, to its putting into discourse by a male writer. Another important question, which has preoccupied many feminist theorists and which Jardine rightly emphasizes at the outset of her book, concerns the problematic relationship between "woman" as discursive entity, or metaphor, and *women* as biologically and culturally gendered human beings. "It is always a bit of a shock to the feminist critic," writes Jardine, "when she recognizes that the repeated and infinitely expanded 'feminine' . . . often has very little, if anything, to do with women" (p. 35). And putting the dilemma even more sharply: "To refuse 'woman' or the 'feminine' as cultural and libidinal constructions (as in 'men's femininity'), is, ironically, to return to metaphysical—anatomical—definitions of sexual identity. To accept a metaphorization, a semiosis of woman, on the other hand, means risking once again the absence of women as subjects in the struggle of modernity" (p. 37). As Jardine points out, the dilemma is especially acute for those American feminist critics who are torn between the heady attractions of (largely French) theory and the no less significant appeal of (largely American) empirical and historical study, where the material situation and the gender of an author are never a matter of indifference. Nancy Miller, who has often and forcefully argued for the materialist view even while admitting the elegant attractions of French theory, summed up the dilemma in another way a few years ago when she asked, half jokingly: "Can we imagine, or should we, a position that speaks in tropes and walks in sensible shoes?"[8]

I would like to take up Miller's challenge by reflecting on a particularly powerful trope associated both with women and with avant-gardes: that of the margin. If, as this trope suggests, culture is "like" a space to be mapped or a printed page, then the place of women, and of avant-garde movements, has traditionally been situated away from the center, "on the fringe," in the margins. One difference is that avant-garde movements have willfully chosen their marginal position, the better to launch attacks at the center, whereas women have more often than not been relegated to the margins: far from the altar as from the marketplace, those centers where cultural subjects invent and enact their symbolic and material rites.

It has become increasingly clear that the relegating of *women* to the margins of culture is not unrelated to the place accorded to "woman" by the cultural imaginary: "Woman, in the political vocabulary, will be the name for whatever undoes the whole."[9] In other vocabularies, "woman" has been the name of the hole that threatens the fullness of the subject, the wild zone that threatens the constructions of reason, the dark continent that threatens the regions of light. What is new, however, is that the "putting into discourse of 'woman'" in modern French thought has gone hand in hand with a revaluation and revalorization of the marginal spaces with which "she" has been traditionally identified. It is because of that reversal that the complicated relations, at the margins of culture, between women writers and the avant-garde in France must occupy our attention.

In *Les Parleuses,* the series of conversations between Marguerite

Duras and Xavière Gauthier published in 1974, the talk turns at one point to why Duras is not really known by the reading public. Gauthier remarks that many people know Duras's name, but few seem to have read her texts—perhaps because they are afraid? Duras replies that very probably things will change after her death, but that indeed "I attract misogyny in a particular way." Gauthier (who often speaks more volubly than Duras in these conversations) then observes: "That doesn't surprise me. Precisely because I think that they are totally revolutionary books, totally avant-garde, both from a usual revolutionary point of view and from a woman's point of view, and most people aren't there yet." To which Duras responds: "Yes, it's something doubly intolerable" ("une double insupportabilité").[10]

Doubly intolerable because "totally revolutionary, totally avant-garde," Duras's work (by 1974 she had published among other works the trilogy comprising *Le Ravissement de Lol V. Stein, Le Vice-Consul* and *L'Amour,* and directed the film *India Song*) is here seen as the quintessence of the marginal. The fact that ten years later, with the publication of *L'Amant,* she would become an international bestselling author does not alter the logic of that characterization (although it did of course alter Duras's own situation.)[11] The avant-garde woman writer is doubly intolerable, seen from the center, because her writing escapes not one but two sets of expectations/categorizations; it corresponds neither to the "usual revolutionary point of view" nor to the "woman's point of view." Gauthier does not explain what she means here by the "woman's point of view"—I would guess that she alludes to a certain view of women's writing which does not include experimentation with language. As for the "usual revolutionary" point of view, it seems to refer to an overtly political kind of writing which adopts an oppositional stance to society. Duras tells Gauthier that in her works there is no "refusal" or "putting into question" of society, because "to put society into question is still to acknowledge it . . . I mean the people who do that, who write about the refusal of society, harbor within them a kind of nostalgia. They are, I am certain, much less separated from it than I am" (p. 62). Her own position is one of total separation, total estrangement. So far out that it escapes the social order altogether? In any case, so far out as to be elsewhere. *L'existence est ailleurs.*

The sudden appearance of the last sentence in the above paragraph, produced as my free association to the word "elsewhere," itself a gloss on Duras's words, suggests to me a curious filiation; for the sentence is the famous concluding sentence of the first Surrealist Manifesto. Breton, declaring the foundation of a radically new movement, states that (his/its) existence is elsewhere; Duras, who accepts to call her works "totally revolutionary, totally avant-garde," declares that she is elsewhere. In one reading of the trope of marginality, "woman," "woman's writing," and "avant-garde" become metaphors for each other. That is one reason why Rosalind Krauss, for example, can write about Surrealist photography that in its practice "woman and photograph become figures for each other's condition: ambivalent, blurred, indistinct, and lacking in, to use Edward Weston's word, 'authority.'"[12]

The opposition Krauss establishes between "straight photography," metonymically represented by Edward Weston and implicitly coded as male ("grounded in the sharply focused image, its resolution a figure of the unity of what the spectator sees, a wholeness that in turn founds the spectator himself as a unified subject") and Surrealist photography, which she explicitly codes as female (blurring all boundaries and threatening the spectator of straight photography to the point that he finds it "unbearable"—which translates exactly into *insupportable,* as used by Duras) is a move that signals Krauss's allegiance to contemporary French thought. It allows her to valorize Surrealist photography as the (metaphorically) "feminine" Other of straight photography; but it is also a move that leads to a significant (symptomatic?) slippage in terminology and conceptualization. Woman, Krauss states, is "the obsessional subject" of Surrealist photography—but in fact, as the illustrations to her essay amply document, woman, or rather the female body, is the obsessional *object* of Surrealist photographic experimentation.[13] Krauss's brilliant discussion of Surrealist "optical assaults on the body" (p. 70) elides the difference between the subject who is agent of the assault (and who is almost invariably a male photographer) and the object that is the target of the "active, aggressive assault on reality" (p. 65), this object being also almost invariably the female body.

To call woman the obsessional *subject* of Surrealist photography is, then, misleading in a particularly interesting way, for it suggests, or rather confirms, that the figural substitution of "woman" or "the feminine" for avant-garde practice (the two being united by their common marginality in relation to "straight" or "mainstream" culture) may end up eliding precisely the question of the female subject; and eliding, as well, the question of history. For if Surrealism, to stick to that example, is studied historically, then the absence or presence of female subjects of Surrealist practice becomes a problem one *cannot* avoid. And I would claim that it is only by working through the problem historically that one can make progress on theoretical ground as well.

Before turning down the historical path, however, I want to emphasize a more positive and empowering aspect of the "woman"/avant-garde/ marginality trope for female subjects. As the remarks by Duras I quoted earlier suggest, there is a way in which the sense of being "doubly marginal" and therefore "totally avant-garde" provides the female subject with a kind of centrality, *in her own eyes.* In a system in which the marginal, the avant-garde, the subversive, all that disturbs and "undoes the whole" is endowed with positive value, a woman artist who can identify those concepts with her own practice and metaphorically with her own femininity can find in them a source of strength and self-legitimation. Perhaps no one has done this more successfully than Hélène Cixous. Her famous essay, "Le Rire de la Méduse" ("The Laugh of the Medusa," 1975), is the closest thing to an avant-garde manifesto written from an explicitly feminist perspective. True to the genre of the manifesto, it is written by an "I" who represents a group ("we," in this case women); it alternates in tone between the aggressive (when addressing the hostile "straight" reader) and the hortatory (when addressing the other members of the group), and it suggests a program that implies both a revolutionary practice of writing and the disruption of existing cultural and social institutions and ideologies.

What distinguishes Cixous's manifesto from its forerunners (Marinetti's Futurist manifestoes, Tzara's Dada manifestoes, Breton's Surrealist manifestoes) is that Cixous explicitly equates the radically new, subversive text with the "feminine text":

> Un texte féminin ne peut pas ne pas être plus que subversif: s'il s'écrit, c'est en soulevant, volcanique, la vieille croûte immobilière, porteuse des investissements masculins, et pas autrement; . . . ce n'est qu'à tout casser, à mettre en pièces les bâtis des institutions, à faire sauter la loi en l'air, à tordre la "vérité" de rire.

> A feminine text cannot fail to be more than subversive. It is volcanic; as it is written it brings about an upheaval of the old property crust, carrier of masculine investments; there's no other way . . . in order to smash everything, to shatter the framework of institutions, to blow up the law, to break up the "truth" with laughter.[14]

Although the "feminine text" that is here projected (not *defined,* but projected into the future as an *écriture à venir*—this too being the hallmark of the manifesto as genre)[15] is not to be restricted to writers who are women, women are nevertheless in a privileged position to practice it: "Thanks to their history, women today know (how to do and want) what men will be able to conceive of only much later" (p. 258).

Cixous's metaphorical equation of "the feminine" with the hyperbolically marginal allows her to envisage *women* as the primary subjects of avant-garde practice. In this she differs not only from Krauss (for whom "the feminine" remains a metaphor, applied to work by male artists), but also from Julia Kristeva; for although Kristeva leaves ample space for the maternal/semiotic in her theory of the avant-garde subject, that subject remains of necessity male. Not only are all of her exemplary avant-garde writers male, from Lautréamont and Mallarmé through Joyce, Artaud, Bataille, and Sollers, but she has even discussed, at various times, why in terms of her theory it is virtually impossible for a woman to achieve a similar status. In order to be truly innovative, one has to be able to risk giving up "la légitimation paternelle"; but if women take that risk, what awaits them more often than not is madness or suicide.[16] For the male subject, the negativity involved in giving up paternal legitimation is compensated by a positive maternal support, and the two coexist in a dynamic balance. For the woman writer, there seems to be no viable alternative to either total paternal identification (which involves the absence of negativity, the conformism of the dutiful daughter) or else a regression to the "archaic mother," which involves yet another conformism equally incapable of producing true artistic innovation—the conformism of those who claim that "it's good because it was done by women."[17]

Even as I am writing these remarks, however, I realize that they are in some profound sense nonpertinent. It is misleading to use the present tense in discussing either Kristeva's or Cixous's theoretical reflections on "écriture féminine" and its possible or impossible intersections with innovation and avant-garde practice. Those reflections are historically situated in the 1970s, at a time when there existed a strong if already splintered women's movement in France, together with an equally strong current of philosophical and literary theorizing about modernity. Today, as we are reaching the end of the 1980s, my sense is that the collective dynamism is gone and there remain only individual efforts, among women as in the French literary and intellectual arena generally.[18] The music has stopped and the dancing is over, at least for a while. This may be the time, therefore, to put on our sensible shoes and take a walk around some real margins in the imaginary garden of the French avant-garde.

From the point of view of one who walks in sensible shoes, it is clear that there is no such thing as *the* avant-garde; there are only specific avant-garde movements, situated in a particular time and place. In order to talk about the real marginalization of women in relation to "the avant-garde" (I mean the exclusion of women from the centers of male avant-garde activity or their exclusion from the historical and critical accounts of that activity), one must look at individual cases in their historical and national specificity. I propose to look at a case that has been much examined by feminist critics of late, in France and in the United States: that of Surrealism. The feminist exploration of Surrealism has proceeded along two tracks, which can be designated, following Elaine Showalter's well-known categorizations, as feminist critique (the rereading of male authors from a feminist perspective) and as gynocriticism (the rediscovery of hitherto "invisible" or undervalued women writers and their work). The pioneering work of feminist critique of Surrealism was Xavière Gauthier's *Surréalisme et sexualité* (1971). Polemical in its effect even though analytical in tone, Gauthier's detailed study of Surrealist poetry and painting sought to show, and to explain in chiefly psychoanalytic terms, "the misogyny of the compact group of male Surrealists."[19] Whether they idealized the female body and their love of it, as they did in their poetry, or attacked it and dismembered it, as they did in their paintings, the male Surrealists, according to Gauthier's analysis, were essentially using the woman to work out their rebellion against the Father.

Gauthier's book appeared a year after Kate Millett's *Sexual Politics;* like Millett's work, it was important because it *posed as a problem* the subject position of male artists in relation to the objects of their representations, women. In recent years, we have seen more nuanced attempts to explore this problem, especially in the field of Surrealist visual art;[20] but there is certainly room for further reflection on the subject position of Surrealism.

As for the gynocritical work, it began with the necessary task of gathering information: who were the women writers and artists associated with Surrealism, and what did they accomplish? The 1977 special issue of the review *Obliques,* entitled *La Femme Surréaliste,* was the first attempt to present a catalogue of "Surrealist women," in alphabetical order, complete with photographs, bibliographies, and brief excerpts or reproductions of their work as well as some interviews and interpretive essays. In 1980 Lea Vergine's *L'Autre Moitié de l'avant-garde,* which sought to document the lives and work of women artists associated with all the major European avant-garde movements between 1910 and 1940, included eighteen women under the heading "Surréalisme"; some of them had also figured among the thirty-six women listed in *La Femme Surréaliste,* while others had not. These two publications are precious reference works, but they were only a first step: neither one made any claim to exhaustiveness, nor did they attempt to draw general conclusions about the participation of women in the Surrealist movement and their contribution to it. In the last few years, important work in that direction has been accomplished by (among others) Whitney Chadwick, Jacqueline Chénieux, and Gloria Feman Orenstein.[21] As a result, it is now becoming possible to engage in a more systematic reflection on the place (and placing) of women in Surrealism.

In the rest of this essay, I want to develop the two lines of thought suggested above. If indeed the subject position of Surrealism was male, what difficulties did that imply for the artistic practice of "Surrealist women," especially of women writers? And what exactly was the position of women artists and writers in the history of the Surrealist movement?

The Surrealist Subject

Since nothing is more instructive than a good example, I shall begin by offering two. The first is a paragraph from an essay by Louis Aragon, one of the founding members of the Surrealist group, published in 1924. He is writing here about the newly established Centre des Recherches Surréalistes (also known as La Centrale Surréaliste), which functioned in its first months as a rallying point for all those wishing to participate in the Surrealist project:

> Nous avons accroché une femme au plafond d'une chambre vide où il vient chaque jour des hommes inquiets, porteurs de secrets lourds. C'est ainsi que nous avons connu Georges Bessière, comme un coup de poing. Nous travaillons à une tâche pour nous-mêmes énigmatique, devant un tome de Fantômas, fixé au mur par des fourchettes. Les visiteurs, nés sous des climats lointains ou à notre porte, contribuent à l'élaboration de cette formidable machine à tuer ce qui est, pour l'achèvement de ce qui n'est pas. Au 15 de la rue de Grenelle, nous avons ouvert une romanesque Auberge pour les idées inclassables et les révoltes poursuivies. Tout ce qui demeure encore d'espoir dans cet univers désespéré va tourner vers notre dérisoire échoppe ses derniers regards délirants: *Il s'agit d'aboutir à une nouvelle déclaration des droits de l'homme.*

> We hung a woman on the ceiling of an empty room, and every day receive visits from anxious men bearing heavy secrets. That is how we came to know Georges Bessière, like a blow of the fist. We are working at a task enigmatic to ourselves, in front of a volume of Fantomas, fastened to the wall by forks. The visitors, born under remote stars or next door, are helping to elaborate this formidable machine for killing what is in order to accomplish what is not. At number 15, Rue de Grenelle, we have opened a romantic Inn for unclassifiable ideas and continuing revolts. All that still remains of hope in this despairing universe will turn its last, raving glances toward our pathetic stall. *It is a question of formulating a new declaration of the rights of man.*[22]

The second example is from an essay by a historian of Surrealism, Robert Short, published in 1976 in an influential volume: "The criterion that the Surrealists apply to a work of art is its susceptibility to provoke a real change in those who encounter it, to call forth an affective response similar in quality to that evoked by the sight of the woman one loves."[23]

Although these texts are very different, one thing they have in common is that the author does not seem to be aware of all that he is saying. Aragon begins by talking about a woman hung on a ceiling and ends by proclaiming the Surrealist project as a desire for "a new declaration of the rights of man"—apparently unaware that the word "man" in his last sentence asks to be interpreted in its gender-specific sense, especially after all the talk about blows of the fist and machines for killing what is. Short begins by talking about the Surrealists' conception of art and ends by evoking "the woman one loves"—apparently unaware that not all spectators of art are heterosexual males. In brief, both the founding Surrealist and the later historian are writing from an exclusively male subject position, and are unproblematically assigning that position to the subject of Surrealist practice. They do this, I would guess, in all innocence, with no malevolent intent: theirs is not the provocation of the self-conscious misogynist, but the ordinary sexism of the man who will reply, when you point it out to him, that he hadn't noticed there were no women in the room.

But in fact, as Aragon tells us, there was a woman in the Surrealist room—her only peculiarity being that she was not made of flesh and blood. The woman in question was a life-size reclining nude figure, a mannequin, armless and headless (was she the inspiration for Max Ernst's 1929 collage novel, *La Femme cent têtes?*), suspended from the ceiling of the Centrale. Her function was evidently to inspire the "anxious men" who came there to unburden themselves of their secrets. Did any anxious women come to unburden themselves of theirs? How might the floating lady have functioned for them?

Aragon does not mention any living women in the room; but a famous photograph by Man Ray, *The Surrealist Centrale* (1924), documents the presence of two living women: Simone Breton and Mick Soupault, wives of the Surrealists André and Philippe. In the standard version of the photograph, the image has been cut off at the top, leaving only the heel of the headless lady visible (just barely) in the upper left hand corner (fig. 1). There exists another version, however, which shows almost the entire figure, occupying the upper third of the photograph (fig. 2); below her, standing and seated in two uneven rows, are twelve men and the two women. The men, dressed in dark suits, white shirts, and ties, are writers and artists: Charles Baron, Raymond Queneau, Pierre Naville, André Breton (sporting a monocle), Jacques-André Boiffard, Giorgio de Chirico, Roger Vitrac, Paul Eluard, Philippe Soupault, Robert Desnos, Louis Aragon, and Max Morise. They look for the most part formal, solemn, almost grim, as befits an official group portrait. The two women look different, both from them and from each other: Mick Soupault, demurely dressed, is smiling slightly, like a good and tolerant wife; Simone Breton (whom Breton was to divorce a few years later,

1. Man Ray, *The Surrealist Centrale*, 1924

2. Man Ray, *The Surrealist Centrale*, 1924

when he met his next *amour fou*) is resting her head sideways on her arm—one eye is covered by her dark hair, while the other looks at the camera with a burning stare. She is the only one who looks openly provocative, almost shocking: in one version, her legs are crossed, exposing a bit of bare flesh above her knee-high stocking (fig. 1).

Why dwell on this image? Because it points up, as clearly and more graphically than Aragon's text, the degree to which the subject position of Surrealism, as it was elaborated at the inception of the movement, was male. The photograph also makes explicit what is only implied in Aragon's text: the problematic position of actual women who might wish to integrate themselves, as subjects, into the male script. I read Simone Breton and Mick Soupault in the photograph as female subjects—but as alienated subjects who have adapted themselves to the male vision of "woman," in what Luce Irigaray calls the masquerade.[24] Together they figure the two poles of femininity between which male desire hovers: the chaste, asexual wife/mother and the burning-eyed whore. Needless to say, I know nothing about the real personalities of Simone Breton and Mick Soupault; my remarks refer to their images in the photograph, which can itself be considered as the construction of a male subject. The photograph fascinates me because it lends itself so beautifully to be read as an emblem: above, the imaginary faceless woman on whom the Surrealist male artist can project his fantasies—fantasies which then become externalized, transformed, elaborated into works, poems, stories, paintings, photographs; below, two flesh and blood women who produced no works, but who *embody* aspects of the imaginary woman hanging from the ceiling.

How much meaning can one extract from a single image or a single text? More examples are needed; for instance, another "official" group portrait, a photomontage published in 1929 in *La Révolution Surréaliste* and often reproduced since then (fig. 3). The montage consists of the photograph of a painting by Magritte, framed by the portraits of sixteen Surrealists with their eyes closed; the painting represents a female nude, standing in a pose reminiscent of Botticelli's Venus, frontally exposed; above and below her, a part of the painting, is the inscription: "Je ne vois pas la / cachée dans la forêt" ("I do not see the / hidden in the forest"), the image of the woman filling in the hole between the words.[25] The Surrealists, all male, who frame her, adopt the position of the "Je," not seeing; at the same time, she is given *to be seen* by the spectator, who sees both the woman and the Surrealists (including Magritte who painted her) with their eyes kept resolutely shut.[26] This too seems to me to be an emblem of the Surrealist subject, who does not need to see the woman in order to imagine her, placing her at the center but only as an image, while any actual woman is now out of the picture altogether.

3. Photomontage of Surrealists around a painting by Magritte, 1929

Now here is the crucial question: given the overwhelmingly male subject position of Surrealism, how did a number of women artists, who *did* produce works, manage to elaborate an imagery and a script that involved neither a masquerade of femininity nor male impersonation—which in aesthetic terms would result in purely formal imitation, the adopting of formal solutions without discovering them as a personal necessity. Luce Irigaray has touched on this problem in an essay dedicated to one of the Surrealist women whose writing has recently become known, Unica Zürn. "If woman is to put into form the *ulè* [Greek: matter] that she is, she must not cut herself off from it nor leave it to maternity, but succeed in creating with that primary material that she is by discovering and exposing her own morphology. Otherwise, she risks using or reusing what man has already put into forms, especially about her; risks remaking what has already been made, and losing herself in that labyrinth."[27] A woman Surrealist, in other words, cannot simply assume a subject position and take over a stock of images elaborated by the male imaginary. In order to innovate, she has to invent her own position as subject and elaborate her own set of images—different from the image of the exposed female body, yet as empowering as that image is, with its endless potential for manipulation, disarticulation and rearticulation, fantasizing and projection, for her male colleagues.

As we are coming to realize, a significant number of women artists and writers did succeed in creating their own version and vision of Surrealist practice, without merely imitating male models. Over the past ten years, there have emerged significant bodies of work produced by women who previously were either never mentioned or mentioned only in the most cursory manner in general histories of Surrealist art or of the Surrealist movement: Leonora Carrington, Dorothea Tanning, Kay Sage, Eileen Agar, Ithell Colquhoun, Toyen, Unica Zürn, Leonor Fini, Valentine Hugo, and the list can be prolonged. These women were (are) primarily visual artists, but some have also produced wonderful written work—notably Leonora Carrington, who is a painter but whose short stories from the 1930s and 1940s, as well as her novel, *The Hearing Trumpet* (written in the 1950s), are finally finding an audience; and Unica Zürn, a graphic artist whose autobiographical texts, *Sombre printemps* and *L'Homme-Jasmin,* written (originally in German) not long before her suicide in 1970, have acquired almost a cult status in Paris.[28] Among the women who are primarily writers, two whose names have found their way into some general studies without receiving sustained attention are Joyce Mansour (1928–1986) and Gisèle Prassinos (born in 1920).[29] One of my own favorites, better known as a filmmaker *(La Fiancée du pirate, Néa, Papa les p'tits bateaux)* but also the author of several books of stories and a novel, whose name appeared in *La Femme Surréaliste* but is rarely mentioned today even by critics interested in Surrealist writing by women, is Nelly Kaplan (born 1936), writing under the pen name Belen.[30]

Only a careful study of individual works and artists will allow us to answer the question of the female subject in Surrealism. In the meantime, however, one can speculate about the strategies employed by women artists and writers, both in the ways they situated their work within Surrealism and in the ways they managed their lives: when and under what circumstances did a given artist become associated with the Surrealist movement? Was her work included in major exhibitions or anthologies organized by male Surrealists? Did she break with the movement, and if so under what circumstances? What was the subsequent evolution of her artistic career? Since the women were generally younger and started producing later than the men who were associated with the movement, it is not unlikely that their version of Surrealist practice included a component of response to, as well as adaptation of, male Surrealist iconographies and mythologies—this being especially the case in the realm of sexuality. Here, Irigaray's notion of "mimicry," the playful or ironic counterpart of the masquerade, might provide a useful analytical category in approaching individual works. In mimicry, a woman "repeats" the male—in this case, the male Surrealist—version of "woman," but she does so in a self-conscious way that points up the citational, often ironic status of the repetition.[31]

Another, specifically stylistic concept that would be useful in looking at the work of women artists is Mikhail Bakhtin's concept of "internal dialogism." The "internally dialogized" word, Bakhtin shows, is often polemically related to another, previous word that is absent but that can be inferred from the present response to it.[32] (And this is also true of the image.) Gloria Orenstein has suggested, relying not on Bakhtin's concept but on the anthropological concept of "muted" versus "dominant" groups, that the work of women who were personally linked—through love or marriage—to well-known male Surrealists like Max Ernst (Leonora Carrington and Dorothea Tanning), Yves Tanguy (Kay Sage), or Hans Bellmer (Unica Zürn) can be read as "a double-voiced discourse, containing both a 'dominant' and a 'muted' story."[33] In Bakhtinian terms, we can speak of the women's work as dialogically related to the men's, often with an element of internal polemic. I would suggest that such internal dialogue is to be found not only in the work of women directly involved with male Surrealists to whose work they were specifically responding, but was a general strategy adopted, in individual ways, by women wishing to insert themselves as subjects into Surrealism.

Women in the History of Surrealism

Henceforth, it will be difficult for any responsible teacher or student of Surrealism not to devote some serious attention to the work of women. And if it is true that the work of women Surrealists is in internal dialogue with that of the "mainstream" male Surrealists, then our understanding of the former will necessarily influence, or even alter, our understanding of the latter. Read in the light of women artists' and writers' responses to it, the aesthetic (and political, in the broad sense) achievement of Surrealism will not necessarily be diminished, but it will look somewhat different.

At the same time, the question arises: will the discovery of a significant body of work by women oblige us to rewrite the history of the Surrealist movement? In one obvious sense, it will—the hitherto invisible women will have to be recognized.[34] In another sense, however, it won't—and to understand why, we can look at a contrasting case, that of Anglo-American modernism. The recent work of feminist scholars has shown that both the nature and the history of Anglo-American modernism begin to look completely different if one takes into serious account and gives full historical weight to the work of early women modernists like H. D., Gertrude Stein, Dorothy Richardson, and Djuna Barnes, among others. The presence of major women writers at the beginning of the modernist movement, in a literary culture that could already boast a long tradition of major writing by women, has allowed contemporary feminist critics to argue that the elimination or belittling of the work of women modernists (including even Virginia Woolf, who fared better than most but whose late novels were often undervalued) was very like a conspiracy perpetrated by both the male modernists and the traditional, largely male historians of modernism. In the Anglo-American case, in other words, one can speak of a concerted exclusion of women's work from the modernist canon, an exclusion which Sandra Gilbert and Susan Gubar interpret as "a misogynistic reaction-formation against the rise of literary women" on the part of the male modernists whose work came to define that canon.[35]

In the case of Surrealism, one cannot make quite the same argument, especially as far as writing is concerned, because women's work was not present in the early years of the movement, when its most significant work was produced and its "project" was elaborated. Here is an instance where the importance of historical and national specificity becomes obvious.

Let us consider some dates. The founding of the Surrealist movement in 1924 was signaled by two publications: Breton's *Manifeste du surréalisme*, and the first issue of *La Révolution Surréaliste*, the "official" organ of the movement, which continued publication through 1929; in 1930, as a result of several years of discussion and internal debate regarding the Surrealists' position vis-à-vis the Communist party, *La Révolution Surréaliste* was replaced by *Le Surréalisme au Service de la Révolution,* which continued publication (although less frequently) through 1933. In the meantime, a number of defections, exclusions, and new arrivals occurred—these can be traced through the signatories to the numerous collective declarations published in the two journals. In 1932 the movement was shaken by the departure of one of its most visible and outspoken founding members, Louis Aragon, who joined the Communist party and began attacking his old comrades. After 1933, when *Le Surréalisme au Service de la Révolution* folded (together with any further hope for active collaboration between the Surrealists as a group and the Communists), the movement no longer had an official journal. (The journal *Minotaure,* published from 1933 to 1938, was largely open to Surrealist work, but it did not have the status of official organ, as the two earlier journals did.)

The movement was further weakened in 1935 by the suicide of another of its founding members, René Crevel, and by continuing attacks from the Communists. Although the Surrealists continued to publish collective statements and to proclaim an anti-Fascist revolutionary politics, their heroic period as an avant-garde movement was coming to an end. According to Maurice Nadeau, the historian of the movement, Surrealism as a genuine avant-garde movement died around 1935. This was, of course, not a view shared by Breton and his friends. Surrealism continued to maintain itself as a movement and to organize collective manifestations in the late 1930s and throughout the war, when many of its members were in New York. After the war, it gained new adherents and staged a major international exhibition (1947), started several new journals with Breton as directeur, and was not officially dispersed until 1969, three years after Breton's death. But for a long time by then, it had been no more than a surviving remnant.[36]

Historically, this is the significant fact: between 1924 and 1933, during the most dynamic and "ascendant" period of the movement, not a single woman was included as an official member. In the twelve issues of *La Révolution Surréaliste,* whose index reads like an honor roll of Surrealism (from Aragon, Arp, and Artaud, through Desnos, Eluard, and Ernst, to Tzara, Vaché, and Vitrac), there is *one* untitled poem by a woman, Fanny Beznos, whose biggest claim to Surrealist status is that she is mentioned in Breton's *Nadja.* A certain Madame Savitsky has a reply to the *enquête* on suicide ("Le suicide est-il une solution?") in the first issue; a woman artist, Valentine Penrose, has a brief reply to the *enquête sur l'amour* published in the last issue. And that is all.

In the six issues of *Le Surréalisme au Service de la Révolution*, there are one-time appearances by three women writers (one of them being Nadezhda Krupskaya, writing about her husband, Lenin—the other two are unknown) and visual work by three women artists, Gala Eluard, Marie-Berthe Ernst, and Valentine Hugo. Of the twenty or so major group declarations published during this period and reproduced in Nadeau's *Histoire du surréalisme*, not a single one carries the signature of a woman. The first major document containing the signatures of women (Dora Maar, Marie-Louise Mayoux, and Méret Oppenheim) dates from 1935 ("Du temps que les surréalistes avaient raison").[37] After 1935, women are fairly regularly included in exhibits and group publications: in the 1930s, in addition to Hugo, Maar, and Oppenheim, we find the names of Fini, Carrington, Agar, Toyen; in the 1940s and 1950s, those of Mansour, Remedios Varo, Tanning, Kaplan, Zürn; in the 1960s, Annie Le Brun.

What conclusions can we draw from all this? First, that it is not only because of sexist bias that historians of Surrealism have tended to exclude women's work from their accounts (although sexism has played a role, since many historians mention the work of younger male Surrealists but not that of the younger women). The fact is that no women were present as active participants in the early years of the movement. Their absence can, of course, be explained as the result of an active exclusion on the part of the male Surrealists, who wanted to maintain their "men's club." But this already suggests a difference from the Anglo-American case, where women were present as active agents at the founding moment of various avant-garde projects, either as writers (H. D. and Imagism, Stein and *transition*) or as publishers and editors who promoted the work of women a well as of men.[38] It was only later that the contribution of these women was either erased from the record or else diminished. In the case of Surrealism, by contrast, women were excluded before they even got started—and this was *especially* true of writers, who even in later years remained a very small minority among women Surrealists.

The relative absence of women writers can be explained in specifically French terms, both sociological and literary. Whereas the nineteenth century in England established a significant tradition of writing by women and integrated several women writers into the major canon (Austen, the Brontës, Eliot), and the same century in the United States produced the phenomenon of bestsellerdom by women writers (who, even if they were belittled by their male colleagues, could still not be ignored), the nineteenth century in France had a quite different literary effect: there were fewer major women, and fewer bestsellers by women, than in the seventeenth and eighteenth centuries. Germaine de Staël and George Sand, recognized by their contemporaries, were eclipsed and belittled by the end of the century, remembered more for their scandalous lives than for their literary achievements. As for the block-buster bestsellers, no woman even came close to Eugène Sue (whose popularity resembled Harriet Beecher Stowe's in the United States).

If one adds to these literary considerations the social fact that France, unlike England and America, did not have a vigorous suffragette move-ment (French women did not get the vote until 1946), one begins to understand why early twentieth-century French women writers had less to build on, and fewer reasons for self-confidence, than their English and American counterparts. The sad fact is that with the single major exception of Colette (and perhaps Anna de Noailles, who never achieved the same degree of recognition), there were no outstanding women writers in France in the first half of this century, and certainly none who had the tenacity to construct an *oeuvre* (much less the kind of innovative, rule-breaking *oeuvre* that can be qualified as "avant-garde" and that requires the self-confidence of, say, a Gertrude Stein) until Simone de Beauvoir. Beauvoir's own achievement looms all the larger when one considers this fact; but one can also understand why, in *The Second Sex,* she lamented the absence of true audacity in women's writing (including her own).

The second conclusion one can draw from the history of Surrealism's relation to women artists and writers is that as the movement grew weaker and more embattled, it became more welcoming to women, especially young women from other countries. It is striking to note how many of the "Surrealist women" are *not* French: Carrington, Colquhoun, and Agar are English; Oppenheim, Swiss, and Mansour, Egyptian; Fini, Argentine and Italian; Kaplan, Argentine; Varo, Spanish; Toyen, Czech; and Zürn, German. There were also a great many non-French male Surrealists (Ernst, Dali, Bellmer, Man Ray among them), but the *writers* of Surrealism remained overwhelmingly French. In the case of the women, the only native French writer in the 1930s was Gisèle Prassi-nos—but she was less a member of the group than a "child prodigy" they discovered and promoted (and was actually born in Turkey, arriv-ing in France as a baby).[39]

One might speculate that competition from foreign women was less threatening to the French male Surrealists' egos than competition from within the French "family." Eileen Agar suggests as much in a recent interview: "André Breton's wife [Jacqueline Lamba, Breton's second wife] was a very talented painter, he wouldn't even look at her work. But they were very nice to me, I think they were so pleased, there were so few surrealists at the time who were giving their heart and soul to it that I think they were pleased to welcome me."[40] Although no dates are mentioned, Agar seems to be referring to the mid-1930s. By then, Surrealism as a movement was on the wane (as her remarks suggest) and needed new blood. Furthermore, most of the women whom it welcomed in the 1930s were ten to fifteen years younger than the founders of the movement.[41] They therefore brought youth as well as renewal—not a small consideration for a movement that prided itself on its youthfulness.

This was even more obviously the case after the war, by which time Breton and his friends were elderly gentlemen, more than eager to welcome young women like Joyce Mansour, Nelly Kaplan, or Annie Le Brun—especially since the young men who might have been their heirs were not about to join a moribund "avant-garde" movement. They were busy founding the new avant-gardes of the period: the rise of the *nouveau roman,* of Situationism and of *Tel Quel* overlaps with the last years of Surrealism.[42]

If it is clear, historically and sociologically, what women brought to Surrealism, it remains to be asked what Surrealism brought to women. In a negative perspective, one could argue that it brought them nothing, since by the time they came to it, the movement's truly dynamic moment was over. Christine Brooke-Rose, writing about avant-garde literary movements in general, has ruefully noted that "women are rarely considered seriously a part of a movement when it is 'in vogue'; and they are damned with the label when it no longer is, when they can safely be considered as minor elements in it."[43] Although the history of Surrealism seems to bear out this assertion, some qualifications are necessary. It seems obvious that for the women who came to it during the late 1930s and 1940s, and even after the war, Surrealism was able to provide both a nourishing environment in the form of group exhibitions and publications, and a genuine source of inspiration.[44] That may explain why some of these women, like Dorothea Tanning and Annie Le Brun, are strongly hostile to any feminist critique of Surrealism, and why Tanning has refused so far to be included in shows or publications devoted exclusively to women's work.[45] It is also true, however, that since they were not present during the founding years of the movement, it is easier to relegate them to the status of "minor elements."

The final conclusion we can draw is that if women are to be part of an avant-garde movement, they will do well to found it themselves. Which, after 1968 (bringing its own problems and divisions, to be sure) was precisely what they did.

Aggressions and Counteraggressions: Readability in Avant-Garde Fiction

The teller's role, he felt, regardless of his actual gender, was essentially masculine, the listener's or reader's feminine, and the tale was the medium of their intercourse.

—JOHN BARTH, *CHIMERA*

To make literature with a gun in hand had, for a time, been my dream.

—RICHARD HUELSENBECK, *EN AVANT DADA*

The fundamental aggressiveness of what Renato Poggioli calls the "avant-garde posture"[1] is inscribed in the military connotations of the term: the avant-garde is the most daring, most fearless group within a fighting force. The early European avant-gardes, starting with Futurism, exploited to the hilt the antagonistic potential inherent in the concept of the avant-garde, directing their aggression both against the (bourgeois) public and against what they perceived as the dominant tradition, in art as in ethics or politics. In this as in some other respects, they had their precursors in the Romantics, with the scandalous opening night of Hugo's *Hernani* (1830), unfailingly evoked in literary histories, as an early prototype.

Today, as everyone knows, the avant-garde isn't what it used to be: the days when an outraged public could be counted on to hurl catcalls and tomatoes at a Dada performance have been over for a long while. Yet, until very recently (certainly through the 1970s), a certain rhetoric of contestation, of embattled action directed against habit, tradition, or the dominant sociopolitical system, persisted and provided the impetus for a great many individual and group activities in the cultural field, especially in France. The idea of *rupture*, a radical break with the past, dominated both the aesthetic and the philosophical and political program of the *Tel Quel* group, for example, which for a few years (roughly, 1967 to 1977) came closest to espousing the doubly revolutionary project of the historical avant-gardes, notably of Surrealism: to transform both language (writing, reading, *text*) and the world, to transform the latter by transforming the former.[2]

Reading and Rupture

When I reread, from the skeptical perspective of today, the revolutionary "Programme" that Philippe Sollers, *Tel Quel*'s chief spokesman and novelist, published in the journal in 1967, I am struck not only by its optimism—confidence in the future seems to be inherent in the concept of the avant-garde—but also by the emphasis that Sollers places on reading. "La théorie est d'abord définie comme une lecture" ("Theory is first defined as a reading")—as if, in order to understand the historical break accomplished by Lautréamont and Mallarmé on the one side, Marx and Freud on the other, one had to learn to read differently. Or perhaps to rethink the very notion of "the readable," of readability or intelligibility. But that, of course, meant that one would have to produce a different kind of writing as well: "This reading is made possible only by a writing that recognizes rupture."[3]

If for *Tel Quel* the idea of rupture was explicitly political as well as philosophical and aesthetic, for the practitioners of the *nouveau roman* (who never formally constituted a movement, but who for a while were treated as if they did) and for theorists of modernity like Roland Barthes (who maintained close ties to both *Tel Quel* and to the *nouveaux romanciers,* especially Alain Robbe-Grillet), rupture remained chiefly an aesthetic, or else a psychological and erotic, concept. Nonetheless, for them too it retained its character of contestation and antagonism: the "modern" text was fundamentally opposed to the norms of classical readability, which for fiction meant the norms of the realist novel.

Looking once again with hindsight, one is struck by how much the theoretical writing that grew up around the *nouveau roman* in the 1960s and 1970s in France presents itself as polemical and programmatic, even when lacking a specifically political cast. The works of Jean Ricardou (himself a practicing *nouveau romancier*), which for a while constituted the most influential discourse on the new fiction, were typical in this respect. They not only provided a largely formalist model for reading the *nouveau roman,* but in the process constructed an antimodel, that of the outdated, aesthetically and ideologically bankrupt "literature of expression and representation" which the new fiction contested: the nineteenth-century realist novel, embodied in particular in the works of Balzac.[4] Balzac was also the preferred counterexample cited by Robbe-Grillet in his manifesto-like essays, collected in 1963 under the title *Pour un nouveau roman (Toward a New Novel).* And, of course, the Balzacian novel became the great negative exemplar of the "readable text" in one of Roland Barthes's most influential and programmatically "pro-modern" works, *S/Z* (1970).

Why was readability a crucial concept in these discussions? Because in terms of the traditional realist aesthetic (which the Surrealists had already demolished in their own way), readability is another word for intelligibility: a readable text is one that "makes sense." It is intelligible because it conforms to certain aesthetic and logical norms that a reader has internalized as a set of expectations; in short, it corresponds to a familiar order, a previously learned code. Furthermore, in the case of the realist novel, the chief expectations that generations of readers have internalized concern some fundamental notions in our culture, perhaps in all cultures: the principle of noncontradiction (an event cannot occur and *not* occur at the same time, a thing cannot exist and *not* exist at the same time), the notions of temporal succession and causality (events follow each other and are related to each other consequentially), a belief in the solidity of the phenomenal world (a table is a table is a table), and a belief in at least a relative unity of the self (a name designates a person who has certain fixed characteristics and a set of identifiable ancestors).

Since a great deal of work has been done recently on the conventions of realism,[5] there is no need to insist on them here. The point I wish to stress is that although we have learned to think of them precisely as *conventions*—that is, as cultural constructs, not as natural phenomena— the conventions of realist fiction correspond to what most of us also think of, in our less theoretical moments, as the "natural order of the world." In our everyday lives we believe, at least we act as if we believed, in the principle of noncontradiction, in temporal succession and causality, in the solidity of objects, and in some sort of unity of the self. We know, to be sure, about relativity and the unconscious, about Freudian slips, perhaps even about Lacan's theory of the split subject— but still we believe that when we see our friend Joe, it really is he and not someone else, that if Joe's eyes were blue yesterday they will be blue tomorrow (if he is wearing postmodern tinted contact lenses, there is still a true color beneath), that if Joe's brother died yesterday he is still dead, and that if Joe tells us a story it is Joe telling us a story.

The conventions of realist narrative correspond, in other words, to what most people (at least in the West) think of as their everyday experience of the world, which may explain why these conventions are so easily internalized that even a very young child can spot and protest against inconsistencies in a story, and why they are so difficult, even for sophisticated readers, to give up. The realist novel invites its readers to make sense of it in a way that is not *essentially* different from the way they try to make sense of the world around them.

The hallmark of what I want to call contemporary avant-garde fiction, however—and I have in mind not only the work of French writers loosely associated with the *nouveau roman* and with *Tel Quel,* but also that of Americans who constituted the "first wave" of postmodernist fiction, from Burroughs to Pynchon, Sukenick, Federman, and others— is that such fiction defies, aggressively and provocatively, the traditional criteria of narrative intelligibility, and correlatively the reader's sense-making ability: where the reader expects logical and temporal development, avant-garde fiction offers repetition or else the juxtaposition of apparently random events; where the reader expects consistency, it offers contradiction; where the reader expects characters, it offers disembodied voices; where the reader expects the sense of an ending, it offers merely a stop. Even typographically, it may assault the reader, either by offering fragments with no indication of the order in which to read them (Raymond Federman does that, as does his French model, Maurice Roche), or else by confronting us—as Philippe Sollers or Pierre Guyotat do, for example—with several hundred pages of unbroken, unpunctuated words forming, apparently, a single monstrous sentence. When faced with the aggression of such a text, it is hardly any wonder if the first reaction of a reader is one of defensive counterattack: the text is called unreadable, that is to say both unintelligible and not worth reading.

In a very interesting article devoted to the question of readability, or rather of unreadability (not by chance, the title of the article is in Latin), Denis Ferraris remarked that "to call a text unreadable comes down to denying it any existence."[6] For readers to adopt such an aggressive position—to pronounce, in Ferraris's words, "a judgment that properly speaking annihilates" the text—they must feel that the text in question is not only scandalous, but also, in a profound way, menacing. Ferraris suggests that perhaps what readers really discover in a confrontation with the "unreadable" text is their own unreadability, their own unintelligibility (p. 285). The reader's counterattack might in that case be seen as a form of self-protection, a way of keeping the self intact against the dangerous fragmentation of the text. The *topos* of the text as mirror of the world and of the self is deeply ingrained in our consciousness.

The psychological implications of the readable/unreadable dichotomy, especially if one introduces the variable of gender (hinted at in my choice of epigraphs), is a question to keep in mind. Another, only slightly less thorny question is one that Barthes asked in an essay devoted to Philippe Sollers's novel *H* (1973): "How is one to read what is attested to here and there as unreadable?" ("Comment lire ce qui est attesté ici et là comme illisible?").[7] Barthes obviously did not share the negative judgment as far as *H* was concerned; his raising the question, and indeed promoting it to a central place in his essay, is a sign of his role as apologist and defender, addressing what he anticipates may be a hostile audience: "What is commented on here is not, properly speaking, Sollers's text; it is, rather, the cultural resistances of reading."[8] Why Barthes felt it necessary to defend himself against the idea that he might be writing a commentary "on" Sollers's text will become clear shortly; for the moment, we may note that for Barthes the question of how to read Sollers was the question of how to overcome the prejudices and habits of the traditional reader.

Although Barthes played in this essay with the distinction between readable and unreadable *(lisible/illisible)*, his own preferred binary opposition was, as is well known, a quite different one; not between the readable and the unreadable, but between the readable and the writable *(lisible/scriptible)*—and in this opposition, the first term was the negative one. As he wrote in the opening pages of *S/Z*, where he first proposed the two terms: "Opposite the writable text is thus established its countervalue, its negative, reactive value: what can be read, but not written: the readable. We call classical any readable text."[9] Tzvetan Todorov has pointed out the Romantic antecedents—indeed, the essential romanticism—of Barthes's notion of the modern text.[10] One finds an implicit recognition of this in Barthes's own equation between the readable and the classical—the canonical opposite of the latter being, of course, the romantic.

There is romanticism, too, in Barthes's insistence on the essentially undefinable—one might say ineffable—nature of *le texte scriptible*. Almost everything he says about this kind of text in *S/Z* is formulated in negative terms; in fact, the very first thing he says is that "about writable texts there may be nothing to say" (p. 4). The writable text is not a thing, a product to be handled or analyzed; it is what defies analysis, "a perpetual present upon which no consequent language (which would inevitably make it past) can be superimposed"; it is "the novelistic without the novel, poetry without the poem, the essay without the dissertation, writing [*écriture*] without style, production without product, structuration without structure"; it is "ourselves writing before the infinite play of the word . . . is traversed, intersected, stopped, plasticized by some singular system (Ideology, Genre, Criticism) which reduces the plurality of entrances, the opening of networks, the infinity of languages" (p. 5).

Thus the writable text, for Barthes, can only be spoken of in terms of what it is not, specifically in terms of its difference from the readable. The readable is serious, fixed, closed, structured, constrained, authoritarian, and unitary; the writable is playful, fluid, open, triumphantly plural, and in its plurality impervious to the repressive rule of structure, grammar, or logic (p. 6). However one extends the parallel series of terms, the ultimate binary opposition comes down to this: the readable is systematic, the writable mocks all attempts at systematization.

There are a number of paradoxes in *S/Z,* not the least of which is that after formulating the difference between the readable and the writable in such stark terms, Barthes appears to undermine those very differences by reading Balzac's *Sarrasine,* which he singles out as a readable text par excellence, *as if* (well, almost as if) it were a writable text. He defines the five codes by means of which the readable text constitutes itself, but he refuses to treat these codes as forming a strictly intelligible system. Instead of structuring the text, the five codes are defined by him as a "tissue of voices," a "vast 'dissolve' which insures both the overlapping and the loss of messages" (p. 20). This way of proceeding is a polemical gesture on Barthes's part. By refusing to structure even a text that he himself has just offered as a model of classical readability, he affirms his own power as a modern commentator, whose work consists in breaking up the unified text, "*maltreating* it, preventing it from speaking [*lui couper la parole*]" (p. 15). First appearances to the contrary, the absolute difference between readable and writable texts is thus not subverted, but on the contrary reinforced by Barthes, for presumably the writable text would not need to be broken up, maltreated, and desystematized by the commentator.[11] Being already nonunified and asystematic, it could only provoke the commentator's silence ("about writable texts there may be nothing to say"). In terms of Barthes's later vocabulary, the writable text elicits not commentary but *jouissance.*

It is here, with the introduction of the erotic metaphor (*jouissance* is a sexual coming), that the variable of gender becomes fully relevant. According to the norms of classical aesthetics, as Naomi Schor has shown, femininity is associated with excessive details, ornamentation, and decadence—a decadent style being defined (in Paul Bourget's words) as one "where the unity of the book decomposes to give way to the independence of the page, where the page decomposes to give way to the independence of the word."[12] By a curious and highly significant reversal, in Barthes's theory this decadent fragmented style—which in classical terms is both "feminine" and negatively valued—is coded as positive and male;[13] and it is the classically readable text, characterized by unity, coherence, and systematicity, that is coded as negative and female: "Any classic (readable) text is implicitly an art of Replete Literature [*Pleine Littérature*]; . . . like a pregnant female, replete with signifieds which criticism will not fail to deliver; like the sea [*la mer,* a homonym of *la mère,* the mother], replete with depths and movements which give it its appearance of infinity, its vast meditative surface" (pp. 200–201). Although Barthes reverses the gender coding, I think it is not accidental that the *value* attached to the texts thus regendered switches accordingly: the "feminine" text, though no longer the same, is still negative, and vice versa.

The commentator who maltreats the (feminine) readable text would seem to be performing a version of the sadistic game that, according to a famous passage in *The Pleasure of the Text*, characterizes modern writing: "The writer is someone who plays with his mother's body . . . in order to glorify it, to embellish it, or in order to dismember it, to take it to the limit of what can be known about the body. I would go so far as to take bliss [*jouir*] in a *disfiguration* of the language, and opinion will strenuously object, since it opposes 'disfiguring nature.'"[14] Conversely, the reader who, yielding to the fragmentariness and asystematicity of the "strong silent" modern text, takes his pleasure without commentary ("The modern work refuses commentary, indeed it defines itself as what refuses commentary; that is the first position on the modern"),[15] in ecstasy, *en jouissant*—that reader appears to take on a feminine role, except that Barthes describes him as unmistakably a man:

> Imagine . . . someone [*un individu*] who would abolish in himself all barriers, all classes, all exclusions, not by syncretism but by simply ridding himself of that old specter: *logical contradiction;* who would mix up all languages, even those said to be incompatible; who would bear, mutely, all the accusations of illogic, of incongruity . . . Such a man would be the abjection of our society . . . In fact, that counter-hero exists: he is the reader of the text, at the moment when he takes his pleasure.[16]

Would it be too improper to suggest that Barthes's model of the bliss provoked by reading the "writable" text functions as a homologue of male homosexual intercourse? If we allow ourselves to entertain that idea, what then happens to the woman reader of the "writable" text: will she have to impersonate the male whose *jouissance* consists in becoming, for the time of his reading, a fragmented, nonunitary subject—in other words, "feminine"? A woman impersonating a man impersonating a woman . . . Or is there a less convoluted correspondence between the fragmented modern text and the woman reader—based on their mutually "plural" eroticism as opposed to "phallic" unity, for example?

Interestingly enough, this homology between the modern text and the woman's body was one of the bases on which French feminist theorists in the 1970s, notably Hélène Cixous and Luce Irigaray, elaborated their notion of *écriture féminine*. For them, as for Barthes and other male theorists of modernity, the traditional realist novel appeared as the negative term against which the new practice of language would affirm itself. But in their terminology the realist novel was codified as male: unitary, phallic, telelogically moving toward a single meaning, a single story. The feminine text, by contrast, was synonymous with the plural, the erotic, the experimental, the new.

The question is: did their mutual rejection of the realist novel put the male theorists and practitioners of *écriture* and the female theorists and practitioners of *écriture féminine* in the same camp? Or did the substantive differences between them (for example, the eroticization and aestheticization of violence, including violence against the female body, that one finds in so much male avant-garde practice) override the sympathies and similarities?

I am not going to try to answer that question now—it will recur in various forms, implicitly or explicitly, in several of the essays to follow (most notably in Chapters 5 and 7). Instead, I will return to the question of readability as it arises in the work of male avant-garde writers; specifically, to the question Barthes posed apropos of Sollers's *H:* "How is one to read what is attested to here and there as unreadable?" Perhaps in reaction to Barthes's (male homosexual?) model of silent *jouissance,* I shall propose two different, complementary ways in which a reader (a woman reader?) might approach certain ostensibly "unreadable" texts— the one consisting in the attempt to discover *new* rules of readability that govern such texts; the other consisting in the attempt to see how such texts inscribe the question of their readability within themselves, thematizing the opposition between readable and unreadable, unity and fragmentation, order and transgression.

I shall look at works by two French writers with impeccable credentials as practitioners of avant-garde fiction, the one associated most closely with the *nouveau roman,* the other with *Tel Quel:* Alain Robbe-Grillet and Maurice Roche.

Robbe-Grillet, or, the Readability of Transgression

In discussing Robbe-Grillet's fiction one can safely invoke the author himself as commentator, for perhaps no avant-garde writer has explained and sought to justify his own work with as much persistence and intelligence as he has. A few years ago, he stopped writing fiction and embarked on a series of autobiographical works (with prominent fictional elements) of which two volumes have so far been published.[17] I shall refer here only to his fiction, however, and to the glosses he made on it over the years when he was still engaged in practicing it. (For the sake of immediacy, I will refer to all this past writing in the present tense.)

In Robbe-Grillet's theoretical writings as in his numerous public appearances, two themes seem to be dominant. First, Robbe-Grillet sees his own fiction, like that of other *nouveaux* and *nouveaux nouveaux romanciers*,[18] as radically "other" and subversive in relation to the order of realistic narrative, which is dominated by the "ideology of representation." This means that his novels are nonreadable in terms of traditional criteria of linearity, coherence, noncontradiction, and psychological depth of characters. It does not mean, however—this is Robbe-Grillet's second theme—that his fiction has no order of its own. On the contrary, he maintains that his works are highly complex and ordered systems; it is all a question of the kind of order one is looking for.

Robbe-Grillet sometimes mentions, with a mixture of wry admiration and dismay, the reading that Bruce Morrissette did of *La Jalousie* shortly after it was published.[19] Through a painstaking process of reordering and rationalization, Morrissette succeeded in demonstrating the narrative, and above all the psychological, coherence of the "story." As a result, noted Robbe-Grillet in a public lecture that was subsequently published in English, "The book became readable . . . and at the same time it was to a certain extent destroyed."[20] By constructing a unified story out of a fragmented text, the critic succumbed to the natural impulse of all readers who reduce the unfamiliar to the familiar, the unreadable to the readable, but in that process erase or repress those aspects of the text that make it new, other, and subversive. Robbe-Grillet has incorporated a similar reader into *Projet pour une révolution à New York,* which contains brief dialogues between the main narrative voice and a hypothetical reader who is constantly pointing out inconsistencies and demanding rational explanations for them. Although the narrative voice obligingly provides the explanations, the effect is that of parody. It is as though the text were saying: "Readers who want coherence will get it, but at their own risk."

In the remark quoted above ("The book became readable . . . and . . . destroyed"), Robbe-Grillet used the word "readable" in a mostly negative sense; yet, as the second dominant theme in his self-explanatory statement shows, he is also aware of another way in which texts such as his may become readable. This second kind of readability does not consist in the operation whereby the reader—or let us say the traditional reader who looks for narrative coherence—makes the unfamiliar familiar; it consists, rather, in an operation whereby the unfamiliar text *makes itself* familiar by insisting on its own codes. Unlike Barthes, who preferred to think of *le scriptible* as resisting all attempts at systematization, Robbe-Grillet knows perfectly well that his own transgressions of traditional narrative logic constitute a code, which means that they are both systematic and susceptible of systematic analysis. One could in fact show—and critics like Jean Ricardou have shown, although they have not expressed it exactly in those terms—that the very procedures in Robbe-Grillet's novels and in those of other *nouveaux romanciers* which function most clearly as transgressions of the code of realist narrative have gradually come to constitute a familiar and therefore highly readable set of devices. In a word, they have gradually moved from transgression to convention.[21]

Let me give some examples. As every reader of Robbe-Grillet's novels from *Le Voyeur* on knows, one of his favorite transgressive devices is what he calls *glissement* ("sliding"). There are many different kinds of *glissement* in his works: from one narrative voice to another (what started out as a story told by X slides into a story told by Y, who has nothing to do with X); from one time-and-place sequence to another (what one thought was a story—or at least a sequence—about a girl named Laura who is attacked in the subway, all of a sudden becomes a story about a girl named Laura who is being raped in her room); from the description of inanimate images to narrative movement (what starts as the description of a picture on the cover of a detective novel suddenly turns into narration), and vice versa (what one thought was narration turns out to be the description of an advertising poster).

All these *glissements* have in common the transgression of rules of continuity and noncontradiction, which function in the realist novel as a means of ensuring readability. The paradox, however, is that after reading a number of Robbe-Grillet's novels, a reader comes to *expect* the *glissements* as part of the code regulating them. This type of transgression begins to function as a familiar device—an element of high probability and consequently of high readability in his works.

The same can be said of any number of other procedures, including one that Robbe-Grillet has taken pains to explain on different occasions. This is the procedure whereby he takes the most debased myths of our society, especially myths of erotic violence, and subjects them to a potentially endless series of permutations and variations, whose ultimate effect (at least so Robbe-Grillet claims) is to deconstruct or demythify them. The repetition-with-variations of popular myths is here seen as a kind of emancipatory gesture, subverting both traditional narrative— which demands linear development, not paradigmatic variations—*and* the dominant ideology, which demands to be reinforced, not deconstructed. Whether or not one is convinced by Robbe-Grillet's explanations of the effect produced by his *bricolage* with sadoerotic myths (I personally have some reservations, which I develop in the next chapter), the fact remains that the procedure has become familiar and predictable, as have the thematic constants (essentially women being raped and tortured) with which his *bricolage* operates.

Indeed, the possibility exists that Robbe-Grillet's novels, both individually and as a corpus, have become all too readable—not in the sense of a readability imposed on them by the traditional reader, but in the sense in which they themselves have codified their own transgressive procedures, and codified as well the *commentary* on those procedures. It is instructive to see how many articles, chapters in books, and book-length studies have been published explaining what Robbe-Grillet the novelist is up to.[22] What is happening, what already happened years ago, is a *récuperation* whereby works that were intended as a "machine of war against order" (the expression is Robbe-Grillet's) have become "classicized" and classified. This kind of *récuperation* is perhaps the tragic fate of every successful avant-garde. As Poggioli remarked: "Like any artistic tradition, no matter how antitraditional it may be, the avant-garde also has its conventions. In the broad sense of the word, it is itself no more than a new system of conventions . . . Disorder becomes a rule when it is opposed in a deliberate and systematic manner to a pre-established order."[23] Mick Jagger, of Rolling Stones fame, put it even more pithily. At a recent black-tie gala at the Waldorf Astoria, inducting the rock group into the Rock 'n' Roll Hall of Fame, Jagger said: "We are being rewarded for 25 years of bad behavior. First we shock you. Then they put you in a museum."[24]

The pronouns are a bit confused, but we ("we") get the point. It was no doubt because he too got the point that Barthes so persistently refused to define or write analytic commentaries on *le scriptible*. The moment one begins to look for rules and order one inevitably finds them, even if they are not the traditional ones. And since the chief raison d'être of the transgressive text is precisely to be—or to appear—transgressive, once one has understood its rules a certain sense of déjà vu and lack of interest ensues. Robbe-Grillet himself spoke, as early as 1978, of the impasse that both the *nouveau roman* and the *nouveau nouveau roman* had reached.[25]

But perhaps I am being too negative—it is possible after all that, having understood the rules of the game, a reader will take great pleasure in playing it over and over, finding delight in the variations presented in each new version. Whether bored or happy, however, there is no doubt that such a reader is no longer dealing with the unfamiliar or the "unreadable." He or she has simply discovered, or created, a new kind of readable text.

I would not be surprised to learn that it was precisely in order to circumvent such mastery (for that is what is involved here) on the reader's part that Robbe-Grillet gave up writing novels, and turned to a genre that (for the moment, at least) appears incongruous and unsettlingly new.

Maurice Roche: Paradigm Lost and Found

Maurice Roche's work poses the question of readability immediately and radically: in Roche's writing, fragmentation and discontinuity occur not only on the level of narrative logic, as in Robbe-Grillet's, but also on the level of individual sentences, paragraphs, and textual segments. What is subverted here is the coherence of any kind of discourse or text as well as the coherence of a story. It is almost as if Roche's writings were meant to illustrate, with a vengeance, Derrida's notion that every text bears within it traces and echoes of other texts: in Roche's work it would appear that a text is *nothing but* a heterogeneous assemblage, a juxtaposition of fragments belonging to different wholes, a collection of verbal (and occasionally iconic) bits and pieces, a cacophony of voices. These novels—for that is what their author calls them—seem really to defy any attempt at systematization.

Is there no way to read such books other than by surrendering to their incoherence? Is there no paradigm, either of writing or of reading, that they allow one to construct? These are rhetorical questions, as my readers have certainly guessed. Indeed, I shall argue that they are questions inscribed in Roche's texts themselves, and that it is precisely their inscription which gives these texts their particular kind of readability.

In 1974, Roche published a novel entitled *Codex*—not an indifferent title, since it means both code and book. It was the codex which, by replacing the parchment scrolls of antiquity, inaugurated a new era and a new mode of reading. The first two pages of *Codex* consist of quotations from two of Roche's previous works: one is from a brief text entitled "Contretypes," published in *Les Lettres nouvelles* in 1970; the other is from Roche's first novel, *Compact,* published in 1966. Two quotations from *Compact,* complete with page references, occupy a page unto themselves. They are as follows:

IL EXISTAIT AUSSI DES LETTRES
:"MON AMOUR, J'écrivais
toujours la même chose, *(t'en rendras-tu compte?)*

and below that, after a large blank space:

JIVARO OU LE PARADIGME PERDU

With these quotations (which in *Compact* occur twenty pages apart) placed as a kind of preface or epigraph to the text of *Codex* proper, Roche performs an autocommentary analogous to Robbe-Grillet's glosses on his own texts. It is also a *meta*commentary, being part of the work rather than a separate text "on" it. This commentary is extremely interesting, for it both poses and answers the question I asked two paragraphs back—but poses and answers it in such a way that it becomes more problematic than ever.

First, the posing: Mon amour, j'écrivais toujours la même chose (t'en rendras-tu compte?)—My love, I was always writing the same thing (will you be aware of it?). The question is presented in three different type styles, with the result that although a coherent interrogative sentence seems to have been formed—and I have emphasized that coherence in my own rendering—we cannot *in fact* be sure that the three segments which form the sentence actually belong together, in other words, that they are readable as a single sentence. This doubt is increased by the fact that the words "Mon amour" are preceded by quotation marks which are never closed, thus creating an ambiguity as to whether the "tu" in the parentheses refers to the same person as "mon amour" or to someone else—and also by the fact that there is no closing punctuation. Having read *Compact,* I know that the different type styles mark independent areas within the text, each of which can be read by skipping the intervening ones. Thus what appeared to be a coherent question disintegrates before my eyes even as I am in the process of registering it.

The answer (if answer it is, and if question there was) comes almost as a mocking anticlimax: JIVARO OU LE PARADIGME PERDU. If the paradigm is lost, how are we ever to notice a repetition ("même chose")? Yet here again, things are not so simple. A Jivaro, my *Larousse en couleurs* tells me, is an Amazonian headhunter and headshrinker—a preserver of skulls, a specialist in the conservation of traces. I know that the image of the skull, as well as the word "crâne" and its semantic variants, are prominently featured in Roche's writings. Finally, if I look up the quotation in *Compact,* I see that it is part of a series of "condensed" titles, preceded by DIGEST DE LA PHYSIOLOGIE DU GOUT and followed by RECHERCHE DU TIME-BINDING. "Jivaro" then begins to resonate with *Jivago,* "le paradigme perdu" with both *Paradise Lost* and *A la recherche du temps perdu.*

The very utterance that seemed to deny all possibility of recognizing repetition becomes a pointer to the repetition by the text of other texts, and a pointer also to the work of transformation that Roche's text accomplishes on others, including his own. But transforming implies preserving as well as changing, and to notice transformation is to notice both identity and difference. The "lost" paradigm cannot, therefore, be altogether lost: it can be multiplied, combined with other paradigms, condensed, disseminated, covered up, transposed.[26] These activities are, I think, the privileged subject of Roche's fictions, and I would like now to look a bit more closely at *Compact*, his first published novel.

Philippe Sollers, in his preface to the book (which appeared under the *Tel Quel* imprint, in a series edited by Sollers), distinguishes four separate *récits* in the text, analogous to the "lines" or "parts" in a musical score. He assigns each *récit* a label—*hypothétique, parlé, narratif, descriptif*—based on the verb tenses and the personal pronouns that characterize it. Visually and materially, however, the text presents itself as much more fragmented than that, for it is broken up into at least twelve different kinds of type styles, all of which occur more than once. Six of these can be thought of as consecutive, for if the segments printed in these types (boldface roman, for example, or small caps or italics) are read consecutively by skipping the intervening ones, they form a single narrative or descriptive space—I hardly think that "line" is the right word, since there is no linear development and since there are times when a textual segment simply trails off or is cut off in midsentence, to be picked up again later but without being *continued* in linear fashion.

These consecutive type styles are what Sollers used in delimiting his four kinds of *récit*. The other six styles are not consecutive in the above sense, but each one is used recurrently in the same way. For example, titles and newspaper headlines appear in capital italics; boldface and capital italics appear twice, both times in German; extra small type is used in footnotes, and so on.

In saying all this I have already begun to systematize the text, however, for at first glance one is not aware of such regularities. Each page presents itself, rather, as a typographical puzzle consisting of the different type styles plus blank spaces of varying widths and heights. As the book unfolds, these puzzles become increasingly heterogeneous: there appear parentheses, brackets, and quotation marks, many of them never closed; parallel and vertical lines between blocks or lines of type; musical notations, fragments in Greek, Hebrew, Russian, German, English, and Eskimo; drawings, figures, and numbers; lines of type run together without any spaces between words; one word superimposed on another as in a palimpsest; lines of nonsense syllables designated as onomatopoeic representations of "cris chaotiques."[27]

In short, the more one reads, the greater is one's sense that the book is becoming unreadable, disintegrating in the very process of constituting itself: "des noms hétéroclites peu à peu délavés, illisibles" ("heterogeneous names gradually washed out, unreadable"—p. 163). And two pages later, the last sentence in the book: "Une texture de signes, de cicatrices, un tissu tactile se décompose" ("A texture of signs, of scars, a tactile fabric disintegrates"—p. 165). At the very instant at which it falls apart, the text comments on its disintegration.

I will certainly not try to put Humpty Dumpty together again, nor try to heal what Laurent Jenny has called, in a different context, "the aggressions of the text against itself."[28] I will simply point out, after having emphasized those aspects of the text that tend to make the very notion of a paradigm—or of readability—derisory, a few counteraspects which, if they do not suffice to create a single totalizing paradigm, nevertheless tend to set up limited continuities and repetitions that a reader can hang on to.

First, from a purely visual perspective, the six consecutive type styles gradually become continuous, for although they interrupt and disrupt each other on the page, a fairly high degree of visual probabililty is created for each one after it has recurred once or twice. This is quite apart from the fact that the narrative or descriptive space signaled by each is characterized by a particular set of syntactic features, and by semantic features as well. Thus the very first style that appears (boldface italics) is characterized by the use of "tu" and the future and conditional tenses, and features the isotopy[29] of blindness; the second consecutive style (boldface roman) is continuous in the use of "on" and the present tense, and features the isotopy of pain *(douleur);* the third consecutive style (standard roman) is continuous in the use of "je" and the imperfect tense, and features the isotopy of death or dying; and so on. Each narrative or descriptive space therefore has a certain homogeneity and fills out a certain paradigm, even if that paradigm is disseminated, Osiris-like, throughout the text.

What is even more remarkable is that linkages are formed not only between the broken-up segments of a single space, but between segments of different spaces as well. On a given page, segments formed by *different* type styles can be read in linear fashion despite their heterogeneity, much like the "question" I discussed earlier ("Mon amour, j'écrivais toujours la même chose . . ."). True, some grammatical anomalies may result, as for example in this: "On ne remarque pas tout d'abord, tant on y est habitué, qu'IL FALLAIT PROFITER DE CHAQUE MINUTE DANS LE SEUL BUT D'OUBLIER CELLE QUI ALLAIT SUIVRE" (p. 66)—"One does not notice at first, being so used to it, that IT WAS NECESSARY TO TAKE ADVANTAGE OF EACH MINUTE WITH THE SOLE AIM OF FORGETTING THE ONE THAT WOULD FOLLOW." The segment beginning "Il fallait" is in a different type style and the verb tenses change accordingly, thus being ungrammatical in relation to the present tense of "remarque" in the first segment. The syntactic armature of the sentence is so strong, however (or is it our habit of reading linearly that is so ingrained?), that this anomaly goes almost unnoticed. We run the heterogeneous segments together and so make "sense"—and a sentence—of them.

Laurent Jenny has noticed a similar process in William Burroughs' textual montages or "cutups," which have a lot in common with Roche's text. Jenny remarks: "The words combine after all [*malgré tout*], and even if their syntax remains suspended one's reading goes on unimpeded, pursuing a tyrannical linearity. Besides, vague isotopies constitute themselves here and there, due to the fact that the montage uses redundant or linked elements over and above the ellipses. This makes one wonder at times whether it is not the materiality of the page that constitutes the text, whether the written text is not condemned to textuality."[30] (By "textuality," Jenny means, here, textual unity or continuity.)

This question seems to me particularly pertinent to *Compact,* but I would expand it to include not only the "materiality of the page" but the "materiality of the book." The "vague isotopies" that Jenny mentions constitute themselves between heterogeneous segments on a single page and between heterogeneous segments throughout the many pages that constitute the book. Thus blindness characterizes not only the "tu" of the first narrative space but also the "je" of the third, prompting one to conclude that they are the same person (indeed, most commentators take it for granted). *Douleur* and *souffrance* become associated with the "on" of the second space and also with the "je" of the third—and here too, the "on" (impersonal "one") can be read simply as a variation on "je," again designating the same person. References to the "Orient" occur both in the space of impersonal descriptions set in capital italics and in the discourse of the Japanese doctor (lowercase italics), who in turn figures as a character in the space defined by "je." With only a bit of effort, one can construct out of all this discontinuity a story.[31]

As I turn the pages, thematic repetitions begin to take shape, linked in some way to the theme of memory. Finally, the more I read and the more the text emphasizes its unreadability, the more I also tend to establish a single thematic category to make sense of it: the category of "mnemopolis," memory as trace, as charting, as inscription—lines on a page, convolutions on the brain, roads on a map.

Now I seem to have done exactly what I said I wouldn't and couldn't do, which is to find the unifying paradigm and heal the self-inflicted wounds of the text. Is it, then, the *reader* who is condemned to textuality? Perhaps. Yet if I have done violence to the text by making sense of it *malgré tout* (and even so, aware of the tentativeness of that enterprise), it has surely not been without the prompting *of* the text:

Mnemopolis que tu pourras hanter sous ton crâne sera une ville seule et obscure. Pas de rues pas de canaux nul labour alentour (ça?—les circonvolutions de ta cervelle), mais des vestiges auxquels tu tenteras de te raccrocher; autant d'objets ou de fragments que patiemment, et non sans hésitations, tu voudras lier les uns aux autres—leur donner un sens en les raccordant.   (p. 16)

Mnemopolis which you will be able to haunt beneath your skull will be a lonely and dark city. No streets no canals no plowing roundabout (this?— the convolutions of your brain), but vestiges to which you will try to cling; so many objects or fragments which, patiently and not without hesitation, you will want to link to each other—to give them a meaning by joining them together.

Etait-ce un syntagme étroit qui venait d'exploser dans cette caboche où j'avais remplacé les objets par des mots?   (p. 106)

Was it a narrow syntagm which had just exploded in that noggin where I had replaced objects with words?

La vie n'est là que pour mémoire.   (p. 107)

Life is there only for memory.

Nous avons la sensation d'être le moule de quelque calligramme fantôme: notre image réduite à la dimension d'un crâne (et nous sommes dedans). (p. 165)

We have the feeling of being the mold of some phantom *calligramme:* our image reduced to the dimensions of a skull (and we are inside).

Surely what Roche's text enacts over and over again, at times in an alternation so rapid that it approaches simultaneity, is the losing and regaining, or rather the losing and *recreating* of the paradigm. JIVARO (headshrinker, preserver) OU LE PARADIGME PERDU (there is nothing to preserve) A LA RECHERCHE DU TIME-BINDING. If to be condemned to textuality means to be condemned to create while destroying, *to make* sense as well as to unmake it, then textuality may not be such a bad thing. And readability neither.

Self-Reflexive Afterthought

What kind of reading have I been practicing on Robbe-Grillet and Roche, and what it does suggest about the theoretical issues raised at the beginning of this essay? It seems obvious that my strategy in reading these works (these authors) has, as its primary effect, neutralized their aggressiveness. In the case of Roche, the text's multiple aggressions—

or, if you will, its negativity—were shown to be dialectically counter-balanced by something positive: the "unreadable" text became readable as a text about reading. Some commentators go so far (I will not follow them) as to say that such works "teach" the reader about "his" (usually used as a universal) own activity; they thus do away with the text's aggression by transforming it into a benevolent didacticism.

In the case of Robbe-Grillet, the text's aggressiveness was given a turn of the screw (as it were): I claimed, somewhat aggressively, that Robbe-Grillet's aggressive/transgressive devices became blunted through familiarity. Obviously, I could have reversed the procedure, applying the arguments in reverse order: showing that Robbe-Grillet's novels are always "about" the activity of reading (and its correlative, writing),[32] and that Roche's dialectic of destruction and creation, of unmaking and remaking sense, has itself become a familiar, coded procedure.

Is the attempt to defuse the aggressiveness of the avant-garde text characteristically "feminine" or "masculine"? Is it the gesture of a woman who refuses to fall into the stereotype of "feminine" receptivity and openness to seduction?

The question is up for grabs. In the meantime, I want to suggest that both of my approaches converge on the problem of repetition, whether for the avant-garde text or for its commentary. In one instance, every new work becomes yet another text on which to demonstrate that the "true" subject of avant-garde (modern, postmodern, what have you) fiction is its own (un)readability—a by now all too familiar deconstruc-tionist move. In the other instance, repetition is itself shown to be the problem faced by the avant-garde text, which, even as it aggressively proclaims its negativity, runs the permanent risk of becoming "recuper-ated" into a familiar canon.

The question for the avant-garde—and for its theory and criticism—comes down, perhaps, to this: Can one ever escape from repetition, or must one discover, as Stephen Dedalus discovers about history, that from some nightmares it is impossible to awake?

THREE

Reading Robbe-Grillet:
Sadism and Text in *Projet pour une révolution à New York*

When this essay was first published, in 1977 (it is in a real sense the kernel out of which the present book grew), the dominant academic way of reading the *nouveau roman*, and Alain Robbe-Grillet's work in particular, was the programmatically formalist one represented in France most forcefully by Jean Ricardou. In the popular press, of course, one did not generally find this approach—like the indignant critic whose words I quote at the beginning of the essay, many "ordinary" readers were simply shocked by Robbe-Grillet's subject matter and did not want to hear about his formal experimentation with narrative. To others, it was the experimentation with narrative that was itself shocking, either to be ignored or denounced as "modish," "elitist," "anti-humanist," or merely "unreadable."

It was in this context of popular indifference or hostility that Ricardou, as I noted in the last chapter, played for a few years the role of chief "defender and illustrator" of the new fiction; his influential, often brilliant readings provided a model for many academic critics and eventually came to constitute a kind of orthodox discourse about the *nouveau roman*, a discourse adopted by some of the novelists themselves when discussing their work.

In turn, it was in reaction to this academic orthodoxy that my own essay was written. The essay has often been cited, perhaps because it was among the first to propose what we would now call a feminist deconstructive approach to avant-garde fiction. In particular, it may have been the first to offer a feminist deconstructive reading of Robbe-Grillet's work; odd as it may seem to us today, no one at the time thought it intellectually respectable to talk about, much less submit to serious critical scrutiny, the obvious, provocatively aggressive erotic content of his novels.

As far as my own writing is concerned, this was the first critical work of mine to be informed by feminism and by psychoanalysis. I wrote it in a state of great intellectual elation, as one writes when one feels one is breaking new ground, yet almost parenthetically, during the off-hours of what I perceived then as a more serious project, my book on the *roman à thèse* (published some years later as *Authoritarian Fictions: The Ideological Novel as a Literary Genre*).

It is for reasons both historical and personal, then, that I have decided not to try and "update" this essay or make any but the most minor revisions. I have added or substituted English translations for what were originally French quotes only, made occasional changes in punctuation and paragraphing, and slipped in one or two extra notes or references. Otherwise, alone among the essays in this book, this one stands un(re)touched. The proof: I have even left in all of the "universal *he*'s" to designate the reader.

L'écrivain est quelqu'un qui joue avec le corps de sa mère.

—ROLAND BARTHES

"Rien d'autre qu'une petite histoire de sadiques," nothing more than a little story about sadists. The indignant journalist who thus dismissed *Projet pour une révolution à New York* (he had been led by the title to expect a treatment of social problems in the United States) was roundly taken to task by Jean Ricardou, in the critical essay he devoted to Robbe-Grillet's novel.[1] *Projet,* affirmed Ricardou, is no more a "little story about sadists" than *Un Amour de Swann* is a "little story about a cuckold." As for the title, only a hopeless obscurantist would expect it to refer to flesh-and-blood revolutionaries in the city of New York. *Projet,* like all of Robbe-Grillet's fictions, is a profoundly subversive work; its subversiveness consists in its rendering impossible any reading that would reduce it to the status of a realistic novel.

One need hardly insist on the pertinence of Ricardou's remarks, or on the eccentricity of the criticism he attacked. Robbe-Grillet's practice as a writer is now too well known—and has been too well analyzed by critics like Ricardou, Roudiez, Heath, and Robbe-Grillet himself—to allow even the kind of sympathetic realistic reading that Bruce Morrissette is known for.[2] As far as *Projet pour une révolution à New York* is concerned, Morrissette himself has abandoned the attempt at a realistic reading: "the true value of *Projet,*" he maintains, "is that it is more of a project for revolution in novelistic forms than a project for revolution in New York, or elsewhere."[3]

Neither a "tale" of revolution nor a "tale" about sadists, *Projet* remains a troubling work—not because it subverts the most cherished traditional notions of what constitutes a "readable" narrative, but for other, less acknowledged reasons. The formal subversion, which has preoccupied most critics, is by now an expected feature not only of Robbe-Grillet's fictions but of the whole body of works we have come to know under the collective, if imprecise label of *nouveau roman*. Discontinuity, *rupture,* autorepresentation, the absolute refusal to "signify" anything other than the process of its own elaboration—these have become canonical features of certain modern texts, and although some tradition-bound readers have not ceased to be infuriated by them, they are no longer the features critics should most insist on in discussing these texts. The danger of a new orthodoxy is never far distant where critical discourse is concerned, and once the *nouveaux romanciers* enter the ranks of "Ecrivains de toujours,"[4] once their writings are analyzed and catalogued as a repertoire of formal devices, no matter how subversive or "revolutionary," it is time to look elsewhere.

I propose to look at what has been most avoided—one is tempted to say, repressed—by critics until now: the thematics of *Projet*, and more precisely its sado-erotic core. This approach does not imply a devious return to a "realistic" or referential reading; it will not culminate in psychoanalytic speculations about Robbe-Grillet in the manner of Charles Mauron; finally, it does not represent a disguised attempt to impose continuity and coherent meaning on a "plural" text. Rather, my aim is to examine the functioning of the text not only on the level of signifiers, as has chiefly been done until now, but also on the level of signifieds.

Stephen Heath sees "the adventure of the writing in a Robbe-Grillet novel" as consisting in an "activity of reassembling, of constructing from, existing elements"—in other words, in what Lévi-Strauss has called *bricolage*.[5] This is an excellent formulation. I would remark, however, that Robbe-Grillet's *bricolage* involves certain highly charged thematic constants, organized into scenic and narrative configurations. These configurations can be analyzed as variants of a controlling fantasy: in Freudian terms, as imaginary enactments of desire.[6] A formalist approach that treats the fantasmatic content of the fiction as a given on which the activity of *bricolage* is practiced bypasses the most interesting questions posed by Robbe-Grillet's texts, and by *Projet* in particular. The questions I shall explore here are: the relationship between the reader and the fantasies enacted in the text; the significance of the intertextual relations between Robbe-Grillet's fictions and those of Sade;[7] finally, the relationship between Sadean fantasy and the theory of the "self-engendered" text.

First, a reminder about *Projet* and about its dominant readings until now. The text, explicitly identified as a *roman,* consists in a discontinuous series of narrative and descriptive sequences, assumed by an equally discontinuous series of narrators—or, more exactly, of narrative voices. The latter are constantly "sliding" into one another: thus, the subway sequence involving three teenagers originates in the voice of "JR" (Fr. p. 105; Eng. p. 86), but is eventually taken over by the voice known as the "Narrator" (Fr. pp. 112, 125; Eng. pp. 92, 103), while the sequence of the abandoned lot is begun by the voice of "Laura" (Fr. p.

159; Eng. p. 134), but is continued by the "Narrator," who reports it as a dream dreamt by him (Fr. p. 172; Eng. p. 145).

Not only the voices but the sequences themselves slide into one another—the subway sequence, for example, whose protagonist is a girl named Laura, slides at several points into another sequence, also involving a girl named Laura, but which takes place inside a house (for example, Fr. pp 137–144; Eng. pp. 114–120). Similarly, descriptions of inanimate objects—for example, the cover of a detective novel—slide into narration (the static, two-dimensional image suddenly "comes to life"), and vice versa: what seemed to be the narration of an animate sequence suddenly turns out to be the description of a subway advertising poster.

Such slidings are characteristic of all of Robbe-Grillet's novels and films, and have become more and more emphasized after *Dans le Labryinthe*. A recent film explicitly refers to them in the title: *Glissements progressifs du plaisir*. The effect of these *glissements* is to undermine any attempt on the reader's or viewer's part to construct a unified story out of the discontinuous textual fragments, and above all to render impossible a traditional reading based on what Ricardou has called the "dogma of representation."[8] Since the text constantly calls attention to itself as a text—as a fabulation, a construction of the writing subject— the reader is prevented from falling into the illusionistic traps set for him by the traditional realistic novel, all of whose devices are essentially devices of naturalization, their aim being to make the reader "forget" that he is reading a text and "believe" that he is witnessing a presentation of reality.

Opposed to the narrative discontinuities of *Projet* is the presence of a limited number of thematic constants. Chief of these, since it is found in every one of the narrative sequences, is the theme of aggression— specifically sexual aggression, in the form of rape, burning, mutilation of the breasts and genitals, forced medical experiments, necrophilia— practiced by men on the bodies of women. Subordinate to this theme, but closely linked to it, are two others: that of ritual sacrifice (repetition of a fixed sequence endowed with collective significance and ending with the immolation of a victim) and that of theatricality. The sacrifice takes place in a clearly defined space (possibly on an actual stage or in front of television cameras) and is lit up by projectors, by a beam of light coming from a single lamp, and so on.

These three themes—aggression, ritualism, theatricality—are related, parodistically, to the theme of revolution. The fusion of themes is accomplished in one of the early narrative sequences, which shows the so-called Narrator witnessing a theatrical lesson in revolutionary tactics.

The conclusion reached by the actors who are reciting the "lesson" is that the perfect revolutionary crime would be

> la défloration opérée de force sur une fille vierge . . . , la victime étant ensuite immolée par éventration ou égorgement, son corps nu devant être brûlé pour finir sur un bûcher arrosé de pétrole. (p. 41)

> the defloration, performed by force, of a virgin . . . , the victim then being immolated by disembowelment or throat-cutting, her naked and blood-stained body to be burned at a stake doused with gasoline. (p. 30)

This particular sequence can be considered as the generator for all of the other sequences; *Projet* would then be a series of textual realizations, or variants, of the revolutionary "project" outlined here.

I stated earlier that the thematics of *Projet,* and specifically the sado-erotic fantasies enacted in it, have been avoided or evaded by most critics. Is this in fact the case? If so, what forms has their avoidance taken?[9]

The first, and most obvious, has been to ignore the thematics altogether and treat the text exclusively as a set of formal variations operating on the level of signifiers. This is what Ricardou does in the greater part of his essay on *Projet.* After demonstrating the discontinuous character of the narration—somewhat along the lines of what I referred to as *glissements,* although Ricardou prefers to speak of "cuts" or "unhealed cuts" (*coupures non-cicatrisées,* that is, nonrationalizable in terms of continuity)—Ricardou concludes that in this kind of world "the fiction [in the sense of "story"] is an immense metaphor of its narration" (p. 221). In other words, the text is *auto*representative.

This means, among other things, a reversal of the traditional status of words: whereas traditionally it is the story that produces or "calls into being" certain words (in a story about a young girl going to a ball, one will necessarily encounter such words as "gown," "partner," "waltz," and so on), in this instance it is certain words that produce the story. Ricardou calls these words *vocables producteurs.* In *Projet,* the major *vocable producteur* is, according to him, the word *rouge,* red. It is the word *rouge* that produces, by what Ricardou calls an operation of "similitude," the blood, the flames, the revolution ("reds"), the red brick floor in the Narrator's house, the Bloody Marys that are the Narrator's favorite drink, the red hair of one female victim, the red dress of another, and the long red-hot needles that are part of one torturer's "regulation tool kit" (pp. 221–223).

Admittedly, Ricardou is working here on the level of signifieds, not on that of signifiers, since what fire, blood, and red-hot needles have in common is the concept (Saussure's term for the signified) of redness. By limiting himself to that single concept, however, Ricardou is unable to pursue other, thematically more relevant similitudes—such as violence, for example. In any case, he soon moves on to the level of signifiers proper: he shows that by an operation of "difference," the word *rouge* generates a whole series of anagrammatic and anaphonic transformations: *orgue, rogue, ogre, orge, roue, rue, grue, gros, or, os,* and so on. Some of these may in turn generate whole chains of signifiers which organize the fiction, such as *rouge-orgue-organiste-organe-orgasme-Morgan* (name of one of the actors) *morts* (dead men) and *gants* (gloves).

Finally, Ricardou moves from the level of single words (*Jeux de mots*) to the level of whole sequences (*Jeux de scènes*), and shows that analogous operations of similitude, inversion, permutation, and combination are at work. Thus, he notes that the major action of the first sequence in the book is the action of penetration (the Narrator looks at, and eventually *through* the design of a wooden door), and then argues that the "idea" of penetration produces, by an operation of similitude, the reiterated scenes of rape, the innumerable pointed objects (knives, keys, needles, pales) and the aggressions of all kinds that proliferate in the fiction. One must conclude that the text is not only autorepresentative but also self-generating: a single concept or a single *vocable producteur* gives rise to entire textual segments.

Ricardou's analysis is, as always, extremely suggestive. Thematic considerations, however, have obviously no place in it. His demonstration of the text's verbal games would in no way be affected if we substituted roses and strawberry ice-cream cones for blood and red-hot needles: his *vocable producteur, rouge,* would account equally for both sets of objects. Paradoxically, Ricardou's analysis accomplishes, on the thematic level, the very sleight-of-hand trick he is so quick to denounce on the formal level in the traditional novel: his analyis "naturalizes" the thematic material of *Projet*, making it appear as the necessary—and therefore "innocent"—consequence of certain formal operations. Thus he writes: "If the fiction is, at a certain level, a metaphor of its narration, then we may infer that a privileged thematics [*une thématique privilégiée*] must generally accompany certain narrative procedures" (p. 221). It is as though the "self-engendered" text were inevitably linked to themes of violence: that may perhaps be true, but if so, the relationship is worth exploring—and explaining.

It was no less a commentator than Robbe-Grillet who first noted the negative implications of Ricardou's work on his text. In his paper at the 1971 *décade de Cerisy* devoted to the *nouveau roman*, Robbe-Grillet addressed himself to the question of how he chose his "generators" and specifically rejected the idea of a *vocable producteur* envisaged as a phonic and graphic matrix out of which all the elements of the fiction could be derived.[10] The chief reason Robbe-Grillet gave for rejecting this notion—which, as he remarked, owes a great deal to the example of Raymond Roussel—is that it leads to a "sneaky consequence" *(conséquence sournoise),* that of "innocence rediscovered" *(l'innocence retrouvée).* If the writer is no longer held responsible for his words, if the text is seen as a "paradise rediscovered where words would mate in liberty, not responsible, not situated, innocent," independent of the writer's intervention, the ultimate consequence will be "an idealization, sacralization or naturalization of language itself: language articulated as the profound—and before long, divine—Nature of the human being."[11]

Robbe-Grillet's insistence on the writer's "will to intervention" *(volonté d'intervention)* seems to affirm the writer's freedom in the choice of his themes. In the latter part of his essay, however, he introduces a significant restriction: the themes of blood, fire, and revolution are, according to him, not freely chosen. They are part of a contemporary mythology, part of the diffuse *parole* (in Saussure's sense of the term) that surrounds us in today's society and that manifests itself in a multitude of forms: pulp fiction, advertising posters, slick magazines, comic strips, pornographic journals sold in sex shops, and so on. The only freedom left to the writer is to consider this *parole* that surrounds him as a *langue,* and to produce his own *parole* with the elements thus furnished to him. The result will be that instead of being dominated by the reigning mythologies, the writer will dominate them: he will exercise over them the power of his freedom, which consists not in ignoring or self-righteously rejecting popular myths but in talking them out—or, as Robbe-Grillet noted elsewhere, in *playing with them.*[12]

Robbe-Grillet's definition of what he is doing goes much further than Ricardou's analysis in accounting for the specificity of his themes. Yet, the possibility exists that Robbe-Grillet may also, in a very subtle and indirect way, be evading the question. If one maintains, as Robbe-Grillet seems to do, that not the writer but the society is responsible for the specific nature of the theme, is that not yet another way of declaring the writer's innocence? The fantasies of mutilation, rape, torture, and murder become then not the products of the writer's imagination, but the *données* on which the writer's imagination works. The writer's activity is not only innocent, it is positively beneficial: its ultimate effect is to expose the myths for what they are, bring them up into the light, and thus deprive them of their alienating power.[13]

This is precisely how Robbe-Grillet envisions the effect of his text: in the programmatic statement included as a *prière d'insérer* in *Projet,* he wrote:

What is new is that such phantons [identified earlier as "the jumble of sexual nightmares: the subway, Blacks, arson, organized assassination, bloody revolution"—oddly enough, no mention of rape, torture, or ritual sacrifice], which in the past rose up mysteriously from the abysmal depths, are today exposed to broad daylight, to their superficiality as *images d'Epinal,* or comic strips. There remain for us only the flat figures of a pack of cards: in themselves they have no meaning or value, but each player will give them meaning, his own, by arranging them in his hand and then throwing them on the table according to his ordering, his own invention of the game being played.

The reference to *images d'Epinal* (simple colored illustrations especially popular in the nineteenth century, forerunners of today's comic strips) and to comic strips invites a comparison of Robbe-Grillet's text with certain kinds of pop art. Just as pop art is an ironic repetition of popular imagery—the irony acting to negate or deconstruct the original that is being repeated—so *Projet* takes the "jumble of sexual nightmares" associated with New York and ironically repeats them, thus exposing them as nothing but two-dimensional images, the "flat figures of a pack of cards."

At this point, Robbe-Grillet's analysis converges rather neatly with Ricardou's; in both instances, the result is an extremely seductive rationalization of the thematic constants of *Projet.* The formalist rationalization treats the thematic constants as the "natural" consequences of certain rules of transformation; the cultural rationalization treats them as mythological *données* that the text seeks to deconstruct. In both cases, the text is seen as profoundly subversive—first, because it subverts traditional forms of narrative and traditional notions of readability; second, because it subverts prevailing cultural myths. These two kinds of subversion can in fact be seen as complementary: it is by its ironic repetition of popular narrative genres, such as the porno detective novel, that *Projet* accomplishes its task of cultural demystification.

As I say, both of these readings are extremely seductive; both are confirmed, moreover, by an experience of the text. The constant *glissements* between narrative voices and sequences, the plethora of sado-erotic scenes unfolding in such "mythical" places as a subway car, an abandoned lot, a Greenwich Village brownstone, a fire escape, a church in Harlem; the association of such scenes with activities involving drug traffic, prostitution, revolutionary conspiracies, double agents—all of this signals, by means of accumulation and hyperbole, the parodistic, subversive nature of the fiction. In addition, *Projet* contains, like most of Robbe-Grillet's texts, numerous self-definitions in the form of *mises en abyme,*[14] which leave no doubt as to the kind of fiction the text is both playing with and subverting. One such *mise en abyme* is the

Narrator's description of Laura's reading habits: she reads detective novels, always the same ones, mixing up their plots, constantly rearranging and reassembling a limited number of "detective-story episodes cannily calculated by the author" (p. 68)—"péripéties policières savamment calculées par l'auteur" (p. 85). This activity of rearranging and reassembling is none other than the *bricolage* that characterizes *Projet* itself.

Still, a certain uneasiness pervades both the formalist and the culturalist readings of this very slippery text. The uneasiness is manifested precisely as concerns the first of the problems I raised earlier: the relationship between the reader and the fantasies enacted in the text. It is surely not an accident that Ricardou, after having successfully avoided the whole question, concludes his essay by positing the existence of "good" and "bad" readers of *Projet*, the difference between them residing in the way they react to the sado-erotic elements in the fiction. "Who can claim," he asks, "that many readers of detective or porno novels won't read *Projet* by ignoring its subversive traits . . . and focusing, through a cannily sanctioned misunderstanding [*un malentendu savamment permis*], on occasional bits and pieces of their favorite reading matter?" (Ricardou, p. 230). The "misunderstanding," even though it is "cannily sanctioned" (that is, in part provoked by the text— a curious concession, considering that *Projet* does not just contain "occasional bits and pieces" of erotica, but that every single sequence is centered around a sado-erotic event), is essentially the reader's fault; the proof is that only habitual "readers of detective and porno novels" would fall into this kind of misunderstanding.

It would appear, then, that to pay attention to the sado-erotic content of the fiction is a sign both of degenerate reading habits and of acute prurience. Little wonder that no critic writing about *Projet* has stopped to linger in this realm! Signifiers are safer.[15]

Fortunately, the text of *Projet* is less reticent than its critics. One of the chief questions in it is that of the reader's reaction to the text— more exactly, the "narratee's" response to the narrator's staging or recounting of certain scenes. At several crucial points, the narration is suspended to give way to a dialogue between the narrative voice and an unidentified voice that can only be that of the narratee. The latter, more often than not, criticizes the narrator for "insisting too much" on the erotic aspects of the scenes he is recounting (for example, Fr. p. 188; Eng. p. 159) The narrator replies by insinuating that it is the questioner who attributes too much importance to such scenes, while ignoring everything else (Fr. p. 191; Eng. p. 162). The effect of these dialogues—whose distant ancestors are the conversations between Tristam Shandy and his "criticks," or the exchange between author and reader in *Jacques le fataliste*—is to "de-realize" the fiction and to insert the problem of the *reading* of the text into the very space of its unfolding.

It is, of course, true that the thrust of these dialogues is essentially identical to the thrust of Ricardou's argument: the insistence on "l'aspect érotique des scènes rapportées" ("the erotic aspect of the reported scenes") is the narratee's problem, not the narrator's. Yet, in other strongly marked places, the text suggests a quite different response to the scenes it stages. Consider, for example, the early sequence in which the Narrator witnesses the theatrical lesson in revolutionary tactics. As I mentioned earlier, this sequence can be considered as a generative matrix for all of the other sequences; its inscription of the narratee's response can also be considered emblematic.

The "lesson" is given by three actors on a stage, who identify and analyze the major liberating actions of rape, fire, and murder, all of them associated with the color red. The narrative voice relates:

> Les comédiens en viennent maintenant à l'identification et à l'analyse des trois gestes choisis. Le raisonnement qui assimile le viol à la couleur rouge, dans le cas où la victime a déjà perdu sa virgnité, est de caractère purement subjectif bien qu'il fasse appel à des travaux récents sur les impressions rétiniennes, ainsi qu'à des recherches concernant les rituels religieux de l'Afrique centrale, au début du siècle, et le sort qu'on y réservait aux jeunes prisonnières appartenant à des races considérées comme ennemies, au cours de cérémonies publiques rappelant les représentations théâtrales de l'antiquité, avec leur machinerie, leurs costumes éclatants, leurs masques peints, leur jeu poussé au paroxysme, et ce même mélange de froideur, de précision, de délire, dans la mise en scène d'une mythologie aussi meurtrière que cathartique.   (pp. 38–39)

> The performers are now dealing with the identification and analysis of the three functions in particular. The reasoning which identifies rape with the color red, in cases where the victim has already lost her virginity, is of a purely subjective nature, though it appeals to recent studies of retinal impressions, as well as to investigations concerning religious rituals of Central Africa, at the beginning of the century, and the lot of young captives belonging to races regarded as hostile, during public ceremonies suggesting the theatrical performances of antiquity, with their machinery, their brilliant costumes, their painted masks, their paroxysmal gestures, and that same mixture of coolness, precision, and delirium in the staging of a mythology as murderous as it is cathartic.   (p. 28)

We recognize, of course, the elements of parody: "recent studies of retinal impressions," "investigations concerning religious rituals"—the text is here adopting a mock-scientific tone, in keeping with the mock-analytic activity of the actors. The word "rituals," however (one of the key words in *Projet*), signals the beginning of a textual *glissement* that takes us away from the scene being enacted on the stage to two other scenes: a scene of primitive ceremonial torture practiced on young female prisoners, and, by association ("rappelant," "recalling"), a theatrical scene of antiquity. The associative complex is constructed by the staged, theatrical nature of the two scenes (costumes, masks and so on); by their ceremonial (ritualistic and collective) function; and by the predominance, in both of them, of an element of violence ("paroxysme," "délire," "mythologie meurtrière").

One difference is that in the African rites the violence is ostensibly "real"—it leads to the actual immolation of the victims—whereas in the antique theater the violence is an *effect* produced by an elaborate *mise-en-scène.* Yet, despite—or rather, because of—its purely formal character, the mythology enacted on the antique stage is both murderous and cathartic, murder "happening" on the stage, catharsis in the audience. But catharsis is a *purgation* of passions: it must be preceded by their arousal. The paroxysm and the delirium of the actors' play is shared by the audience, and the murder enacted is ultimately collective.

Now if we recall that violence, theatricality, and ritual are precisely the thematic constants of *Projet,* then we may consider the above-quoted description to be one of the text's *mises en abyme:* it is a reduced model of the text's own mode of functioning. We may assume that *Projet* too stages some "murderous myths" and that these myths are not meant to leave the reader cold.

As if to illustrate this point, the very next paragraph of the text stages a scene inspired by the African rites; the focus of the scene is not the immolation of the victims but the effect it produces on the spectators:

> La foule des spectateurs face à l'hémicycle déterminé par la rangée courbe des palmiers à huile, danse d'un pied sur l'autre en martelant l'aire de terre rouge, toujours au même rythme lourd qui s'accélère cependant peu à peu de façon imperceptible. Chaque fois qu'un des pieds touche le sol, le buste s'incline en avant tandis que l'air sort des poumons en produisant un sourd ahan, qui semble accompagner quelque travail pénible de bûcheron avec sa cognée ou de laboureur avec sa houe à bras . . .
>
> . . . Et, pendant ce temps, le martèlement des pieds nus sur le sol d'argile continue avec une cadence de plus en plus rapide, accompagné d'un halètement collectif de plus en plus rauque, qui finit par couvrir le bruit des tam-tams frappés par les musiciens accroupis sur le devant de la scène, dont la rangée ferme d'une ligne droite le demi-cercle des palmiers. (pp. 39–40)

> The crowd of spectators, facing the semicircle formed by the curved row of oil palms, dances from one foot to the other, stamping the red-earth floor, always in the same heavy rhythm which nonetheless gradually accelerates.

Each time a foot touches the ground, the upper part of the body bends forward while the air emerging from the lungs produces a wheezing sound which seems to accompany some woodcutter's laborious efforts with his ax or some farmer's with his hoe . . .

. . . And meanwhile, the stamping of bare feet on the clay floor continues in an accelerating cadence, accompanied by an increasingly raucous collective gasping, which finally drowns out the noise of the tom-toms beaten by the musicians crouched in front of the dancing area, their row closing off the half-circle of palm trees.   (pp. 28–29)

The spectators, who are apparently only *witnessing* the ritual sacrifice (they are *outside* the space of the ceremony, "facing the semicircle" and separated from it by the line of musicians), are at the same time involved in it to the point of reaching a collective orgasm. The ceremony requires the participation—indeed, the "laborious efforts"—of the spectators, and the consequence of their participation is pleasure.

Here, I would propose, and not in the Shandian dialogues, is the real inscription of the reader in *Projet.* As if to reinforce the programmatic value of this inscription, the text repeats the sacrificial scene forty pages later, with a slight variation. This time the African rituals are performed on television and are watched separately by two individuals: the red-haired victim, JR, who watches the program while standing naked, ironing a dress; and her male torturer, who watches from his hiding place on the fire escape. "Au moment le plus intéressant" ("at the most interesting moment"), when the blood begins to flow down the thighs of the young prisoners being impaled on the phallus of the fertility god, a small smile of satisfaction passes over JR's face and she begins to caress herself against the pointed end of the ironing board (Fr. p. 80; Eng. pp. 63–64). As for her torturer, he announces when he enters that he will begin by raping her, because "that television program has worked me up a little" (p. 80)—"ce reportage, à la télévision, m'a un peu ému" (p. 98). The male figure is not only aroused sexually while watching the scene but is inspired by his role as spectator to perform a variant of the scene on the first female body he meets.

The difference between spectator and actor—or, on other levels, between narratee and narrator, reader and scriptor—is thus practically eliminated; more exactly, the spectator becomes an actor (and the reader a potential scriptor) by inventing and performing his own version of the scene he has just witnessed.

One question we might ask is why, in *Projet,* all of the active (aggressive) roles are assumed by male figures and why, concurrently, only the male spectator can become an actor, the male narratee become a narrator—and presumably, the male reader become a scriptor. For the moment, it is sufficient to remark that the inscription of the reader, whether male or female, implies a strong erotic involvement with the scenes staged by the text. If Artaud was right in proclaiming that theater is a "communicative delirium," then the only proper way to respond to the theater of cruelty, be it Artuad's or Robbe-Grillet's, is to participate in the delirium. The bad reader of *Projet* may be not the one who is aroused by the erotic aspects of the text, but the one who would deny the text's delirium by concentrating only on the "signifiers."

Delirium, however, is dangerous; he who would participate in it and remain sane must be protected. In the theater the protection is provided by the space between the spectator and the stage. The empty, transparent space allows full participation in the spectacle, which "nothing" separates from the viewer. At the same time, the space functions as a screen between the spectacle and the audience: it sets a limit to the spectacle, which thereby becomes perceived as "only [a] play." The distantiating effect of theatrical space is achieved, in Robbe-Grillet's text, by the de-realizing devices I have already mentioned: parody, *glissement, coupure.* The sado-erotic scenes enacted in the fiction are interrupted or parodistically undercut at moments of tension, and are thus exposed as "only play." The reader, consequently, is caught up in two contradictory movements: one pulling him into a fiction that provokes erotic excitement, the other keeping him at a safe distance.

The de-realizing devices serve a double function. By interrupting the scene at a moment of tension—before climax—they help to maintain the excitement it arouses. As Jacques Derrida might put it, they defer *jouissance.* At the same time, by exposing the scene as "only play," they enable the reader (as well as the subject who is elaborating them) to experience the excitement as *pleasure,* devoid of the anxiety that would accompany such scenes enacted in real life. In this second function, the de-realizing devices act as mechanisms of censorship or defense: they permit the staging of desire to unfold relatively unimpeded— except by the defense mechanisms themselves, which of course do impede or deform them.

In this context we might recall Freud's notion of the relationship between daydream (*Tagtaum* is one of his words for fantasy) and works of literature: literary works (at least those that contain an element of representation) are elaborate, partly disguised or deformed versions of fantasy.[16] Freud's emphasis is chiefly on the relationship between the writer and the fantasy; at the end of his essay, however, he shifts his attention to the reader and suggests that "the true enjoyment of literature" results perhaps from "the writer's putting us into a position in which we can enjoy our own day-dreams without reproach or shame." In Norman Holland's more recent formulation, "The unconscious fantasy at the core of a work will combine elements that could, if provided full expression, give us pleasure, but also create anxiety . . . The literary work . . . acts out the defensive maneuvers for us: splitting, isolating, undoing, displacing from, omitting (repressing or denying) elements of the fantasy."[17]

Splitting, isolating, undoing—Holland could almost be referring to the de-realizing devices of *Projet*. Is it also true, then, that what these defensive maneuvers shield us from is an unconscious fantasy? On the contrary, it would appear that the fantasy is perfectly conscious: the "scenes" of *Projet* could not be more explcit. Each of them centers around a rape or some other form of sexual aggression against one or more female victims, ranging in age from early adolescence (Laura) to the early twenties (JR).[18] Besides their youth and their passivity (marked by their being bound, gagged, or physically overpowered), the other constant characteristic of the victims is their stereotyped beauty: each is described as "splendid," "charming," "doll-like," with blue eyes, long blond or red hair, a creamy porcelain-like complexion, and so on. Yet another constant is that the more alluring the victim's body, the more prolonged and refined the aggression practiced on it. Finally, the aggression, when allowed to run its course, is accompanied by orgasm, on the part of the victim as on that of the aggressor.

The single most complete version of this scenario occurs in the empty lot sequence (Fr. pp. 176–184; Eng. pp. 149–155); significantly, the sequence grows out of the narrator's description of a dream (Fr. p. 172; Eng. p. 145) and is thus doubly marked as fantasmatic. The scenario involves the ritualistic torture (burning and cutting of the genitals) of JR, identified as "cette belle créature rousse," "that splendid red-haired creature." The "splendid" victim is alternatively designated as a young woman or as a store dummy ("mannequin"—the ultimate female object), but at the crucial moment she is definitely animate: as she reaches a "paroxysm of suffering,"

> Une sorte de râle sort de sa gorge, avec des halètements et des cris de plus en plus précipités, jusqu'au long gémissement rauque final . . .   (p. 180)

> A kind of rattle emerges from her throat, with gasps and increasingly frequent screams, until the long final harsh moan . . .   (p. 152)

The paroxysm of suffering is indistinguishable from a paroxysm of pleasure.[19] Further on, the pubis of the victim will be observed to be "smeared with sperm" (p. 156)—"barbouillé de sperme" (p. 185).

Despite some notable differences, an allusion to Sade is inescapable. The fixed components of the controlling fantasy in *Projet*—beauty and powerlessness of the victim, direct proportion between the victim's capacity to arouse the aggressor sexually and the energy invested in the aggression, interdependence of orgasm and violence—as well as the occurrence of certain verbal patterns (for example, the stereotyped, hyperbolic descriptions of the victim's beauty, or the coupling of adjectives like "charmant" with nouns like "contorsions"), all point to a Sadean intertext. The Sadean victim, as Barthes has noted, is always described in hyperbolic and stereotyped terms; she is in a position of greatest possible humiliation or "objectification" vis-à-vis the aggressor;[20] the more she excites the aggressor, the greater his cruelty (thus the arch-libertine Saint-Fond, having to dispose of three victims, gleefully "reserves the best" torture for the one who "excited him the most," "l'échauffait le plus);[21] and, of course, *volupté* in Sade is impossible without the presence of unprovoked violence, perhaps the ultimate form of transgression against "natural" law. The Sadean intertext appears, too, in the ritualistic and theatrical nature of the scenes, as well as in a religious vocabulary: in Sade as in Robbe-Grillet, the victim is often designated as sacrificial, the place of her immolation is referred to as an altar.

One major difference between text and intertext would seem to be that in Sade both victims and aggressors can be either male or female (even though female victims and male aggressors are by far the more numerous), whereas in *Projet* the victims are always female, and the aggressors are always male. The difference, however, is only apparent, and it can be shown that in Sade *and* in Robbe-Grillet, the male-female opposition operates as the opposition between aggressor and victim. As Gilles Deleuze has argued, Sadism is essentially a paternal and patriarchal structure: Sade's libertine heroines may successfully appropriate the role of aggressor, but "the undertakings they conceive imitate man, require the gaze and the direction [*présidence*] of man, and are dedicated to him."[22]

The predominance of the male figure in Sade is apparent even in *Juliette,* where the triumphant libertinism of the heroine is made possible only by the presence of male models and protectors, and where the only limit to Juliette's dominance is precisely in her relation to Saint-Fond and Noirceuil: "Here, you will be nothing but a whore" ("Ici, vous ne serez plus qu'une putain"), Saint-Fond tells her, at the very moment when he gives her total immunity—and power—in her dealings with others.[23] As Nancy Miller has remarked, "Juliette is . . . granted freedom to perform—sexually and criminally—but that freedom is mediated by a higher authority."[24]

Viewed in the light of the Sadean intertext, *Projet pour une révolution à New York* takes on a curiously nonsubversive aspect. Far from deconstructing male fantasies of omnipotence and total control over passive female bodies, *Projet* repeats them with astonishing fidelity. Indeed, it not only repeats them but adds another element to them: as we saw, the victims in *Projet* are described as if they experienced pleasure in the course of their torture, which is never the case in Sade. To the fantasy of total domination is added the fantasy that "if it's done right, she will enjoy it." Just as Sade himself, despite his modern reputation as a libertarian saint, was no revolutionary in his view of the relation between the sexes,[25] so Robbe-Grillet appears to be no demystifier in this domain. Whatever else *Projet* may be, it is definitely a man's book.

It is a man's book in more ways than one—first of all, in the relation it posits between language and sex. Here again, the Sadean model is enlightening. As Barthes has shown, the only trait besides that of murderousness that the libertine *always* possesses in opposition to his victim is control over language: "The master is the one who speaks, who disposes of language in its entirety; the object is the one who is silent."[26] The aggressor, in Sade, is first of all a manipulator, the subject who invents and directs the staging of Sadean fantasy. And since all fantasy is ultimaely *textual* ("the fantasmatic operation is indissolubly *text* and *scene*"),[27] the subject of Sadean fantasy can be none other than the speaking subject of the Sadean sentence. "We understand better," writes Barthes, "the foundation and ultimate end-point of Sade's whole erotic system [*combinatoire*]: its origin and sanction are of the order of rhetoric."[28]

We also understand better why, in *Projet,* all of the narrative sequences are eventually appropriated by the male narrator who says "Je," and why it is only male figures who can alternate between the roles of spectator and actor, narratee and narrator. Language, rhetoric, and above all the right to *invent* (narrate) belong to the aggressor. This rule is confirmed even in the insances that seem to constitute exceptions to it; I mean the narrative sequences that are first narrated by female voices: the subway sequence, whose narrative source is the voice of JR, and the empty lot sequence, first introduced by Laura. In both instances the female narrative voice soon "slides" into that of the chief narrator (the one who begins and ends the book), and he does not relinquish control from then on.

Even more to the point, in both instances the female narrator begins to narrate under *constraint*, and at the prompting of a male voice. JR, for example, is being interrogated by the male figure who proposed to rape her after watching the television program, and who now threatens her unless she produces a "story":

> —Ne bougez pas tant, ou je vous attache tout de suite. Et arrangez-vous pour inventer des faits précis et significatifs.
> —Oui. Je vous en supplie. Le métro. Voilà, c'est ça: le wagon de métro

et la scène avec les trois blousons noirs. Ben Said se trouve, en pleine nuit, dans une voiture vide qui roule à toute allure sur une voie express . . . (p. 105)

"Don't move so much, or I'll tie you up right away. And try to invent details that will be exact and meaningful.

"Yes. Oh please, don't do that. The subway. There, that's it: the subway car and the scene with the three hoodlums in leather jackets. Ben-Saïd is riding, in the middle of the night, in an empty car hurtling on the express track . . . (p. 86)

The story is certainly born under "the direction of man." It is, furthermore, not only "dedicated" to man but expressly addressed to a man who has the power of life and death over the female narrator.[29]

But *Projet* is a man's book in other ways as well. The relation it posits between language and sex is intimately linked to fantasies that are specifically masculine. "The writer is someone who plays with his mother's body" ("L'écrivain est quelqu'un qui joue avec le corps de sa mère"), wrote Barthes in *Le Plaisir du texte*.[30] Body of language, body of the mother (-tongue): the writer's games are irremediably Oedipal. This brings us to the last of the three questions raised earlier: the relationship between Sadean fantasy (which we have been considering as homologous with "Robbe-Grilletian" fantasy) and the theory of the self-engendered text.

At the start, we run up against a problem about the nature of fantasy that Freud himself never fully resolved: it concerns the relative status of conscious fantasy, unconscious fantasy, and primal fantasy *(Urphantasie)*.[31] According to one of Freud's formulations, conscious fantasy or daydreaming differs from unconscious fantasy only in that the latter has been repressed, whereas the former has not—the logic and elaboration of the two are identical. Both of them, however, are "secondary" in relation to primal fantasy, which is always unconscious. The notion of primal fantasy (which entered Freud's writings relatively late—around 1915—and which never became an "official" psychoanalytic concept) is extremely useful from our point of view, because it posits the existence of a kind of storehouse of unconscious fantasies, all of them relating to *origin*, which can be found "in all neurotics and probably in all the children of men."[32]

The term *Urphantasie* is semantically overdetermined, for it can designate both a "first fantasy" from which others follow, and a "fantasy of origins"—which Lévi-Strauss calls myth. In the sense that primal fantasy is a "fantasy of origins," it is obviously linked to the notion of engenderment; in the sense that it is a "first" or "founding" fantasy, it enables us to consider the fantasies we have been discussing (in Sade and in Robbe-Grillet) as secondary, analogous to the manifest content of dreams. The primal fantasy can then be considered analogous to latent content and can be arrived at by further analysis. Let us note, however, that primal fantasy, like all others, is a staging of desire; furthermore, in the absence of clear indications to the contrary, one may hypothesize that certain primal fantasies are predominantly masculine or predominantly feminine.[33]

Given all this, what can we say about the primal fantasies of Sadean texts? Is there a "founding" scenario—staging a "founding" desire— behind the Sadean fantasy we have already described? According to Deleuze—and I find his argument most convincing—the founding desire behind Sadean fantasy is *the active negation of the mother*.[34] The Sadean hero's antinaturalism, evidenced by his repeated infraction of "natural" laws such as those governing incest, parricide, or infanticide, goes hand in hand with his hatred of mothers, identified as the "natural" source of life.

In this context one can understand the Sadean hero's aversion toward the womb and the breasts (favorite loci of torture, but not of pleasure), and in general his refusal to accomplish the sexual act in a way that might lead to procreation. One can also understand why several Sadean heroes actually kill their mother. One such hero—Bressac, in *Les Infortunes de la vertu*—justifies his murder of his mother by invoking an argument at least as old as the *Oresteia*: the father alone is responsible for the creation of a child—the mother simply furnishes a resting place where the fetus can grow.[35] Here, surely, is something that can be called a predominantly masculine fantasy: that of a world where man is not born of woman. Let us recall that in mythology the birth of heroes is rarely "natural." And not only in mythology: if Macduff is a conqueror, it is precisely because he is not "of woman born." Woman, the irreducible Other, is eliminated to make way for the engenderment of the same by the same. Perhaps the most succinct version of the fantasy is given by the title of one of Hemingway's volumes of stories: *Men without Women*.

One might ask where *Projet pour une révolution à New York* fits into all this. There are no mothers in the fantasies of *Projet*, only nubile young women. It seems safe to assume, however, that women and mothers are related. According to one Sade specialist, "Tenacious hatred of mothers in Sade's characters has everything to do with fury toward women."[36] We can easily reverse the formula and perceive its relevance for *Projet*: Fury toward women has everything to do with tenacious hatred of mothers. The degraded young victim is in a sense a stand-in for the mother.

But it would be overly simple to see either in Sade's or in Robbe-

Grillet's fictions only destructive fantasies directed against the mother. There is another fantasmatic possibility, analyzed by Freud, in which the mother is not negated but rather maintained as an idealized love object. According to Freud, it is in cases where the first incestuous attachment to the mother is not overcome by the finding of a substitute love object that there occurs "the most prevalent form of degradation in erotic life"—the dissociation of erotic life into two channels, one exclusively sensual, the other exclusively "tender." Sensual feelings are aroused only in the presence of women totally different from the idealized mother—prostitutes and other "degraded" objects; tenderness is reserved for the mother.[37]

The total degradation of the object-victim that forms a constant of Sadean fantasy may therefore be considered as a manifestation of incestuous fantasies attached to the mother. The victim, instead of being a substitute in whom the mother is destroyed, functions rather as a "deflector" who deflects desire directed toward the mother and satisfies that desire, even while keeping the mother inviolate.

The mother destroyed, the mother idealized—these seem to be the two poles between which the Sadean imagination wavers. There is, however, yet another possibility, which we see realized in Robbe-Grillet's text, and not in Sade. The last *mise en abyme* of *Projet* will illustrate what I have in mind. It occurs toward the end of the book, in the sequence describing the torture of "Sarah Goldstücker." The victim is tied up, naked, on the floor, and will eventually be killed by a giant black spider, after which her still-warm body will be raped by one of the standard assailants, disguised as a peeping locksmith. (The elements of parody are, as usual, present). Toward the beginning of the sequence, a very long sentence describing the positions of the victim and of the spider ends with the evocation of a "feuille blanche," a white page:

> Ses yeux agrandis d'horreur fixent l'araignée géante . . . qui vient d'échapper au chirurgien, dérangé dans sa monstrueuse expérience, et s'est immobilisée pour l'instant à vingt centimètres de l'aisselle, juste à la limite du cercle de lumière vive projeté sur le sol par la très forte lampe à tige articulée dont le pied est vissé au coin du bureau en métal, tout encombré de paperasses, au milieu desquelles *une feuille blanche ne porte encore que de brèves notes manuscrites,* en haut et à droite, *accompagnées d'un dessin d'anatomie* à symétrie axiale, aux contours précis et compliqués, qui figure la vulve, le clitoris, les petites lèvres et l'ensemble des organes externes féminins. (p. 193, my emphasis)

> Her eyes wide with horror stare at the giant poisonous spider . . . which has just escaped from the surgeon, disturbed in his monstrous experiment, and has come to rest for the moment about six inches from the armpit, at the very edge of the circle of bright light cast on the floor by the powerful

lamp with its jointed shaft whose base is screwed to the corner of the metal desk covered with papers, among which *one white page as yet bears only brief manuscript notes,* in the upper right corner, *accompanied by an anatomical drawing* of axial symmetry, the outlines precise and complicated, representing the vulva, the clitoris, the inner lips, and the entirety of the external female genitals.   (p. 164, my emphasis)

The external feminine organs—these, and not the color red, are the real "generators" of *Projet;* and of course, quite properly they appear near the very end. The text here points to its own beginning, when it was nothing more than a few "manuscript notes" accompanying an anatomical drawing. Robbe-Grillet's Muse, like that of other poets, is feminine. She is simply represented by a synecdoche. Let us note, however, that the part, while it fertilizes the mind of the poet, is not itself the fertile part of woman, but only the entrance to it: no danger of procreation here. Indeed, the part itself is not what generates the text: the blank page contains only a drawing of it. The source of the text is scriptural, like the text itself. The role of mother has been appropriated by the one who writes; the mother's parts have become, literally, a *pre-*text.

In Robbe-Grillet, but not in Sade: therein lies more than a small difference. The Sadean text, despite its militant espousal of transgression, excess, antinaturalism, remains paradoxically within the formal boundaries of the realist novel: Sade's "scenes," however unimaginable as lived events, are narrated "as if" they had really happened. Even Justine, that consummate storyteller, ostensibly tells not "stories" but *the* story of her *life.* If one defines the fundamental impulse of realist fiction as the impulse to naturalization or *vraisemblabilisation* (rendering "believable" what never happened), then Sade's texts must be called realist: the fictions they enact are never designated *as* fictions; the text never explicitly calls attention to itself as invention, as *text;* its origin, like its destination, is ostensibly the world of flesh and blood.[38]

In *Projet* the world of flesh and blood is explicitly negated by the text. Ricardou's statement that the fiction of *Projet* is an immense metaphor of its narration turns out to be true, with a vengeance. *Projet'*s "murderous mythology," consisting in the repeated violation of the maternal organs, can indeed be seen as a metaphor of the modern writer's activity. "For the modern writer necessarily replays with his *tongue* the scenario the Narrator plays with his mother," writes Serge Doubrovsky.[39] The narrator he is referring to is not that of *Projet,* but his conclusion is general: "The desire to write is a form of the drive to dominate [*pulsion d'emprise*]."[40]

One can go further: the desire to write, in modern times, is not only the desire to dominate—be it one's language or the body of one's mother—but also the desire to *be* one's mother (and father). "For what strong maker," asks Harold Bloom rhetorically, "desires the realization that he has failed to create himself?"[41] The ultimate masculine fantasy, of which *Projet* is the enactment, is the fantasy of self-engenderment.

Postscript: 1989

Noticeably, in the concluding paragraph I waver between attributing the fantasy of self-engenderment to "modern writing" (or rather, the modern writer) in general, and attributing it specifically to modern *masculine* writing. I also avoid the question of whether, being a "man's book," *Projet* can be read with pleasure—even with a certain sexual pleasure—by women readers. The fact that I myself spent enormous amounts of time over the book, analyzing not only its sado-erotic aspects but its numerous elements of play and parody, provides, I think, at least an indirect answer to the question. It is not a matter of simplemindedly "denouncing" Robbe-Grillet, but of reading him by according his novels *all* of their due, including their due as "man's books."

That having been said, I believe there is room for a critical as well as a merely "appreciative" or explicative stance toward novels like Robbe-Grillet's *Projet*,[42] or like Bataille's *Histoire de l'oeil*, to which I now turn.

FOUR

Transgression and the Avant-Garde: Bataille's *Histoire de l'oeil*

> One can find everything in a text, provided one is irrespectful toward it.
>
> —UMBERTO ECO

Mainly, this essay will be about reading. Specifically, it will be about different ways of reading literary pornography, as exemplified by one of the great works of the twentieth century belonging to that genre. In order to understand what is at stake in this enterprise (my discussion is not meant to be purely academic), we must take a few steps back and look more fully at the figure of Georges Bataille.

At the time of his death in 1962 (at age sixty-five), Bataille was known to a rather limited public—in France, that is; outside France, he was almost totally unknown. The French public knew him as the editor of a small but influential journal, *Critique,* which he had founded after the war and to which he contributed regularly (his first article, in the inaugural issue, was on Henry Miller), and as the author of a few books of essays—notably a study on eroticism, a volume on modern literature and evil, and a volume of philosophical fragments on what he called "the inner experience," to which Jean-Paul Sartre had devoted a long and rather negative review when it was first published in 1943.[1]

Some readers knew Bataille as the author of two novels with scabrous subjects: *L'Abbé C.* (1950), which deals with the sexual and political torments of a priest during the French Resistance; and *Le Bleu du ciel* (1957), which deals with the sexual and political torments of a Parisian intellectual during the mid-1930s (it was written in 1935). Finally, to the intellectual elite, Bataille was also known as the author of *Histoire de l'oeil (Story of the Eye)* and *Madame Edwarda,* short pornographic novels that had appeared in extremely limited editions under two different pen names.

Histoire de l'oeil, first published in 1928, occupies the privileged position of liminary text in Bataille's *Oeuvres complètes;*[2] but, like *Madame Edwarda* (1941), it never appeared under Bataille's own signature during his lifetime. This is one indication of the pornographic status of these texts, at least in a legal and sociological sense—a good place to start if one wants to define pornography. A pseudonymous author cannot be prosecuted, especially if his work appears in a very limited edition and bears a false place of publication.[3] Although in our permissive days such prudence may be deemed unnecessary, one does well to recall that only a few years before Bataille's death the Editions J.-J. Pauvert was brought to trial in Paris and heavily fined for publishing the works of Sade.[4]

By a remarkable turn of cultural history, in the space of a few years Bataille became one of the central references, a veritable culture hero, of the French literary and philosophical avant-garde.[5] In the decade following his death, his work elicited major essays by Roland Barthes, Julia Kristeva, Jacques Derrida, Philippe Sollers, Maurice Blanchot, and Michel Foucault, to mention only those who subsequently became culture heroes in their own right, in France and elsewhere. In fact, Bataille's writings functioned as a major intertext in the theories of cultural subversion and of (literary) textuality that were being elaborated around the *Tel Quel* group during the years immediately preceding and following the explosion of May 1968.

In 1970 the prestigious publishing house Gallimard began publishing his complete works (which now run to twelve volumes), with a preface by Foucault that began: "It is well known now: Bataille is one of the most important writers of his century."[6] In 1972 the *Tel Quel* group organized a *décade de Cerisy* devoted to Bataille and Antonin Artaud; in his opening remarks, Sollers stated flatly that no worthwhile thought could take place after 1968 that did not take account of—indeed, that was not in some way determined by—the thought of Artaud and Bataille, touching on sexuality, knowledge, the family, speech and writing, representation, madness; in short, on every subject worth thinking about.[7] No wonder that Susan Sontag, with her usual intuition for significant intellectual trends on the Continent, devoted a long essay chiefly to Bataille as early as 1967.

The obvious question is why Bataille's work should have been felt so deeply to correspond to a certain notion of textual and cultural modernity. It was not only, as some might think, a matter of promoting to a central place that which had been marginal—one of the characteristic gestures of any avant-garde. The French literary and philosophical avant-garde of the 1960s and 1970s found in Bataille's work an *exemplariness* that went far beyond a mere desire for paradox. But it will not be enough to suggest or even analyze the reasons for this correspondence; it will also be necessary to criticize them, in the radical, etymological sense: to make decisive, to separate, to choose. For we are not dealing with some safely distant question of cultural or literary history. The question of Bataille's relation to the problematics of modernity is contempoary, it concerns *us*. And this is nowhere more evident than in his practice of literary pornography.

Pornography as Textuality

In her essay "The Pornographic Imagination" (1967), which remains one of the rare attempts to analyze the relations between pornography and modern writing, Susan Sontag stated that "books like those of Bataille [she was referring to *Histoire de l'oeil* and *Madame Edwarda*] could not have been written except for that agonized reappraisal of the nature of literature which has been preoccupying literary Europe for more than half a century."[8] Pornography, as practiced by a writer like Bataille, was one of the ways in which modern art fulfilled its task of "making forays into and taking up positions on the frontiers of consciousness," one of the manifestations of the modern artist's constantly renewed attempt to "advance further in the dialectic of outrage," to make his work "repulsive, obscure, inaccessible; in short, to give what is, or seems to be, *not* wanted" (p. 45).

By situating Bataille's pornographic fictions in the French tradition—or, more exactly, antitradition—of transgressive writing, a tradition whose founding father was Sade, Sontag manifested her own allegiance to the adversary values of the European avant-gardes of this century. For of course the avant-garde of the 1960s was not the first in our century to valorize an aesthetics of transgression. That process had begun much earlier, with the Futurists and Dada, and was consolidated by the Surrealists via their own reading of Sade and Lautréamont. It was the Surrealists, too, who placed eroticism at the center of their preoccupations with cultural subversion. But it was in the 1960s that the potential for a metaphoric equivalence between the violation of *sexual* taboos and the violation of *discursive* norms that we associate with the theory of textuality became fully elaborated. And it is here that both Bataille's practice as a writer and his thought as a philosopher became a central reference.

Philippe Sollers, in a long essay devoted to Bataille's book on eroticism (the essay appeared in *Tel Quel* in 1967), suggested that all of modern literature, from Sade's *Juliette* to Bataille's *Histoire de l'oeil*, was haunted by the idea of a "bodily writing" *(écriture corporelle)*, to the point that the body had become the "fundamental referent of [modern literature's] violations of discourse."[9] Derrida, in an essay on Bataille published in the same year, suggested that the transgression of rules of discourse implies the transgression of law in general, since discourse exists only by positing the norm and value of meaning, and meaning in turn is the founding element of legality.[10] And already in 1963, in an essay devoted to *Histoire de l'oeil,* Barthes had explicitly stated: "The transgression of values, which is the declared principle of eroticism, has its counterpart—perhaps even its foundation—in a technical transgression of the forms of language."[11]

The importance of this idea—which suggests that the transgressive content of a work of fiction, and of pornographic fiction in particular, must be read primarily as a metaphor for the transgressive use of language effected by modern writing—cannot be overestimated. What we see here is the transfer (or, to use a very Bataillean term, the "sliding," *glissement*) of the notion of transgression from the realm of experience—whose equivalent, in fiction, is representation—to the realm of words, with a corresponding shift in the roles and importance accorded to the signifier and the signified. The signified becomes the vehicle of the metaphor, whose tenor—or as Barthes puts it, whose foundation—is the signifier: the sexually scandalous scenes of *Histoire de l'oeil* are there to "signify" Bataille's linguistically scandalous verbal combinations, not vice versa.

To appreciate fully the importance of this shift, we must consider briefly Bataille's own notion of transgression. For Bataille, transgression was an "inner experience" in which an individual—or, in the case of certain ritualized transgressions such as sacrifice or collective celebration *(la fête),* a community—exceeded the bounds of rational, everyday behavior, which is constrained by considerations of profit, productivity, and self-preservation. The experience of transgression is indissociable from the consciousness of the constraint or prohibition it violates; indeed, it is precisely by and through its transgression that the force of a prohibition becomes fully realized.

The characteristic feeling accompanying transgression is one of intense pleasure (at the exceeding of boundaries) *and* of intense anguish (at the full realization of the force of those boundaries). And nowhere is this contradictory, heterogeneous combination of pleasure and anguish more acutely present than in the inner experience of eroticism, insofar as this experience involves the practice of sexual "perversions," as opposed to "normal," reproductive sexual activity. In eroticism, as in any transgressive experience, the limits of the self become unstable, "sliding." Rationalized exchange and productivity—or, in this case, reproductivity—become subordinated to unlimited, nonproductive expenditure; purposeful action, or work, becomes subordinated to free play; the self-preserving husbandry of everyday life becomes subordinated to the excessive, quasi-mystical state we associate with religious ecstasy and generally with the realm of the sacred.

These ideas were already present in Bataille's 1933 essay "La Notion de dépense" ("The Notion of Expenditure"). They were developed and refined in his later works, in particular in *L'Erotisme* (1957), which presents a theory of eroticism in the historical and cultural perspective of transgressive practices in general.

What theorists of textuality like Barthes, Derrida, and Sollers accomplished was to transfer, or perhaps more specifically to extend, Bataille's notion of transgression to modern writing—to *écriture*. For *écriture,* in the sense in which they used that term, is precisely that element of discursive practice which exceeds the traditional boundaries of meaning, of unity, of representation; and just as for Bataille the experience of transgression was indissociable from a consciousness of the boundaries it violated, so the practice of *écriture* was indissociable from a consciousness of the discursive and logical rules, the system of prohibitions and exclusions that made meaning, unity, and representation possible but that the play of *écriture* constantly subverted.[12]

It now becomes clear why Bataille's writing, read in a particular way, could function as a central reference and as an exemplary enterprise for the French theorists of modernity of the 1960s and 1970s. His theoretical texts provided a set of concepts or "key words" whose applicability extended from the realm of cultural and individual experience to the realm of writing: expenditure, transgression, boundary, excess, heterogeneity, sovereignty—this last being a key term in Bataille's vocabulary, whose implications, as Derrida brilliantly demonstrated, are the very opposite of Hegel's term "mastery." Mastery is linked to work, and above all to the affirmation and preservation of meaning; sovereignty, by contrast, is precisely that which enables an individual to expose himself to play, to risk, to the destruction or "consumation" of meaning.[13]

Accompanying and complementing the theoretical texts, Bataille's pornographic fictions provided metaphoric equivalents for his key concepts, as well as a locus for their elaboration: the eroticized female body. Finally, Bataille's writing practice, tending toward the fragmentary and the incomplete, provided the example of a writing which (as Derrida put it) "will be called *écriture* because it exceeds the logos (of meaning, of mastery, of presence)"; the sovereignty of the Bataillian text, as of all *écriture,* resides in the text's "commentary on its absence of meaning."[14]

As I say, what is involved here is a particular reading of Bataille—a very powerful reading that has (or had) at least two advantages: first, it is integrative, allowing the commentator to consider *all* of Bataille's varied writings as part of a single artistic and intellectual quest. In this integrative view, the pornographic narratives Bataille did not sign with his own name or did not publish even under a pseudonym during his lifetime become as much a part of Bataille's signature as any of his other writings; thus, Julia Kristeva noted in her 1972 essay on Bataille that "Bataille's novels are inseparable from his theoretical positions and give them their real value."[15] Maurice Blanchot, in a similar way, began one of his essays by stating that central to an understanding of Bataille's thought are not only his theoretical works but also "the books he published under a name other than his own," whose "power of truth is incomparable."[16]

The other advantage of this kind of reading—let us call it the "textual" reading—is that it is generalizable: Bataille's varied writings are seen as parts of a single enterprise, and that enterprise becomes emblematic of modern transgressive writing in general.

If there is one thing, however, that the theorists of textuality have taught us, it is that no reading is innocent. Every reading is an interpretation, and every interpretation is an appropriation of a text for its own purposes. Every interpretation has its blind spot, which I like to think of not only as the spot or place from which the interpreter cannot "see" his or her own misreading of a text, but also as the spot or place *in* a text from which the interpreter averts his or her gaze.

What is the spot in Bataille's text from which the powerful textual reading averts its gaze? To answer that question, it is necessary to turn to an *other* reading, one that has its own significant blind spot but that nevertheless has the advantage of making us see Bataille—as well as the theory of textuality in whose service he was so powerfully enrolled—in a new, problematic light: I refer to the recent feminist reading of Bataille's pornographic fiction and of his theory of eroticism and transgression.

Pornography as "Reality"

I know at least two versions of the feminist reading, which complement rather than contradict each other. In the United States, Andrea Dworkin has discussed *Histoire de l'oeil* in the context of a political attack on pornography. In France, Anne-Marie Dardigna has discussed Bataille in a sophisticated analysis of the modern (male) erotic imagination.[17] What Dworkin and Dardigna both succeed in doing, albeit in different ways and with different degrees of persuasiveness (I find Dardigna's detailed readings more persuasive than Dworkin's), is to focus our attention on that from which the textual reading averts its gaze: the representational or fantasmatic content of Bataille's (and other modern writers') "pornographic imagination," and the political (in the sense of sexual politics) implications of that content. I stated earlier that the textual critics considered Bataille's pornographic narratives inseparable from his other writings. At the same time, it is striking to note how very few have devoted any kind of sustained analysis to these narratives. Blanchot and Kristeva insist on the importance of the pornographic novels but then go on to more general and abstract considerations. Sollers writes thirty pages of close commentary on *L'Erotisme* but devotes only a few (extremely intelligent ones, it is true) to a work of fiction, *Ma mère*.[18] Derrida at no point explicitly mentions Bataille's novels.

As for Barthes, his essay on *Histoire de l'oeil* remains one of the most interesting—as well as one of the rare—detailed commentaries on that text. The whole thrust of Barthes's analysis, however, is to bracket the representational content of the fiction and to insist on the play of metaphoric and metonymic transformations (egg-eye-testicle, milk-urine-sperm, etc.) that underlie and ultimately determine the surface progression of the narrative. It is only at the end, in a comment I have already quoted, that Barthes makes explicit mention of the transgressive content of the story of *Histoire de l'oeil*—but he does *that* only in order to affirm the primacy of Bataille's linguistic violations over the sexual and cultural violations that the narrative represents.[19]

No doubt this averting of the gaze by textual critics is due more to their general suspicion and critique of representation in art, and in narrative fiction in particular, than to sexual timidity, or what the French call *pudeur*. Nevertheless, it seems not insignificant that in their pursuit of the metaphoric equivalences between textual violation and the violation of bodies, what they passed over was precisely the *view* of the body and of the body's generally hidden organs, which were displayed and verbally designated on almost every page of Bataille's pornographic texts.[20]

"But let us leave the scene and the characters. The drama is first of all textual." This remark by Derrida (which I am quoting slightly out of context, for Derrida was referring not to Bataille's fiction but to the "story" of Bataille's relationship to Hegel)[21] sums up, I think, the strategy—and the symptomatic swerve away from representation—that characterizes the textual reading of Bataille. What characterizes Dworkin's reading is exactly the opposite. I am going to concentrate on hers rather than on Dardigna's, because it is more concise and also a lot simpler, allowing me to make my point by exaggeration, as it were. I am calling this reading not thematic but "ultra-thematic," for reasons that will become evident.

Here is how Dworkin begins her discussion of *Histoire de l'oeil:*

> The story is told by a narrator in the first person. He grew up alone and was frightened of the sexual. When he was sixteen he met Simone, the same age. Three days after they met they were alone at her villa. Simone was wearing a black pinafore. She wore black silk stockings. He wanted to pick up her pinafore from behind to see her cunt, the word he considers the most beautiful one for vagina. There was a saucer of milk in a hallway for the cat. Simone put the saucer on a bench and sat down on it. He was transfixed. He was erect. He lay down at her feet. She stayed still. He saw her cunt in the milk. They were both overwhelmed.[22]

And so on for seven more pages of deadpan summary, detailing Simone's and the narrator's sexual exploits, which culminate in the rape and murder of a priest in a church in Seville, followed by their embarking on a schooner from Gibraltar to sail to further adventures. By means of this unwavering attention to "the scene and the characters," Dworkin flattens Bataille's narrative into a piece of pulp pornography. *Histoire de l'oeil* becomes, in the space of her summary, indistinguishable from novels with titles like *I Love a Laddie* or *Whip Chick* (which she summarizes in exactly the same way), or the photograph in *Hustler* magazine entitled "Beaver Hunters," showing a spread-eagled naked woman tied to a Jeep, the trophy of two gun-carrying male hunters (Dworkin describes and analyzes this photograph and the accompanying caption in detail, pp. 25–30).

In effect, Dworkin recontextualizes Bataille's novel, or in more technical terms relocates it in what Gérard Genette would call a new "architexte," a new generic category.[23] This was precisely the kind of reading, or misreading, that Susan Sontag foresaw and tried to ward off, when she insisted that Bataille's novels had to be read in the context of European avant-garde writing: "lacking that context," she wrote, the novels "must prove almost unassimilable for English and American readers—except as mere pornography, inexplicably fancy trash" (Sontag, p. 44).

Now the interesting thing is that Dworkin has read Sontag—but she refuses to "buy" Sontag's argument. In the analysis that follows her summary of *Histoire de l'oeil*, she seems to be replying to Sontag, and indirectly to Barthes as well, whose essay Sontag had evidently read although she didn't refer to it explicitly. Where Sontag, following Barthes, admired Bataille's "spatial principle of organization," which consists in "the obscene playing with or defiling" of a limited number of objects (chief among them being the eye of the title), Dworkin merely notes, sarcastically, that "high-class symbols are . . . essential to high-class pornography: eggs, eyes, hard-boiled, soft-boiled . . ." (p. 175).

Where Sontag saw the power of Bataille's writing in its dark view of sexuality, "as something beyond good and evil, beyond love, beyond sanity; as a resource for ordeal and for breaking through the limits of consciousness" (p. 58), and above all in the fact that "Bataille understood more clearly than any other writer I know of that what pornography is really about, ultimately, isn't sex but death" (p. 60), Dworkin replies:

> The intellectual claim made for the work is that Bataille has revealed a sexual secret: the authentic nexus between sex and death . . . But in fact, Bataille has obscured more than he has uncovered. He has obscured the meaning of force in sex. He has obscured the fact that there is no male conception of sex without force as the essential dynamic . . . The grand conceptions—death, angst—cover the grand truth: that force leading to death is what men most secretly, most deeply, and most truly value in sex. (p. 176)

Obviously, the crucial words here are "male" and "men." What Sontag saw as the revelation of a troubling truth about human sexuality, Dworkin diagnoses as the particular truth of *male* desire, or the male imagination of sex, in our culture.

Now I am going to embark on a series of spiraling "Yes, but's."

Yes—politically, I find Dworkin's argument important, in the same way that Kate Millett's argument in *Sexual Politics* was important. There is something in our culture that endorses and reinforces violence against women, as any daily newspaper will confirm; and this violence seems to be inextricable from very old, deeply ingrained, essentially masculine attitudes toward sex.

But—rhetorically, as a reading of Bataille, or even as a reading of a single work by Bataille (for Dworkin claims no general knowledge of Bataille's *oeuvre*), Dworkin's pages on *Histoire de l'oeil* are by any standard less than satisfying. If the textual critics avert their gaze from representation, Dworkin cannot take her eyes off it. She is so intent on looking at "the scene and the characters" that she never sees the frame. I am using "frame" here as a shorthand for all those aspects of a fictional narrative that designate it, directly or indirectly, as constructed, invented, filtered through a specific medium: in short, as a *text* rather than as life itself. Not unlike those consumers of pornography who skip the descriptions to get to the "good parts," Dworkin reads too quickly: she devours the text in order to get to its "core," or (to change metaphors) she traverses it without attention to its shape or the grain of its surface. Where the text says: "I stood for some time before her, without moving, the blood rushing to my head and trembling while she looked at my stiff prick make a bulge in my knee-pants," Dworkin reads: "He was transfixed. He was erect." Where the text says: "Then I lay down at her feet without her having moved and, for the first time, I saw her 'pink and black' flesh cooling itself in the white milk,"[24] Dworkin reads: "He lay down at her feet. She stayed still. He saw her cunt in the milk."

As you notice, I have not chosen anodyne sentences as my examples. Bataille's text is without a doubt pornographic.[25] But certainly one thing that contributes to its effect—even to its pornographic effect—is the contrast one feels between the long, sinuous, grammatically "exquisite" sentences (which in French appear even more so because of the use of the past historic tense [*passé simple*] and the imperfect subjunctive, indices of classical literary narration) and the explicitly sexual, obscene words ("stiff prick") that crash through the structure of the syntax, as Simone's transgressive behavior crashes through the stillness of a summer afternoon.[26] In the second sentence the text avoids naming Simone's sexual part explicitly, using instead a periphrasis set off by quotation marks, which suggest a literary or pictorial allusion: "her 'pink and black' flesh" ("sa chair 'rose et noire'"). The allusion is to Baudelaire's famous verses about Lola de Valence, who was also represented in a famous painting by Manet:

Mais on voit scintiller en Lola de Valence
Le charme inattendu d'un bijou rose et noir.

But one sees scintillating in Lola de Valence
The unexpected charm of a pink and black jewel.

In Baudelaire's poem there is a "displacement upward" (to use Freud's phrase) from the woman's genitals to the jewel she wears or possesses. This displacement is founded on both a metaphoric and a metonymic equation between genitals and jewel (Lola's sex is "like" a jewel and is surrounded by jewels)—a very nice coup, rhetorically speaking. Bataille does Baudelaire one better, however. He characteristically displaces things downward, for "sa chair rose et noire" (which here clearly refers to the lower part of Simone's body) could also refer to a woman's face, with the adjective "noire" having slid over, in both cases, from hair to flesh by means of a transgressive metonymy: flesh cannot, literally or logically, be both pink and black, but one can have pink flesh framed by black hair—as in Proust's recurrent descriptions of Albertine's face, for example, or as in the narrator's view here of Simone's genitals framed by black pubic hair.[27]

Bataille's implicit equation of face with genitals—which, as in Baudelaire's poem, can be read both metaphorically and metonymically—is much more shocking and violent, especially if it is read as metaphor, than Baudelaire's equation of jewel with genitals.[28] This rhetorical violence, whose milder manifestation is the metonymic sliding of the adjective *noire* (pink *and* black flesh?), is consonant with the transgressive behavior represented in the scene. Without losing sight of the scene, we must remark (and our remark will be a great deal closer to Barthes than to Dworkin) how closely the language of the text "repeats" or "doubles" the content of its representation.

Yes, but. Dworkin, responding to my reading, would no doubt accuse it, and me, of a culpable formalism. She is obviously aware of the language of the text, even in English translation, but the argument of her book—that pornography is harmful to women because of the scenes or images it represents—requires that she consider Bataille's language as mere ornament, and as a dangerous ornament, since it "stylizes the violence and denies its meaning to women" (Dworkin, p. 176).

Yes, but. Dworkin's argument also obliges her to see, in every book she reads, simply more of the same thing. This prevents her from noticing differences that might lead to a more significant questioning— and a more persuasive critique—of Bataille's text. For example, Dworkin writes about the character of Simone that "she exists in the male framework: the sadistic whore whose sexuality is murderous and insatiable . . . She is a prototypical figure in the male imagination, the woman who is sexual because her sexuality is male in its values, in its violence. She is the male idea of a woman let loose" (p. 176). It may be true that Simone's sexuality is male; but if so, then it is precisely the nature of male sexuality that is figured in Bataille's text as problematic. Simone is presented throughout the novel as a sister soul of the narrator, who in true Bataillian fashion is never more tormentedly aware of the Law than when he is trangressing it. Neither she nor the narrator fits the description of "sadistic whore." The significant thing about Simone is precisely that she is not a whore but a "young girl from a good family," a virginal-looking adolescent who, like the narrator himself, experiences sex as profoundly scandalous (from Greek *skandalon:* trap, snare, stumbling block).[29]

And just as she is not a whore, Simone is not sadistic in Sade's sense: the Sadean hero, or heroine, puts a premium on transgression, but transgression in Sade occurs when a sovereign subject defies an external Law. In Bataille, the Law is internalized; the drama of transgression occurs *within* the subject. (He did not have a Catholic childhood for nothing.)

It is also the case that in Bataille's fiction the privileged locus of this drama is the female body. Bataille's internally divided subject is, emblematically, a woman: Simone, Madame Edwarda, Marie in *Le Mort,* the narrator's mother in *Ma mère,* Eponine in *L'Abbé C.,* Dorothea ("God's gift," whose nickname is Dirty) in *Le Bleu du ciel.* The question one should ask, it seems to me, is: Why is it a woman who embodies most fully the paradoxical combination of pleasure and anguish that characterizes transgression—in whose body, in other words, the contradictory impulses toward excess on the one hand and respect of the boundary on the other are played out? Dworkin cannot ask this question, for she has not read Bataille's text carefully enough to notice its specificity.

And yet (this is my last "yes, but"), despite its obvious flaws—perhaps even because of them—Dworkin's willful misreading, or flattening, of *Histoire de l'oeil* provokes at least one important question of anyone interested in modern writing: To what extent are the high-cultural productions of the avant-gardes of our century in a relation of complicity rather than in a relation of rupture vis-à-vis dominant ideologies? From the Surrealists to the *Tel Quel* group and beyond (including some "wings" of postmodernism), twentieth-century avant-gardes have proclaimed their subversive relation to the dominant culture; in a sense, they have lived on (or off) this relation. But insofar as the dominant culture has been not only bourgeois but also patriarchal, the productions of most male avant-garde artists appear anything but subversive.

This was already a conclusion I reached in my reading of Robbe-Grillet in the previous chapter. It is also the chief argument of Anne-Marie Dardigna's book, *Les Châteaux d'Eros.* Dardigna reads Bataille, Klossowski, and other French avant-garde writers not, like Dworkin, as "ordinary pornographers," but precisely as pseudo-subversive ones. "The twentieth-century," she writes in her conclusion,

> is characterized in literature by the total freedom of the subjective instance; the subject can finally tell all about its fantasies, its perversions, its hidden desires. That is well and good . . . But what voices are heard then? Always those of men. And what do they say? Nothing new: that women are dangerous, that they must be dominated, that their "flesh" must be conquered by assimilating them [to a male model] or by putting them to death . . . in any case, that they must be suppressed.[30]

In this conclusion Dardigna rejoins, by a different route, the critique of masculine sexual economy—based on the suppression of what is "other" in female sexuality—that one finds in the work of those women writers and philosophers who constituted the French feminist avant-garde of the late 1960s and 1970s: Hélène Cixous, Luce Irigaray, and others associated with what in the United States has come to be known as "new French feminism." I will discuss the feminist avant-garde in later chapters. In the meantime, I want to return to a question I raised only implicitly in my discussion of Robbe-Grillet's *Projet pour une révolution à New York:* What kind of reading is a "good" feminist reading (in quotation marks to acknowledge that the answer can only be subjective, my own) of texts like the ones we have been considering? Texts to which we could add a great many others, from every realm of male avant-garde artistic practice since Surrealism: Hans Bellmer's dolls (both the objects and the photographs), paintings by Magritte or Dali or David Salle, novels by Sollers or John Hawkes or Robert Coover, photographs by Man Ray or Raoul Ubac, films by Godard or Warhol or Robbe-Grillet, the list is virtually endless.

Feminist Poetics and the Pornographic Imagination

Should we, echoing Simone de Beauvoir's question about Sade, ask whether to "burn Bataille"? That question, which Beauvoir asked only rhetorically, but which was also asked (equally rhetorically?) by a French Communist journal around the same time about Kafka, is perhaps—as Bataille suggested in his own essay on Kafka—the permanent temptation of any dogmatism when faced with texts it considers harmful, or even merely irresponsible.[31] But contemporary feminist criticism is, or has been at its best, precisely the opposite of a rigid dogmatism.

If, as I believe, a genuine theory of the avant-garde must include a poetics of gender, and if (as I also believe) a genuine poetics of gender is indissociable from a feminist poetics, then a feminist reading of Bataille's and other modern male writers' pornographic fictions must seek to avoid both the blindness of the textual reading, which sees nothing but *écriture,* and the blindness of the ultra-thematic reading, which sees nothing but the "scene and characters." Such a reading, necessarily thematic but not "ultra," will look at a text, or at a whole *oeuvre* if time and space allow, patiently and carefully, according the work all due respect—but also critically, not letting respect inhibit it.[32]

Patiently and carefully, because like all modern writing with any claim to significance, the fictions of Bataille and other transgressive writers go a long way toward providing the necessary commentary on themselves. Just as *Projet pour une révolution à New York* is also (not only, but also) a book about reading, so *Histoire de l'oeil* is also a book about the very processes that nourish the pornographic imagination. It is no accident that in *Histoire de l'oeil* the narrative of sexual excesses is only part 1 of the work. The second part—which, curiously, none of the commentators I have cited finds worthy of attention—consists of a commentary that traces the fantasmatic elaboration of the obscene narrative from a number of events and people in the narrator's life. The representational content of the fiction is thus retrospectively designated as fantasy—and not only that, but as a fantasy whose source is Oedipal.

The turning point in the narrator's life, we are told, came one day when he heard his mad, blind, syphilitic father cry out, while his mother was in the next room consulting with his doctor: *"Say, doc, when you will finish screwing my wife!"* (*"Dis donc, docteur, quand tu auras fini de piner ma femme!"*). "For me," writes the narrator,

> this sentence, which destroyed in one instant the demoralizing effects of a strict upbringing, left behind it a kind of constant obligation, which until now has been involuntarily and unconsciously felt: the necessity to continually find its equivalent in every situation in which I find myself and that is what explains, in large part, *Story of the Eye.*

> Pour moi, cette phrase qui a détruit en un clin d'oeil les effets démoralisants d'une éducation sévère a laissé après elle une sorte d'obligation constante, inconsciemment subie jusqu'ici et non voulue: la nécessité de trouver continuellement son équivalent dans toutes les situations où je me trouve et c'est ce qui explique en grande partie *Histoire de l'oeil.*[33]

"This sentence which destroyed in one instant the demoralizing effects of a strict upbringing . . .": what the father suddenly reveals (or recalls?) to the son is that the mother's body is sexual. The knowledge that a "strict upbringing" has always tried to repress, in a male child, is that his mother's body is *also* that of a woman. The recognition of the mother's body as female, and desirable—a recognition forced on the son by his blind but still powerful father—is thus designated as the source of the narrator's pornographic imagination. This, I think, might explain why in Bataille's fiction it is always a woman (and in the posthumous *Ma mère,* is the mother herself) in whose body the drama of transgression is played out. For the female body, in its duplicity as asexual maternal and sexual feminine, is the very emblem of the contradictory coexistence of transgression and prohibition, purity and defilement, that characterizes both the "inner experience" of eroticism and the textual play of the pornographic narrative.

One could also, in a more classically Freudian perspective, suggest that the mother's sexual body traumatizes the son by exhibiting its (and his own potential) "castration." In Bataille's pornography the male protagonist is often split between a passive and an active sexual role; this split is most clearly evident in *L'Abbé C.,* where one of the identical twin brothers is the desired woman's lover, while the other brother, a priest dressed "in skirts," repeatedly witnesses their lovemaking and leaves behind him his own feces as a trace of his *jouissance.* This is strikingly similar to Freud's reconstitution of the primal scene in the case history of the Wolf Man, in which a crucial supposition is that the child reacted to witnessing his parents' lovemaking by passing a stool (it's true that he was only eighteen months old!). Freud interprets this reaction as a sign (or a source?) of his patient's repressed homosexuality, his anal identification with the passive role of the mother.[34]

As far as Bataille's text is concerned, it is clear that whichever interpretation one emphasizes, the focus is on the son's view of the mother's
genitals, which invariably leads him to a recognition of sexual difference
and to a split in his own experience: either through the combination of
fascination and terror provoked by the mother's sexuality (in the first
interpretation), or through the combination of fear and desire, manifested in active *versus* passive sexual roles, as concerns his own castration (in the second interpretation). Paradoxical as it may seem, in both
instances the real drama exists between the son and the father (who is
at once "real" and "symbolic" in Lacan's sense), not between the son
and the mother. The mother's body functions as mediation in the Oedipal narrative, whose only true (two) subjects are male.[35]

These observations are the result of a careful reading of Bataille's
own text, not against itself but insofar as it comments on itself. Kristeva,
in one of her general remarks on Bataille's fiction, wrote: "Contrary to
'objective,' historical or simply novelistic narratives which can be blind
to their cause and merely repeat it without knowing it, [Bataille's]
'opération souveraine' consists in 'meditating' . . . on the Oedipal cause
of the fiction and therefore of the narrating-desiring subject."[36] In its
self-conscious meditation on its own Oedipal sources, Bataille's pornographic fiction (one finds this meditation, in one form or another, in all
of Bataille's novels) is a far cry from the pulp novels or trashy magazine
photos that serve up their fantasies straight. The difference between
them is, one could argue, the difference between blindness and insight.

But the insight provided by Bataille's text about itself has its own
limits. And that is why it must be read critically as well as carefully.
Among the questions that Bataille's text cannot ask about itself—because in order to do so it would have to have both a historical and a
theoretical distance from itself that it cannot have—are these: Is there
a model of sexuality possible in our culture that would not necessarily
pass through the son's anguished and fascinated perception of the duplicity of the mother's body? Is there a model of *textuality* that would
not necessarily play out, in discourse, the eternal Oedipal drama of
transgression and the Law—a drama which always, ultimately, ends by
maintaining the latter?[37]

Harold Bloom, in a moment of mock prophecy (and, one suspects,
with some anxiety of his own) once predicted that "the first true break
with literary continuity will be brought about in generations to come, if
the burgeoning religion of Liberated Woman spreads from its clusters
of enthusiasts to dominate the West. Homer will cease to be the inevitable precursor, and the rhetoric and forms of our literature may then
break at last from tradition."[38] That time is still a while off, nor am I
certain that it is what we should be waiting for. What does appear to

me certain is that there will be no genuine renewal, either in a theory of the avant-garde or in its practices, as long as every drama, whether textual or sexual, continues to be envisaged—as in Bataille's pornography and in Harold Bloom's theory of poetry—in terms of a confrontation between an all-powerful father and a traumatized son, a confrontation staged across and over the body of the mother.

FIVE

Love Stories:
Women, Madness, and Narrative

> Parler d'amour, en effet, on ne fait que ça dans le discours analytique.
>
> —JACQUES LACAN, *ENCORE*

> He wants to put his story next to hers.
>
> —TONI MORRISON, *BELOVED*

This essay is about entanglements—what Lacan would have called knots. Entanglements among persons, characters, texts, discourses, commentaries and cross-commentaries, glosses and footnotes and further footnotes to stories real and imagined, scenes seen and recounted, reconstructed, revised, denied; knots between desire and frustration, mastery and loss, madness and reason, illness and cure, men and women. In a word, love. Which some have called transference. Which some have called reading. Which some have called writing. Which some have called *écriture*. Which some have called displacement, slippage, gap. Which some have called the unconscious. Which some have called the discourse of the Other. Which, if it can be spoken (of), written (of) at all, produces knots.

That would be a way to begin. Or I can begin at the beginning, asking questions. How does modern writing move from André Breton's *Nadja* (1928) to Marguerite Duras's *Le Ravissement de Lol V. Stein* (1964), and why is that move important? What does it have to do with a theory of the avant-garde? With women, madness, and narrative? And what do these questions have to do with us?

In an article published some years ago, Shoshana Felman raised the question of women, madness, and the writing and reading of fiction apropos of a story by Balzac.[1] The central figures in the story are an army officer who had participated in the Napoleonic wars; a woman he had loved and lost, and whom he found again years later, transformed into a mad creature unable to recognize him or to utter any but a single word ("Adieu," the story's title); and an old, benevolent doctor who is the madwoman's uncle and caretaker, with whose help the officer undertakes to cure her of her madness by recreating the traumatic event (an episode in the French army's retreat from Russia) that precipitated her madness.

Felman's reading emphasized two interrelated points: first, that the traditional academic criticism of this story (represented, in her edition, by a Preface and a didactic Notice) literally *did not see* the woman, being interested only in Balzac's "realistic" portrayal of the Napoleonic wars; and second, that the story itself is both a dramatization and a subversion of the representational logic which, seeking to cure the woman's madness by means of recognition, re-presentation, attains its aim only at the price of killing her. The story's hero, like its academic critics, cannot see the woman; he wants only to see himself recognized by her, as in a mirror, which, "reflecting his image, will thereby acknowledge his narcissistic *self-image*" (p. 9). The academic critics also see only what they want to see: the "real," as reproduced by Balzac's "realism." Balzac's text itself, however, by its ironic ending (at the instant when she recovers her reason, the woman dies) subverts both the critics' and the hero's project and "can be read as a kind of preface to its own Préface, as an ironic reading of its own academic reading" (p. 10).

Felman's reading of Balzac and of his critics, which struck me (and still does) as so suggestive and new, could not have been intelligible, indeed could not even have existed without the conjunction of three major moments or movements in recent French thought: the psychoanalytic—more exactly, Lacanian—moment, with its emphasis on specularity and the problematics of self and Other; the deconstructive moment, with its emphasis on textual rhetoric and self-reflexiveness; and the feminist or "feminine theoretical" moment, with its emphasis on the exclusion of women from traditional discourse, including the discourse of Freudian and Lacanian psychoanalysis. It is precisely at this conjunction—which is not only intertextual but interdiscursive, a multidimensional space where literature and psychoanalysis, theory and fiction, politics and poetics, meet—that we encounter Nadja, Dora, and Lol V. Stein.

Nadja has been called, by Michel Beaujour in an admirable essay, "the account that an honest man can give of a shattering and failed adventure."[2] The same could be said, with some qualification, about *Le Ravissement de Lol V. Stein.* And yet, the distance that separates these two books and these two adventures seems to me more significant than their resemblances, which are strikingly numerous. In both, a male narrator who says "I" tells a story, fragmented and discontinuous in its presentation *(récit)* and excruciatingly self-conscious in its mode of telling *(narration);* the story is about the narrator's involvement with a woman, who by "normal" societal standards is mad, and whose madness constitutes the chief fascination she holds for the narrator.

Aside from these internal homologies, the two texts have in common a certain historical similarity: they are probably the best known and most commented-upon of their author's works, having achieved the status of "modern classics" (to put it antithetically) within a few years of their writing. They both constitute inaugural texts—*Nadja* being the first of four autobiographical narratives about the ultimate Surrealist adventure according to Breton, love; *Le Ravissement de Lol V. Stein* being the first of a series of fictions and films in which Duras has reworked, elaborated, and expanded a single narrative kernel: the night of the ball at T. Beach, where Lol watches, fascinated and ravished, the ravishing of her fiancé, Michael Richardson, by a "woman dressed in black," Anne-Marie Stretter. Finally, in addition to the outpouring of commentaries that both books have elicited from literary critics and historians, cultural theorists, feminist critics, and, in the case of *Lol V. Stein,* from Lacanian analysts including Lacan himself, they have received extensive glosses and reworkings by their own authors.

Breton revised *Nadja* and added a preface and notes, to a new edition published thirty-six years after the original version; and he kept coming back to it, quoting from it and commenting on it, in published interviews, in the second Surrealist Manifesto (1935), and in other writings.[3] As for Duras, she has stated, in interviews and self-commentaries, that *Lol V. Stein* was the real beginning of a new way of writing for her and that she is still obsessed by the figure that obsesses Lol, Anne-Marie Stretter.[4] The three films *(La Femme du Gange, India Song, Son nom de Venise dans Calcutta désert)* and two novels *(Le Vice-Consul, L'Amour)* that followed *Lol V. Stein* can themselves be read as developments and glosses on that book.

No need to continue the demonstration, these are obviously pivotal texts: pivotal in their author's *oeuvre,* in contemporary literary history, and in an intertextual and interdiscursive space of commentary and self-commentary. They are also (and this is not exactly the same thing) *exemplary* modern texts: *Nadja* is *the* Surrealist prose narrative; *Lol V. Stein* is (so far, at least) the most important single narrative in which literary modernity and *écriture féminine* are self-consciously merged.[5]

And *Dora?* Where is *Dora?* Crucial question. In one sense she—or rather it, Freud's text—is exactly where the others are, for everything I have said about *Nadja* and *Lol V. Stein* is also true of *Dora:* self-conscious male narrator, woman considered mentally ill as main character, inaugural text in a major series (the five case histories), pivotal in its author's *oeuvre* (here, Freud tells us, is where he discovered the importance of transference) and in the history of modern culture; finally, even more than the other two, this text has generated a seemingly endless series of commentaries, revisions, qualifications, and rewritings by both its author and interpreters ranging from other psychoanalysts to literary critics, cultural historians, playwrights, novelists, and film-makers.[6]

In another sense, *Dora* separates *Nadja* from *Lol V. Stein;* it divides them more radically than their many similarities unite them. I know, I know—*Dora* is not *Dora* but "Fragment of an Analysis of a Case of Hysteria," written in 1901, published in 1905, expanded with additional footnotes in 1923—all well before Breton's *Nadja* saw the light. The space I am referring to, however, is not chronological. Back in the late 1960s and early 1970s, one might have evoked (especially around *Tel Quel*) "la coupure épistémologique freudienne."[7] Today, it may be more evocative to say that *Dora* is the difference between *Nadja* and *Lol V. Stein,* as Freud is the difference between Charcot and Lacan. Or we can say that to move from Surrealism to *écriture féminine,* modernity must traverse *Dora,* and that to traverse *Dora* is to put into question the subject: the subject of discourse and of sexual difference. The subject of narrative and of desire. The subject of interpretation. The subject of transference.

Mastery and Transference: The Significance of *Dora*

Let us begin, then, once again—once again citing Shoshana Felman, who I believe first developed the enormously fruitful idea that the analytic experience of transference can also serve to define the experience of literature.[8] More recently, Peter Brooks has proposed a "trans-ferential model" of reading in which the relation between narrator and narratee, and between author and reader, is analogous to the relation between analysand and analyst.[9] Between Felman and Brooks, how-ever, there is a difference. Brooks's model is classically Freudian: for him, transference is the effect of the *patient's* desire, to be "read" by the analyst; Felman's model is Lacanian: for her, transference is also the effect of the *analyst's* desire.

According to Brooks, the "task of the analyst is to recompose the narrative in order to represent better the story of the patient . . . , to account better for its dominant themes and to capture better the force of [the patient's] desire" (p. 65). Correlatively, the task of the reader is "not only to recapture [*ressaisir*] the . . . story, but to judge its relation to the narrative and to make himself the critic of the narrative in relation to the story, seeking not only to understand what the narrative says but also what it wants to say" (p. 72).

For Felman, this one-way relation, in which the reader/analyst is in a position of judgment, of mastery over the other's desire, is impossible. Interpretation, whether analytic or literary, is an enterprise of mutual seduction and displacement. Felman can thus read Freudian interpretation itself through and with Lacan, seeing its blind spot: "to his great astonishment" (this is Lacan talking about Freud, quoted by Felman), "he noticed that he could not avoid participating in what the hysteric was telling him, and that he felt affected by it. Naturally, everything in the resulting rules through which he established the practice of psychoanalysis is designed to counteract this consequence, to conduct things in such a way as to avoid being affected" (p. 118).

What Freud was blind to, contemporary Freudians have said, was the unavoidable necessity and presence of countertransference, "the effects of the analyst's own unconscious needs and conflicts on his understanding or technique."[10] Donald Spence, for example, argues that far from being a "possible source of error, something to be 'analyzed away' so as not to contaminate the therapeutic conversation . . . , countertransference may be a necessary part of active listening," so that "unless the analyst is continually supplying his own private associations, he can never hope to understand the clinical encounter."[11] This view, however, is still not the same as Lacan's, which sees transference itself as the entanglement of two desires. "Transference," Lacan said in one of his many pronouncements on this subject, "is a phenomenon in which the subject and the analyst are included together. To divide it in terms of transference and countertransference, no matter how bold and daring the propositions one allows oneself to make on that theme, is never anything but a way of eluding what is involved."[12]

What is involved, I would suggest, is not only who desires what and whose desire "comes first," but also, more importantly, the aim of the clinical encounter itself.

The aim of the encounter is the cure, Freud would say—Freud did say, in "Fragment of an Analysis of a Case of Hysteria" among other places. And in what does the cure consist? In the removal of symptoms and in the construction, or reconstruction, of an "intelligible, consistent, unbroken" story:

> It is only toward the end of the treatment that we have before us an intelligible, consistent, and unbroken case history. Whereas the practical aim of the treatment is to remove all possible symptoms and to replace them by conscious thoughts, we may regard it as a second and theoretical aim to repair all the damages to the patient's memory. These two aims are coincident. When one is reached, so is the other; and the same path leads to them both.[13]

If the sign of true neurotics is their "inability to give an ordered history of their life" (*Dora,* p. 31), then the analyst's task is to help them achieve that capacity. As Steven Marcus has remarked, in his brilliant and path-breaking essay on *Dora,* "No larger tribute has ever been paid to a culture . . . which had produced as one of its chief climaxes the bourgeois novels of the 19th century" than this faith of Freud's in the healing capacity of coherent storytelling.[14]

Donald Spence's influential recent book, *Narrative Truth, Historical Truth,* criticizes Freud's notion that the story thus reconstructed corresponds to historical truth. Yet, Spence remains faithful to the notion that the analytic cure consists in the production of narrative coherence: "Gaps must be filled; explanations must be supplied; puzzles must be clarified. What we are after, it seems, is a narrative account that provides a coherent picture of the events in question" (p. 180). Spence's thesis that this narrative does not necessarily have to correspond to "historical truth," that it can be effective by virtue of its aesthetic unity and pleasingness alone, is a revision of Freud—more exactly, Spence carries to its logical conclusion what Freud himself saw but was loath to admit, as his defense of the "story" he constructed for the *Wolf-Man* makes clear.[15] Spence's thesis does not, however, change or put into question the fundamental premise that the aim of analysis is interpretation, and that interpretation consists in the construction, by the analyst, of a unified, aesthetically pleasing, plausible story for, about, and ideally with the collaboration of, the patient.

This is precisely where Lacan's notion of transference complicates and entangles things. For it is not at all clear, reading Lacan, that the aim of analysis, or of analytic discourse, is to construct a coherent—plausible, finished—story. I would go so far as to say that this is precisely *not* the aim of analytic discourse, according to Lacan.

But I am getting ahead of myself, rushing prematurely from Vienna to Paris. My subject here is *Dora*—and I realize that my apparent reluctance to stick to it, my desire to rush beyond her, manifests anxiety of a transferential kind. In order to reach Dora, will I have to displace all the other texts around her? Or will I have to settle for writing commentaries on the commentaries? But what kind of text will that produce? Perhaps it will be hysterical.

At the end of his 1912 paper "The Dynamics of Transference," Freud speaks about "the struggle between physician and patient, between intellect and instinct . . . This is the ground on which the victory must be won, the final expression of which is lasting recovery from the neurosis."[16] In the postscript to *Dora* he says it was because he did not "succeed in mastering the transference in good time" that he lost the struggle. But as many commentators, starting with Lacan, have pointed out, Freud's real error lay not in failing to master the transference but in trying too hard to master Dora and her story.[17] Indeed, Freud tried to ram down Dora's throat the story of her love for Herr K.: "'So you see that your love for Herr K. did not come to an end with the scene, but that (as I maintained) it has persisted down to the present day—though it is true that you are unconscious of it.'—And Dora disputed the fact no longer" (p. 125).

Dora did not dispute the "fact," but she opened the next sitting by informing him that it was her last.[18] Whereupon Freud continued the love story by supplying (via the governess Dora told him about) motives of jealousy and revenge for her slapping Herr K. in the crucial "scene by the lake," as well as for her subsequently telling her parents about his attempted seduction: "You waited for [a fortnight] so as to see whether he would repeat his proposals; if he had, you would have concluded that he was in earnest, and did not mean to play with you as he had done with the governess" (p. 129). Finally, Freud even began to envisage an alternate "happy ending" to the story, in which Dora would have married Herr K., whom his wife would have been only too happy to divorce given her relations with Dora's father! Dora did not dispute this either, but "she said goodbye . . . and came no more" (p. 130). Marcus's comment seems most apt: "Dora refused to be a character in the story that Freud was composing for her."[19]

The most common explanation for why Freud was so intent on forcing this rather unsavory story on Dora is that he himself identified too much with Herr K., a man "still quite young and of prepossessing appearance," as he put it in a footnote (p. 44). Here, then, would be an example of unrecognized countertransference (or, more simply, transference) on the part of the analyst. I would suggest, however, that Freud's love story for Dora was inspired not only by his putting himself in Herr K.'s place, but also by his putting himself in the place of an omniscient narrator who, having a limited number of "characters" to work with, must find the most plausible and psychologically motivated solution to their entanglements. In other words, it was the desire for narrative coherence *as such* (based on the only model Freud appreciated, that of the nineteenth century realist novel, whose privileged subject, as Tony Tanner has shown, was adultery) that may have been a central driving force.

Freud's own transference, then, was not only to Herr K. but to Balzac—by which I do not mean that Freud desired to write fiction (he vigorously defended himself against that idea, incompatible in his mind with scientific truth); rather, to the extent that Freud had to construct stories, he desired to possess the authority of a Balzacian narrator. It is extraordinary, in fact, how tenaciously and single-mindedly Freud pursued the construction of the love story for—and to—Dora, from the first kiss in Herr K.'s "place of business" when Dora was fourteen right through the interpretation of the second dream and after. He did not miss a single occasion to draw connections that would reinforce the tale, providing ever more subtle motivations, establishing ever tighter links between events.

At the same time, even as he was hammering home his tale of heterosexual jealousy and passion, he set in motion a major counterstory, that of Dora's homosexual love for Frau K.—*but it was not a story he told to Dora herself*. This story is elaborated in digressions: first in a four-page digression in the text just before the analysis of Dora's first dream (pp. 77–81), then in three long footnotes, which all appeared in the 1905 text (pp. 126, 133, 142). Whereas the heterosexual love story is addressed to Dora, who is both narratee and recalcitrant protagonist (this is most clear in the bit of second-person narration I quoted earlier: "You waited . . . so as to see," where Dora is supplied with both action and motives, in the best nineteenth-century tradition), the alternate, homosexual love story is communicated, as a "complication," (p. 77), only to the reader.

What links, if any, can we establish between Freud's desire for narrative mastery (what I have called, somewhat facetiously, his transference to Balzac) and his splitting of Dora's story into two versions? The simplest answer would be this: the desire for narrative mastery is part of Freud's therapeutic desire for the cure (his mistake being that he was too impatient, forcing the story on Dora before she was ready to accept it), and the splitting is the result of the delay between the treatment itself and its being written up into the case history. In other words, Freud was not aware, during the treatment itself, of the "other story," that is why he made no use of it in his interpretations to Dora.[20] He himself suggests as much, in a note toward the end of the text: "The longer the interval of time that separates me from the end of this analysis, the more probable it seems to me that the fault in my technique lay in this omission: I failed to discover in time and to inform the patient that her homosexual (gynaecophilic) love for Frau K. was the strongest unconscious current in her mental life" (p. 142).

As one group of commentators has pointed out, this remark appears surprisingly disingenuous on Freud's part, since "he had long since abandoned the notion that it was sufficient for the analyst to inform the patient of the contents of her unconscious to effect a cure." In order to make Dora realize her homosexual love for Frau K., the authors argue, he would have had to "fight it out in the sphere of transference," which means that he would have had to be willing to accept identification with Frau K. This, however, he was unable to do, not only because Frau K.

was a woman, but because she was a "woman that is the object of a love that is homosexual."[21]

This explanation—which suggests not that Freud was lying, only that he was "blind"—seems to have some validity, especially if we compare Freud's footnote (which implies that it took him some time to realize that he "had failed to discover in time" Dora's love for Frau K.) with a remark he made to Fliess in a letter dated January 30, 1901, less than a month after Dora's last visit. In the letter he refers to his already finished manuscript, "Dreams and Hysteria" (the original title of the case history, which he finished on January 24 according to another letter), and describes it as follows: "The main thing in it is again psychology, the utilization of dreams, and a few peculiarities of unconscious thought processes. There are only glimpses of the organic, that is, the erotogenic zones and bisexuality. *But bisexuality is mentioned and specifically recognized once and for all,* and the ground is prepared for detailed treatment of it on another occasion. It is a hysteria with tussis nervosa and aphonia . . . and *the principal issue in the conflicting thought processes is the contrast between an inclination toward men and an inclination toward women.*"[22]

Could it be that Freud discovered "the principal issue in the conflicting thought processes" only in the course of writing up the case history— that is, in the three weeks following termination of the treatment? Even if that is so, we may wonder why he insists in his footnote (added later, perhaps, but certainly by 1905) that it took him a long time to realize Dora's love for Frau K.? And why does he return to the question again so emphatically at the end of the footnote? "Before I had learnt the importance of the homosexual current of feeling in psychoneurotics, I was often brought to a standstill in the treatment of my cases" (p. 142). This remark seems curiously at odds with a much earlier digression *in the text,* in which Freud was at pains to establish that even in normal people, adolescence is a period when there exists "an affection for people of their own sex" (p. 77). All the more so will one find such affection in neurotics, *"for I have never yet come through a single psychoanalysis* of a man or a woman without having to take into account a very considerable current of homosexuality" (p. 78, my emphasis).

If this digression in the text is a revision added after the first writing in 1901, perhaps around the time Freud was writing the *Three Essays on the Theory of Sexuality* (which were published in the same year as *Dora,* 1905), that only heightens the contradiction, for the footnote—in which Freud claims not to have had any inkling of a "homosexual current" in Dora—seems also to have been written quite a while after the end of the treatment. Whatever its date of writing, the note's purpose was evidently to emphasize Freud's "ignorance of the homosexual current" in this particular case at the time of the treatment. But textually, the digression occurs sixty-five pages *before* the note, so that textually both the reader and Freud "knew" long before the note what he now claims he didn't know until much later. And besides, there is the letter to Fliess, which insists that "bisexuality is mentioned and specifically recognized once and for all" already in the very first draft.

Curiouser and curiouser, Alice would say. So curious, in fact, that a stronger explanation is needed than the one founded on Freud's inability to let himself be placed in the position of Frau K., or even of Dora's mother. Such an explanation has been offered by Neil Hertz. According to Hertz, the real problem involved Freud's possible or impossible identification not with transference objects but with Dora herself. Freud had, above all, to defend himself against the possibility of being confused with Dora—not so much because he feared feminization (although that was surely a factor), but because *this* feminization would lead to an "epistemological promiscuity, in which the lines would blur between what Dora knew and what Freud knew and, consequently, in which the status of Freud's knowledge, and of his professional discourse, would be impugned."[23] In other words, Freud did not want his own discourse and knowledge to be contaminated with the discourse and knowledge of the hysteric.

This, it seems to me, is the most interesting entanglement of Freud in Dora's case. The desire for narrative mastery would then turn out to be a therapeutic desire for the cure *and* a personal and intellectual defense against the contamination of psychoanalysis and of the psychoanalyst's discourse by its object. A year before he began the treatment of Dora, Freud already expressed anxiety about mastery in talking about the style of his "dream book," which he had just finished. He wrote to Fleiss: "Somewhere inside me there is a feeling for form, an appreciation of beauty as a kind of perfection; and the tortuous sentences of my dream book, with their parading of indirect phrases and squinting at ideas, deeply offended one of my ideals. Nor am I far wrong in regarding this lack of form as an indication of insufficient mastery of the material."[24] The "material" in this case was chiefly his own dreams. In Dora's case the material was Dora's dreams, Dora's history, and Dora's desire. Freud could not "sufficiently master" these either, no matter how hard he tried. The splitting of Dora's love story may be read as one indication (as a symptom?) of the way in which the case history itself becomes "hysterical," caught up in the "conflicting thought processes . . . between an inclination toward men and an inclination toward women."

But perhaps even more interesting, from my point of view, is a single moment in the case history where it is not Freud's *narrative* that is contaminated by hysteria but Freud's own unconscious that seems to become indistinguishable from Dora's. Neil Hertz notices this moment, but fails to notice what is really significant in it. It occurs during the interpretation of Dora's second dream, the one in which a thick wood (*Wald*), a train station (*Bahnhof*), and a cemetery (*Friedhof*) figure prominently. Associating to this dream, Dora produces yet another memory of the scene by the lake ("The wood in the dream had been just like the wood by the shore of the lake"—p. 119), and then recalls that she saw a similar wood the day before in a picture at an exhibition ("In the background of the picture were nymphs"). Following this is a paragraph Hertz quotes in its entirety:

> At this point a certain suspicion of mine became a certainty. The use of *Bahnhof* and *Friedhof* to represent the female genitals was striking enough in itself, but it also served to direct my sharpened curiosity to the similarly formed *Vorhof*—an anatomical term for a particular region of the female genitals. This might have been no more than a witty error. But now, with the addition of "nymphs" visible in the background of a "thick wood," no further doubts could be entertained. Here was a symbolic geography of sex! "Nymphae," as is known to physicians though not to laymen (and even by the former the term is not very commonly used), is the name given to the labia minora, which lie in the background of the "thick wood" of the pubic hair. But any one who used such technical names as *Vorhof* and "nymphae" must have derived his knowledge from books, and not from popular ones either, but from anatomical text-books or from an encyclopaedia—the common refuge of youth when it is devoured by sexual curiosity. If this interpretation were correct, therefore, there lay concealed behind the first situation in the dream a phantasy of defloration, of how a man seeks to force an entrance into the female genitals.[25]

What strikes Hertz as most curious are the last three sentences, and the logic by which Freud arrives at the very last sentence. Hertz asks, "is the shift to the masculine pronoun ["any one who used such technical names . . . must have derived *his* knowledge"] a way of suggesting that such reading habits, though indulged in by women, are essentially masculine, and hence coordinate with male fantasies of defloration?" He concludes that this would be in line with Freud's "persistence in characterizing Dora's love for Frau K. as masculine," but that it is above all a sign of Freud's anxiety "to preserve certain clarities in his thinking about the transfer of psychoanalytic knowledge. It required a vigilant effort, it would seem, to draw the line between the operations in the hysteric which produce the text of her illness, and those in the analyst which seek to interpret and dissolve that text" (p. 236).

I agree with Hertz's conclusion, but am surprised that he did not notice the astonishing way in which the beginning of Freud's paragraph fails, precisely, to "draw the line" between operations in the hysteric and those in the analyst. For the really curious slippage in this text is not the use of the masculine qualifier, which in the German construction of the sentence is grammatically required (*"Wer* aber solche technische Namen . . . gebrauchte, *der* musste seine Kenntnis aus Büchern geschöpft haben"—the "Wer . . . der" construction is obligatory).[26] The really curious slippage is the way Freud, not Dora, produces the word *Vorhof* in association with *Bahnhof* and *Friedhof,* and *then* proceeds to say that "anyone who used such technical names as *Vorhof* and 'nymphae' must have derived his knowledge from books . . ."[27] At this point, we can no longer be certain whose associations are being interpreted, since Freud has merged his own *Vorhof* with Dora's "nymphae" to produce the "fantasy of defloration."

Whose rape fantasy, exactly, is this? And is the position of the subject of the fantasy "masculine" or "feminine"? (Dora fantasizes being raped, Dora fantasizes raping; Freud fantasizes Dora fantasizing she is being raped, Freud fantasizes Dora raping, Freud fantasizes being raped, Freud fantasizes raping . . .)

Psychoanalysis, we have known for a long time, is about the unconscious and about human sexuality. It is also, as Marcus, Brooks and others have reminded us and as any reading of Freud confirms, about the possibilities and limits of narrative. One great virtue of the Dora case—which may explain its apparently endless capacity to generate commentaries and rewritings—is that it dramatizes, as perhaps no other of Freud's writings does, the ways in which the desire of the narrating and of the interpreting subject is caught up, entangled with, contaminated by its object. Freud's multiple entanglements with Dora—on the levels of discourse, of desire, and of sexuality—can be read as an allegory of the failure of psychoanalysis, which is at the same time its greatest success: the failure to achieve complete "mastery of the material."

Such a reading is, of course, itself necessarily caught up in a process of displacement, as the reader/writer, I, is (am) contaminated by other texts, other "sexts" (Hélène Cixous's portmanteau word). Interpreters beware: desire is contagious.

Breton, Charcot, and the Spectacle of Female Otherness

If we turn, or return, now to Breton and Duras, it may become clear why *Nadja* lies on one side and *Le Ravissement de Lol V. Stein* on the other of "la coupure épistémologique freudienne." It may also become clear that what is at stake here is a radical difference that runs across and within modern writing, at least modern French writing; and that the implications of this difference are not trivial either for psychoanalysis or for literature.

That *Nadja* and *Lol V. Stein* are both resolutely *modern* texts is clear enough. They privilege the fragment, the gap, incompletion, postponement, they are written in a language that perturbs—the one by its baroque syntax (Breton's sentences, although grammatically correct, often strike one as positively tortuous), the other by its repetitive, almost hallucinatory quality and its love of silences. Using the vocabulary of the avant-garde, one could say that both these texts self-consciously contest and subvert traditional narrative authority and coherence, the authority and coherence on which "the great tradition" of mimetic fiction is founded, and to which Freud, as we have seen, still pledged theoretical allegiance. Where, then, lies the difference? I believe that it lies in the acceptance or refusal of genuine entanglement, on the part of the male narrating subject, with the woman and her madness. The implications of this acceptance or refusal—in the realm of gender as in that of narrative—are precisely what must be explored.

Nadja opens with a quintessentially analytic question: "Qui suis-je?" ("Who am I?"). This question, which Breton addresses to himself, is immediately rephrased with a play on words produced by the particular genius of the French language: "Si par exception je m'en rapportais à un adage: en effet pourquoi tout ne reviendrait-il pas à savoir qui je hante?" (p. 9)—"If for once I relied on a proverb, why would it not all come down to knowing whom I 'haunt'?" Tell me whom you haunt, I'll tell you who you are, says the proverb. But Breton expresses worry over the word "haunt," which threatens to "lead him astray" ("ce dernier mot m'égare"):

> Il dit beaucoup plus qu'il ne veut dire, il me fait jouer de mon vivant le rôle de fantôme, évidemment il fait allusion à ce qu'il a fallu que je cessasse d'être, pour être *qui* je suis. Pris d'une manière à peine abusive dans cette acception, il me donne à entendre que ce que je tiens pour les manifestations objectives de mon existence, manifestations plus ou moins délibérées, n'est que ce qui passe, dans les limites de cette vie, d'une activité dont le champ véritable m'est tout à fait inconnu.   (pp. 9–10, Breton's emphasis)

> It says a great deal more than it means to say, it makes me play, while alive, the role of a phantom, obviously it alludes to what I had to have ceased being in order to be *who* I am. Taken, with only a slight exaggeration, in this sense, it leads me to think that what I take to be the objective, more or less deliberate manifestations of my existence are merely what passes, into the limits of this life, from an activity whose veritable field is wholly unknown to me.

He then goes on to say what the word "phantom" means to him:

> La représentation que j'ai du "fantôme" avec ce qu'il offre de conventionnel aussi bien dans son aspect que dans son aveugle soumission à certaines contingences d'heure et de lieu, vaut avant tout, pour moi, comme image

finie d'un tourment qui peut être éternel. Il se peut que ma vie ne soit qu'une image de ce genre, et que je sois condamné à revenir sur mes pas tout en croyant que j'explore, à essayer de connaître ce que je devrais fort bien reconnaître, à apprendre une faible partie de ce que j'ai oublié.   (p. 10)

The representation I have of a "phantom," with all of its conventional trappings—its appearance as well as its blind submission to certain contingencies of place and time—suggests to me the finished image of a torment that can be eternal. It may be that my life is but an image of this kind, and that I am condemned to retrace my steps even while believing that I am exploring, to try and know [*connaître*] what I should be able to recognize [*reconnaître*], to learn a small part of what I have forgotten.

I would suggest that Breton's refusal to take on the role of "phantom" is tantamount to refusing both the existence of the unconscious ("an activity whose veritable field is wholly unknown to me") and the elaboration of continuous narrative. For to retrace one's steps while believing one is exploring, to try to know for the first time what one should be able to recognize, to learn a small part of what one has forgotten—isn't this one possible description of the enterprise of psychoanalysis? And wouldn't it be one possible description, as well, of a narrative project like that of, say, *A la recherche du temps perdu?* Breton is not interested in that kind of project. What he wants to discover is his "differentiation" from other men (p. 11), not from himself. And he wants to discover his uniqueness not by seeing his life whole, moving through time, but in flashes, unexpected moments of revelation, chance encounters, fortuitous associations, dizzying coincidences. The whole first part of *Nadja* consists of a string of such coincidences and encounters, presented "without established order," as they occur in his memory (p. 22).

The fact that many of these encounters involve women is not surprising, given the enormous prestige accorded to heterosexual love (and specifically to *amour fou,* passionate "love at first sight") in the mythology of Surrealism. As Breton wrote years later, commenting specifically on *Nadja,* the "mental climate" of the early years of Surrealism which produced that text was one in which "a taste for aimless wandering [*errer*] . . . is carried to its extreme limits. An uninterrupted quest is given free rein: it is a question of seeing, of revealing what is hidden behind appearances. The unexpected encounter which always tends, explicitly or not, to take on the features of a woman [*prendre les traits d'une femme*] marks the culmination of this quest."[28]

I will concentrate here on a single encounter, which leads almost directly to the central section of the book, to what Breton calls the "entrance onto the stage" ("entrée en scène") of his ostensible main character, Nadja. This preparatory, or premonitory, encounter is literally theatrical. Persuaded by the unanimous critical condemnation of a play that it couldn't be all bad, Breton goes to see it—and is marked by it for life: "*Les Détraquées* ["The Deranged Women"—literally, "Women off the track"] . . . remains and will remain for a long time the only dramatic work (I mean, written exclusively for the stage) that I will want to remember" (p. 46). His fascination—increased by the fact that the play is being performed in a theater near the Place Clichy, hangout of the lowlife—is such that, contrary to his aesthetic principles, he proceeds to give a continuous, coherent account of the play's plot. This account, nine pages long, is the longest single fragment in the book before Nadja's appearance.

"The action takes place in a boarding school for young girls" (p. 46). It is almost time for the end of the year celebration; the Headmistress is feverishly awaiting the arrival of a friend, a certain Solange. After a while, the noise of a carriage is heard.

> Une femme adorable entre sans frapper. C'est elle. Elle repousse légère-ment les bras qui la serrent. Brune, châtain, je ne sais. Jeune. Des yeux splendides, où il y a de la langueur, du désespoir, de la finesse, de la cruauté. Mince, très sobrement vêtue, une robe de couleur foncée, des bas de soie noire. Et ce rien de "déclassé" que nous aimons tant.   (p. 49)

> An adorable woman enters without knocking. It is she. She lightly pushes away the arms that embrace her. Blackhaired, brownhaired, I don't know. Young. Magnificent eyes, full of languor, subtlety, cruelty, despair. Slender, very soberly dressed, a dark colored dress, black silk stockings. And that touch of the *déclassé*, which we like so much.

To cut a long story short: the Headmistress and Solange are lovers; Solange injects herself with morphine, "displaying a marvelous thigh there, just above the dark garter" (p. 49). A ball bounces into the room, followed by a young girl. Curtain. In the second act the young girl has disappeared. The doctor, having been called, is suspicious—already last year one of the boarders disappeared mysteriously and her body was later found in the well. The search continues. Finally, the Headmistress opens a medicine closet and:

> Le corps ensanglanté de l'enfant apparaît la tête en bas et s'écroule sur le plancher. Le cri, l'inoubliable cri . . . Je ne sais si le cri dont je parle mettait exactement fin à la pièce, mais j'espère que ses auteurs (elle était due à la collaboration de l'acteur comique Palau et, je crois, d'un chirurgien nommé Thiéry, mais aussi sans doute de quelque démon) n'avaient pas voulu que Solange fût éprouvée davantage et que ce personnage, trop tentant pour être vrai, eût à subir une apparence de châtiment que, du reste, il nie de toute sa splendeur.   (pp. 53–55)

> The bloody body of the child appears, head down, and spills out onto the floor. The cry, the unforgettable cry . . . I don't know if the cry I am

referring to was the exact end of the play, but I hope that its authors (it was due to the collaboration of the comic actor Palau and, I believe, a surgeon named Thiéry, but also doubtless to some demon) did not want to expose Solange to further trials, wishing to spare the character, too tempting to be true, from any appearance of punishment—a punishment which, in any case, it denies with all its splendor.

As a matter of fact, the play did *not* end with the cry—and we know this because almost thirty years after the publication of *Nadja*, Breton published *Les Détraquées* in the first issue of his journal, *Le Surréalisme, Même*. The play ended with the arrest of the Headmistress and Solange, after several long, didactic, and moralizing scenes in which the doctor, a psychiatrist, explains to the police commissioner exactly what ailment the women were suffering from ("folie circulaire et périodique") and exactly what they did to the poor girl: "ces dames pratiquaient le grand jeu," torturing her with pen-nibs before strangling her in a "fit of sadistic passion." As for Solange, the doctor diagnoses her as "une détraquée, érotomane, morphinomane . . . avec perversion des instincts sexuels." The author of the play, P. L. Palau, explained in a postface that he wanted absolute scientific accuracy and obtained, through the intervention of a doctor friend named Paul Thiéry, great help from "the eminent Joseph Babinsky."[29]

Now here is something to sharpen our curiosity, as Freud might say: Breton, neither in the 1928 version of *Nadja* nor in its 1962 revision (after he had presumably read the script), makes any mention of the doctor/*raisonneur* role in the play. In fact, he doesn't merely "forget" but *actively negates* this role. In the fragment immediately following the plot summary, he returns once again to the play, specifically to the "gap" between acts 1 and 2: "The lack of sufficient indications about what happens after the fall of the ball, about exactly what Solange and her partner might be prey to, in becoming those superb beasts of prey [*ce dont Solange et sa partenaire peuvent exactement être la proie pour devenir ces superbes bêtes de proie*] remains par excellence what confounds me" (pp. 56–57). This after stating that he had returned to see the play two or three more times!

Either what Breton saw was not the play that Palau wrote; or what Breton wanted to see, and remember, was not the play that Palau wrote. For what Breton sees, in his recounting, and what excites and mesmerizes him, is the spectacle of female "otherness": madness, murderousness, lesbianism. In order for the spectacle to work, to produce its voyeuristic pleasure, it has to remain two-dimensional, lacking psychological motivation and depth. The last thing a voyeur wants is a psychiatrist to explain to him "what those ladies were doing and why." His pleasure comes precisely from the distance between him and "the scene," from the gap ("curtain," at once cut and screen) into or onto which he can project his own fantasies.

The repressed returns, however: in the 1962 version, Breton added a long footnote giving the reference to the published version of the play. (Astonishingly, no one seems to have followed up his reference until now, or been interested enough to write about it.) And then he mentions Palau's postface: "Great was my surprise when I learned that Dr. Babinsky had had a role in the elaboration of *Les Détraquées*. I remember the great neurologist well, having assisted him for a while as a 'temporary intern' in his service at la Pitiée. I still feel honored by the kindness he showed me—going so far as to predict a great medical future for me!—and, in my own way, I think I have put his teaching to good use" (p. 54). Good use indeed. But who was Joseph Babinsky? The son of Polish immigrants, one year younger than Freud, he had been Charcot's most famous pupil; after Charcot's death, he became one of the leading French specialists on hysteria. His chief contribution to the study of that disease was his theory of "simulation," according to which it was extremely difficult, if not impossible, to tell a "real hysteric" from one who was merely "acting."[30] We may speculate with some delight on Babinsky's own pleasure in helping Palau elaborate *Les Détraquées*. His name calls to mind another spectacle, however, for he was immortalized, as a young man, in Louis Brouillet's famous painting "Une leçon clinique à la Salpêtrière" (fig. 4). The painting shows the great Charcot lecturing to a group of seated men. To his left, slightly behind him, a young woman stands, half-swooned, throat and shoulders bared, supported at the waist by Babinsky. Her eyes are half closed, her lips slightly parted, as if smiling in sensual bliss. Charcot, aging, portly, balding, beardless, faces his students while pointing at the woman. Babinsky's face, handsome and bearded, topped by a headful of wavy brown hair, is turned down toward her; his eyes are on her face and throat.

At this point, we may digress for a moment to number 11 of the Surrealist journal *La Révolution Surréaliste,* which appeared in 1928, the same year as *Nadja*—and the same year as the first French translation of Freud's "Fragment of an Analysis of a Case of Hysteria." In this issue we find, among many other interesting things (including a full-page ad by the NRF imprint of the Gallimard publishing house, in which *Nadja* and three other Surrealist works are framed by Freud's *Interprétation des rêves, Trois essais sur la théorie de la sexualité, Un Souvenir d'enfance de Léonard de Vinci,* and *Ma vie en psychanalyse*) a short article co-signed by Breton and Louis Aragon, entitled "Le Cinquantenaire de l'hystérie." This "fiftieth anniversary of hysteria" refers not to Freud's *Studies on Hysteria* but to Charcot's famous lessons

4. Louis Brouillet, A Clinical Lesson at la Salpêtrière, 1887

on that ailment. Indeed, the article is illustrated by six large photographs drawn from the *Iconographie de la Salpêtrière*, showing Charcot's star patient, Augustine, in various "attitudes passionnelles," as Charcot called them, lying or sitting, her hair loose, on her bed.

Perhaps the most memorable sentence in this short text by the two Surrealist poets is the following question, which contains the only mention of Freud's name: "Does Freud, who owes so much to Charcot, remember the days when, according to the testimony of survivors, the interns at la Salpêtrière confused their professional duty and their taste for love, when, at nightfall, the patients joined them outside or received them in their beds?"[31] One can only dream about how Freud, the scrupulous author of "Observations on Transference-Love" (in which he warned male analysts against the dangers of succumbing to the seduction of women patients)[32] would have responded to this question.

The madwoman observed, theatricalized, photographed, eroticized— this was clearly the aspect of Charcot's legacy to which Breton most deeply responded. Much has been written about the photographs that accompany the text of *Nadja:* their function is to emphasize the documentary quality of the work, its "antiliterariness," its abhorrence of descriptions too reminiscent of the nineteenth-century novel, and so on. No one has suggested, however, that the photographs (which are not all of women, to be sure) may have an affinity with the nineteenth-century observation of hysterics—no one except Breton, that is. In the 1962 preface to *Nadja,* he unites in a single sentence a mention of the photographs with what he calls the "medical" tone of his narrative: "Just as the abundant photographic illustration has as its object to eliminate any description . . . , the tone adopted for the narrative copies [*se calque sur*] that of medical, above all neuropsychiatric, observation, which tends to keep a trace of all that the examination and the interrogation [*interrogatoire*] can yield, without taking the least trouble, in reporting it, to prettify the style" (p. 6).

One can doubt whether Breton did not take quite a bit of trouble over his style, but that's not the interesting thing about this statement. I react above all to the association of the words "neuropsychiatric observation" with photographs (Charcot's works on hysteria were all accompanied by abundant illustrations, and Charcot's "visual" approach to the hysteric has often been noted), and to the words "examination" and "interrogation." For Charcot and the whole school of French neuropsychiatry that followed him, the psychiatric encounter consisted of looking at, pointing to, and interrogating the patient: this model was fixed and has come down to us in that illuminating multivolume document, Charcot's *Leçons de mardi à la Salpêtrière,* consisting of verbatim

transcripts of the famous lessons. At each session, Charcot would inter-
rogate several patients, addressing didactic remarks to his audience
above the patient's head.[33]

Breton, who at one time thought of becoming a doctor, who had
studied with Babinsky, who had spent several months as an "apprentice"
doctor in a psychiatric hospital during the war, had internalized this
model to a degree that he was probably not aware of. One of the most
famous passages in *Nadja* is the diatribe directed against asylums and
psychiatrists (which, for Breton, meant *French* psychiatrists). And yet,
Breton's own encounter with Nadja, his own recounting of that encounter, his own role and stance and attitude in that encounter, evoke nothing
so much as the fantasy embedded in the article "Le Cinquantenaire de
l'hystérie": to "play doctor" with the madwoman, to know her carnally
and otherwise, without ever forgetting *who* one is (*"qui* je suis"). Without
becoming entangled with her, without "ceasing to be oneself," without
"haunting" her.

Breton met Nadja on the afternoon of October 4, 1926, on rue La-
fayette, behind the Opera, during one of his aimless wanderings:

> Tout à coup, alors qu'elle est peut-être encore à dix pas de moi, venant en
> sens inverse, je vois une jeune femme, très pauvrement vêtue, qui, elle
> aussi, me voit ou m'a vu. Elle va la tête haute, contrairement à tous les
> autres passants. Si frêle qu'elle se pose à peine en marchant. Un sourire
> imperceptible erre peut-être sur son visage. Curieusement fardée, comme
> quelqu'un qui, ayant commencé par les yeux, n'a pas eu le temps de finir,
> mais le bord des yeux si noir pour une blonde. Le bord, nullement la
> paupière . . . (p. 72)

> Suddenly, when she is still perhaps ten steps away from me, I see coming
> toward me a young woman, very poorly dressed, who also sees or has seen
> me. She goes with her head high, unlike all the other passersby. So frail
> that she barely touches the ground while walking. An imperceptible smile
> may be wandering over her face. Curiously made up, like someone who,
> having started with the eyes, didn't have time to finish, but the rims of the
> eyes so dark for a blond. The rims, not the lids . . .

And after a long parenthesis: "I had never seen such eyes." The parenthesis contains an explanation that such an effect of brightness is
obtained only if one carefully applies the eyeliner under the lid (a
surprisingly "feminine" piece of information), followed by the apparently incidental remark ("Il est intéressant de noter à ce propos . . .")
that Blanche Derval, the actress who played Solange, even seen close
up, appeared to have no makeup on. After this, Breton, who said earlier
that to his great shame he never found out more about Blanche Derval,

stops Nadja and speaks to her. She replies. And so begins their "failed adventure," whose first and most intense phase Breton recounts in the form of a diary. Interestingly, the only two pieces of extended, continuous (or nearly continuous, as in a diary) narrative in *Nadja* are the plot summary of *Les Détraquées* and the diary entries recounting Breton's first meetings with Nadja. As if the encounter of the Surrealist poet—whose aesthetic is founded on discontinuity—with the discontinuous self of the madwoman provoked a kind of textual reverse reaction: the usually fragmented text does not allow itself, here, to be "contaminated" by the madness it reports; it is fascinated but keeps its distance.

This phase of intense involvement ends nine days after the first meeting, on the afternoon of October 13 in a hotel room in Saint-German-en-Laye, where certain "scenes of her past life," recounted by Nadja to Breton, almost "drove me away from her forever" ("ont failli m'éloigner d'elle à jamais"—p. 134). In fact, they do seem to have driven him away from her, for after this, the narrative becomes generalized and atemporal: "J'ai revu Nadja bien des fois" (p. 136)—"I saw Nadja again many times." Here is where Breton resembles most the "neuropsychiatric observer," giving us examples of Nadja's enigmatic drawings (reproduced in photographs), quoting her strange utterances, citing her uncanny ability to make unexpected associations (like Surrealist metaphors) and arrive at "correct" interpretations of Surrealist paintings—such as a "particularly difficult" painting by Max Ernst, whose meaning she explicates with exactly the words Ernst himself had written on the back of the canvas (p. 149).

This phase of observation ends with a general reflection, by Breton, on his fundamental difference from Nadja ("I had, for a long time already, ceased having an understanding with [*m'entendre avec*] Nadja. To tell the truth, perhaps we never understood each other"—p. 157). Finally, there comes the last shattering fragment: "On est venu, il y a quelques mois, m'apprendre que Nadja était folle" (p. 159)—"Some people came to tell me, a few months ago, that Nadja was mad." Breton was very far from her by then, as the curiously impersonal construction of the sentence indicates. The next sentence is equally distanced: "A la suite d'excentricités auxquelles elle s'était, paraît-il, livrée dans les couloirs de son hôtel, elle avait dû être internée à l'asile de Vaucluse" ("As a result of eccentricities in which, it seems, she had indulged in the hallways of her hotel, she had had to be committed to the Vaucluse asylum").

The sentence after that raises the disturbing possibility that Breton himself played a determining role in Nadja's madness. This question is deflected by the seven-page diatribe against psychiatrists and asylums (pp. 160–167), but to his credit Breton returns to it at the end of the fragment. Had he perhaps encouraged her too much along her road to absolute freedom and flaunting of conventions, unaware that she lacked the essential instinct for self-preservation which he and his friends never lost? This question is left unanswered. The final section of the book, separated by a blank page, is written after a hiatus of several months and is addressed to an unnamed woman with whom Breton is in love.

Who, then, was Nadja, and why—and for whom—was Breton's adventure with her a failure? The commentators on this subject have been numerous, and, whatever the particular judgment they adopt, on some things they are generally in agreement. Nadja was the very embodiment of Surrealism, because she lived out, in her own life, to an extreme limit and beyond, "the Surrealist aspiration to total availability [*disponibilité*], to the refusal of any ethics based on calculation, to the acceptance of risk."[34] Nadja was the mediator and mirror through whom Breton found himself, she "emancipated the poet and freed his imagination."[35] She allowed him to recognize that the passion of love "was the absolute law of his being and of his destiny."[36]

Breton's biographers applaud this role; some of his critics deplore it. Roger Shattuck voiced the negative view years ago: "By his prolonged spying on her, Breton has swallowed Nadja . . . devoured her . . . Nadja emerges not as the subject of the book but as its victim."[37] More recently, Gloria Orenstein has criticized Breton for failing to understand Nadja's drawings and gnomic utterances from *her* point of view. Orenstein proposes an elaborate interpretation of Nadja's drawings and statements as reported or reproduced by Breton but not understood by him. According to her, Nadja was a female visionary who attempted (but failed because of Breton's blindness) to disclose to him "the sacred knowledge of her ancient psychic powers and of her lost matriarchal heritage connected with the Celtic mythological tradition that she identifies with."[38]

The view of Nadja as a symbol of female visionary knowledge is intriguing but strikes me as no less "appropriative" than the view of her as a symbol of the Surrealist quest. The truth is, we'll never know who Nadja was or what she "meant to say." Nor is that the most interesting question posed by Breton's book.[39] The question of Breton's attitude toward Nadja and of his possible role in precipitating her madness, which Breton himself poses, comes closer to the heart of the matter. And whatever criticism one might make of Breton as a "character" in the story, one must give him credit as *author* for providing the very evidence on which any criticism must be based; in this, he does resemble Freud, whose account of the Dora case is the basis on which his critics have elaborated even their most hostile interpretations. Breton's answer to his own question, both in the book and in his later commentaries on it, was that he did not love Nadja: despite all her attractions and seductions, she did not succeed in inspiring in him "l'amour pur et simple" that the woman to whom the last part of the book is addressed did inspire.[40]

Are we to blame him for this? Certainly not: the ways of love are mysterious, and besides, Nadja was crazy.[41] But we may not be entirely wrong in saying that Breton's conception of "pure and simple" love—which, by a supreme irony again produced by the French language, he called *l'amour fou*—precluded precisely the possibility of his being *touched* by madness, or simply by the "otherness" in femininity. Observed on a stage, distanced from him by the screen of fantasy, female madness excited him. Close up, he fled from it. The "scenes" Nadja told him about on October 13 almost drove him away forever, he says, because he judged that they had "compromised her dignity." The only one he actually reports, however, has more to it than that:

> Une histoire de coup de poing en plein visage qui avait fait jaillir le sang, un jour, dans un salon de la brasserie Zimmer, de coup de poing reçu d'un homme à qui elle se faisait le malin plaisir de se refuser, simplement parce qu'il était bas—et plusieurs fois elle avait crié au secours non sans prendre le temps, avant de disparaître, d'ensanglanter les vêtements de l'homme. (p. 134)

> A story of a punch in the face that made her blood spurt, one day, in a private room at the brasserie Zimmer, a punch in the face received from a man whom she gave herself the nasty pleasure of refusing simply because he was common [or short?]—and several times she had called for help, not without taking the occasion, before disappearing, of bloodying the man's clothes.

The question we cannot fail to ask, I think, is this: Was Breton sickened by the loss of Nadja's dignity or by the image of a man spattered with female blood?

Duras/Lacan: Not Knowing as Entanglement

This brings me, finally, to *Le Ravissement de Lol V. Stein*. Published in 1964, thirty-six years after *Nadja* (but the same year as the revised version), fifty-nine years after *Dora,* during the year in which Lacan gave his seminar on the "four fundamental concepts of psychoanalysis" (and during which he was definitively expelled from the International Psychoanalytic Association), *Lol V. Stein* is yet one more story about a doctor and a madwoman. But the author of the story was a woman, aware of herself writing "as a woman," although not ready to theorize about that fact; nor did she need to be (the conversations with feminists came later, after 1968).

Without claiming it as a general truth, valid for all times and all books, I want to argue that the difference between *Nadja* and *Lol V. Stein,* a difference more significant than their mutual participation in the aesthetics of modernist narrative (I am using that term here in opposition not to "postmodernist" but to "traditional realist"), is ultimately a difference in the gender, or more exactly the gender politics, of their authors. It is also, concurrently, a difference in their conceptions of the individual self and its relation to others—a difference that corresponds, historically, to the one between pre-Freudian and post-Freudian conceptions of the speaking (and writing) subject.

The fictional narrator created by Marguerite Duras is a man, Jacques Hold, thirty-six years old, a doctor, probably a psychiatrist, although this is only suggested, not affirmed. He tells the story of Lola Valérie Stein, Lol V. Stein. He tells the story haltingly, uncertainly, retracing his steps while exploring. He says that where he does not know, he imagines; he says that he knows Lol V. Stein the only way he can, by love.[42]

The first scene he imagines, over and over, is the scene of the ball at T. Beach, where Lol watched all night as her fiancé, Michael Richardson, danced with Anne-Marie Stretter. In the morning he went away with Anne-Marie, and Lol went mad. Mad because she had lost him? Mad because she had lost the sight of him and Anne-Marie Stretter, because she never saw the end of the scene, where Michael Richardson would take off Anne-Marie Stretter's black dress. Deprived of this last image, the ball continues to unfold eternally in "the cinema of Lol V. Stein" (p. 46).

Jacques meets Lol years after this ball, when she has returned to S. Tahla, her native city, married and a mother. Before recounting the scene of their first meeting, he tells—imagines—another scene, which took place a few days earlier: Lol follows a man through the city to its outskirts, to his rendevous with a lover; the woman he meets is Lol's childhood friend, Tatiana Karl; the hotel where they meet is the hotel where Lol used to meet Michael Richardson. Stretched out in a field of rye, Lol watches through a lighted window while the man and Tatiana make love.

The man is Jacques Hold. A few days later, Lol pays a visit to Tatiana, who is with her husband and her lover. Lol looks at Jacques Hold, who sees her looking at him and wants to "see her eyes on [him] again" (p.

83). So begins, in the middle of the book, the account of the entanglement which prompted Jacques Hold to begin his narration; which has
been present, although unspecified, from the very beginning of that
narration ("l'écrasante actualité de cette femme dans ma vie," p. 14—
"the crushing presentness of this woman in my life"); and which, the
novel's ending suggests, may perhaps never end.

The entanglement, the love, is chiefly between Jacques and Lol. But
it could not come into being, and continue, without the "third term,"
Tatiana. Tatiana and Jacques making love, watched by Lol; Tatiana
and Lol with their arms around each other, talking, watched, and over-
heard—at Lol's arranging, knowing that she has arranged it *for him*—
by Jacques; Lol and Jacques dancing, watched by Tatiana, who
does not know; Jacques making love to Tatiana in their hotel room,
knowing this time that Lol is watching; Jacques and Lol making love,
but Lol calling herself, in the midst of cries, insults, and supplications,
"Tatiana Karl and Lol V. Stein." And once again, Jacques in the
hotel room, waiting for Tatiana, his eyes on Lol who has preceded
him in the field of rye. The narrative stops here, but it could obviously
go on.

Lacan, in what I think is the only piece he wrote about a living author,
spoke about *Le Ravissement de Lol V. Stein* in his "Hommage fait à
Marguerite Duras." "Marguerite Duras shows that she knows without
me what I teach."[43] The apparent arrogance of this statement is atten-
uated by the sentence just before it, which, despite its tortuous syntax,
succeeds in telling us that Lacan agrees with Freud: "the artist always
precedes [the psychoanalyst], who therefore does not need to act like a
psychologist [*faire le psychologue*] where the artist shows him the way"
(p. 133). To say, then, that I wish to read *Lol V. Stein* "with" Lacan is
not to suggest that Lacan's theories "apply" to this novel or that this
novel "illustrates" his theories. Rather, it is to suggest that each can be
read as a commentary on the other—subject to subject, not subject to
object. A couple, in sum.

Lacan writes about Jacques Hold that as narrator he is not "a simple
demonstrator of the machine [*montreur de la machine*] but one of its
inner springs [*un de ses ressorts*], who does not know everything that
holds him in it [*ne sait pas tout ce qui l'y prend*]" (p. 132).[44] When I say
that Jacques Hold becomes entangled with Lol, becomes ravished by
Lol as he reinvents her own ravishment, I mean precisely that. To be
a demonstrator is to be outside, to observe. It is to be where Breton
was, where Freud wished (but happily failed) to be. Jacques Hold is,
and wishes to be, inside: he is *riveted* to Lol. "Nous voici chevillés
ensemble" (p. 113—*cheviller:* to peg, to bolt, to pin together). Lol's
desire has chosen him. "Je suis l'homme de S. Tahla qu'elle a décidé

de suivre," he is the man of S. Tahla she has decided to follow—and he follows her, across the city and into her dreams:

> Lol rêve d'un autre temps où la même chose qui va se produire se produirait différemment. Autrement. Mille fois. Partout. Ailleurs . . . Ce rêve me contamine. (p. 187)

> Lol dreams of another time when the same thing that is about to happen would happen differently. Otherwise. A thousand times. Everywhere. Elsewhere . . . That dream contaminates me.

He follows Lol into her memories:

> Lol regardait. Derrière elle j'essayais d'accorder de si près mon regard au sien que j'ai comencé à me souvenir, à chaque seconde davantage, de son souvenir. (p. 180)

> Lol was looking. Behind her I tried to adjust my gaze so closely to hers that I began to remember, more and more each moment, her own remembrance.

Is Jacques Hold Lol's phanton, the one who haunts her? There is a wonderfully complicated moment in Lacan's "Hommage à Marguerite Duras" where that idea is suggested and where the word *hanter* occurs; it is complicated because Lacan tells us, in the next sentence, that this idea is not his but comes to him from Marguerite Duras. And in the sentence after that, he puts it, in his own name, into question. Here is how it goes:

> Cet être à trois pourtant, c'est bien Lol qui l'arrange. Et c'est pour ce que le "pense" de Jacques Hold vient *hanter* Lol d'un soin trop proche, à la fin du roman sur la route où il l'accompagne d'un pélerinage au lieu de l'événement [the ballroom of T. Beach]—que Lol devient folle.
>
> Dont en effet l'épisode porte des signes, mais dont j'entends faire état ici que je le tiens de Marguerite Duras.
>
> C'est que la dernière phrase du roman ramenant Lol dans le champ de seigle, me paraît faire une fin moins décisive que cette remarque. Où se devine la mise en garde contre le pathétique de la compréhension. Etre comprise ne convient pas à Lol, qu'on ne sauve pas du ravissement. (p. 135, my emphasis)

This three-fold being, however, is indeed arranged by Lol. And it is because the "thinking" of Jacques Hold comes to haunt Lol with too much solicitude, at the end of the novel, on the road where he accompanies her on a pilgrimage to the place of the event—that Lol becomes mad.

Which, in effect, is suggested by certain signs in the episode, but about which I want to state that I have it from Marguerite Duras.

For the last sentence of the novel, bringing Lol back to the field of rye, seems to me to create a less decisive ending than this remark. Wherein one sees a warning against the pathos of understanding. To be understood does not suit Lol; she is not one to be saved from ravishment.

The first paragraph offers an explanation, even a kind of plot summary: Lol "arranges" the triangle that will allow her to repeat the scene of the ball (herself as observer, Jacques and Tatiana observed). And because Jacques Hold's "thinking," his attempt to reinvent Lol's story, comes too close to her, because he "haunts" her too much with his own solicitude [*soin trop proche*] when he accompanies her on a visit to the scene of the original "event," she becomes mad.

The second paragraph states that, although in effect there are signs in the last episode (the return to T. Beach) to support this interpretation, Lacan wishes to emphasize that he has it directly from Marguerite Duras.

For as far as Lacan is concerned, says the third paragraph, the final sentence of the novel, which brings Lol back to the field of rye, suggests a "less decisive" ending than this remark. Does the "wherein" in his next sentence refer to the novel's ending, or to Duras's remark? It's not clear. I tend to think that it refers to the ending, which offers a warning—even against the author's own remark—against the "pathos of understanding." The novel's ending, Lacan suggests, appears less "decisive" than Duras's summary of it ("Lol becomes mad"), and thus both gives and heeds its own warning.

I agree. And I dare think, since her name has been invoked, that Marguerite Duras would agree too. Lol does not "become" mad at the end, not any more than she has been throughout. The warning about trying to understand her is directed not at Jacques Hold but at a reader who would be content with the too easy "plot summary" offered in paragraph one. Jacques Hold does not need a warning, for he makes no claim to understand Lol V. Stein, or to save her from ravishment.[45] For him, nothing ends at the end of the novel, no more than for her. The last sentence (in fact, it's the last two paragraphs that Lacan refers to) is not an ending, but a suspension:

> Le soir tombait lorsque je suis arrivé à l'Hôtel des Bois.
> Lol nous avait précédés. Elle dormait dans le champ de seigle, fatiguée, fatiguée par notre voyage. (p. 191)

> Night was falling when I arrived at the Hotel des Bois.
> Lol had preceded us. She was sleeping in the field of rye, tired, tired by our voyage.

The voyage can continue, nothing says it won't. And Jacques Hold (but let us not forget, behind him, Marguerite Duras) can go on speaking, writing, not what he knows, but what he does not know. For the very

first moment he saw Lol, he understood one thing: "to have no knowledge at all about Lol was to know her already. One could, I realized,
know even less, ever less and less, about Lol V. Stein" ("ne rien savoir
de Lol était la connaître déjà. On pouvait, me parut-il, en savoir moins
encore, de moins en moins sur Lol V. Stein"—p. 81).

If Jacques Hold "haunts" Lol, it is to the exact degree that she haunts
him. "Nous voici chevillés ensemble. Notre dépeuplement grandit. Nous
nous répétons nos noms" (p. 113). What does it mean to say "Our
depopulation increases," right after: "We are riveted together"? And
what does it mean to repeat for each other, to each other, to ourselves
[nous nous répétons] our names, our "no's" (phonetically, the homonymic
[nonō])? We are being emptied, riveted together. Our names do not
name us, we are not our names.

When (the moment before this) Lol pronounces his name, Jacques is
ravished:

> Virginité de Lol prononçant ce nom! Qui avait remarqué l'inconsistance de
> la croyance en cette personne ainsi nommée sinon elle, Lol V. Stein, la soi-
> disant Lol V. Stein? Fulgurante trouvaille . . . Pour la première fois mon
> nom prononcé ne nomme pas. (pp. 112–113)

> Virginity of Lol pronouncing that name! Who had noticed the unsubstan-
> tiality of the belief in that person so named if not she, Lol V. Stein, the so-
> called Lol V. Stein? A blinding discovery . . . For the first time my name
> pronounced does not name.

Who had ever noticed the fragility—the lack of solidity—of the person
called Jacques Hold, of the person so called, if not she, if not Lol V.
Stein, the so-called Lol V. Stein, whose name of "stone" does not harden
her any more than his holds him? She has found in him what no one
else has found, recognized in him what no one else has recognized, what
he himself didn't see—the absence in his name, precisely that in him
which his name does not name. And he does the same for her:

> —Lola Valérie Stein.
> —Oui.
> A travers la transparence de son être incendié, de sa nature détruite, elle
> m'accueille d'un sourire. Son choix est exempt de toute préférence. Je suis
> l'homme de S. Tahla qu'elle a décidé de suivre. Nous voici chevillés en-
> semble. Notre dépeuplement grandit. Nous nous répétons nos noms. (p.
> 113)

Two transparencies, two names emptied of solidity, two beings depop-
ulated, riveted together. That is what Jacques Hold's ravishment by
and of Lol V. Stein is about.

This reading of Le Ravissement, and of Jacques Hold's position in that text, situates me at a critical distance from the influential "anti-Lacanian" feminist reading proposed by Marcelle Marini. According to Marini's reading, Jacques Hold behaves in typically male fashion by appropriating both Lol's gaze and her story:

> Jacques Hold will live out other scenes of love by giving himself to be seen by Lol, whose gaze remains his surest support: she, confined to her watching-place, will henceforth support by her gaze . . . the unchanging splendor of the masculine sex . . . And furthermore it is he who controls the discourse whereby he can narrate, at a distance, their story at will, putting himself in the first person while Lol becomes the one he speaks about, the one in whose place he most often speaks in order to sketch her portrait. He is the one who will reconstitute the pieces of the puzzle that is a woman.[46]

In Marini's reading, Jacques Hold remains "untouched" by Lol, using her to affirm both his sexual and discursive centrality; in that reading, Duras's authorial stance would have to be seen as *ironic,* even downright sarcastic, toward the male narrator. My reading, on the contrary, assumes a significant merging between Duras's authorial voice (and vision) and the voice of Jacques Hold—as if the subversive quality of the novel resided precisely in the feminization of the male narrator, who is "contaminated" by femininity both on the diegetic or story level (his involvement with Lol) *and* on the discursive level: Jacques' mode of narration, despite Marini's and some other feminist critics' claim to the contrary, is anything but "masculine"; it is hesitant, uncertain, full of silences, corresponding precisely to Duras's notion of what a "feminine writing" might be.[47]

It is important, I think, that Jacques Hold's narrative discourse is *similar* to the narrative discourse of other Duras texts (beginning with *Moderato Cantabile,* 1958, which according to Duras constituted a first break in her writing), where the narrator is either a woman *(L'Amant)* or else of unspecified gender *(Moderato Cantabile, L'Amour).* One might see in Duras's feminization of Jacques Hold a decentering of the masculine, its displacement toward the margins where femininity—and madness—have traditionally been lodged; and see this move, in turn, as a profoundly *feminist* one.[48] Wherein there lies a warning against the exclusive privileging of feminist irony. Irony and sarcasm toward the "male" are not the only feminist moves possible. To be ironic about heterosexual passion—her version of *l'amour fou*—does not suit Marguerite Duras.

Lacan, on the last two pages of his 1973 seminar, *Encore,* operates a breathtaking reversal. Having spent the whole book explaining a few provocative opening statements, such as "il n'y a pas de rapport sexuel" ("there is no sexual relation"), and "il sera à jamais impossible d'écrire comme tel le rapport sexuel" ("it will be forever impossible to write the sexual relation as such"), he ends by speaking—not for the first time, but for the first time in *this way*—about love. Love, he says, is not a sexual relation, if by that one means the orgasmic reunion of two bodies; instead, it is a momentary, oh so vulnerable *recognition* between two subjects, two split subjects inhabited by lack. It is only this recognition, this encounter of two absences that, as if by miracle, can produce for a moment the illusion that the sexual relation, thus redefined, can cease not being written, *cesse de ne pas s'écrire*. And to displace the negation once again, from *cesse de ne pas s'écrire* to *ne cesse pas de s'écrire* (does not cease being written, writing itself), that is the (impossible?) aim toward which love tends. "Tout amour, de ne subsister que du *cesse de ne pas s'écrire*, tend à faire passer la négation au *ne cesse pas de s'écrire*, ne cesse pas, ne cessera pas" ("All love, subsisting on the *ceases not to be written*, tends to displace the negation to *does not cease to be written, to write itself*, does not cease, will not cease").[49]

I will not dot the *i*'s and cross the *t*'s by pointing out the ways in which this magnificently pessimistic and at the same time inspired and inspiring, totally modern, yet surprisingly romantic view of love and of its relation to writing responds and corresponds to the pessimistic, inspired and inspiring, extravagantly romantic, totally modern vision of love and of *écriture* that Marguerite Duras has pursued in her novels and films since *Le Ravissement de Lol V. Stein*. Instead, I shall end by raising (very briefly) the question of how a feminine discourse—both as criticism and as *écriture*—might situate itself in relation to the discourse of psychoanalysis today. I tried to suggest, in my reading of Freud, that the desire to "master the material"—whether it be dreams, the unconscious, the woman's body, sexual difference, or narrative itself—was both the generating impulse and the Achilles' heel of the psychoanalytic project. I also tried to suggest that insofar as it *is* the Achilles' heel, it is a good thing—to be vulnerable, to be open to the risk of pain and death, is the sign of being human. For a long time and in very specific ways, it has been the additional sign, in our culture, of being a woman. Women bleed, women give birth, women have holes in them. The discourse of psychoanalysis becomes obnoxious, and noxious, during those moments when, faced with the openness of women, which it suddenly calls castration, it transforms women into Woman, and Woman into the flawed opposite of Man.

When he was not being willfully obnoxious ("La femme n'est pas toute," "Woman is not all," etc.), Lacan, I think (I like to think) knew this. Reading Lacan with Duras, we see emerging the possibility of a psychoanalytic discourse that would be not a discourse of mastery but a discourse of mutual entanglement. Who writes, or speaks, in the "ne cesse pas, ne cessera pas" that Lacan leaves us desiring? Who speaks, or writes, the ravishment of Lol V. Stein? Feminine discourse, which is not always where one expects to find it, reminds us that when it comes to being human, we are all in a position of ravishment—call it lack, if you must; our only hope for survival—call it love—being, against all odds and through all our divisions, to keep on writing.[50]

SIX

The Politics and Poetics of Female Eroticism

> I had the feeling that Pandora's box contained the mysteries of woman's
> sensuality, so different from man's and for which man's language was inad-
> equate. The language of sex had yet to be invented.
>
> —ANAIS NIN

As the general outcry that followed the publication of Kate Millett's
Sexual Politics in 1969 made clear, the question of women's bodies and
women's sexuality is a highly loaded one, with implications both for
politics—that is, for the relations of power and control that govern a
society—and for literature, or the production of verbal constructs that
in some ways reflect and in some ways help to create those relations.
The program implicit in Millett's analyses, which were soon to be followed by others and which coincided with the rise of the women's
movement as an international phenomenon, seemed as clear as it was
urgent. Women, who for centuries had been the *objects* of male theorizing, male desires, male fears, and male representations, had to discover and reappropriate themselves as *subjects;* and the obvious place
to begin was the silent place to which they had been assigned again and
again, that dark continent which had ever provoked assault and puzzle-
ment ("Was will das Weib?"). The call went out to invent both a new
poetics and a new politics, based on women's reclaiming what had always
been theirs but had been usurped from them: control over their bodies
and a voice with which to speak about it.

Over the past two decades, we have seen this program, if not fully
realized, at least fully embarked on. There have occurred real, mea-
surable changes in women's lives—for example the laws liberalizing
abortion in the United States and in France—as a result of it.[1] At the
same time, the program itself, both in its theoretical formulations and
in the kind of imaginative writing that can be thought to correspond to
it, has evolved over the years. What seemed, at first, an unproblematic
desideratum—let woman speak her own body, assume her own subject-

hood—has become problematized, complicated by increasingly difficult questions: what exactly do we mean when we speak of woman as subject, whether of speech or writing or of her own body? Is there such a thing as a (or the) subject? Is there such a thing as woman's body, woman's sexuality? Is there such a thing as woman—or, for that matter, man? These questions—which become inevitable the moment one begins seriously to think about the body or about sexuality, whether male or female—did not originate in the contemporary women's movement or in contemporary feminist thought; but the latter has evolved to encompass them and has infused them with a new urgency, whether in the form of analytical discourse or imaginative elaboration.

I would like to support and illustrate this statement by discussing what I see as three exemplary gestures of reappropriation in the works of some contemporary American, French, and English women writers. I call these gestures "exemplary," not in order to suggest that they ought to function as models to follow, but because they represent three different possibilities for—and constitute so many actual manifestations of—the contemporary attempt, by women, to rewrite and rethink the female body and female sexuality.

Equal Rights, or, Telling It with Four-Letter Words

The two novels, both American, that I shall focus on first were published in the same year, 1973. Erica Jong's *Fear of Flying* became a national bestseller, with several million copies sold in hardback and paperback editions; Rita Mae Brown's *Rubyfruit Jungle,* first published by a small feminist press in New York, sold seventy thousand copies in that edition before being bought and distributed by Bantam Books, after which it sold a great many more. Whatever their flaws, both of these works are exceptionally good first novels, by poets who have a real flair for language. It could be argued that neither Jong nor Brown has written anything as good since, but that is another matter; what interests me here is not their work in general but these particular books.

Why these two? Because they correspond, although in somewhat different ways, to what might be called the first wave of the American women's movement. They can be thought of as fictional counterparts to books like *Our Bodies Ourselves,* also first published in 1973, or Shere Hite's *Sexual Honesty, By Women for Women,* published in 1974 and later expanded into the *Hite Report on Female Sexuality.* The impulse behind these works was perhaps most succinctly summed up in one of the editorial statements of the *Hite Report:* "researchers must stop telling women what they *should* feel sexually, and start asking them what they *do* feel sexually."[2]

Fear of Flying and *Rubyfruit Jungle* are fictional manifestations of the same impulse. Both are autobiographical, narrated in the first person by heroines who are struggling to define themselves sexually and artistically, and who are aware of the tangle of contradictions implied by that combination where women are concerned. Both novels have an undeniable freshness and vitality in the use of language; I think that this is due partly to their lack of inhibition in using "unladylike" four-letter words, and partly to their ironic awareness of their own unconventionality. The uninhibited, humorously flaunting use of obscenities in a novel signed by a woman and published by a major press (*Fear of Flying* was published by Holt, Rinehart and Winston) in the year 1973 constituted in itself a significant gesture, both in terms of sexual politics and in terms of what I am calling sexual poetics.

The story told in *Fear of Flying* is well known, so I do not need to repeat it. What I wish to argue is that Jong's use of obscene language—which was generally recognized as a "first" in American fiction by a woman—was a self-conscious reversal of stereotypes, and in some sense a parody of the language of the tough-guy narrator/heroes of Henry Miller or Norman Mailer. I did a quick count of the number of times the word "fuck" or its variant appears in the first chapter of the novel; in the space of fourteen pages it appears fourteen times, including once in the title of the chapter (the famous "zipless fuck"). That kind of accumulation must, I contend, be interpreted as parodic. What is involved here is a reversal of roles *and* of language, in which the docile or bestial but always silent, objectified woman of male pornographic fiction suddenly usurps both the pornographer's language and his way of looking at the opposite sex. In one of the passages analyzed by Kate Millett, the narrator/hero of Miller's *Sexus* says about a woman: "She had a small juicy cunt, which fitted me like a glove."[3] Jong's narrator/heroine, Isadora, says about her husband: "I fell in love with Bennett partly because he had the cleanest balls I had ever tasted."[4]

Among the negative reviewers of *Fear of Flying,* some of the most harshly critical were women: "Complaints, complaints, all in the same vacuous language . . . Endless discontent," wrote Patricia Meyer Spacks about the heroine.[5] And Millicent Dillon, writing in the *Nation* about what she called the "new bawd" (as opposed to the old bawds we find in Chaucer or Cervantes), spoke disapprovingly of the attempt to fuse "vulgarity with self-discovery and self-conscious art."[6] What I find surprising is that no one noticed—or at any rate, no one gave its due to—the self-irony that accompanied the complaints and the vulgarity; nor did anyone give proper weight to the allusions that occasionally surfaced in the text, undercutting both the heroine and her male predecessors. At the end, for example, when Isadora looks at her body soaking in the bathtub, what does she see? "The pink V of my thighs, the triangle of curly hair, the Tampax string fishing the water like a

Hemingway hero" (p. 310). This is neither self-pitying, nor vacuous, nor vulgar; it is self-ironic, and a wonderfully irreverent reflection on the *machismo* of "Papa."

Am I suggesting that *Fear of Flying* is a great novel, with no lapses in taste or style, no unevenness in language or tone or vision? No, I am not. I am not even suggesting that it is a great *feminist* novel, despite the repeated, often quite moving reflections of the heroine on the difficulties of being both a sexual woman and an artist—or even merely a daughter—in our world. It is, however (or certainly was in 1973) a significant book, both stylistically and in terms of feminist politics. For the latter, its significance lies not so much in the occasional didactic commentaries (some of which are, as I say, quite moving, but others, especially today, sound merely like clichés), but rather in the usurpation of four-letter words to talk about a woman's sexual desires and fantasies. A phrase like "how to make peace between the raging hunger in my cunt and the hunger in my head" (p. 154) is shocking, not only because it implies that a woman feels hunger in both places (indeed, that she possesses both places), but perhaps above all because of the coupling of the first person possessive pronoun with the obscene noun—a combination that did not exist in serious fiction in English before Jong's book.

At this point, it becomes interesting to take another look at the "flying" of its title: by a felicitous coincidence, Isadora Wing (whose name is already a program) is preoccupied with precisely the activity that French feminists were proclaiming during the same years as the emblem of women's writing: flying, *voler*, which in French also means to steal. Claudine Herrmann, in a well-known book, called women writers *les voleuses de langue*—the thieves of language, or more exactly, the usurpers and subverters of a certain kind of "male" language.[7] An anonymous reviewer writing in the *London Observer* noted that in *Fear of Flying*, "Most of the narrative tricks are filched from the men, to be brandished in their faces and elsewhere, with undisguised relish."[8] That filching is, I think, what makes this book significant.

Rubyfruit Jungle is a somewhat different case. Whereas the "message" (to put it heavy-handedly) of a book like *Fear of Flying* might be stated as "women too are entitled to speak of their fantasies obscenely, and to view men as sexual objects," the "message" of *Rubyfruit Jungle* is that women have a right to speak of—and to recount in detail their enactments of—their sexual desire for other women. The narrator/heroine of *Rubyfruit Jungle* is unabashedly, enthusiastically, a lover of women. She has had sex with men too, but they simply don't compare—as she puts it, the difference is like the "difference between a pair of roller skates and a Ferrari."[9]

Here again, we have to see the tradition against which this kind of statement—which of course is funny but also serious—is being made.

One finds plenty of lesbian sex scenes in male pornography; in fact, sex between women is a stock element in pornography from Sade on. But as a number of commentators, including Nancy Huston in her book *Mosaique de la pornographie* have pointed out, lesbian scenes in Sade and elsewhere are always subordinated to a male gaze and above all to male desire. "To the enigmatic question 'What do women do together?' the pornographers give the answer that is most reassuring to them: 'the same thing.' To imagine a genuinely other kind of relation would be too threatening."[10] In other words, what is absent from the lesbian scenes of pornographers (and Huston rightly insists that pornography, even when not written by men, has always traditionally been written for a male public) is the reality of women's *desire* for other women. It is against this background that *Rubyfruit Jungle,* with its celebration of lesbian desire and lesbian pleasure, becomes fully significant.[11]

One must be careful not to overstate the case, however, either for *Rubyfruit Jungle* or for *Fear of Flying.* If the continuing popularity of these books is, on the one hand, a positive sign, suggesting that the American public has admitted some real changes in what is considered an acceptable story or an acceptable use of language by women, it may also be a sign that neither book is felt to imply a genuine threat to existing ways of seeing and being between the sexes. Like modern capitalism, modern patriarchy has a way of assimilating any number of potentially subversive gestures into the mainstream, where whatever subversive energy they may have possessed becomes neutralized. The two blurbs on the front and back covers of the paperback edition of *Rubyfruit Jungle* are, in this sense, extremely revealing. On the front, above the title, one reads: "A novel about being different and loving it." By the time we turn to the back, however, what we see is: "Being different isn't really so different." And indeed, the adventures of Molly Bolt, who rises from "a dirt-poor ole Southern girl" to become a New York filmmaker, fits into the schema of any number of American picaresque tales, just as the adventures of Isadora Wing fit into the familiar pattern of the *Bildungsroman* with an artist-hero, where the moment of self-discovery coincides with the decision to write a novel.[12]

This suggests that what may be needed is not merely the usurpation of old narrative structures and the old words by new speakers (however important these may be as a first step), but the inventing of new structures, new words, a new syntax that will shake up and *transform* old habits of thought and old ways of seeing.

Celebrating Difference, or, Writing (and Reading) Otherwise

As the reader has probably guessed, the writers I shall discuss under this heading are among those known in the United States as "new

French feminists."[13] Although their work is much more recent than that
of the "new novelists," who started publishing in the 1950s, the "new
feminists" have also, in a sense, become historical—which does not mean
that they are dépassé (all of the major figures associated with that
movement are still active and writing); but they are no longer in exactly
the same place, theoretically, as they were in the 1970s and their work
can now be seen with a certain temporal and emotional distance. I shall
try to take account of this time lag in my discussion, but like the hare
in the old story, I shall inevitably never catch up—especially if one
takes into account the time lag between even the final revisions of this
book and its own publication.

How has the injunction: "Reclaim your body!" functioned in the
context of recent French feminist writing and theory? To answer that
question one must begin with the work of Luce Irigaray, who in her
book *Speculum de l'autre femme* (1974) was the first to present a
massive, closely reasoned critique of the Freudian theory of feminine
sexuality, not only as it was formulated by Freud but also as it was
developed and reformulated by the "French Freud," Lacan. At the risk
of a tremendous generalization, one can say that all of Irigaray's critique,
both as presented in *Speculum* and in its sequel, *Ce Sexe qui n'en est
pas un,* is directed against the cornerstone of Freudian and Lacanian
theory: the primacy of the phallus. It is the erection (so to speak) of the
phallus to the status of transcendental signifier that enabled Lacan to
theorize the exclusion of women from the symbolic: from the Law of
the Father and from language.

Furthermore, Irigaray argues, it is the phallus—or rather its physical
counterpart, the penis—posited as the single standard for the measure
of sexual pleasure that has rendered Freudian-Lacanian theory incapable of recognizing, much less accounting for, the real existence and the
specific nature of feminine sexuality and feminine pleasure. The insistence on the uniqueness, and the unicity, of the erect phallus has rendered impossible the realization that woman's sexuality is not one but
multiple, not based on the gaze that objectifies but on the touch that
unites, not on the stiffness of strictly localized, free-standing forms but
on the melting together of diffuse, multiple, functionally nondifferen-
tiated elements: "Woman's sex is all over [her body] . . . the geography
of her pleasure is much more diversified, multiple in its differences,
complex, subtle, than is imagined . . . within an imaginary that is too
strictly centered on one and the same."[14]

How is this view of the female body and its pleasure linked to language and writing? Putting it slightly differently, how can the recognition of a hitherto repressed female eroticism embody itself in texts that
might be called "feminine?" Irigaray's claim is that the recognition of

the specificity of female eroticism necessarily implies a recognition of the specificity of women's relation to language. In opposition to the logic of "phallic" discourse—characterized by linearity, self-possession, the affirmation of mastery, authority, and above all unity—feminine discourse must struggle to speak otherwise. "Si nous continuons à nous parler le même langage, nous allons reproduire la même histoire"—"If we continue to speak the same language, to each other and to ourselves ["nous parler" has both meanings], then we shall reproduce the same story and the same history"; so begins the concluding text of *Ce Sexe qui n'en est pas un,* "Quand nos lèvres se parlent" ("When Our Lips Speak Together"), in which Irigaray attempts not so much to theorize about, but actually to *write,* a "feminine" text. I will not analyze this text in detail but will simply point out those elements in it that appear to me most significant in the context of the present discussion.[15]

First, it is a text that celebrates love between women. What is most specific about such a love? The fact that the lovers are not "enigmas" for each other, do not represent "the other" for each other, which is always the case between a man and a woman—but are, rather, in a relation of absolute reciprocity in which the notions of "giving" and "receiving" have no place. "When you say I love you—here, close to yourself, close to me—you are saying I love me. You don't 'give' me anything in touching yourself, in touching me: touching yourself again through me" (p. 206). In the perfect reciprocity of this relation, there is no place for an economy of exchange, or of opposition between contraries. The lovers are neither two nor one, neither different nor the same, but un-different *(indifférentes).*

Second, this text celebrates a state of being, and a form of communication, in which binary oppositions become nonpertinent. If we recall that all of the traditional linguistic and logical categories in Western thought are based on binary opposition, then the "scandalousness" of Irigaray's attempt becomes immediately evident. Not only the scandalousness, but also, in a sense, the impossibility: Irigaray's text is haunted by the question, "How to speak without using the 'old' male language?" This question punctuates her text with a kind of obsessive regularity: "But how to say otherwise, I love you?" "How to say it?" "How to speak in order to get out of their partitions, checkerings, distinctions, oppositions . . . How to disenchain ourselves, alive, from their conceptions?" (pp. 207, 211).

At one point, she raises the possibility that perhaps there is no point in trying to say it at all—since the two bodies feel the same things at the same time, there is no need to speak. But she immediately rejects that idea: "If we do not invent a language, if we do not find *its* language, our body will have too few gestures to accompany its (hi)story" (p. 213).

For women to be silent is not the solution: "Don't cry. One day we will succeed in saying ourselves. And what we shall say will be even more beautiful than our tears. All fluid" (p. 215).

To invent a language in which to speak about woman's pleasure and woman's love for woman—indeed, a language that will be addressed exclusively *to* women—this, I think, is the utopian ideal that Irigaray's text seeks both to project and in some approximate way to exemplify.

A number of feminist theorists, in England and in France, have criticized what they see as the essentialism of Irigaray's position, which seems to base everything on the female body without asking to what extent the body (whether male or female) is a cultural construct, rather than a "natural" given. Some of these attacks are, as Carolyn Burke has pointed out, themselves quite reductive and do not take sufficient account of the complexity—nor, one might say, of the metaphorical quality—of Irigaray's discourse.[16] And yet, it seems increasingly clear that the ideal of a "woman-language" modeled on, even if not actually produced by, the female body—a language that women alone can speak, for other women "together" and whose privileged subject, in every sense of the term, is woman—is unsatisfactory. For although Irigaray's ire—and irony—are rightfully directed at the male logic of exclusion, which cannot take account of the real existence of "the other" and which divides the world into simple binary categories, the logic of her own discourse leads to a similar exclusion in reverse. The structure of the pronouns in "Quand nos lèvres se parlent" is revealing: *je, tu, nous, eux*—I, you, we, them. They are outside us, they are what we are not, they are the enemy. Even if we assume that "they" refers not to all or only men but to a particular and particularly pernicious mode of discourse or of thought, I am bothered by the absolute nature of the opposition.

In fact, Irigaray's subsequent work suggests that she did not consider the exclusionary logic of "Quand nos lèvres se parlent" as her permanent ideal. In *Amante marine* (1980), a set of essays "about" Nietzsche, the first long essay consists of meditative fragments addressed directly to the male philosopher. Although the tone is accusatory, the fact that the female speaker chooses the form of direct address (using the familiar *tu*) suggests a recognition of the other as a possible interlocutor. This possibility is even more emphasized in *Passions élémentaires* (1982), a set of fragments addressed to a male lover. The lover is accused of a certain blindness, and of the traditional male attempt to imprison the beloved woman in his rigid conception of her. At the same time, it is—albeit tentatively—suggested at the end that a real dialogue and a genuine encounter between the lover and the female speaker might be possible, one in which each would retain his/her difference even while uniting with the other.

Furthermore, it is interesting that Irigaray's poetic *language* (should we call it "feminine"?) does not change in moving from the celebration of love between women to the (tentative) celebration of a (possible) love between a man and a woman. Jane Gallop was no doubt right in suggesting that the emphasis on a "female homosexual economy, a female narcissistic ego" may be, for Irigaray, but the first step—necessary for women in order to find an adequate representation of themselves and an adequate language, and necessary too in order to avoid being "engulfed by the male homosexual economy," but not something "raised to an ideology."[17]

Besides Irigaray who is primarily a theorist, two other French women writers have emerged as exemplary in their attempt to forge a new language to speak about the female body, and to fuse this language with a radical, female-centered politics: Hélène Cixous and Monique Wittig. It has become almost a critical commonplace to *oppose* Cixous's and Wittig's writing practices as well as their conceptions of female sexuality.[18] Indeed, they were for a number of years associated with two ideologically opposed groups in France: Cixous with the Psych et Po group and with its publishing house, Editions des Femmes, Wittig with the Marxist feminist journal *Questions féministes*. In the context of my present discussion, however, Cixous and Wittig rejoin each other in at least two important ways: in their theoretical as in their fictional writing, they explicitly or implicitly criticize and seek to displace patriarchal language, culture, and narrative. And this critique appears, in both, to lead to the elaboration of a fictional world—and to a corresponding poetics—that is exclusively female.

Cixous's is the more complicated itinerary. In her first novels, before 1975 (such as *Portrait du soleil*, 1973) and early scholarly writings (for example, the major study of Joyce that was her doctoral dissertation),[19] she seems to have identified primarily with male poets and traditional male symbols like the sun. Somewhat later, in her first theoretical writings about *écriture feminine* (I have in mind especially her long essay, "Sorties," in *La Jeune Née* and her essay "The Laugh of the Medusa," both published in 1975), she alternated between a view one could call essentialist—affirming that women should "write their bodies," write with "white ink," (mother's milk), and so on—and a more ambiguous view that insisted on the potential bisexuality in writing. In good Derridean fashion, she was careful to point out that the bisexuality she had in mind was not that of the hermaphrodite, who represents a "fantasy of unity" or a myth of totality, but rather the bisexuality of a "dual" or even multiple subject, who is not afraid to recognize in him- or herself the presence of both sexes, not afraid to open her- or himself up to the presence of the other, to the circulation of multiple drives and desires. She then went on to say, however, that for historical and cultural reasons, it is women who today have the greatest potential for realizing this kind of bisexuality, and for practicing the kind of writing that results from it. Men, with a few notable exceptions among the poets, have been too prone to fall victim to the ideology of phallocentrism—whence their submission to the rules of logic, syntax, linearity, homogeneity, and realist representation. Cixous called, instead, for a kind of writing that would break open the chains of syntax, escape from the repressiveness of linear logic and teleological "storytelling," and allow for the emergence of a language "close to the body"; this language, linked, for Cixous, to the voice and the body of the mother, would allow the "wildness" of the unconscious to emerge over the tame reasoning of the superego or the Law."[20]

After these essays were published, Cixous produced close to a dozen long texts she calls "fictions," all of which are both reflections on and examples of the kind of writing she had theorized. The first one in the series, *Souffles,* which inaugurated Cixous's collaboration with Editions des femmes, is a wonderfully rich and complex book, whose title recalls one of the programmatic statements of "Sorties": "By writing herself [the verb "to write" is being used transitively], woman will return to that body that has been more than confiscated from her . . . In censuring the body, one censures at the same time breathing [*le souffle*] and speech."[21]

The title of *Souffles,* then, suggests both the breathing and the speech that come when censorship over the body is lifted; it also suggests strong emotion, labor, or passion, in all of which one "breathes hard." Cixous's text exploits these multiple associations of the word and merges all of them into a single metaphoric complex that runs throughout the book: that of giving birth (*naissance, accouchement, enfantement*). The primary voice who speaks in the text and who says "I" fantasizes several violent scenes of birth, both by herself and by another (perhaps her own) mother. She herself harbors a number of mothers within her and eventually gives birth to a young woman who is perhaps another version of herself. She also gives birth to this text, which is "delivered" from her body.

Throughout *Souffles* there is a tremendous verbal energy and a kind of breathlessness. Although the book is divided into sections of varying length, each one further divided by variations in typography and by blank spaces between passages, the feeling one has is not of fragmentation but rather of effusion, as if everything were being written in a single breath. In one of her subsequent works, *Ou l'art de l'innocence* (1981), Cixous writes that she has never been able to revise and reread her texts in order to make them easier to follow. On the contrary, she says: "I have never been able to turn back, I've never been able to write with a reading following the text and leading it along, I'm always following behind sentences running forward with all their might. I have never thought of writing a beginning for a text, I have always been carried along by a high-strung writing moving with the wind, coming from I don't know where."[22]

To return to *Souffles:* besides the metaphoric complex of birth images, one very interesting feature of this text is the way it sets in motion two different kinds of intertextuality. First, there is a positive or affirmative intertextuality, consisting (for example) of quotations from and allusions to the writings of Jean Genet, who actually appears as a "character"— to the extent that there are any characters—in the fiction, as well as a whole series of puns on Genet's name (such as *Je-nais,* "I am born," which brings us back to the birth images). Second, there is a negative or critical intertextuality, which consists of ironic rereadings of major texts in our culture, especially of *the* major text, Genesis—which brings us back yet again to the problematics of birth and of origins.

At the end of a long section that recounts the narrator's simultaneous discovery, as a little girl, of beauty, theft, and the ridiculousness of the "great white master" (this section recounts an incident in which the little girl saw a beautiful medallion in a store and stole it, but was caught and punished—to no avail, for she didn't succeed in feeling any guilt whatsoever), she tells us that it was around that time she first read Genesis, "in her own way." Her favorite character in that story was the serpent:

> un grand nègre-serpent tout en tête et en queue ornée de diamants. Je le trouvai d'une rassurante beauté, en contraste avec les membres en sucre des autres personnalités. Quant à Eve, que je trouvais niaise, (toujours aussi infantile alors qu'elle était adulte) je la pressais de manger le fruit: c'est là décelai-je, que se greffe la falsification masculine, et tout est dans le commentaire.   (pp. 180–181)

> a tall black serpent, all head and a tail covered with diamonds. I found his beauty reassuring, in contrast to the sugariness of the members of the other characters. As for Eve, whom I found silly (still just as infantile, even though she was grown up), I urged her to eat the fruit. It was there, I discovered, that masculine falsification comes in, and everything is in the commentary.

If "everything is in the commentary," then an integral part of the new "feminine" poetics was to reappropriate, by means of ironic rereadings— and rewritings—the dominant cultural productions of the past. Cixous made this explicit about her work in an interview published in 1977: "I found myself in the classic situation of women who, at one time or another, feel that it is not they who have produced culture . . . Culture was there, but it was a barrier forbidding me to enter, whereas of course, from the depths of my body, I had a desire for the objects of culture. I therefore found myself obliged to steal them . . . So that in a sense [culture] is always there [in her works], but it is always there in a displaced, diverted, reversed way. I have always used it in a totally ironic way."[23]

The subject of feminist irony will preoccupy us at length in the next chapter. For now, I want to come back for a minute to the figure of Jean Genet, and the role he plays in *Souffles*. He figures not only as the emblematic thief who is outside the Law of the "great white masters," but also as the emblematic bisexual writer. The narrative "I" refers to him as her "precursor," her ally, and as the "mother" of his texts; at the end of the book she speaks about a "maternal father . . . a man of that kind, of good and transparent femininity" ("un père maternel . . . un homme de ce genre, d'une bonne et transparente féminité") who has given her a child (p. 220). Significantly, however, if one looks at Cixous's fictions subsequent to *Souffles,* one discovers that this figure of the feminine man—as well as that of the bisexual woman—has been gradually eliminated, to be replaced by figures who are all female, not to say "all woman." *Ou l'art de l'innocence,* for example, begins by saying that men, the men the narrator used to know, don't really like language, that they are afraid of language, and goes on to develop a quite absolute opposition between the way women—that is to say "we," *nous*—view language and the way men ("they") do. From her first celebration of Joyce, Kleist, Genet, and other male poets in whom she saw allies or precursors in "bisexual writing," Cixous moved toward an emphatic celebration of the feminine, as embodied in women.[24]

And Wittig? Although her intellectual allegiances and theoretical statements place her in strong opposition to both Cixous and Irigaray, her imaginative works manifest a number of similar preoccupations, both formal and thematic. Wittig categorically rejected the concept of *écriture feminine* even at a time (during the 1970s) when it was an enabling concept for a number of French and francophone women writers, including Cixous, Irigaray, Chantal Chawaf, Annie Leclerc, and Madeleine Gagnon, among others; indeed, Wittig rejected the very idea of "woman" (*femme*) or of "femininity." In an often-cited essay first published in the Marxist-feminist journal *Questions Féministes,* known for its scathing critiques of what it called the "neo-femininity" theories of the Psych et Po group, Wittig denounced the concept of an ontological difference between the sexes as a creation of heterosexual bourgeois capitalist thought. For her, the difference between the sexes is not ontological (or even biological), but political:

> For us there is no such thing as being-woman or being-man. "Man" and
> "woman" are political concepts of opposition . . . It is the class struggle
> between women and men which will abolish men and women. The concept

of difference has nothing ontological about it. It is only the way that the masters interpret a historical situation of domination . . . for us, this means there cannot any longer be women and men, and that as classes and as categories of thought or language they have to disappear, politically, economically, ideologically. If we, as lesbians and gay men, continue to speak of ourselves and to conceive of ourselves as women and as men, we are instrumental in maintaining heterosexuality.[25]

This leads Wittig to the provocative conclusion that "it would be incorrect to say that lesbians associate, make love, live with women, for 'woman' has meaning only in heterosexual systems of thought and heterosexual economic systems. Lesbians are not women" (p. 110).

This essay suggests that, just as the aim of the Marxist class struggle is to abolish all social and economic classes, the aim of the feminist class struggle is to abolish sexual categories as we have known them. Lesbians and gay men seem designated to lead this struggle, since they are already outside the confines of sexual categorization. Wittig's imaginative works—starting with *Les Guérillères,* which was her second book but the first to deal explicitly with this problematic—can be read as attempts to embody this program in a new kind of writing; but they also, paradoxically, manifest the most radical kind of binarization and the most radical elimination of "the other" that it is possible to imagine.

Les Guérillères, published in 1969, has become a classic in the genre of the feminist Utopia—a genre inaugurated by Charlotte Perkins Gilman's *Herland* (1915). *Les Guérillères* is different, however, for it is not, strictly speaking, a narrative text. In the traditional Utopia (*Herland* conforms to this model) a basically descriptive impulse—describing how things might be "elsewhere," as a corrective to the "here and now"—is grafted onto a simple narrative schema: a stranger arrives in the land, finds out all about it, then returns to tell the tale. Wittig does away with the narrative frame and writes a series of descriptive fragments in the present tense, all of them having as their subject (both grammatically and in terms of content) "elles"—the *guérillères* of the title, who are modern reincarnations of the Amazons. Theirs is an exclusively female world of warriors, with its goddesses, its sacred book—called *le féminaire*—its history, myths, rituals, games, celebrations, and symbols, the chief of these being the circle, symbol of the vulva. The word "femme" occurs extremely rarely and is never used to designate "elles." But the descriptive fragments are interspersed with pages bearing a series of women's names, of all nationalities, from antiquity to the present, printed in capital letters. Even more insistently, the language of the text feminizes the French indefinite pronoun, "quelqu'un," which is morphologically masculine, to yield the "ungrammatical" pronoun "quelqu'une," a somebody who is female; it also systematically uses the female designation of animals, so that even the animal world around the *guérillères* consists (linguistically, at least) only of the female of the species.

Wittig, like Cixous, practices both a positive and a negative intertextuality. Among the positive intertexts in *Les Guérillères* are works by Marx, Mao Tse-Tung, and the Vietnamese tactician of guerilla warfare, General Giap. The negative intertexts include Lacan, but Wittig's more characteristic move, in this book and subsequent works, is to present rewritten, feminized versions of classical and Christian myths:[26] the golden fleece, for example, is described as "one of the names given to the hairs that cover the pubis" (p. 60); the Grail cycle is reread and rewritten in terms of the symbol of the vulvar circle, which explains the round table, the spherical cup, and the blood it contains. As for Eve, she appears in the story of a naked woman who walks among the fruit trees in an orchard. Her "beautiful body is black and shining," and her hair consists of "thin moving snakes that produce music at each of her movements"; thus the biblical Eve (who is here shown *alone* in a garden, with only her snakes for company) is conflated with the Medusa, who is also a key figure in Cixous's writing and whose name always evokes an indirect mockery of Freud's theories about female castration.[27]

These rereadings and rewritings accomplish two complementary things: they appropriate positive but male-oriented symbols like the golden fleece or the Holy Grail by feminizing them; and they reverse negative, female-associated symbols like the head of the Medusa by endowing them with positive value.

Although I have said that there is no narrative line in *Les Guérillères*—an absence reinforced by the exclusive use of the present tense—there is something like an internal evolution among the fragments. Near the middle of the book, for example, there is a fragment that *criticizes* the earlier symbolism of the circle and the glorification of the vulva. Such symbols belong to a dead culture, not to the new world toward which "elles" are advancing (p. 102). Similarly, there is a movement toward what might be called a reconciliation with the enemy: at the end of the book, when something like a final struggle has been won, "elles" make peace with the surviving men, who are young, long-haired, and nonviolent. The very last fragment, where suddenly the pronoun "nous" appears (together with a first-person possessive signaling the presence of a personal narrator who is part of "elles"), describes a triumphant celebration at which the assembled crowd—designated only by the feminine form "nous toutes"—sings the International and remembers those who died for liberty.

Les Guérillères, then, combines a massive feminization of culture, history, and language, with a Marxist vision of class struggle followed by the abolition of all conflict. But the fact that only "nous toutes" are left suggests not so much a decategorization of masculine/feminine as the assimilation of one category by another, which is what traditionally happens with the use of masculine forms as universals. Here, the assimilation is reversed: the universal becomes female.

An alternative interpretation would be that the female has not so much assimilated the male as eliminated it. This is what happens, I think, in Wittig's two books subsequent to Les Guérillères: Le Corps lesbien (1973), a series of lyrical, often violent erotic fragments addressed to a beloved, with echoes of Sappho and Ovid, and Brouillon pour un dictionnaire des amantes (1976). The latter, written in collaboration with Sande Zeig, consists of a series of alphabetically arranged fragments, which do not quite "add up to" but nevertheless do produce a fractured account of human history from an original Golden Age through an age of chaos to a new age of glory. There are two extremely striking things about this account: first, it traces all the conflicts of human history to a primordial conflict between "mothers" (also called "women"), who gradually became sedentary, and the bands of Amazons, or amantes, who continued the migratory way of life that characterized the Golden Age. (It was the "mothers" who insisted on building houses and cities, thus initiating the decline into chaos.) Second, the dictionary does not contain a single mention of the word "man" or any of its cognates. It is, quite simply, as if one half of the human race had never existed. This may be read as a parodic—but also grimly polemical— reversal of the way men have written human history, eliminating women, throughout the ages, just as Wittig's systematic feminization of grammatical categories may be read as a critical reversal of the traditional norm, according to which the masculine form is the "universal" one.

I admire Wittig's writings enormously, but I have serious reservations about the separatist politics implicit in her poetics.[28] Other commentators have praised Wittig for the "all female contexts and texts" she has created,[29] or for the fact that in her texts "male culture is eliminated," male language "overthrown by lesbian language," and male discourse is silenced "to allow textual and linguistic space for the development of the new language."[30] I am troubled by the conflictual vocabulary— elimination, overthrow, silencing—of such praise, which echoes (but without the poetic resonances and ambiguities) the conflictual vocabulary of Wittig's own texts.

This may be a heterosexual bias on my part, or even a kind of fear— the heterosexual woman's fear of being "contaminated" by lesbianism. But there are theoretical reasons for my demurral as well. Is one going to do away with the confines of sexual categorization, whether in language or in life, by eliminating one of the terms altogether? Does not the eliminated term become reinscribed by its very absence? Feminist critics (including me, in Chapter 3) have often criticized and demystified the masculine fantasy of "men without women," which is deeply anchored in our culture and has a very long history. A book like *Brouillon pour un dictionnaire des amantes* makes me realize that I find the opposite fantasy no less distressing, and, ultimately, no less impoverishing.

It can be persuasively argued that the violence Wittig does to traditional (male?) syntax and vocabulary, and to a corresponding mythical and historical memory, is—and certainly was, in 1973—necessary and salutary, in the face of centuries of similar violence directed against women's words, language, and memory by patriarchal institutions and patriarchal writing. In *Le Corps lesbien,* the female speaker, identified as a "split subject" by the slashed orthography of "j/e," alludes humorously to the heel of "Achillea, the well-named one who very much loved Patroclea." It can also be argued that Wittig's commentators are more simple than she, for has she not, after all, said that "lesbians are not women"? Perhaps Wittig's *amantes,* whom I read as "female lovers," are not women, not female at all. Perhaps they represent a whole new species, neither man nor woman, the age of glory being precisely that age in which the strict boundaries of sex, as of class, will have been transcended.[31] But if so, then we are once again entrapped by language, which does not have a "third term"—a term that would not be neuter, genderless, but gender-undecidable (or better still, gender-multiple). Today, if I am reading French, I must read *amantes* as female, and Wittig's age of glory as single-sexed.

Have we hit a dead-end? Is there no alternative to "equal rights," in which all the old structures remain in place, only the roles are reversed—women on top—or to a celebration of difference that turns into the celebration of one sex, not two? From here on, we can only dream. But that is what stories, poems, have always invited us to do.

Dreaming beyond the Number Two

My reflections here were inspired by the intersection of a number of heterogeneous texts. I would like therefore to begin by quoting a few fragments of theoretical or speculative writing, which I shall not try to explicate individually but whose resonance with each other—and with the discussion thus far—will be evident. I should emphasize that I present these fragments deliberately out of context, not in their own argumentative frame but in my own.

The first is from an essay by the English feminists Beverly Brown and Parveen Adams, "The Feminine Body and Feminist Politics":

What can be said of the political task of feminism set up as a control of the feminine body and feminine sexuality is that it is dominated by the conception of unities—the unity of the body, the unity of sexuality, the unity of control, the overarching unity of the individual formed by their coincidence and ultimately, a unity of the body of women. Analyses in terms of unities hold out the prospect of liberation—unities can be grasped and will not finally escape us.[32]

The second is from another essay by Parveen Adams:

It could be said that one of the paradoxical effects of feminism as a political force has been to force the recognition of the diverse and unexpected character of the organisation of sexual differences. It has proved a difficult and contentious problem as to how to analyse the effects of anything from social policy to artistic practices in respect to the organisation of sexual differences. But to reduce these problems to the simplifications of an always already antagonistic relation between two social groups who are frozen into a mutually exclusive and jointly exhaustive division is an obstacle both to feminist and political practice.[33]

Finally, there is this fragment from a text consisting of a written dialogue between Jacques Derrida and Christie V. McDonald. At the end of this dialogue, McDonald asks the question:

If we do not yet have a "new" "concept" of woman, because the radicalization of the problem goes beyond the "thought" or the concept, what are our chances of "thinking 'difference' not so much before sexual difference, as you say, as taking off 'from'" it? What would you say is our chance and "who" are we sexually?

To this question Derrida replies not by proposing an answer (what kind of answer, in the sense of a stated position, or a position statement, could one give?) but by speaking about desire, and a dream:

As I dream of saving the chance that this question offers, I would like to believe in the multiplicity of sexually marked voices. I would like to believe in the masses, this indeterminable number of blended voices, this mobile of non-identified sexual marks whose choreography can carry, divide, multiply the body of each individual, whether he be classified as "man" or as "woman" according to the criteria of usage. Of course, it is not impossible that desire for a sexuality without number can still protect us, like a dream, from an implacable destiny which immures everything for life in the figure 2. And should this merciless closure arrest desire at the wall of opposition, we would struggle in vain; there will never be but two sexes, neither one more nor one less ... But where would the "dream" of the innumerable come from, if it is indeed a dream? . . . Then too, I ask you, what kind of a dance would there be, or would there be one at all, if the sexes were not exchanged according to rhythms that vary considerably? In a quite rigorous sense, the exchange alone could not suffice either, however, because the desire to escape the combinatory itself, to invent incalculable choreographies, would remain.[34]

The dream, then, is to get beyond not only the number one—the number that determines unity, of body or of self—but also beyond the number two, which determines difference, antagonism, and exchange conceived of us as merely the coming together of opposites. That this dream is perhaps impossible is suggested. Its power remains, however, because the desire it embodies is a desire for both endless complication and creative movement.

What would a story—or a text—inspired by such a dream look like? Cixous, in one of her later texts, writes about love as a dance between persons of undecidable gender:

> Et alors si je parlais d'une personne que j'ai rencontrée et qui m'a bouleversée, elle-même étant émue, et moi émue de la voir émue et elle de me sentir émue, émue à son tour, et que cette personne soit une elle et un il et un elle et une il et une ellil et une ilelle, je veux avoir la permission de ne pas mentir, je ne veux pas l'arrêter si elle transe, je le veux, je la veux, je la suivrai.[35]

> And then if I spoke about a person whom I met and who shook me up, herself being moved and I moved to see her moved, and she, feeling me moved, being moved in turn, and whether this person is a she and a he and a he and a she and a shehe and a heshe, I want to be able not to lie, I don't want to stop her if she trances, I want him I want her, I will follow her.

Language is here shaken up, the way the speaking "I" is shaken up: *ellil, ilelle,* shehe, heshe. But if there is a story, it is only fleetingly suggested. If we want narrative, we must turn to fantasy, or science fiction. Or we can turn to Angela Carter's novel, first published in England in 1977, *The Passion of New Eve.*[36]

As its title suggests, this is yet another rewriting of an old story. In fact, it is a rewriting of many stories, ranging from Greek mythology and the Bible to *Faust, Wuthering Heights, Pilgrim's Progress,* and Virginia Woolf's comic novel, *Orlando.* Like Orlando, the hero of Carter's novel is a modern-day Tiresias, a hero who becomes a heroine. Evelyn, a young fair-haired Englishman, comes to the United States and follows the labyrinthine path of his destiny, which leads him to a violent birth: Evelyn becomes Eve. This is no mere story of a sex-change, however—no transsexual fantasy where everything remains the same and the signs are simply inverted (Gore Vidal's *Myra Breckenridge* is a good example of that genre). Evelyn's story—which, unlike Orlando's, is narrated retrospectively in the first person, adding a new sexual twist to the quintessentially modern question: who speaks?—is a heterogeneous combination of mythic realism, science fiction, and allegory, with elements of a *Bildungsroman,* a picaresque tale, a quest romance, and a Hollywood love story. It is also—and that is another reason I find it so interesting in the present context—a lyrical, quasi-hallucinatory exploration of some of the questions I have been raising, first and foremost the question of the female body, female selfhood, and the problematic relation between masculine and feminine.

Well, what is the story? It quite defies summary—that is one of its charms and one of the ways in which Carter succeeds in producing a new kind of writing even while apparently remaining within the bounds of a certain "traditional" narrative logic. Whereas Cixous and Wittig innovate by refusing linear narrative, preferring the serialization of lyrical and descriptive fragments to continuous storytelling, Carter *multiplies* the possibilities of linear narrative and of "story," producing a dizzying accumulation that undermines the narrative logic by its very excessiveness.

"The last night I spent in London, I took some girl to the movies and, through her mediation, I paid you a little tribute of spermatozoa, Tristessa" (p. 5). So the narrative begins. Tristessa, we find out, is an aging Hollywood screen idol, now in seclusion in Southern California but at one time the very embodiment of melancholy femininity and the focus of Evelyn's adolescent fantasies. (The cultural referent for Tristessa is obviously Greta Garbo.)

The day after this renewed—and, it will turn out, prophetic—encounter with the woman of his dreams, Evelyn flies to New York: a mythical New York where packs of rats roam the streets and civil war is about to break out between blacks and whites. Here he meets a young black prostitute, Leilah, "the night's gift," whom he follows "deep into the geometric labyrinth of the heart of the city" (p. 21), in an erotic chase that Carter lifted brazenly from one of her male Surrealist predecessors, Robert Desnos.[37] Leilah, as seen by Evelyn, is all flesh and all woman, at once infinitely seductive and infinitely repugnant: "She seemed to be a born victim" (p. 28). She becomes pregnant, gets an illegal abortion, which almost kills her, and winds up in the hospital, sterilized.[38] Evelyn then leaves New York and heads West for the desert, where, "among the bleached rocks and untenanted part of the world, I thought I might find that most elusive of all chimeras, myself" (p. 38).

That is indeed what he finds, although not quite as he expected. In the California desert he is captured by an underground community of women, whose emblem, which they wear imprinted on their T-shirts, is a broken phallus. This is a scientific-military society of Amazons (with some intertextual echoes of *Les Guérillères,* which Carter may or may not have intended), led by a black female doctor they call Mother. She is an excessive, "self-created" symbol of maternity, with four breasts (the other women, by contrast, have only one breast) and a gigantic belly. But she is also a highly skilled plastic surgeon, who proceeds to perform the operation that converts Evelyn into Eve—not before mating with him, however, in a union for which the text evokes, among other antecedents, Oedipus's encounter with his mother and Faust's encounter with the Mothers.

Textually, as well as in terms of its narrative content, this episode is fascinating, with its combination of lyricism, grotesque comedy, and a kind of epic grandeur. When Mother tells Evelyn, shortly before his operation, "Embrace your fate, like Oedipus—but more brave than he! . . . I am the Great Parricide, I am the Castratrix of the Phallocentric Universe, I am Mama, Mama, Mama!" (p. 67), one does not know whether to guffaw or to shrink in awe. The particular flavor of this text owes much to its tonal heterogeneity, which is unfortunately difficult to convey without extensive quotations.

Evelyn, then, is castrated to resounding Hosannah's piped into the operating room. And not only castrated but turned into a biological female, with all the necessary organs including a uterus. Mother's idea is to produce her own version of the Virgin birth by impregnating the "new Eve" with Evelyn's sperm, which was collected after his mating with Mother herself. This plan is prevented from being carried to completion by Eve's escape from Beulah—for that, ironically, is the name of this underground Amazonia (Beulah is the name given to Israel in the book of Isaiah and also appears in *Pilgrim's Progress* as the land of peace).

No sooner does Eve escape from Mother, however, than she falls into the clutches of a demonic Father. The Southern California desert is a place of symmetries, for only a few miles away from Mother and her army of virgins lives Zero the poet, with his harem of slavishly devoted wives. Just as Mother is at once a mythical and monstrous version of the feminine, Zero is a mythical and monstrous version of manhood. He worships his own phallus and demands its worship by his wives. His only way of relating to women—who he believes are "fashioned of a different soul substance from men, a more primitive, animal stuff" (p. 87)—is by rape. Like Mother, Zero dreams of instituting a totalitarian rule by reproducing his own kind. Corresponding to her dream of re-making the world by producing a child who would be born of a single being is his dream of "printing out new Zeros" and repopulating the continent with his own offspring.

But alas, he is sterile, and he is convinced that the fault for this lies— here the plot thickens and becomes circular—with Tristessa. Zero believes that she is a "dyke" and has cast a spell over him. Or as he puts it: "She's magicked the genius out of my jissom, that evil bitch! And it won't come back until I stick my merciless finger into this ultimate dyke, like the little Dutch boy" (p. 91).

So Zero spends his time flying over the desert in his helicopter, hunting for Tristessa's hideaway. And one day he finds it. Here begins the most extraordinary of Eve's adventures, the one prepared from the very beginning of the novel and now encountered in its circular movement. For what Zero and his harem discover, when they invade Tristessa's crystal palace and find her, still beautiful beneath her white hair, lying on top of a glass coffin—what they discover, when they strip her naked, is that Tristessa is a man. Or rather, he has the physical appendages of maleness even while continuing to manifest the famous signs, and beauty, of her quintessential femininity.

What follows is a mock wedding, where two people are married but both are the bride and both the groom. Eve is dressed as the groom in this ceremony, while Tristessa is outfitted with the wedding gown he/ she wore in *Wuthering Heights*. All of this is grotesque, but also eerily beautiful. The same can be said of the fact that Eve has fallen in love with Tristessa, as a woman loves a man, as a woman loves another woman, as a man loves a woman, and (although this possibility is not exploited by the text) as a man loves a man. Their union in the desert, after they escape from the crystal palace, leaving Zero and his wives to die a fantastic death, is, if not the enactment of an incalculable choreography, certainly that of a dizzying dance in which it is impossible to say who is woman and who is man, where one sex or one self begins and the other ends. I find this one of the most extraordinarily sensual and bewildering love scenes in recent literature, despite its obvious elements of parody and comic exaggeration.[39]

I shall not continue telling the story—in any case, it becomes increasingly difficult to summarize, and increasingly fantastical. I have offered this partial reading not because I think that Carter's novel provides an "answer" to the riddle of sexuality, whether male or female.[40] Or that it provides a model for a kind of eroticism—or even a kind of writing— that one ought to imitate. It does accomplish, and I think superbly, two other things: it suggests a direction for postmodern feminist fiction, based on parody and the multiplication of narrative possibilities rather than on their outright refusal (I shall develop this idea in the next chapter); and it expands our notions of what it is possible to dream in the domain of sexuality, criticizing all dreams that are too narrow. Mother, who seeks to break all phallic towers, and Zero, who seeks only to erect them, are both caricatures, living by outmoded symbols. It is to the desire, or dream, of going beyond the old dichotomies, of imagining "unguessable modes of humanity" (p. 77), that *The Passion of New Eve* succeeds in giving textual embodiment.

Feminist Intertexuality and the Laugh of the Mother

To write, of course, is to rewrite.

—CHANTAL CHAWAF

Nothing sacred.

—ANGELA CARTER

Parody and Politics

How is this for a putdown? "Women's share in poetry is a tremendous share of parody, in the most serious and formal sense of the word. *Feminine poetry is an unconscious parody of both poetic inventions and remembrances.*"[1] Osip Mandelstam, the great Russian poet, made these remarks in 1922. As Svetlana Boym aptly notes, the crucial word here is "unconscious": "the poetess lacks precisely that authentic artistic subjectivity that would enable her to turn upon the poetic tradition and critically comment on it."[2]

To a reader in 1988, Mandelstam's bon mot may call to mind the witticism of another great modernist, Jacques Lacan; seeking one day to formulate the difference between himself and the objects of his discourse, women, Lacan famously stated: "they don't know what they are saying, which is all the difference between them and me."[3] In both cases, what is humorously denied to women is self-consciousness and agency in the symbolic field, specifically in language. If we recall that Lacan's remark occurred during a session of his seminar on female sexuality, and further recall how deeply Western notions of self-consciousness and agency—in other words, subjectivity—are implicated with thinking about the body as locus and symbol of sexual difference, then the sentences following the above remarks in Mandelstam's essay take on a particularly suggestive resonance: "The majority of Moscow poetesses have been struck by metaphor. These poor Isises are doomed to an eternal search for a forever-lost second part of the comparison, which would return to the poetic image-Osiris its primordial unity."

There is hardly a need to name, for a post-Lacanian reader, the missing part that Mandelstam's "poor Isises" are forever deprived of. It is worth pointing out, however, that in his evocation of the Egyptian myth, Mandelstam manages to transfer, by means of his own double metaphor, the marker of lack from the castrated god, Osiris, to his sister-wife and to her metaphoric substitutes, the Moscow poetesses; he then transfers the marker back again (*metaphorein:* to carry across, transfer), not to the god but to *his* metaphoric substitute: the incomplete poetic image produced by women poets.

Which goes to show that there is nothing like a myth to make a point: by appropriating the old story for his own purposes, the poet proves both his argument and his mastery as an innovator in language.

Poetesses too have learned this lesson, especially of late. "Some of the best-known recent poetry by women," wrote Sandra Gilbert and Susan Gubar in 1979, "openly uses . . . parody in the cause of feminism: traditional figures of patriarchal mythology like Circe, Leda, Cassandra, Medusa, Helen, and Persephone have all lately been reinvented in the images of their female creators, and each poem devoted to one of these figures is a reading that reinvents her original story."[4] Alicia Ostriker, in a more recent study, sees such parodic appropriations or revisionist mythmaking as part of "the extraordinary tide of poetry by American women in our time," whose effect is not only to challenge and transform the history of poetry, but to "change the way we think and feel forever."[5] In a more explicitly theoretical mode, Patricia Yaeger and Mary Russo have sought to demonstrate both the political force and the poetic power of parody and of other playful uses of tradition by feminist writers and critics. "As women play with old texts," writes Yaeger in a pithy sentence, "the burden of the tradition is lightened and shifted; it has the potential for being remade."[6]

Obviously, neither the theory nor the practice of parody as a form of critical rereading (and rewriting) of traditional texts and mythologies originated with contemporary feminism. The contemporary feminist critical emphasis on "writing as re-vision" (Adrienne Rich's famous phrase) can itself be seen as an appropriation of earlier theoretical and historical work by male, nonfeminist (sometimes even misogynist) critics—most notably of Mikhail Bakhtin's writings on carnival and on the "carnivalesque": the heterogeneous, multivoiced, multilingual (Bakhtin's terms are "heteroglossic" and "polyglossic") discourses of medieval and Renaissance popular culture, and their gradual integration into the high-cultural genre of the novel.[7] It was Bakhtin's work that chiefly inspired Julia Kristeva's theory of intertextuality, which subsumes parody as one of its forms.[8] And it was Bakhtin who formulated, in one of his wide-ranging historical discussions of parody, the politically as well as aesthetically suggestive notion that "parodic-travestying forms . . . destroyed the power of myth over language; they freed consciousness from the power of the direct word, destroyed the thick walls that had imprisoned consciousness within its own discourse."[9]

Parody, according to Bakhtin, had from its very inception in Greek theater and performance the salutary effect of establishing a distance between language and reality: "Language is transformed from the absolute dogma it had been within the narrow framework of a sealed-off and impermeable monoglossia into a working hypothesis for comprehending and expressing reality" (p. 61). Extrapolating a bit, we arrive at the contemporary—and contemporary feminist—insight that the stories we tell about reality *construe* the real, rather than merely reflect it. Whence the possibility, or the hope, that through the rewriting of old stories and the invention of new forms of language for doing so, it is the world as well as words that will be transformed.[10]

Bakhtin himself had an optimistic view of the emancipatory potential of carnival and carnivalized discourse. This may explain why his model of carnival has been adopted by so many contemporary theorists interested in the adversary possibilities of literature and other artistic practices in relation to dominant culture. Peter Stallybrass and Allon White have noted that "everywhere in literary and cultural studies today, we see carnival emerging as a model, as an ideal and as an analytic category."[11] They also note, however, that Bakhtin's theory of carnival lends itself to a more conservative interpretation and has been criticized as such, by historians and anthropologists as well as by literary theorists. Stallybrass and White quote Terry Eagleton, for example: "Carnival, after all, is a *licensed* affair in every sense, a permissible rupture of hegemony, a contained popular blow-off as disturbing and relatively ineffectual as a revolutionary work of art."[12] If the transgressions of carnival are licensed and "contained" by the dominant culture, then such transgressions are no more than a particularly clever ruse of the Law.

So runs what might be called the "realist" or "hard-headedly political" critique of Bakhtin's theory. While this critique is no doubt a salutary corrective to overly idealized views of carnival as an emancipatory strategy (to use Patricia Yaeger's phrase), it is itself too simplistic in its assumption that symbolic modes like carnival—or like "revolutionary works of art"—have no actual, political effects. Personally, I am more persuaded by Stallybrass and White's argument that "the politics of carnival cannot be resolved outside of a close historical examination of particular conjunctures: there is no a priori revolutionary vector to carnival and transgression" (p. 16). Neither, I would add, is there an a priori conservative vector. Everything depends on the context; and only a fine-grained analysis of the relations beween context and individual event (which is what I take Stallybrass and White to mean by the "historical examination of particular conjunctures") will reveal the meanings and effects, including the political effects, of (a) carnival—or of a "revolutionary work of art."[13]

It is a fine-grained analysis that I would like to undertake for Leonora Carrington's comic novel, *The Hearing Trumpet,* in the double context of Surrealist experimentation and contemporary feminist experimentation with parodic rewriting. One of the most interesting aspects of Carrington's novel—a feminist parodic rewriting of, among other old stories, the quest of the Holy Grail—is that it must be situated historically, as well as formally and ideologically, in this double context. My contextual reading aims to accomplish at least two things: first, to explore the possible alliances as well as the irreducible differences between the work of male avant-garde artists (in this instance, Surrealists) and the "similar but different" work of women; second, to explore the differences that may exist between and among contemporary women avant-garde writers, especially as concerns the broader cultural and political implications of their works.

Carrington, an English painter and writer who has spent most of her life outside England, was closely associated with the Surrealist movement during the late 1930s and early 1940s and has continued to produce an impressive body of work since then. She is one of the very few women artists who started out in the relatively heroic period of Surrealism before the war and are still working today. (The only others who come to mind are Leonor Fini, Gisèle Prassinos, and Dorothea Tanning; but Tanning became associated with Surrealism only in the 1940s.) And she is the only one of those, to my knowledge, who has identified herself in recent years as a feminist.[14] She wrote *The Hearing Trumpet* in Mexico City, where she had been living for several years, in the early 1950s; at that time she was still in close touch with a number of Surrealist artists and poets, including Benjamin Péret and his wife, the painter Remedios Varo, who were also living in Mexico.[15]

By the time the novel was published—first in a French translation, in 1974—Surrealism and its principal protagonists were dead. The French feminist movement, however, was flourishing and producing some of its most interesting experiments in rewriting traditional mythologies. Monique Wittig's *Les Guérillères,* whose intertextual strategies I discussed in Chapter 6, had appeared in 1969, soon to be followed by other works in the same vein (*Le Corps lesbien,* 1973; *Brouillon pour un dictionnaire des amantes,* 1976). Hélène Cixous's "The Laugh of the Medusa," perhaps the single best known feminist revision of a classical myth and of its orthodox psychoanalytic interpretation, appeared in 1975. Although Carrington's novel (in French, *Le Cornet acoustique*) was quite at home in this context, it received almost no attention in Paris.

The Hearing Trumpet first appeared in English in 1976 and was duly if somewhat perfunctorily reviewed in the *Times Literary Supplement* and a few other journals.[16] Here again, the context was right, or almost (several English and American women writers whom we now associate with postmodern feminist revision were just becoming known or were about to start publishing),[17] but Carrington's place in it went unnoticed. She seemed to be caught between nationalities, between languages, between generations.

The renewal of interest in Surrealism, particularly in the work of women Surrealists, which gathered momentum in the mid-1980s, has finally brought Carrington's work some of the attention it deserves. The recent publication, in English, of two volumes of her stories, originally written in French, English, or Spanish over a period of more than thirty years, should introduce her to a whole new generation of readers.[18]

Among Carrington's works I single out *The Hearing Trumpet* not only because it is brilliant, outrageously inventive, and comically "carnivalesque," occupying a significant place between Surrealism and (feminist) postmodernism; but also because, quite uniquely, Carrington's novel associates the subversive laughter of carnival with the figure—and even more important, with the voice—of the mother. This is certainly not the case in Surrealism or in any of the other male avant-garde movements of this century, nor would we expect it to be. The emblematic subject of male avant-garde practice is, I have suggested, a transgressive son who may, in Roland Barthes's words, "play with the body of his mother" but who never imagines (let alone gives voice to) his mother playing. More surprisingly, however, one almost never finds the figure or the voice of the playful (laughing) mother in contemporary feminist experimental writing either—this despite the well-known revalorization of the mother and of the "maternal metaphor" in some of that writing.

What is at stake, aesthetically and politically, in the figure of the playful mother is the driving question behind this essay. In order to understand the full import of the question, as well as why I find Carrington's novel so pertinent to it, we will need to take a few detours and keep some further questions in mind. Why, and how, have the repudiation of the mother or the unwillingness to imagine her playing been so prevalent in our culture? Why have they been so prevalent even in the work of writers and artists who greatly value and promote the ideas of play, innovation, and radical antipatriarchal politics? And what consequences, in writing and in life, might result from a change in this?

As a first step, let us venture into the wide-open territory of Surrealist parody.

Parody, Perversion, Collage: Surrealists at Play

> True playing always involves an element of perversion.
>
> —GÉRARD GENETTE

> Perversion is dedicated to the father. But without knowing it.
>
> —PHILIPPE SOLLERS

The Surrealists' predilection for punning and other verbal games, as well as for the humorous, often scatological or otherwise "scandalous" rewriting of traditional texts or images, is well known; so is their predilection for collage and collage-like techniques of juxtaposing heterogeneous elements, which Peter Bürger considers the hallmark of "the avant-gardiste work."[19]

We find all of the above in one of Louis Aragon's earliest works, *Les Aventures de Télémaque* (*The Adventures of Telemachus,* 1920), which rewrites—and appropriates the title of—a French classic that was already a rewriting of Homer, the Abbé Fénelon's didactic novel-cum-treatise on government (1695).[20] Like one of the Surrealists' heroes, Lautréamont, who wrote "corrections" of French classics in his *Poésies* (the work on which Kristeva based her original discussion of her newly coined term, "intertextuality"), Aragon "corrected" the seventeenth-century cleric's work by changing both the story and its moral: his Telemachus, instead of learning from his travels the art of living and of kingship, dies an absurdly farcical death to prove a philosophical point; he is not chaste, not moderate in love or anything else, and never does go home.

In addition to this perversion of the meaning of a classic (perversion in its etymological sense: *per* + *vertere,* "turning around"), Aragon incorporated into his *Télémaque* a whole series of unidentified quotations from Fénelon and other authors, as well as a number of previously published (and some unpublished) Dada poems and manifestoes written by himself. His book thus functions as a stylistic and textual collage spanning several centuries—an extreme form of Bakhtin's "carnivalized discourse"—and as a parody of a specific anterior text. Not surprisingly, it also includes some characteristic Dada wordplay, such as a poem consisting of a single name repeated in regular lines (save for two brief interruptions to break up the regularity) for three pages.[21]

One could cite many other examples of early Surrealist work in the same vein: irreverent, bookish, raunchy, self-celebratory, and outrageously playful. One of my own favorites is Robert Desnos's *La Liberté ou l'amour!* (published in 1927, written in 1925), a fragmented prose narrative that includes, among other scandalous tidbits, a rewriting of Christ's imprisonment and crucifixion as a battle between two advertising emblems: the smiling "Bébé Cadum" of billboards for Cadum soap playing Christ, and the Michelin tire man in the role of adversary. This chapter of the book was considered sufficiently blasphemous to be cut from the original edition by the censor—the offending pages appeared as blanks.[22]

A somewhat more minor effort, but no less interesting in its perversion of traditional wisdom, is the collaborative work between Benjamin Péret and Paul Eluard, *152 Proverbes mis au goût du jour* (1925), consisting of French proverbs "updated" by the two Surrealist poets. Example: "Il faut battre le fer pendant qu'il est chaud" ("One must strike the iron while it's hot") becomes, by the simple substitution of two words and their corresponding articles and pronouns, "Il faut battre sa mère pendant qu'elle est jeune" ("One must beat one's mother while she's young").[23] The offense to propriety and good taste was altogether intended.

Was all this just child's play, the nose-thumbing antics of young boys drawing mustaches on the Mona Lisa? For the Surrealists of the 1920s, graffiti and defacement were more than "just play"—they were a veritable program for liberation. Aragon, prefacing his 1919 collection of poems and prose texts, *Le Libertinage,* in 1924, the year of the first Surrealist Manifesto and of the official founding of the Surrealist movement, could combine a truculent celebration of scandal for scandal's sake ("Je n'ai jamais cherché autre chose que le scandale et je l'ai cherché pour lui-même"—"I have never sought anything but scandal, and have sought it for its own sake") with an impassioned defense of the "spirit of the French Revolution": "I am irreducibly a man of the left, and if that expression makes you laugh, you're nothing but a clown" ("je suis irréductiblement un homme de gauche, et si cette expression vous prête à rire, vous n'êtes qu'un pître").[24] Then, to make clear just how high the stakes were in his and his friends' libertarian politics, Aragon added:

> So we are defending the cause of the devil. Paul Eluard said to me one day that it's God's fault if there is a devil: and that there never would have been devil's advocates, if there hadn't been the stupid advocates of God. Let's accept once for all the epithet "messianic." It's silly, it's empty: we didn't choose it. But finally that's what's held against us, we are messianics. Fine. To the traditional idea of beauty and the good, we will oppose our own, however infernal it may appear. Messianics and revolutionaries, I

agree. And you, you are traditionalists and christians, for example.   (pp. 271–272)

By claiming for Surrealism not only the place of a Robespierre but also that of Lucifer, Aragon staked out for the young movement a position it would long consider its own: one of absolute revolt, opposed to every form of authority; and by accepting the label "messianic," he suggested Surrealism's commitment to the future. Here too, of course, he was perverting the religious meaning of the word. But that may simply underline the fact that the parodic perversions of Surrealism were meant to be understood as (among other things) a strategy for radical political and cultural change.

So far, I have used the word "perversion" only in its etymological sense, without considering its psychosexual connotations. If I am right, however, in claiming that Surrealist play was essentially that of a transgressive son, then the psychoanalytic meaning of the word must be given its due. And it has been, by some critics. Rosalind Krauss, for example, has argued that Surrealist photography "fetishizes reality" by doing away with the "naturalness" of the photographic object (fetishism, she reminds us, is that perversion which substitutes a fabicated object for a natural one perceived to be missing), and that it is precisely this fetishization which constitutes Surrealist photography's difference from—and its scandalous challenge to—"straight" photography.[25] By her superimposition of psychoanalytic and aesthetic categories, Krauss suggests—as Julia Kristeva had done in *La Révolution du langage poétique*—a more than coincidental link between the psychosexual dynamics of perversion and radical artistic innovation.

The psychoanalyst Janine Chasseguet-Smirgel has made an even more explicit case for translating the analytic concept of perversion into general aesthetic and philosophical terms. On the one hand, she states categorically: "The pervert is trying to free himself from the paternal universe and the law." On the other hand, "perversion is one of the essential ways and means [man] applies in order to push forward the frontiers of what is possible and to unsettle reality"[26]—which is a pretty good definition of Surrealist aesthetics (indeed, of the aesthetics of early twentieth-century European avant-gardes in general) as well as of Surrealist philosophy and cultural politics.

According to Chasseguet-Smirgel, the interest of the law has always been to maintain separations and distinctions—witness the many biblical injunctions against mixing heterogeneous kinds, or the meaning of the Greek word for law, *nomos:* "divided into parts." Basing her analysis not on Surrealism but on the works of Sade, Chasseguet-Smirgel argues that perversion, in contrast to the law, espouses mixture and the hybrid;

it aims for the erosion or "homogenization" of differences: "The man who does not respect the law of differentiation challenges God. He creates new combinations of new shapes and new kinds . . . Notice that the word *hybrid* comes from *hybris,* which means violence, excess, extremeness, outrageousness" (p. 298).

Although one might want to question Chasseguet-Smirgel's equating of all perversion with sadism ("perversion is inevitably sadistic"—p. 296), and question as well her notion of "homogenization" (does the erosion of differences, or their recombination into "new kinds," necessarily imply the uniformity of homogenization?), I find her argument extremely suggestive because it allows for a discussion of perversion as a *figure,* or as an aesthetic choice, rather than as a clinical disorder. We might see such a figure at work, for example, in the poetics of Surrealist collage and Surrealist metaphor, both of which emphasize "new combinations of new shapes and new kinds." Lautréamont's famous dictum about the encounter of a sewing machine and an umbrella on an operating table, so often cited as a model in Surrealist discussions of metaphor and collage, is a case in point.

Another is the Surrealist exploration of hybrids (recall Chasseguet-Smirgel's gloss on the word, and her example of the hybrid as a "perverse" erosion of differences), both in formal and representational terms. Formally, a work like Breton's *Nadja* is a hybrid, combining fiction, autobiography, case history, photographic essay, and literary manifesto. Collage, especially Surrealist collage, is by definition a hybrid form, combining heterogeneous verbal, visual, and tactile elements. The collage novels of Max Ernst, perhaps the greatest and most consistent Surrealist practitioner of collage as an art form, "hybridized" popular Victorian illustrations and Surrealist dream images by selectively superimposing the latter on the former, and superimposed as well the possibilities of verbal and visual narrative. In addition, Ernst thematized the hybrid by his hallucinatory inventions of animal-and-human, animate-and-inanimate creatures: bird-headed and lion-headed men, women with bats' wings sprouting from their shoulders, men with the heads of Easter Island monoliths.[27]

Finally, the Surrealists' preference for the fragment and their avoidance of continuous forms, whether as teleological narrative or as integrated image, could also be transposed into the vocabulary of perversion. For according to Freud, the law of the father and of adult sexuality—the law from which, Chasseguet-Smirgel argues, the pervert is trying to free himself—requires not only the recognition of (sexual) difference but also the integration of the fragmented "component instincts" of infantile sexuality "under the primacy of a single erotogenic zone" and their teleological directedness toward a single sexual aim:

"the union of the genitals in the act known as copulation." In adult (genital) sexuality, "the pursuit of pleasure comes under the sway of the reproductive function."[28]

Could we see, in the Surrealists' refusal of integration and hierarchy, and in their pursuit of heterogeneity in all its various forms—from parody to punning to collage—an analogue of the pervert's refusal of "normal' adult sexuality?

Why not?

In that case, the choice of perversion would turn out to be the quintessentially transgressive, antipatriarchal act, in aesthetics as in socio-psychosexual politics; and the "revolutionary and messianic" politics of early Surrealism would indeed be all of a piece with its parodic perversions, in sexuality as in art. This is the conclusion that Krauss's analysis of Surrealist photography hints at. It is also the idea that grounds the celebrations, by the avant-garde of the 1960s and 1970s, of the perverse fictions of Bataille. But if I was right in suggesting, in my discussion of *Histoire de l'oeil*, that the founding scenario of Bataille's work is Oedipal, what does that do to the notion of perversion as quintessentially antipatriarchal? Is perversion a way out of the classic Oedipal scenario—which always involves, in the end, an alliance of the son with the father and the elision and repudiation of the mother—or is it merely a more roundabout way into it?

One thing Krauss does not mention, in her celebration of the scandalous potential of fetishism, is that fetishism, as Freud (to whom she refers) analyzes it, is not only the substitution of the fabricated for the natural, nor only an imaginative defense against the fear of castration, nor only a brilliant "blurring" of sexual difference; it is also, as Freud explicitly puts it, a choice that "saves the fetishist from being a homosexual by endowing women with the attribute which makes them acceptable as sexual objects." The fetishist is not a lover of women: "Aversion from the real female genitals . . . is never lacking in any fetishist."[29]

If fetishism is a perversion that reaffirms the primacy—indeed, the unique predominance—of the phallus, how far can it go as an escape from the law of the father, which is founded on that very same predominance?

This question, perhaps surprisingly, leads us back to Mona Lisa's mustache. More exactly, it leads us to 1919 and Marcel Duchamp's ultra-famous "assisted readymade"—the Mona Lisa with a mustache and beard (fig. 5). A slightly different version of this picture—showing the Mona Lisa with a mustache but minus the beard—became part of a Dada Manifesto signed by Duchamp and Francis Picabia in 1920, thus underlining the programmatic value of Duchamp's work.[30] Al-

5. Marcel Duchamp, *L.H.O.O.Q.*, 1919

though strictly speaking this picture belongs to "late Dada" rather than to Surrealism, that distinction is not relevant to our present concerns.

Now part of a private art collection in New York City, the 1919 work consists of a mass-produced color reproduction of the Leonardo painting, to which Duchamp added, in pencil, a Dali-like mustache (an inverted *V* with curlicues at both ends) and a small goatee (another *V*) from whose point there hangs something resembling a short black tail. The bottom left and right corners bear the inscriptions "Paris" and "Marcel Duchamp," respectively. Beneath the reproduction, on a strip of white paper that acts as a partial frame, a hand-lettered inscription in capital letters reads: L.H.O.O.Q.

Since this work has been much commented on, and appears in all the standard histories of Dada/Surrealism and of modern art, I won't belabor the obvious: the playful, pointedly "childish" and at the same time crudely aggressive defacement of the most famous painting in Western art; the scurrilous but explosively funny punning of the title (when pronounced aloud, LHOOQ yields "Elle a chaud au cul," "She's got hot pants"); and the sly playing around with sexual identities, evocative both of Leonardo's homosexuality and Duchamp's own feminine alter ego, Rrose Sélavy.[31] What is worth emphasizing, for it is not usually mentioned by commentators, is the self-conscious (perhaps even parodic) Oedipal drama being played out in this bit of "impish cultural irreverence."[32]

A first reading of the drama will focus on the signature: Marcel Duchamp, the irreverent modern son living in the capital of modern art, has displaced the dead but burdensome Father of tradition—he has erased the Father's name—and appropriated both the painting and the lady represented in the painting for himself. The graffiti-mustache and beard and the scurrilous pun all point to an infantile persona for the signatory to this work—as does the bilingual pun on "LOOK," which suggests the antics of a little boy wanting to be seen performing by (usually) his mother.[33] Here is a case, then, of a classic Oedipal scenario in its "ascendant" phase: the son, counting on the complicity of his mother, declares his rebellion against the name—and the law—of the father.

The straight reading of the scenario is soon complicated, however, by the intervention of a more perverse scenario and *its* reading: for if we focus not on the signature but on the mustache and beard, it becomes obvious that the two *V*'s, minus their appendages, are mirror images of each other—and are also fairly standard iconographic representations of a woman's pubic hair. It would appear that by a humorous "displacement upward," Duchamp has produced not, or not only, the Mona Lisa as a sexpot ("elle a chaud au cul"), nor the Mona Lisa as a young man,

but the Mona Lisa as a phallic mother (pubis plus "appendages")—
indeed, a phallic mother doubly marked, redundantly phallic. We are
no longer in Oedipus but in its fetishistic perversion: sexual difference
no sooner recognized than denied.

One could argue, following Krauss's lead, that Duchamp's comic *mise-
en-scène* of fetishism is precisely what makes this picture scandalous.
The "normal" Oedipal scenario, after all, would end in the son's recognition of castration and his submission to the father's law; by perverting
the scenario in the direction of fetishism, Duchamp maintains its transgressive, antitraditional, and antipatriarchal force.

The interpretation is seductive, but it is not the only one possible.
Given our cultural knowledge of Leonardo's homosexuality and Duchamp's feminine alter ego, so often mentioned by commentators, we
may ask: If the Father who is being assaulted/displaced desires not
women but men, what does that do to the son's desire—especially to
the desire of a son who, cross-dressed, becomes a "woman with a phallus"? Should we perhaps take literally the "cul" (ass) of the scurrilous
pun ("she is hot in the ass") and read the "she" as referring not to the
Mona Lisa of Leonardo's painting but to the Mona Lisa here represented, the Mona Lisa with a phallus? Or perhaps to the other "woman
with a phallus," Rrose Sélavy? Could one of the underlying fantasies
fueling this programmatic avant-garde picture be not the "straight"
Oedipal fantasy of displacing the father and sexually possessing the
mother, but its homosexual variant: the fantasy of being sexually possessed by the father? That fantasy is perverse, to be sure. But is it a
sign of rebellion against the father?

Leaving that question in suspense for now, let us look at a properly
Surrealist "picture-manifesto" (so labeled by the artist), Max Ernst's
1926 painting, *The Blessed Virgin Chastising the Infant Jesus before
Three Witnesses* (fig. 6).[34] This work too has been much commented on.
Like Duchamp's *L.H.O.O.Q.*, it is humorous and iconoclastic, parodying
a masterpiece of Italian painting: Parmigianino's *Madonna of the Long
Neck* (dated 1540; fig. 7). Unlike the Duchamp work, it is blatantly
blasphemous (it was publicly denounced by the archbishop of Cologne
in 1926); and it is a much more elaborate painterly effort, signaling in
style as well as in content the displacement of the old by the new, the
traditional father by the modernist son.

Ernst has replaced the Italian master's muted colors, soft draperies,
fluid forms, and classical allusions (the columns in the background, the
amphora in the left foreground) by starkly drawn primary colors on the
Virgin and child (whose yellow hair is echoed by the triangle of yellow
wall in the background) and by flat, geometric shapes in tones of ochre,
reminiscent of de Chirico's metaphysical landscapes, in the background.

6. Max Ernst, *The Blessed Virgin Chastising the Infant Jesus before Three Witnesses*, 1926

7. Parmigianino, *Madonna with the Long Neck*, sixteenth century

The soft, tasseled pillows beneath the Virgin's foot in Parmigianino's painting have been replaced by two angular boxes, on one of which the Virgin is uncomfortably sitting—it is too small for her huge pelvis, and protrudes beneath her tightly stretched skirt. By a formal and thematic reversal that functions as one kind of signature (the actual signature is in the right foreground, in the circle of the child's fallen halo), Ernst has replaced Parmigianino's ephebic angel witnesses by the heads of three Surrealist voyeurs: Paul Eluard, André Breton, and himself. It is worth noting that of the three only Ernst is looking directly at the scene, and by extension at the viewer of the painting.

Finally, of course, there is the icon of Mother and Child. Parmigianino's Madonna—who was considered somewhat scandalous in the painter's own time because she is so obviously sexual, naked beneath her gauzy dress—gazes with a tender smile at her sleeping son; and his infant Jesus, although Manneristically elongated, is clearly a baby. Ernst's Madonna, although sexually female, her breasts and belly bulging beneath her tight, lowcut dress, is anything but "feminine": taut, muscular, eyes hypnotically staring at her son's buttocks, she is a hulking figure totally engrossed in her punitive task. As for the infant Jesus, although we cannot see his face, he is clearly not a baby: he has the muscular body and legs, and the full head of hair of a four- or five-year old child. This fact is, to be sure, not the first thing we notice about him. The first thing we notice, like a slap in the face, is the physical inversion of the child's body and of the child's relation to the mother, and the inversion/perversion of meaning that results from it: by a simple flip-flop, Ernst has transformed centuries of pious veneration into an explosive moment of sacrilegious laughter.

But not only laughter: the sight of a child being beaten evokes other feelings as well. Margot Norris, in her very interesting recent discussion of this painting, writes: "The viewer is forced to abandon a virtuous posture and obliged to contend with an array of libidinal affects: outrage, secret pleasure and recognition, shame, and so forth."[35] In particular, she notes that the viewer is "embarrassed because Ernst, Breton, and Eluard function as witnesses not only of the scene, but also to our voyeurism in seeing the scene. We are seen seeing." In fact, it is only Ernst who "sees us seeing," for Breton's head is turned the other way and Eluard is in a three-quarter profile, his eyes lowered. But this would seem only to confirm Norris's remark that here, as in many of his other works, "Ernst teases, traps, discomfits, and shocks [his viewers] by outraging their expectations and ideals, confronting them with the limitations of their reason, and extorting from them libidinal responses by implicating them in *his* unholy fantasies" (p. 135, my emphasis).

According to Norris, Ernst's critique of the Christian myth (in addition to the Madonna and Child, Norris discerns in the painting allusions to the Nativity and the Crucifixion) "is both psychoanalytical and political, revealing the extent to which religious imagery and belief mask sadism and masochism and, by a similar fraudulent signification of suffering, justify political and social oppression in the name of discipline and self-sacrifice" (p. 151). Norris's reading thus emphasizes the subversive, emancipatory, antipatriarchal aspects of the work accomplished by this Surrealist parody. In terms of this reading, Ernst's perverse picture-manifesto (voyeurism is, in Freudian terms, a bona fide perversion) appears as a perfect example of what Stallybrass and White call transgression, and what the cultural anthropologist Barbara Babcock has called "symbolic inversion": "any act of expressive behaviour which inverts, contradicts, abrogates, or in some fashion presents an alternative to commonly held cultural codes, values and norms, be they linguistic, literary or artistic, religious, social and political."[36] Ernst's painting, as read by Norris, seems to invert not just some but all of the codes that Babcock mentions.

Is there another, more ambiguous, less "politically correct"—in short, more unexpectedly perverse—way to read this painting? One that would not necessarily contradict, but complicate, our understanding of it as an antipatriarchal statement? And that would also resonate with our reading of Duchamp's *L.H.O.O.Q.*?

It strikes me as curious that Norris, who obviously knows Freud and uses his vocabulary, should fail to mention the one Freudian text which Ernst's painting immediately evokes: the essay of 1919 entitled 'A Child Is Being Beaten': A Contribution to the Study of the Origin of Sexual Perversions." Freud begins this essay as follows: "It is surprising how frequently people who come to be analyzed for hysteria or an obsessional neurosis confess to having indulged in the phantasy: 'A child is being beaten.' Very probably it occurs even more often with other people who have not been obliged to come to this decision by manifest illness."[37] Freud suggests, in the last sentence, that one need not be clinically neurotic in order to have entertained this fantasy; the ordinary, garden variety neurotic or "pervert"—in other words, everybody—may have indulged in it too. I mention this because I want to ward off a misunderstanding: what is at stake for me in this analysis of Ernst's painting, as of Duchamp's *L.H.O.O.Q.,* is not a matter of individual biography, and even less a matter of individual sexuality. Max Ernst's and Marcel Duchamp's sexual habits and preferences, whether straight or perverse, are not the issue. The issue is how a certain *figure of perversion* functions in their work, and possibly in male Dada/Surrealist practices of collage and parodic intertextuality in general.

One interesting feature of Freud's essay is that, although he begins by saying he will restrict his remarks to the functioning of this fantasy (which displays "the essence of masochism") to women, Freud goes on to distinguish a specifically male version of the fantasy from the female version—only to conclude, in the end, that they have a single common character of a kind he did not expect: *"In both cases the beating-phantasy has its origin in an incestuous attachment to the father"* (p. 127, Freud's emphasis).

How does Freud arrive at this conclusion, and what does it have to do with a reading of Ernst's painting? I will not attempt to summarize Freud's unusually tortuous argument—suffice it to say that behind the conscious beating fantasy (which turns out not to be exactly the same in men and women), Freud reconstructs for both sexes a repressed childhood fantasy of being beaten by the father, which he interprets in the case of the boy to mean: *"I am loved by my father"* (p. 127, Freud's emphasis).[38] This unconscious fantasy is then transformed, he posits, into a conscious fantasy. The girl's version becomes that "a child is being beaten" by an authority figure—a replacement for the father—while she and other children look on. The boy's version becomes: *"I am being beaten by my mother"* (p. 127, Freud's emphasis). Freud concludes from this that "the boy evades his homosexuality by repressing and remodeling his unconscious fantasy [of being sexually loved by his father]; and the remarkable thing about his later conscious fantasy [of being beaten by his mother] is that it has for its content a feminine attitude without a homosexual object-choice" (pp. 127–128).

The male masochist, like the fetishist, invents a way to remain heterosexual despite his fundamental desire for the (father's) phallus.[39] And, also like the fetishist, although by a different means, he converts the woman into a simulacrum of a man: he "endows the women who are beating him with masculine attributes and characteristics" (p. 128).

In Ernst's painting a child is being beaten by someone who is clearly a woman, but with masculine attributes of size, muscularity, and authority, while Max Ernst looks on; the artist thus seems to be occupying the subject position in the female conscious fantasy as Freud describes it. This fact is interesting enough, in light of Freud's speculations about the "feminine attitude" sought by the male subject. The only trouble with it is that, according to Freud's analysis, the subject with the "feminine attitude" in the male fantasy is the child who is being beaten, not the witness. Is the child in Ernst's painting also a stand-in for the artist, then?

As it happens . . . Evan Maurer, in a recent essay devoted to a quite different topic, has demonstrated, almost in passing, that the figure of the blond, curly-haired Jesus in Ernst's painting is autobiographical, derived from a specific event in the artist's early childhood. Maurer quotes a few sentences from Ernst's autobiographical fragments of 1948, "Some Data on the Youth of M. E.," to back up his claim. But the only conclusion he draws from this evidence (which, in light of our present discussion, is an astonishing find) is disappointingly bland: "From the evidence of both text and painting we can see how the events of Ernst's life merged with his later artistic and philosophical concerns and were transformed into images which he endowed with a combination of mythic dignity and ironic humor."[40]

The anecdote in Ernst's autobiographical fragments from which Maurer draws this conclusion occurred in 1896, when the artist was five years old. It is short enough to be quoted almost in full:

> To scrutinize the mystery of the telegraphic wires (and also to flee from the father's tyranny) five-year-old Max escaped from his parents' house. Blue-eyed, blond-curly-haired, dressed in a red night shirt, carrying a whip in the left hand, he walked in the middle of a pilgrims' procession. Enchanted by this charming child and believing it was the vision of an angel or even the infant of the virgin, the pilgrims proclaimed "Look, little Jesus Christ." After a mile or so little Jesus Christ escaped from the procession, directed himself to the station and had a long and delightful trip beside the railroad and the telegraphic wires.
>
> To appease father's fury, when the next day a policeman brought him home, little Max proclaimed that he was sure he was little Jesus Christ. This candid remark inspired the father to make a portrait of his son as a little Jesus-child, blue-eyed, curly-haired, dressed in a red night shirt, blessing the world with the right hand and bearing the cross—instead of the whip—in his left.
>
> Little Max, slightly flattered by this image, had however some difficulty in throwing off the suspicion that daddy took secret pleasure in the idea of being God-the-Father, and that the hidden reason of this picture was a blasphemous pretension. Maybe Max Ernst's picture "Souvenir de Dieu" (1923) has a direct connection with the remembrance of this fact.[41]

Curiously (or perhaps, in light of Freud's essay, symptomatically), Ernst does not associate this childhood memory with his painting of the Virgin chastising her son. And yet, Maurer is surely right in claiming that the blond curly-haired child in the painting—whose body, we recall, is not that of an infant but of an older child—bears an unmistakable association to the five-year-old Little Max whose father painted him as a little Jesus. Philippe Ernst's *Portrait of His Son Max as the Christ Child* (fig. 8) is done in a sentimental "Italianate" style: the child stands in a niche, surrounded by a nimbus of light; he is wearing a tunic with draped folds; under his feet is a soft tasseled pillow (or is it a cloud?); from the upper corners, two heads of cherubs with wings look down as witnesses.[42]

8. Philippe Ernst, *Portrait of His Son Max as the Christ Child*, 1896

Its playfully ironic tone notwithstanding, Max Ernst's reminiscence emphasizes the Oedipal conflict that pitted the five-year-old Max against his father. The painting Ernst alludes to, *Souvenir de Dieu (Remembrance of God)*, is the portrait of a grotesque personage, apparently a hybrid of goat and man; we see the creature's face and hands, and huge gaping mouth—but the mouth, a circle bisected by a rod, also looks vaguely like an artist's palette.[43]

In light of Ernst's reminiscence, we could see in his *Blessed Virgin Chastising the Infant Jesus before Three Witnesses* (in which the child has exactly the same hairdo as Little Max in his father's portrait of him but is "turned around" and naked) not only a parody of Parmigianino's masterpiece, but also a parody of Philippe Ernst's awful little painting. And that would tally rather nicely with Norris's reading of the painting as subversive and antipatriarchal: the Oedipal dynamics of Ernst's multilayered parody would then appear to be all of a piece with his—and Surrealism's—revolutionary aesthetics and politics. (The idea for the painting, Ernst has told us, came from Breton.)[44] But what about Freud? If he is right that the male masochist fantasy of being beaten by the mother—a fantasy which we now recognize as stunningly staged in Max Ernst's painting—masks an earlier homosexual fantasy of being loved by the father, what does that do to our understanding of this picture-manifesto?

Could it be that the son's rebellion, whether "straight" or "perverse," and no matter how outrageously innovative on the level of artistic practice, is always, in the last analysis, phallocentric—and to that extent in alliance with the father and repudiating the mother?

What a lot of effort to arrive at this obvious conclusion.

On second thought, the conclusion may not be so obvious. Julia Kristeva has argued, apropos of Lautréamont, that the male avant-garde writer (in her model, the avant-garde writer is always male) uses his mother, and even appropriates her place, in his "battle against the Name-of-the-Father."[45] This appropriation (which may be called perverse) leads, Kristeva argues, to a revulsion from genitality and a putting into question of "family structures and the rules of filiation" (p. 471); but it does not imply that the son/subject gives up his "phallic position." In fact, sadism and aggression against the mother's body accompany the son's appropriation of it.

Kristeva concludes that the son's "implacable war against an absolutely present father," enacted in Lautréamont's *Chants de Maldoror*, signals a historical crisis of identity for the phallic subject (p. 472). Which may be another way of saying that the son's battle against the father is rendered ambiguous by their mutual fascination with the phallus.

We might see in Surrealism's antipatriarchal politics and aesthetics a symptom of the same historical crisis, and the same ambiguity. And we might conclude, as Gayatri Spivak does (in a different context) that contemporary *feminist* versions of antipatriarchal parody and rewriting have little to gain from being associated with the work of male predecessors; indeed, that the feminist works derive all of their power from "their *substantive* revision of, rather than their apparent *formal* allegiance to, the European avant-garde."[46]

As I think I have made clear throughout this book, I share Spivak's desire to emphasize the substantive (ideological and existential) differences between feminist avant-garde practice and the practice of male avant-garde artists who, for all their formal innovations, are still deeply implicated in patriarchy. However, I believe that two points need to be made: First, it is not the case that all feminist avant-garde practices are identical in their substantive implications. In some cases, there may be substantive agreement between some feminist writers and their male predecessors, and there may be substantive differences among feminists: attitudes toward the mother are one such case, as I shall show in a moment.

Second, the existence of substantive differences should not blind us to the potentially *positive* aspects of a "formal allegiance" between contemporary feminists and the European avant-garde. One may—one should—criticize or point up the ambiguities of male avant-garde sexual and cultural politics, and still recognize the energy, the inventiveness, the explosive humor and sheer proliferating brilliance of much male avant-garde "play." And one may delight in seeing similar energy, inventiveness, humor, and brilliance in the work of women.

Some of the best contemporary feminist writing—and parodic rewriting—has an obvious formal allegiance to earlier male avant-garde practice; and, as I have suggested, even the substantive differences between them are not monolithic. The antipatriarchal and antitraditional impetus of Dada/Surrealist parody, no matter how ambiguous on a "deep" psychological level, provides a positive substantive link, as well as a formal allegiance, to contemporary feminist work—and to feminist play with tradition. It in no way diminishes Angela Carter's achievement, for example, to suggest that she may have learned a few tricks from Robert Desnos.[47] Nor does it take away from her feminist/postmodernist credentials to point out that her motto, "nothing sacred" (the title of a collection of wide-ranging radical essays)[48] has something substantive in common with Aragon's "revolutionary and messianic" flippancy.

This double allegiance—on the one hand, to the formal experiments and some of the cultural aspirations of the historical male avant-gardes; on the other hand, to the feminist critique of dominant sexual ideologies, including those of the very same avant-gardes—can be found not only in Angela Carter's work, and before her in the work of women Surrealists like Leonora Carrington, but in that of other experimental women artists working today as well.[49] The "double-voicedness" of women's writing and the general doublings and redoublings in women's lives have often been noted by feminist critics. The double allegiance I am referring to here may be the most innovative as well as the most specifically "feminine" characteristic of contemporary experimental work by women artists.

Yes, we *are* moving closer to *The Hearing Trumpet*. One more detour, and we will be there.

Daughters Playing: Some Feminist Rewritings and the Mother

> She said stories helped you to understand the world.
>
> —JEANETTE WINTERSON

> Humor is not resigned; it is rebellious.
>
> —SIGMUND FREUD

A scene toward the beginning of Jeanette Winterson's first novel, *Oranges Are Not the Only Fruit* (1985), thematizes, in a wonderfully comic way, the antipatriarchal impetus of feminist parody.[50] Significantly, the scene occurs in a chapter entitled "Genesis" (all of the novel's chapters bear titles corresponding to books of the Old Testament) and involves a little girl's playing with a sacred text. The female first-person narrator recounts this incident, which occurred when she was seven years old. Brought up by her strictly Evangelical adoptive mother,[51] the little girl spends a lot of time in church. One day, a visiting pastor, eager to make a point about the ubiquity of evil, points to our innocent heroine and intones: "This little lily could herself be a house of demons." As it happens, the heroine will grow up to be a "house of demons" (in her mother's and the pastor's eyes) by becoming a lesbian. In the meantime, her unorthodox penchants reveal themselves in play:

> I felt a bit awkward to so I went into the Sunday School Room. There was some Fuzzy Felt to make Bible scenes with, and I was just beginning to enjoy a rewrite of Daniel in the lions' den when Pastor Finch appeared. I put my hands into my pockets and looked at the lion.
>
> "Little girl," he began, then he caught sight of the Fuzzy Felt.
> "What's that?"

"Daniel," I answered.

"But that's not right," he said, aghast. "Don't you know that Daniel escaped? In your picture the lions are swallowing him."

"I'm sorry," I replied, putting on my best, blessed face. "I wanted to do Jonah and the whale, but they don't do whales in Fuzzy Felt. I'm pretending those lions are whales."

"You said it was Daniel." He was suspicious.

"I got mixed up."

He smiled. "Let's put it right, shall we?" And he carefully rearranged the lions in one corner, and Daniel in the other.   (p. 13)

The pastor is outraged, then mollified; the little girl, wily—a contrast to the open defiance of the graffiti-drawing boy. The overall effect is humorous, at the pastor's expense; in the end, the little girl leaves him playing out his own biblical fantasies in Fuzzy Felt.

As the novel progresses, more and more old stories enter its texture: other Old Testament stories, fairytales, Perceval's quest for the Holy Grail. Their presence, increasingly unmotivated in realist terms, fragments the text and gives it something like the heterogeneity of collage, the hybrid, or carnival. The narrator's humor, however, gives way to anger and eventually to a kind of despair—as if the parodic lightness of the beginning could not be sustained after she becomes an outcast from home and church, both of them her mother's house.

And her mother? Repressive and fanatical, she looms large; as a fictional creation, she is a triumph for the novelist. As a character within the fiction, however, she is more disastrously hampering to her daughter than any male (the male characters all appear weak, or ridiculous). Although I am simplifying somewhat for the sake of the argument, I think it is not a misreading to say that the mother is represented here as being wholly on the side of patriarchy, indeed as the most vigorous defender of patriarchal values. Surrounded and sustained by women friends and totally dominating her husband, the mother is nevertheless in thrall to male authority figures: God, and his earthly representatives, a few fundamentalist pastors. Fortunately for her, they are all quite distant, which allows her to wield considerable local power even while disclaiming it.

Winterson's novel allows us to see why the figure of the mother often fares badly even on the surface, not merely in the depths of the psyche, in the work of radical artists, whether male or female; and it also provides one example of substantive agreement, rather than difference, between a strand of contemporary feminist parody and Surrealist parody.

In discussing Surrealist parody, I emphasized the "deep" psychoanalytic dimension of the son's alliance with the father and repudiation of the mother; but on the surface level, where the father's function appeared unambiguously negative, there was a much more obvious way, and reason why, the Surrealists repudiated the mother—and why other avant-garde artists, including some feminist women, have repudiated her as well. To the extent that she is perceived as a defender and an instrument of patriarchy, the mother takes on all of the father's negative attributes even while lacking his power: as such, she is the perfect target for both the son's and daughter's anger. Robin Lydenberg has written, apropos of William Burroughs, that "it is the figure of the mother who arouses his most vitriolic resentment," because he "perceives that the mother, as defined by conventional notions of sexual difference and family structure, is a necessary instrument in a larger system of patriarchal power which seeks to dominate the individual from his earliest moment of life."[52]

This kind of surface analysis complements rather than contradicts my psychoanalytic one. Ernst's figure of the mother chastising her son, for example, could be seen in terms of such an analysis as the "instrument in a larger system of patriarchal power" that Burroughs despises. One of the most vitriolic Surrealist documents, signed by Ernst and every other major male Surrealist (thirty-two signatories in all, an unusually large number) was the eight-page diatribe against Mrs. Charlie Chaplin, who sued her husband for divorce and a large financial settlement (she was the mother of his two children) in 1927. Entitled "Hands off Love!" the document was an impassioned defense of poetry and free love, embodied in the person of Charlie Chaplin, and an attack on the petit bourgeois mentality of "those bitches who become, in every country, the *good* mothers, *good* sisters, *good* wives, those plagues, those parasites of every sentiment and every love," represented by his wife. Narrow-minded, money-grubbing, moralizing, deriving her raison d'être solely from the "manufacture of brats" ("la fabrication des mioches"),[53] Mrs. Chaplin as painted in this Surrealist portrait is the very embodiment of the patriarchal mother (not to be confused with the phallic mother!) that both male and female Surrealists despised.[54]

Winterson, a very young writer (she was born in 1959) is not a Surrealist. But her portrayal of the heroine's mother in *Oranges Are Not the Only Fruit* is negative for the same reason as theirs: the mother is perceived as the narrow-minded defender of the law (in this case, the law of heterosexuality), even when the male figures around her have given up on that policing role. In the absence of a strong father, it is the mother who functions as repressive authority—thus doubly betraying her daughter.

I have discussed, in Chapter 6, Monique Wittig's distinction between Amazons and mothers—the latter functioning as upholders of the father's law and therefore enemies of the former. A slightly revised version of this separation between the lesbian daughter/warrior and the heterosexual mother occurs in *Virgile, non* (1985), Wittig's rewriting of Dante's *Inferno*. Like her great male predecessor's, Wittig's comedy is not funny but by turns sarcastic, angry, lyrical, vituperative, sorrowful. The damned souls that Wittig's poet-protagonist sees during her journey— all of them women, most of them willing victims of the patriarchal system—elicit her pity or her scorn, and none more so than the creatures "permanently accompanied by one or several annexes." To Wittig's continual surprise, the women actually love these millstones around their necks. "Will we ever be able to rid them of their damned annexes?" she asks Manastabal, her guide who is "not Virgil." Manastabal replies that she and Wittig are "not in hell to blame the damned souls but to show them the way out, if necessary."[55]

In other words, mothers have become alienated victims of patriarchy, rather than its self-righteous accomplices. Not much progress, from the Amazon's point of view. And nothing to laugh about.

Nancy Miller, in her study of a certain tradition of fiction by French women writers (which she calls a "feminist literature of dissent") remarks that in the typical feminist plot the heroine not only refuses to marry but also refuses to become a mother. "Is this bypassing of maternity the ultimate effect of the indictment of patriarchy?" Miller asks rhetorically.[56] Judging by the figure of the patriarchal mother, it would indeed seem to be the case that a woman cannot be a mother and outside the father's law at the same time: whether as alienated victim or as self-righteous accomplice, the mother appears necessarily on the side of patriarchy.

It is partly in reaction to this view that theorists like Cixous and Irigaray began, in the mid-1970s, to elaborate the "maternal metaphor" for women's writing *and* women's cultural politics. Cixous's simultaneous affirmation, in "The Laugh of the Medusa," that "a woman is never far from 'mother'" ("La femme n'est jamais loin de la 'mère'") and that "now, I-woman, am going to blow up the Law" ("maintenant, je-femme vais faire sauter la Loi") seems directed specifically against the notion that the mother is always patriarchal.[57] On the contrary, here it is the mother who, as metaphor ("I mean outside her role functions: the 'mother' as nonname and as source of goods"—p. 251), allows the woman to oppose both the Name-of-the-Father and the father's parsimonious economy.

Nor does the mother remain exclusively metaphoric, in Cixous's manifesto. A woman who wants a child should not be afraid of falling into the patriarchal trap, "engendering all at once child—mother—father— family. No; it's up to you to break the old circuits" (p. 261). Cixous thus suggests, in a significant reversal of the avant-garde (and sometimes avant-garde feminist) stereotype, that a woman can be politically radical, artistically innovative, and yet a mother.

Domna Stanton, who has submitted the maternal metaphor to a thoroughgoing critique, admits that it served in its time as an "enabling mythology."[58] I would say that (among other things) it enabled a number of French women writers to imagine a feminist avant-garde practice that would retain the historical avant-gardes' subversive/parodic energy but would revise and critique their negative attitude toward women— an attitude which, as Cixous and others rightly understood, had its source in, and was exemplified by, their repudiation (whether "deep" or "surface") of the mother.

It is just such a critical revision that is effected by Cixous's famous evocation of the Medusa:

> Tant pis pour eux s'ils s'effondrent à découvrir que les femmes ne sont pas des hommes, ou que la mère n'en a pas. Mais est-ce que cette peur ne les arrange pas? Est-ce que le pire, ce ne serait pas, ce n'est pas, en vérité, que la femme n'est pas castrée, qu'il lui suffit de ne plus écouter les sirènes (car les sirènes, c'étaient des hommes) pour que l'histoire change de sens? Il suffit qu'on regarde la méduse en face pour la voir: et elle n'est pas mortelle. Elle est belle et elle rit.   (p. 47)

> Too bad for them if they fall apart upon discovering that women aren't men, or that the mother doesn't have one. But isn't this fear convenient for them? Wouldn't the worst be, isn't the worst, in truth, that women aren't castrated, that they have only to stop listening to the Sirens (for the Sirens were men) for history to change its meaning? You only have to look at the Medusa straight on to see her. And she's not deadly. She's beautiful and she's laughing.   (p. 255)

The punch line is in the last sentence—and I do mean "punch line," because its effect is similar to the aggressive and scandalous effect of Surrealist parody. Cixous's figure of the beautiful and laughing Medusa, a reversal of the traditional hideous image, is formally equivalent to any number of Surrealist reversals (whether positive to negative, like Ernst's punitive Virgin, or negative to positive, like Aragon's Lucifer). It is the meaning of the figure, as determined by the context of the paragraph and by that of the essay as a whole, that is different.

Within the paragraph, the figure alludes both to the Greek myth and to Freud's reading of it. According to the myth, as retold by Ovid, the Gorgon Medusa was once beautiful, "the hope of many an envious suitor," until one day Neptune raped her in Minerva's temple—whereupon the Goddess, "punishing the outrage as it deserved," turned Medusa into a monster. Ovid also tells us that after the hero Perseus severed the Gorgon's head, "from that mother's bleeding / Were born the swift-winged Pegasus and his brother."[59] The Gorgon's head became a powerful weapon, turning all those (men) who looked at it into stone. In Cixous's revision, Medusa is restored to her beautiful state before the rape, and her head invites looking at, by men and women ("Il suffit qu'on la regarde," "on" being an impersonal pronoun) rather than aversion.

Freud, as is well known, read the decapitated Medusa's head as a symbol of the mother's (and by extension, women's) castrated genitals, seen from the "terrorized" point of view of the male spectator. Cixous's revision of this reading consists in imagining a female spectator who finds the very notion of women's castration laughable;[60] and who, looking at her body through her own eyes rather than the man's, finds all of it beautiful. (Does the equation of the Sirens with men suggest that once women stop listening to them they will become Odysseuses—explorers and heroes?) Cixous's Medusa, in short, figures the woman who laughs at being taken for the Medusa, that "symbol of horror."[61]

Enlarged to the context of the essay as a whole, the laughing Medusa becomes a trope for women's autonomous subjectivity and for the necessary irreverence of women's writing—and rewriting. A powerful trope it is, too. In fact, Cixous's Medusa could be the perfect reply to Mandelstam's witticisms about women's parody and women's metaphor, with which we started.

But if the maternal metaphor (and recall that in the Greek myth Medusa actually became a mother, giving birth to Pegasus) was empowering to some women writers, opening up to them possibilities for verbal invention and "freeplay," little of the writing thus produced was playful in the ordinary sense of lighthearted, or just plain funny. Annie Leclerc, Chantal Chawaf, and Julia Kristeva, who all at some point wrote about motherhood and maternal love not (or not only) as a metaphor but as an actual experience, opted for the expansive lyric mode when writing as mothers.[62] Although lyric can be full of invention, it does not offer much possibility for humor or parody.

The lyric genre also, of course, stands in contrast to the epic—that is, narrative. Cixous's fictions after "The Laugh of the Medusa" exploited the maternal as a metaphor for the mutually nurturing relations between women and as a metaphor for her own writing (the author giving birth to her texts). These works delight in verbal invention, including puns and other "play of signifiers"; they are intertextual, reworking Greek myths (*Illa, Le Livre de Promethea*) or texts by contemporary writers (*Vivre l'orange*). But their overall effect is effusively lyrical, or else essayistic, rather than narrative; and although they may at times provoke laughter, they are not comic works.

Am I being obtuse, desiring that women's play be humorous and narrative, as well as inventive—and especially humorous about, and in the voice of, the mother? Erma Bombeck's humor is not what I have in mind—it is not a matter of mothers grinning and bearing the age-old travails of motherhood. I have in mind something closer to Freud's notion that humor is both pleasure-producing and rebellious.[63] And I have in mind, finally, a desire for laughter coupled with a desire for *story*. (Metaphors are fine, but stories spun out are better—does this thought mark me as "postmodern," or merely as having lived too long in the country of Hollywood?)

Not the same old story, to be sure, or if the same old story, then rewritten, rewritten. But something that takes place in time, no matter how unlinear; that tells about events occurring in a world with characters (and "characters"), no matter how preposterous (the more preposterous, the better). In short, something that moves and changes, yet continues too.

We have arrived, at long last, at *The Hearing Trumpet*.

The Hearing Trumpet: Marian Leatherby and the Holy Grail

> If it's not blasphemous, why bother to make it?
>
> —ANGELA CARTER[64]

The narrator-heroine of *The Hearing Trumpet* is ninety-two years old and stone deaf. (Carrington was in her early thirties when she wrote the novel.) She is toothless, but her sight is still excellent; she has a "short grey beard which conventional people would find repulsive" but which she "personally" finds "rather gallant" (p. 3). Her name is Marian Leatherby, she was born in England but now lives in a country that sounds like Mexico; she lives in the house of her son and his family, in a room overlooking the backyard ("the back yard which I share with my two cats, a hen, the maid and her two children, some flies and a cactus plant called maguey"—p. 2). Her son's name is Galahad.

The people Marian lives with do not consider her quite human: "The Maid, Rosina, is an Indian woman with a morose character and seems generally opposed to the rest of humanity. I do not believe that she puts me in a human category so our relationship is not disagreeable" (p. 2). Her grandson calls her "the monster of Glamis," "a drooling sack of decomposing flesh"; to her daughter-in-law, she is a senile old woman ("'Remember Galahad,' added Muriel, 'these old people do not have feelings like you or I'"—p. 10); to her son, she appears merely as an "inanimate creature"—on which Marian comments: "He may be right, but on the other hand the maguey cactus seems alive to me, so I feel I can also make claims on existence" (p. 9).

As I have tried to suggest by my quotations, the first thing that strikes a reader of this novel is the heroine's voice; in particular, the contradiction between the humorous intelligence of the subject to whom this voice belongs, and the absolute denial of intelligence—indeed, of sub-jecthood—to which her age, her physical state, and her dependent status reduce her in the eyes of her family. Only by having the old "senile" crone tell her own story is this contradictory effect achieved. Marian's sharp wit counteracts her "decomposing flesh," and her dependent status is belied by her narrative mastery: "All this is a digression and I do not wish anyone to think my mind wanders far, it wanders but never further than I want" (p. 3).

Even more quotations are necessary to show the sustained effect of Marian's narrative voice—an effect that, I suggest, is cumulative and is made possible because there is a *story,* albeit an increasingly "mad" and fantastical one. Here, for example, is Marian's description of her friend and fellow ancient lady, Carmella, who changes Marian's life by giving her a hearing trumpet to alleviate her deafness:

> She lives in a very small house with her niece who bakes cakes for a Swedish teashop although she is Spanish. Carmella has a very pleasant life and is really very intellectual. She reads books through an elegant lorgnette and hardly ever mumbles to herself as I do. She also knits very clever jumpers but her real pleasure in life is writing letters. Carmella writes letters all over the world to people she has never met and signs them with all sorts of romantic names, never her own. Carmella despises anonymous letters, and of course they would be impractical as who could answer a letter with no name at all signed at the end? These wonderful letters fly off, in a celestial way, by airmail, in Carmella's delicate hand-writing. No one ever replies. This is the really incomprehensible side of humanity, people never have time for anything.   (p. 4)

Carmella's romantic imagination extends not only to names but to sto-ries: she picks her correspondents' names out of phone directories in far away places and writes to them after outfitting them with a life story. Monsieur Belvedere Oise Noisis of Paris, for example, she sees as "a rather frail old gentleman, still elegant, with a passion for tropical mushrooms which he grows in an Empire wardrobe. He wears embroi-dered waistcoats and travels with purple luggage" (p. 6).

Marian tells her she must be more realistic, not try to impose her imagination on people she has never seen. Suppose, for example, that Monsieur Belvedere Oise Noisis "is fat and collects wicker baskets? Suppose he never travels and has no luggage, suppose he is a young man with a nautical yearning?" To which Carmella replies that Marian is too "negative minded": "although I know you have a kind heart, that is no reason that poor Monsieur Belvedere Oise Noisis should do any-thing so trivial as collecting wicker baskets" (p. 6).

This is a charmingly Lewiscarrollesque way to remind us of the power of imagination and fancy (Marian's "realist" story is no less fanciful than Carmella's romantic one)—but where is the bite? you may ask. Are these two old playful ladies "avant-garde"? Is this novel critical? Radical? Parodic? Antipatriarchal? Surrealist? Postmodern?

Patience. Slow-burning fuses make big blasts.

Not long after Marian receives her hearing trumpet, she discovers—with its help—that her family is planning to ship her off to a home for senile ladies. Although forewarned is forearmed, there is nothing she can do about it. So she says goodbye to her cats and to Carmella (who makes contingency plans to rescue her with a getaway car and a machine gun, should the institution turn out to be too horrible), and lets her daughter-in-law and her son (whose name, recall, is Galahad) take her to the Well of Light Brotherhood old age home, presided over by one Dr. Gambit.

Marian's entry into this institution—consisting of gardens and courtyards, and buildings in the shape of medieval castles, towers, toadstools, a boot, an Egyptian mummy, and even a few "ordinary bungalows" (p. 24)—is a crossing over the threshold from the (more or less) real world to a world elsewhere. Some years before *The Hearing Trumpet*, Carrington recounted another such crossing, in her autobiographical narrative, *Down Below*, which tells of her temporary internment in an insane asylum in Spain in 1940.[65] Having crossed the border into Spain from the south of France, where she had been living with Max Ernst, after Ernst was taken into custody by French police, Carrington suffered a mental breakdown and was diagnosed as "incurably insane" by a Spanish doctor, then shipped off to the asylum with her family's approval. *Down Below*, first published in the American Surrealist journal *VVV* in 1944, recounts in detail the hallucinations and delusions she constructed in her states of madness. It is a harrowing account, not least because the Carrington who is telling the story (about three years after it occurred) refuses to adopt a safely "distant" perspective; she tries, instead, to convey the experience of madness as it was lived, from the inside—as in the following passage: "The son was the Sun and I the Moon, an essential element of the Trinity, with the microscopic knowledge of the earth, its plants and creatures. I knew that Christ was dead and done for, and that I had to take His place, because the Trinity, minus a woman and microscopic knowledge, had become dry and incomplete. Christ was replaced by the Sun. I was Christ on earth in the person of the Holy Ghost" (p. 195).

The Hearing Trumpet can be read as a self-conscious, artistically controlled transposition and expansion of some of the delusionary constructions described in *Down Below* (including the one I have just quoted), with an accompanying change in mood and color from the tragic to the comic. Marian is not mad, and the old ladies' home is not an insane asylum: but the male god is displaced by a female, Christian symbols and mythology become mixed up with pagan (above, the Trinity with the Sun and Moon), the world becomes topsy-turvy. Obviously, this association between the two works does not provide a complete reading of either one. But it does suggest a certain continuity in Carrington's preoccupations, as well as her ongoing relationship to Surrealism. *Down Below* is a kind of *Nadja,* but told from the point of view of the madwoman, not the male observer. *The Hearing Trumpet* is closer to Surrealist parody in the manner of Aragon, Desnos, or Péret, but again told from a different subject position.

Galahad, in the Arthurian legends, is the knight pure in heart destined to succeed in the quest for the Holy Grail. In Carrington's rewriting, it is not Galahad but his mother who delivers the Grail. The Grail itself becomes a pagan symbol originally associated with the goddess of love (but also of motherhood), Venus, the Christian version being a later usurpation.[66] And so on. We recognize here the feminist parodic reversal (or, as is often the case, reappropriation) of a sacred text or consecrated myth. In *Les Guérillères,* Wittig also alludes briefly to the Grail cycle, which the women read in terms of female symbols. What distinguishes Carrington's feminist parody is not only its meaning, its sly but unmistakable emphasis on the mother;[67] it is also the sustained, narratively and textually complicated way in which this revised meaning is achieved.

That is why a summary of the novel's feminist meaning, which does not take into account its formal complexities, can only fall flat. It is certainly not incorrect to say that Marian's "quest marks a voyage to the gynocentric past—a time when the Goddess was the center of creation."[68] But it is not this meaning, no matter how appealing it may be politically, that makes Carrington's parody a pleasure to read. Gayatri Spivak has noted that there is an unfortunate tendency among academic critics to "restore [avant-garde] texts back to propositional discourses."[69] She had in mind chiefly the work of male avant-garde writers, but the pitfall is also there—perhaps even more so—in the case of feminist avant-garde works, whose polemical content may tempt one to overlook the way it is framed, and the fact that the framing is part of the content. This is yet another version of the "how to read" question, which I explored in the chapters on Bataille and Robbe-Grillet.

What should one emphasize about *The Hearing Trumpet,* besides its obvious (and admittedly important) feminist reversals of meaning? Personally, I find most interesting Carrington's play with narrative representation and framing—texts within texts within texts, overlapping in curious ways; her "carnivalesque" accumulation of intertexts, ranging from the Bible and the Grail cycle to classical and Celtic mythology, the lives of saints, fairy tales, Goddess lore from various traditions, alchemical doctrines and Surrealist theories of collage and the hybrid; her use of humor, especially to create instabilities and moments of self-directed irony; and finally, the ways in which she situates this novel both as a prolongation of and a (feminist) divergence from Surrealist aspirations.

The play with narrative representation and framing begins, quite literally, with a representation in a frame: on her first day at the institution, while Dr. Gambit is explaining to the ladies gathered in the dining room that the purpose of Lightsome Hall is to "follow the inner Meaning of Christianity and comprehend the Original Teaching of the Master," Marian notices a large oil painting, a portrait of a nun, on the wall facing her: "The face of the Nun in the oil painting was so curiously lighted that she seemed to be winking, although that was hardly possible . . . However the idea that she was winking persisted, she was winking at me with a most disconcerting mixture of mockery and malevolence" (p. 28).

This painting, which Marian studies at every meal, begins to obsess her. Is the nun really winking? Georgina Sykes, one of the other pensioners with whom she discusses this question, has no doubt about it: "She is definitely winking; the bawdy old bag is probably peeking at the monastery through a hole in the wall, watching the monks prancing around in their knickers" (p. 41). Marian, although concluding from this that Georgina has a "one track mind," is nevertheless convinced. Henceforth the leering abbess (as she calls her) becomes the subject of her fantasies: she gives her a name, Dona Rosalinda Alvarez Della Cueva, and begins to invent a story for her: "She was abbess, I imagined, of a huge Baroque convent on a lonely and barren mountain in Castile. The convent was called El Convento de Santa Barbara de Tartarus, the bearded patroness of Limbo said to play with unbaptised children in this nether region. How all these fancies occurred to me I do not know" (p. 43).

As it happens, Marian's fancies will be "objectively" confirmed when one of the other pensioners, a black woman named Christabel Burns, gives her a book written by an eighteenth-century monk and telling the life story of Dona Rosalinda, "Abbess of the Convent of Santa Barbara of Tartarus," who was "canonized in Rome in 1756" (p. 72). Even before that, however, Carmella writes to say she has been having recurrent dreams about "a nun in a tower" with a winking face (p. 52). And another pensioner, Maude Wilkins, tells Marian about a very detailed dream involving Maude's search for a "magic cup" and her eventually stumbling on a woman in a fourposter bed who is winking at her and whom she recognizes as the nun in the painting (p. 58).

By the time Christabel gives Marian the book, then, the nun's story has the ontologically multiple status of pictorial representation, dream, and daydream (fantasy), elaborated independently by four different subjects. The eighteenth-century book adds yet another ontological layer: that of a written account purporting to be "a true and faithful rendering of the life" (p. 72). The effect is that of a multiple *mise en abyme,* with the usual unsettling and destabilizing of "reality" characteristic of such mirrorings.

The book about the painted nun, technically a framed or embedded tale occupying almost one fifth (twenty-eight pages) of the novel, includes some framed tales of its own, in various languages. The book itself is "translated from the original Latin," with a few Latin passages kept intact; and some of *its* framed tales, in the form of letters by or to the abbess or in the form of scrolls discovered by the monk/author, were translated, we are told by him, from Hebrew or Greek. It is as if Carrington had grafted the Surrealist preoccupation with doubling and with the boundaries between dream states and reality onto the postmodernist preoccupation with doubling and with boundaries between ontological levels, levels of narration and narrative representation, and levels of transmission or translation[70]—all this as part of a generally dizzying collage of texts and mythologies, of which the name "Santa Barbara de Tartarus," with its anachronistic joining of a Christian virgin martyr to the netherworld of Greek mythology, is but a small example. And all this underpinned, of course, by the primary structure of the feminist revision.

The story that emerges as Dona Rosalinda's life, told by what turns out to be an unsympathetic narrator, is a story of antipatriarchal and anti-Christian subversion: the good abbess and her homosexual friend, the bishop of Trêves les Frêles, are devotees of "the Goddess," working to destroy the Christian edifice from the inside—which means, to *rewrite* its story. The means for this rewriting are offered to them first by a "precious liquid" or ointment discovered near the mummy of Mary Magdalen, about which Dona Rosalinda writes to her friend:

> The ointment which was found on the left side of the mummy may very well release secrets which would not only discredit all the gospels but which would crown all the arduous work we have shared during recent years . . . You may imagine the transports of delight which overcame me when I learnt that Magdalen had been a high initiate of the mysteries of the Goddess but had been executed for the sacrilege of selling certain secrets of her cult to Jesus of Nazareth. This of course would explain the miracles which have puzzled us for so long. (p. 75)

By the next twist of the tale, the origin of the magic (aphrodisiac) ointment is pushed even further back, to merge with the rewritten origin of the Grail. This time, it is the bishop who is the narrative source, although he got his own tale from others in a receding series:

> One evening the boy Angus . . . let me understand that the Knight Templars in Ireland were in possession of the Grail. This wonderful cup, as you know, was said to be the original chalice which held the elixir of life and belonged to the Goddess Venus. She is said to have quaffed the magic liquid when she was impregnated with Cupid, whereupon he leapt in the womb and, by absorbing the pneuma, became a God. The story follows that Venus, in her birth pangs, dropped the cup and it came hurtling to earth, where it was buried in a deep cavern, abode of Epona the Horse Goddess.
>
> For some thousands of years the cup was safely in the keeping of the subterranean Goddess, who was known to be bearded and a hermaphrodite. Her name was Barbarus. (p. 91)

Carrington's emphasis on Venus as mother is in keeping with the early Greek meanings of the goddess of love: Aphrodite was thought to be of Asiatic origin, associated with the mother-goddess Ishtar. However, there was a general tendency even by the Greeks to efface Aphrodite's maternal meaning in favor of her erotic meaning (thus confirming the Western prejudice against associating sexuality with motherhood).[71] In Carrington's version, both meanings are maintained: the "magic liquid" is an aphrodisiac, and the child Venus gives birth to is Cupid.

With the mention of the bearded hermaphroditic goddess Barbarus in the bishop's tale, we sense that the narrative, like the serpent of alchemical symbolism, will soon bite its own tail (remember that Marian too has a beard).[72] One of the alchemical meanings of the serpent with its tail in its mouth is metamorphosis; another is the union of opposites or the coupling of contraries, as in hermaphroditism.[73] More generally, this symbol may stand for self-reflexiveness and the crossing of boundaries, whether ontological or narratological.

Indeed, Dona Rosalinda's story spills over onto Marian's story, and the Grail sought by Dona Rosalinda (who infiltrates the Templars' castle disguised as a "bearded cavalier," has a solitary encounter with the Grail, and eventually gives birth to a "boy, no bigger than a barn owl, luminously white and winged"—p. 99) is the Grail eventually found by Marian and her "army of bees, wolves, six old women, a postman, a Chinaman, a poet, an atom-driven ark, and a werewoman" (p. 157).

How Carrington gets us from there to here is a whole story. Suffice it to say that after Marian reads the life of Dona Rosalinda, life at the institution—and outside it—becomes increasingly strange. Maud Wilkins is poisoned by two of the pensioners, the victim of an error (their real target was Georgina Sykes), and turns out to have been an old gentleman, not an old lady; Christabel Burns turns out to be a devotee of the Goddess, and gives Marian three riddles to solve; Carmella arrives for a visit, bearing chocolate biscuits and port wine, and counseling rebellion; Marian and the other ladies dance around the bee pond, invoking Hecate and the Queen Bee,[74] then stage a coup d'état, exiling the poisoners and deposing Dr. Gambit; Carmella returns, a millionaire after she dug up a uranium mine in her backyard; a new ice age begins; the earth quakes, the Tower in the courtyard splits open and there springs forth a winged creature, "entirely covered with glittering feathers" (p. 133); Marian solves the riddles and descends under the Tower to the womb of the world, which is also a kitchen—where she meets herself, stirring a broth.

> She looked me up and down from head to foot and then from foot to head, rather critically I thought, and said finally, as if to herself, "Old as Moses, ugly as Seth, tough as a boot and no more sense than a skittle. However meat is scarce so jump in" . . .
> I tried to nod and move away at the same time, but my knees were trembling so much that instead of going towards the staircase I shuffled crabwise nearer and nearer the pot. When I was well within range she suddenly jabbed the pointed knife into my back side and with a scream of pain I leapt right into the boiling soup and stiffened in a moment of intense agony with my companions in distress, one carrot and two onions.
> A mighty rumbling followed by crashes and there I was standing outside the pot stirring the soup in which I could see my own meat, feet up, boiling away as merrily as any joint of beef. I added a pinch of salt and some peppercorns then ladled out a measure into my granite dish. The soup was not as good as a bouillabaisse but it was a good ordinary stew, very adequate for the cold weather.   (p. 138)

Such is Carrington's homely version of the alchemical broth, in which the self dissolves everything but its own essence. When Marian next looks at herself in a piece of polished obsidian, she sees, in sequence, "the face of the Abbess of Santa Barbara de Tartarus grinning at me sardonically," then the Queen Bee, and finally her own face (p. 138).

Glossing this passage, Gloria Orenstein writes: "Marian, after a series of adventures, has a revelation of her previous incarnations, all of which symbolize aspects of the spirit of the Mother Goddess . . . The three-faced female is the image of the Triple Goddess or the Triple Muse, who, according to Robert Graves, is woman in her divine character. Each lifetime is revealed to be one step in the karmic cycle, and the conclusion of the process yields a total knowledge of all-time."[75] Orenstein is no doubt right, but she misses the humor of Carrington's tribute to the Great Mother. Marian, after her vision of the three faces, adds:

"This of course might have been an optical illusion." But curiously, her self-deprecating humor does not undercut the force of Carrington's feminist critique: on the contrary, it makes it even stronger—as if one did not need to be ultra solemn in order to be taken seriously, in order to be heard.

Which does not mean that all playing is alike in its effects or implications, however. The Monty Python version of the story, *Monty Python and the Holy Grail,* which came out roughly at the same time as Carrington's novel in England, is zany and self-reflexive, full of fake blood and nonsequiturs, as we would expect from that irreverent bunch. (It is noteworthy that Monty Python films are usually characterized as "surrealistic.") But in the end, all the play is safely put in its place when the police interrupt the shooting (by the camera, in this case) and pack the actors off in a paddy wagon: one of them had chopped off the head of a "famous historian" who narrated part of the story in an earlier sequence. To me, that ending seems to say (not as flatly as this, of course): "Playing is fun, but let's not confuse it with reality. Cut up as many people as you like in fantasy, but remember that in real life murder is punishable by the law. And a good thing, too."

Obviously, it's a good thing. Civilization is there to remind us of what is possible and permissible in the social world; a child can be all the more wildly inventive and anarchic in his play, knowing that the Law of the Father will keep him from going too far.

Carrington's version of the Holy Grail does away with that safety rail—without advocating murder, I hasten to say. *The Hearing Trumpet* ends neither in murder nor in a return to reality as usual. It ends, instead, with a victory for the Goddess, to whom is restored her cup full of honey, wrested away from the "Revengeful Father God" (p. 146). And it ends very far indeed from reality as usual—in a quite unique (but still humorous) surreality.

Marian, before she became an old crone, had known the Surrealists, she tells us. And she had had a great friend, Marlborough, a poet, who loved to see Marian laugh, and who "always seemed to be present when I was overtaken by my spasms, which he was pleased to call Marian's maniac laughter. He always enjoyed seeing me making an exhibition of myself" (p. 37). As it happens, Marlborough turns up again after Marian's kitchen scene, while she and her friends (who now include Carmella's Chinese valet, Majong, and the postman Taliessin, a.k.a. the Celtic bard who already figured in Dona Rosalinda's story) are pondering how to capture the Holy Grail. Marlborough arrives in an atom-powered Ark, accompanied by a pack of wolves and his wolf-headed sister, Anubeth—perhaps a cousin of the Egyptian dog-headed god, Anubis? Or of Max Ernst's bird-headed alter ego, Loplop? Anubeth's hybrid form is explained by the fact that she, like her brother, is related to a "Hungarian nobleman whose Mother was a well-known Transylvanian Vampire" (p. 153). Anubeth is a talented artist specializing in (oh, surprise!) collage.

The interior of Marlborough's ark is "like the opium dream of a gypsy"—or like a Surrealist metaphor/object: "perfume sprays shaped like exotic feathered birds, lamps like praying mantis with moveable eyes, velvet cushions in the form of gigantic fruits, and sofas mounted on prostrate werewomen beautifully sculptured in rare woods and ivory" (p. 152). One of the more famous objects displayed at the 1938 International Surrealist exhibition was Kurt Seligmann's *Ultra-Furniture,* a chair mounted on women's legs; and the praying mantis—an insect whose outstanding characteristic is that the female eats the male after copulation—was a favored Surrealist stand-in for the *femme fatale.*[76] Carrington's homage to her friend Max Ernst (with whom she spent a few crucial years of her life) and to the Surrealist aesthetic of parody and collage is unmistakable, though teasing—and apparently without illusions about the place of women in Surrealism.

In the end, Marian's army captures the Grail, which is borne off by bees to a secret part of the cavern they all share; and Marian can write: "This is the end of my tale. I have set it all down faithfully, without exaggeration either poetic or otherwise" (p. 158). But as we might expect from such a truthful statement, Marian's tale is not quite at an end yet. It continues for a few more paragraphs, which tell us that Anubeth, pregnant by the wolf King Pontefact, has given birth to "six young werewolf cubs which improved in appearance after their fur grew"; that Marian is continuing her job as scribe; and that, with the poles shifting, Marian and her crew are now where Lapland used to be—where Marian had always dreamed of going.

> Ice ages pass, and although the world is frozen over we suppose someday grass and flowers will grow again. In the meantime I keep a daily record on three wax tablets.
>
> After I die Anubeth's werecubs will continue the document, till the planet is peopled with cats, werewolves, bees and goats. We all fervently hope that this will be an improvement on humanity, which deliberately renounced the Pneuma of the Goddess . . .
>
> If the old woman can't go to Lapland, then Lapland must come to the Old Woman.   (p. 158)

The seriousness behind Carrington's "maniac laughter" is obvious: it is no small thing to write off the human race.[77] At the same time, the novel's concluding sentence suggests the hope that if the world becomes sufficiently topsy-turvy, even the peaceable desires of old women (of the Old Woman—a mother) may be satisfied.

It is the perennial hope of carnival, is it not?

The Laugh of the Mother

> Normal mothers are teaching their kids the alphabet, but I'm saying, "Now, Mabel, how does the Good Witch talk in 'The Wizard of Oz'"?
>
> —TRACEY ULLMAN

"Imagine the mother playing," I wrote in the beginning of this book. "Imagine the mother laughing," I have suggested here. But why? Why should we imagine the mother playing and laughing? And why are the stakes political (in the broadest sense) as well as aesthetic?

Playing, as Freud and Winnicott (among others) have shown us, is the activity through which the human subject most freely and inventively constitutes herself or himself. To play is to affirm an "I," an autonomous subjectivity that exercises control over a world of possibilities; at the same time, and contrarily, it is in playing that the "I" can experience itself in its most fluid and boundaryless state. Barthes speaks of being "liberated from the binary prison, putting oneself in a state of infinite expansion."[78] Winnicott calls the play experience "one of a non-purposive state, as one might say a sort of ticking over of the unintegrated personality"—and adds a few pages later that "it is only here, in this unintegrated state of the personality, that that which we describe as creative can appear."[79]

To imagine the mother playing is to recognize her most fully as a subject—as autonomous and free, yet (or for that reason?) able to take the risk of "infinite expansion" that goes with creativity. Some feminist critics have expressed worry over the idea of the female subject, mother or not, playing with the boundaries of the self, given the difficulties women in our culture have in attaining a sense of selfhood to begin with. As Nancy K. Miller, who has most forcefully argued this view, has put it, speaking of the signature: "Only those who have it can play with not having it," and women's signatures, even for those who "have" them, are still undervalued. Naomi Schor has argued, in a similar vein, that feminists should not abandon the notion of feminine specificity in favor of "the carnival of plural sexualities."[80]

Although I share Miller's and Schor's desire to hold on to a notion of female selfhood, it still seems important to me to admit the possibility of playing with the boundaries of the self—especially if Winnicott is right in seeing such play as a necessary part of artistic creativity. I believe that women—women artists in particular—must be strong enough to allow themselves this kind of play; and that one way to achieve such strength is for girls to imagine—or better still, see—their mothers playing.[81] Jessica Benjamin has argued that if the mother were really recognized in our culture as an independent subject, with desires of her own, this recognition would revolutionize not only the psychoanalytic paradigms of "normal" child development (which have always been based on the child's need to be recognized by the mother, not on the idea of *mutual* recognition), but the actual lives of children in this culture as they develop into adults.[82] Could it be that it would change the way we in the West think about the constitution of human subjectivity?

Maybe this is too big a claim, or at least one that would have to be argued more fully than I am doing here. In fact, I will be content with a more modest vision; of boys (later to be men) who actually enjoy seeing their mother move instead of sitting motionless, "a peaceful center" around which the child weaves his play;[83] of girls (later to be women) who learn that they do not have to grow up to be motionless mothers.

To imagine the mother laughing as she plays brings a touch of lightness to what otherwise could appear as too solemn a dream (there is nothing so self-defeating, or so grim, as the idea of required or regimented play). And it may allow us to envision a new, lighter—though no less inventive and free—mode of play than the sadistic, narcissistic, angst-ridden games of transgressive children.

Tracy Ullman is a British comedian who specializes in mimicry, impersonating imaginary characters of her invention. Ullman associates her talent with memories of her mother: after her father died when she was six years old, "my Mom used to get out this pistol Dad had, and we'd have competitions in her bedroom to see who could die the best." Laughing at her mother's playing, says Ullman, "was the greatest defense we had against the misery."[84]

Patricia Yaeger quotes Herbert Marcuse paraphrasing Friedrich Schlegel: "Man is free when the 'reality loses its seriousness' and when its necessity 'becomes light.'"[85] As Yaeger points out, this is not a recipe for learning to live with the way things are, but rather one possible recipe for wanting to change them.

EIGHT

Feminism and Postmodernism:
In Lieu of an Ending

> ... and to this day young authors sally forth in fiction like majes-
> tic—indeed, divinely ordained!—*picaros* to discover, again and
> again, their manhood.
>
> —ROBERT COOVER

> To write a quality cliché you have to come up with something
> new.
>
> —JENNY HOLZER

Une Histoire Bien Postmoderne

As I prepare to write this final essay, in Paris during the whole month
of February 1989 (the preparation takes a long time, every new week
seems to bring yet another book or special issue devoted to the "postmodernism debate"), I follow each day, with an obsessed fascination,
the unfolding of "L'Affaire Rushdie." The *International Herald Tribune*
reports it fairly thoroughly, but *Libération* does better. For several days
running, it devotes numerous pages to the story, including interviews
and editorials; it prints photos of the demonstrations in Teheran, Bom-
bay, New York (the shock of seeing thousands of bodies prostrated
toward Mecca on Fifth Avenue), and of the book burning in Bradford,
England, back in January. It also prints, early on (Thursday, February
16), a large dark portrait of Rushdie himself, his face with its high
balding pate and quizzically raised eyebrows the only white thing
emerging from the black background: Satanic-looking author of *The
Satanic Verses,* whose opening chapter *Libération* will publish in French
translation a week later. (No chance of finding the original these days
in any of the English-language bookshops in Paris. I read the translation
avidly—is this what *samizdat* felt like in the days before *glasnost?*)

The day the portrait of Rushdie appears, together with excerpts from
an interview with him in the *Guardian,* in which he states that he is

and remains a Moslem and that it is not his fault if the Islamic orthodoxy has declared a holy war against the twentieth century, I reread Fredric Jameson's famous essay, one of the major documents in the debate I am tracing, "Postmodernism, or the Cultural Logic of Late Capitalism." Among the ills Jameson diagnoses (and deplores) about postmodernism, that quintessential expression, according to him, of late capitalist society, is that it lacks any and all oppositional force: in the "society of the spectacle," as Guy Debord already showed in the 1960s, opposition becomes simply one more image, one more simulacrum of the real instead of the thing itself. It is as if (say I to myself, free-associating) the revolvers so prized by the historical avant-gardes had all turned into toy guns distributed by the culture industry—"Take one, they're free, part of our new advertising campaign!" The modernist avant-gardes, Jameson writes, still had the power to offend; the "offensive features" of postmodernism, by contrast, including "overt expressions of social and political defiance, which transcend anything that might have been imagined at the most extreme moments of high modernism," no longer offend anyone. Indeed, they "are not only received with the greatest complacency but have themselves become institutionalized and are at one with the official culture of Western society."[1]

As the days go by, I read and ponder: Are the three million dollars offered by the Ayatollah for the head of Salman Rushdie, the author of novels usually qualified as "postmodernist," a proof that Jameson was wrong and that, in the non-Western world at least, literature still has the power to offend? And is the justified outcry in the Western world, together with the courageous actions of the writers who gathered in New York to read excerpts from the novel and of the publishers who have refused to withdraw it from circulation, a proof that in the West the value of free speech remains sacrosanct? Or is this whole story a macabre illustration of the very point that Jameson was making? Is the story of the Author and the Ayatollah itself caught in the late capitalist logic of the simulacrum, where no one is in control yet real people get killed in demonstrations over a work of fiction none of them has read, and where governments as well as individuals shift and weigh their words in accordance not with their beliefs (whatever they might be) but with what they perceive to be economic necessities?

Rushdie, when it looked as if the death sentence might be lifted by an apology, apologized publicly for any offense his novel might have caused—and who can blame him? As for the Ayatollah, it seems he was the master, when it suited him, of the self-canceling message. After demonstrators in Paris shouted the Ayatollah's death sentence against the author and provoked a sharp response from the French government and its allies, including the cancellation of some commercial deals Iran had counted on, the Iranian embassy in Paris suddenly issued a disclaimer of Iran's involvement in all violent actions linked to the affair. Such actions, the communiqué stated, were the work of "enemies of Islam [who] have decided to undertake, in certain countries, provocations and violent actions and to attribute them to the Islamic Republic in order to deform the meaning of the religious verdict, clear and without ambiguity, of the Imam Khomeiny."[2]

If I read this sentence right, it says that the Imam's verdict was clear and necessary but strictly "religious," not meant to lead to real-life violence (or, presumably, to real-life cancellation of commercial contracts). Was the verdict just words, then, and should Rushdie come out of hiding? Was the Ayatollah simply doing his job, with no offense intended?[3] High tragic drama of "les droits de l'homme," in this two-hundredth anniversary year of the French Revolution, suddenly veers into black comedy.

In the meantime, the popular British author Roald Dahl straight-facedly accuses Salman Rushdie of having engineered all of the above just to "get an indifferent book on to the top of the best-seller list, but to my mind, it is a cheap way of doing it."[4] Various British officials, secular and religious, declare that although *The Satanic Verses* is a deeply offensive book, they do not think the author's life should be threatened. A headline in the *Tribune* on March 7 sums up the latest developments: "Britain's Wall of Support for Rushdie is Developing Cracks."

This way, ladies and gentlemen, welcome to postmodernity.

Discourses on the Postmodern and the Emergence of Feminist Postmodernism

> The absence of discussion of sexual difference in writings about postmodernism, as well as the fact that few women have engaged in the modernism-postmodernism debate, suggests that postmodernism may be yet another masculine invention engineered to exclude women.
>
> —CRAIG OWENS, "FEMINISTS AND POSTMODERNISTS"

> Typically male-dominated organizations open doors to women only after their power is on the wane.
>
> —ROZSIKA PARKER AND GRISELDA POLLOCK, *FRAMING FEMINISM*

Contrary to what some recent commentators on postmodernism seem to think, there was life before Jean-François Lyotard. The term "postmodernism," designating a cultural sequel and/or challenge to modernism (however one defined that term) existed well before the publication of *La Condition postmoderne* (1979).[5] It is ironic that Lyotard's book, or rather its English translation, *The Postmodern Condition* (1981), should have become the required starting point for all current discussions of postmodernism by American and English critics, when Lyotard himself, in what I have called elsewhere a "rare instance of 'reverse importation' in the French-American theoretical marketplace," credited his use of the term to American critics, notably to Ihab Hassan.[6]

One would not be altogether wrong to see in this displacement, whereby the French philosopher "takes the place of" all his American predecessors, a sign of what Jameson diagnosed as the absence of historical consciousness in postmodern culture—as if the memory of those who discussed postmodernism in the 1980s did not extend beyond the confines of the decade itself; or perhaps, more ironically, to see in it a sign of the snob appeal of "genuine French imports" (or what are mistakenly thought to be such) in a certain sector of American intellectual life. But if this view would not be altogether wrong, it would not be altogether right either, for although Lyotard's book did not initiate the discourse on postmodernism, it did place it on a new theoretical and philosophical footing. Most notably, it articulated the links between French poststructuralist philosophy and postmodern cultural practices (including science and everyday life as well as the arts), so that the latter could be seen—at least in the ideal sketched by Lyotard—as an instantiation of the former.

All of the concepts Lyotard invoked to define the innovative aspects of postmodern knowledge—the crisis of legitimation and the refusal of "grand narratives," the choice of models of dissent and heterogeneity over models of consensus and systemic totality, the view of cultural practices as overlapping language games with constantly shifting rules and players—are concepts grounded in poststructuralist thought, as the latter was elaborated in France in the 1960s and 1970s by Lyotard, Derrida, Foucault, and others. *The Postmodern Condition* can thus be read as a poststructuralist manifesto or "manifesto of decentered subjectivities," expressing the optimism for the future that the manifesto genre requires. Although Lyotard is aware of the nightmarish possibilities offered by the "computerization of society" (his model of postmodern knowledge invokes and seeks to generalize the new technologies and conceptualizations—such as Mandelbrot's fractals—made possible by the computer), he emphasizes instead its potentialities as a positive dream. The dream is of a society in which knowledge would consist of language games that would be "non-zero-sum games," where there would be no losers or winners, only players in a constantly evolving process; where openness would be the rule, with information and data banks available to all; where instability and "temporary contracts" would lead neither to alienation nor to anarchy, but to "a politics that would respect both the desire for justice and the desire for the unknown" (p. 67).

In short, a utopian—or cautiously utopian, if such a thing is possible—version of Babel, a positive counterargument to the pessimistic views being elaborated, during the post-1968 decade, by Jean Baudrillard. Lyotard was seeing the same things as Baudrillard but interpreting them differently: what to Baudrillard appeared as the increasingly horrifying world of simulacra evacuating the real, indeed evacuating the very concept of a *difference* between the simulacrum and the real, appeared to Lyotard—at least potentially—as a world of increasing possibilities for innovation, brought about precisely by the breakdown of stable categories like "the real." Where Baudrillard saw the "postmodern condition" (a term he did not use) as the end of all possibility for (real) action, community, resistance, or change, Lyotard saw it as potentially a whole new game, whose possibilities remained open.[7]

That difference marked one of the stakes in what was soon to become, with the entry of Jürgen Habermas into the fray, the best known version of the "modernism-postmodernism debate."[8] Since then, the debate has shifted again: What is now in question is not so much whether postmodernism constitutes a totally new development or "break" in relation to modernism (most people, it seems to me, have now accepted that as a given, even if they don't agree on all the details of why and how), but rather the current significance and future direction of the new development as such.

What does all this have to do with women or feminism? And with the earlier American discourses about postmodernism, which I accused other recent commentators of ignoring and then proceeded to ignore myself? Obviously, this is not the place to undertake a full-scale history of discourses on the postmodern.[9] Suffice it to say that, like a number of other important "isms" (romanticism, modernism, classicism), postmodernism has functioned as both a formal/stylistic category and a broadly cultural category. From the start, the most provocative discussions have been those that linked the formal or stylistic to the broadly cultural. Irving Howe's 1959 essay, for example, "Mass Society and Postmodern Fiction," which is generally credited with first use of the term "postmodern" in its current sense, saw in the emergence of a new kind of American fiction (roughly, that of the beat generation) both a stylistic sequel to modernism—exemplified by Joyce, Mann, and Kafka, as well as Hemingway and Fitzgerald—and a cultural symptom of the transformations that had occurred in Western countries after World War II.[10]

A similar argument, although adopting a different, more positive judgment on these transformations and on the literature that accompanied them, was made by Leslie Fiedler a few years later; it was also suggested, again in positive terms, by Robert Venturi and Denise Scott Brown around the same time regarding architecture, in the essay that was to become the basis for their famous (or infamous) manifesto of postmodern architecture, *Learning from Las Vegas*.[11]

A few years ago, I argued that as far as literature was concerned, it made no sense to try and establish clearcut formal differences between the "modernist" and the "postmodernist," for such an attempt invariably involved oversimplification and flattening out of both categories.[12] Although I would now want to change some of the premises of that earlier argument, I still believe that the effort to define postmodernism chiefly as a formal (or even as a formal and thematic) category and to place it as such in opposition to modernism is, even when successful, of limited interest.[13] If postmodernist practice in the arts has provoked controversy and debate, it is because of what it "does" (or does not do), not because of what it "is." In other words, it is as an object "to be read," an intervention in the sense of an action or a statement requiring a response, rather than as an object of descriptive poetics, that postmodernism, whether in literature or in the other arts, strikes me as significant today.

This position, whether explicitly stated or not, seems to me to be shared by all those who are currently involved in the "postmodernism debate." Where is postmodernist practice going? Can it be political?—should it be? Does it offer possibilities for opposition, critique, resistance to dominant ideologies? Or is it irremediably compromised by its complicity with the market, with mass culture, capitalism, commercialism? Familiar questions, questions that have been asked in one form or another, at one time or another, about every avant-garde movement and experimental practice since Impressionism. Which does not make them less significant when asked about postmodernism, though it suggests that no definitive answers may be forthcoming.

And women? And feminism?

It should come as no surprise, knowing what we know about earlier avant-garde movements and their historians, to learn that the first writings about postmodernism made absolutely no mention of the work of women. One could argue that if early commentators like Irving Howe and Leslie Fiedler, whose prime examples of the postmodern were the Beats (Fiedler also included Pop art in the visual arts), did not mention women's work, it was because there was little or no such work around to be mentioned at the time. Restated in terms of my argument in

Chapter 1, this would mean that the Beats and the Pop artists were male avant-gardes similar to Surrealism, excluding women during their most dynamic period. In fact, there were a few women active in both movements, if not at the very beginning, then close enough to it (Diane Di Prima among the Beats, Marisol among the Pop artists). Still, as in the case of Surrealism, one can ascribe the early critics' silence not only to ordinary sexism ("not seeing" women who are there), but also to a real scarcity of women's work in those movements.

Critics who started to write about postmodernism in the 1970s or 1980s had less of an excuse for excluding the work of women; for in what I take to be a genuinely *new* (*inédit,* as they say on bookcovers in Paris) historical development, women's participation in experimental literary and visual work during those two decades reached a level, both in terms of quantity and quality, that could no longer be ignored. Some critics, of course, even among the most brilliant, managed to ignore it, as late as the mid-1980s; others, less brilliant, went so far as to theorize its absence. (A few years ago, I received a letter from a European doctoral student who asked whether I agreed with her professor that "women have not produced any postmodernist fiction," and if so, to what I attributed that lack. I replied that the lack may have been in the beholder rather than in the object.)

In the 1980s women's work began to be mentioned, and even featured, in academic discussions of postmodernism, especially in the visual arts. Rosalind Krauss's important article, "The Originality of the Avant-Garde: A Postmodernist Repetition" (1981), which made a strong, polemically "pro-postmodernist" case for the difference between postmodernism and its modernist or historical avant-garde predecessors (the difference residing, according to Krauss, in postmodernism's "radical questioning of the concept of origin . . . and originality"), cited as exemplary postmodernist works the photographs of Sherrie Levine; two years earlier, in the pages of the same journal, Douglas Crimp had argued for the innovativeness (originality?) of postmodernist "pictures" and cited, among other examples, the photographs of Levine and Cindy Sherman.[14]

To discuss the work of women as part of a new movement, trend, or cultural paradigm one is defending is undoubtedly a desirable thing. As Renato Poggioli showed, every avant-garde has its critical defenders and explicators;[15] their work, in turn, becomes a basis on which the movement, once it goes beyond its "scandalous" phase, is integrated into the standard literary and cultural histories. It is quite another thing, however, to take into account not only the existence of women's work, but also its (possibly) feminine or feminist specificity; and to raise, furthermore, the question of how the specificity, whether sexual or political, of women's work within a larger movement affects one's understanding of the movement itself.

In his 1983 essay "The Discourse of Others: Feminists and Postmodernism," Craig Owens made one of those conceptual leaps that later turn out to have initiated a whole new train of thought. Simply, what Owens did was to theorize the political implications of the intersection between the "feminist critique of patriarchy and the postmodernist critique of representation."[16] He was not the first to suggest the political potential of poststructuralism (which, in the preceding sentence and in Owens's argument, is virtually interchangeable with postmodernism); the ideological critique of the "unified bourgeois subject" and of classical representation had been a continuing theme in French poststructuralist writing from the late 1960s on and had been part of the political platform of *Tel Quel* in its most revolutionary period. Nor was the linking of the feminist critique of patriarchy with poststructuralism surprising, since French feminist theory had from the beginning acknowledged its link to deconstruction and even proclaimed it in its famous portmanteau word, "phallogocentrism." The novelty, indeed the pathbreaking quality of Owens's essay was that it placed the feminist issue *at the center of the debate on postmodernism* (which was also, if one wishes, a debate on poststructuralism), as that debate was unfolding in the United States (and, with a bit of delay, in England) after the publication of Lyotard's *The Postmodern Condition*.[17]

On the one hand, Owens quite rightly criticized the major players in the debate for ignoring both the "insistent feminist voice" in postmodern culture and the whole issue of sexual difference in their discussions of postmodernist practices: thus even those critics who, like Crimp, Krauss, and Hal Foster (and Owens himself, in an earlier essay), discussed women's work as an important part of postmodernist art, could be faulted for ignoring the specifically feminist—or even "feminine"—meanings of that work (pp. 73–77). On the other hand, Owens suggested that if the feminist/critical aspect of postmodernist work *was* taken into account, there would result a new and more politically sharpened view of postmodernism itself—for feminism, after all, is not only a theory or an aesthetics, it is also a politics.

By linking feminist politics with postmodernist artistic practice, Owens provided the pro-postmodernists in the debate with a precious argument, whose advantages they were quick to grasp. Feminism provided for postmodernism a concrete political edge, or wedge, that could be used to counter the accusatory pessimism of a Baudrillard or a Jameson: for if there existed a genuinely *feminist* postmodernist practice, then post-

modernism could no longer be seen only as the expression of a fragmented, exhausted culture steeped in nostalgia for a lost center. Indeed,
such a view of postmodernism, with its sense of irremediable decline
and loss, could now itself be shown to be implicated in the Western,
patriarchal logic of the "grand narratives"—the very logic that feminism,
and feminist postmodernism, contested. As Hal Foster, in an essay that
I read as a response to and development of Owens's argument, elo-
quently noted: "Here, then we begin to see what is at stake in [the] so-
called dispersal of the subject. For what is this subject that, threatened
by loss, is so bemoaned? For some, for many, this may indeed be a
great loss, a loss which leads to narcissistic laments and hysterical dis-
avowals of the end of art, of culture, of the west. But for others, precisely
for Others, it is no great loss at all."[18]

Andreas Huyssen, around the same time, was arguing that feminism
and the women's movement, together with anti-imperialism, the ecology
movement, and the growing awareness of "other cultures, non-Euro-
pean, non-Western cultures," had created a new "postmodernism of
resistance" that would "satisfy the needs of the political *and* those of
the aesthetic."[19] Most recently, following up on these arguments, Linda
Hutcheon has spoken of the overlapping agendas between postmodernism and "ex-centrics": blacks, women, and other traditionally margin-
alized groups.[20]

In short, feminism brings to postmodernism the political guarantee
postmodernism needs to feel respectable as an avant-garde practice.
Postmodernism, in turn, brings feminism into a certain kind of "high
theoretical" discourse on the frontiers of culture, traditionally an exclusively male domain.[21]

If this summary sounds cynical, the effect is only partly intended.
There is, I believe, an element of mutual opportunism in the alliance
of feminists and postmodernists, but it is not necessarily a bad thing.
The opportunism operates not so much, or perhaps not at all, in the
actual practice of feminist postmodernist artists, but rather in the public
discourse about that practice: influential critics who write about the
work of feminist postmodernists, especially in the realm of the visual
arts, are both advancing their own reputations as "high theorists" and
contributing to—or even creating—the market value of those artists'
work, while other, less fashionable feminist work may go unnoticed.
And once it becomes valuable on the market, the feminist postmodernist
work may lose its critical edge.

This is not a new problem, as I have already suggested and will
suggest again. In a world in which everything, even the discourse of
high postmodernist theory, has an exchange value, should one reject the

advantages of the feminist-postmodernist alliance for the sake of an ideal of aesthetic or intellectual purity? If every avant-garde has its public defenders and promoters, why not feminist postmodernism?

Oh dear, oh dear, now I do sound excessively cynical. Let me therefore quickly affirm that I take the theoretical arguments advanced by Owens, Foster, Huyssen, and Hutcheon in favor of the feminism-postmodernism alliance extremely seriously, and indeed subscribe to them (mostly); that I believe it is important to look for the critical and political possibilities of avant-garde practices in general, and of postmodernism in particular; and that I think women and feminists rightfully belong in the center of such discussions and practices—in the middle of the margin, as it were.[22] As I said earlier, with postmodernism we have arrived at a totally new situation for women artists: for the first time in the history of avant-gardes (or in history *tout court*), there exists a critical mass of outstanding, innovative work by women, both in the visual arts and in literature.[23] Simone de Beauvoir's complaint, in *The Second Sex,* that women artists lacked genius—that is, the audacity to take real risks and to carry "the weight of the world on their shoulders"—is no longer true, if it ever was. Today, thanks in part to the existence of predecessors like Beauvoir, there are women artists who possess genius in her sense— *and* who are aware at the same time that "genius," like every other abstract universal category, is determined by particulars: race, sex, nationality, religion, history. As Christine Brooke-Rose has recently noted, "genius" has the same Indo-European root as gender, genre, and genesis.[24]

Still, it would be unwise to celebrate postmodernism, even more so feminist postmodernism, without keeping one's ears open to dissenting voices, or without acknowledging things that don't "fit." Feminist postmodernism, like postmodernism in general, must confront anew some of the dilemmas that have plagued every successful avant-garde for the past century or more: the dilemma of political effectiveness versus stylistic indirection and innovation, numbingly familiar to students of the 1930s; or the dilemma of the market and the avant-garde's relation to mass culture, which dominated, as Andreas Huyssen has shown, the "Greenberg and Adorno decades" after World War II. In addition, feminist postmodernism must confront the specific questions and challenges posed to it from within the feminist movement, notably as concerns the political status of the "decentered subject."

Not a short order, in sum. Enough to fill another whole book, in fact. But I shall fill only a few more pages, with thoughts and notes for future reflection and work, whether by me or others.

Opposition in Babel? The Political Status of Postmodern Intertextuality

> Then I shall enter with my hypotheses and sweep the detritus of civilization.
>
> —CHRISTINE BROOKE-ROSE, *AMALGAMEMNON*

> The vital thing is to have an alternative so that people will realise that there's no such thing as a true story.
>
> —JEANETTE WINTERSON, *BOATING FOR BEGINNERS*

The appropriation, misappropriation, montage, collage, hybridization, and general mixing-up of visual and verbal texts and discourses, from all periods of the past as well as from the multiple social and linguistic fields of the present, is probably the most characteristic feature of what can be called the "postmodern style." The question, as it has emerged in the debate on postmodernism, is: Does this style have a critical political meaning or effect, or is it—in Fredric Jameson's words—merely "blank parody," a "neutral practice" devoid of any critical impulse or historical consciousness?

Having extolled the virtues—including the political/critical virtues— of feminist irony and parody in the previous chapter, I do not need to restate my own position. Nor is it necessary to reformulate the arguments over the political effects of "carnivalized" discourse, which I summarized in that chapter. (Note that the affair of *The Satanic Verses* has confirmed the complicated status of carnival: what may appear as simply one more case of "authorized transgression," immediately recuperable or ignorable by the system, can, under certain circumstances, take on a life-threatening seriousness; which means that the political and ideological effects of carnival, or of the language games that correspond to it, can never be totally controlled or foreseen.) It will be useful, however, to consider the question again from a theoretical perspective, not as a prelude to a single interpretive reading.

What does it mean to talk about the political effect of a novel or painting or photograph? If one means that in a particular historical circumstance an artwork can be used for political ends, well and good: Picasso's "Guernica," exhibited in major European and American capitals between 1937 and 1939, earned a lot of sympathy as well as material support for the Spanish Republic before coming to rest for a few decades in the Museum of Modern Art. If one means that the work elicits a political response, whether in the form of public commentaries or private reactions, including the production of other art works that build on it ("Guernica" is again a good example), that is also well and good.[25] What seems to me wrongheaded, or at the very least problematic, is talking about the political effect or meaning of a work—especially of a self-conscious, insistently intertextual, often multiply ironic work—as if that meaning were clear, immutable, and immanent to the "text," rather than determined by its interpretive context.

Political readings—indeed, all interpretations—tend to speak of works as if their meanings and effects were immanent; to convince someone else of the validity of one's reading, one has to claim, or at least imply, that it is the best reading, the reading most closely corresponding to the "work itself." When Jameson made his often-quoted claim that postmodern pastiche "is a neutral practice of . . . mimicry, without any of parody's ulterior motives, amputated of the satiric impulse, devoid of laughter and of any conviction that . . . some healthy linguistic normality still exists," implicit in the claim (which was used to support his general argument that postmodernism lacked authentic historical awareness) was the assumption that works of art determine their own meaning and reading. Linda Hutcheon, who strongly criticizes Jameson for not citing any examples, offers many examples of her own to show that postmodern parody does *not* lack the "satiric impulse" and is not apolitical or ahistorical. She is no doubt justified in her critique; but as the very act of citing counterexamples shows, she shares Jameson's assumption that political meanings reside in works, not in their readings.

I assumed the same thing, or acted as if I did, in my reading of, say, Carrington's *The Hearing Trumpet*. But precisely in the case of *The Hearing Trumpet* I also tried to suggest that how a work is read depends very much on who is reading it, when, and to what ends. My own reading, clearly situated in the late 1980s and almost unimaginable at the time the novel was written (the early 1950s), was determined by a particular set of ideological preoccupations, as well as by my appreciation of a certain kind of formally complex, humorous, feminist, postmodernist narrative fiction—a category I *constructed* and in which I placed the novel, not in which it necessarily or eternally belongs. It must be noted, furthermore, that my own reading, although individual, can be shown to be part of a collective discourse. As Stanley Fish and other theorists of "reader-oriented criticism" have argued, reading is a *shared* activity; every reading, no matter how personal or original (or "quirky") can be analyzed historically and ideologically as characteristic of a group, or what Fish has called an interpretive community.[26] To be part of an interpretive community, one does not need a membership card; it is a matter of having learned, in the classroom or through scholarly exchange, or through more informal modes of communication, certain shared ways of approaching a text: asking certain questions of it, and elaborating a language and an interpretive "strategy" for answering them.

Displacing the political effect from the work to its reading has the advantage of moving the debate from the question of what postmodernism "is" to the question of what it does—in a particular place, for a particular public (which can be a public of one, but as I have just suggested, every individual is part of a larger interpretive community) at a particular time. That displacement does not, however, alter the basic questions about the politics of intertextuality or of irony, or more generally about the relation between symbolic action and "real" action in the world. It merely . . . displaces them, from the work to its readings and readers.

Jameson, reading postmodernist intertextuality as an expression of advanced capitalism, "a field of stylistic and discursive heterogeneity without a norm," calls it "blank parody, a statue with blind eyeballs" (p. 65). But postmodernist intertextuality (is it the "same" one?) can also be thought of, for example in the British artist Mary Kelly's terms, as a sign of critical commitment to the contemporary world. According to Kelly, this commitment distinguished British postmodernist art of the 1970s and early 1980s from its American counterpart: whereas the Americans merely "purloined" previous images and "pilfered" the contemporary world's "cultural estate," the British were "exploring its boundaries, deconstructing its centre, proposing the decolonisation of its visual codes and of language itself."[27]

It is not clear from Kelly's comparison how one can distinguish, objectively, "mere pilfering" from political deconstruction and decolonization. Similarly, Jameson's recent attempt to distinguish the "ahistorical" postmodernism he deplores from its "homeopathic critique" in the works of E. L. Doctorow, works he admires and finds salutary, strikes me as dubitable at best.[28] So, for that matter, do all the other attempts that have been made to distinguish a "good" postmodernism (of resistance) from a "bad" postmodernism (what Lyotard calls the "anything goes" variety).[29]

It seems a good bet that almost any given work can be shown to belong to either of those categories, depending on how one reads it. Cindy Sherman's early work, the series of "Untitled Film Stills" from nonexistent Hollywood films (figs. 9, 10), which the artist interprets as being "about the fakeness of role playing as well as contempt for the domineering 'male' audience who would read the images as sexy,"[30] and which some critics have read in those terms as a form of feminist ironic critique, have been read by other critics as works that play up to the

9. Cindy Sherman, *Untitled Film Still #7*, 1978

10. Cindy Sherman, *Untitled Film Still #13*, 1978

"male gaze" for the usual profit: "the work seems a slicked-up version of the original, a new commodity. In fact, much of this work has proved quite salable, easy to show, easy to write about, easy to sell."[31] Even the "Third World" and "women of color," those brave new banners under which (together with feminism) the postmodernism of resistance has sought its political credentials, can be shown, if one is so inclined, to be caught up in the logic of the simulacrum and in the economics of multinational capitalism. In today's world, one can argue, there are no more places *outside*; the "Third World" too is part of the society of the spectacle.

Perhaps it all comes down, in the end, to how one understands Christine Brooke-Rose's evocative phrase about "sweeping the detritus of civilization." Does (can?) the sweeper hope to *clear* the detritus, or is she merely making new patterns with it and thus adding to the heap? And if the latter, should the sweeper put away her broom?

Yet another twist: If postmodernist intertextuality can be read both ways, that fact itself is open to interpretation. For Linda Hutcheon, it proves that postmodernist works are ambivalent and contradictory, "doubly encoded," and that they therefore constitute not a "break" but a "challenge to culture from within."[32] For Craig Owens, it proves that postmodernism is the true art of deconstruction, for it recognizes the "unavoidable necessity of participating in the very activity that is being denounced precisely in order to denounce it."[33] But one could call this apology for postmodernism itself part of a strategy of "anything goes," with the added proviso: "as long as I recognize that I am not innocent." This was already, in an ethical and existential perspective, the strategy of Camus's "penitent judge" in *La Chute* (1956): Clamence is more than willing to admit his own guilt, as long as it allows him to denounce everyone else. But Clamence is not exactly an admirable character.

And so it goes—the twists may be unending.

Does that mean we should no longer play?

Martha Rosler, who calls her work "didactic" but not "hortatory," and whom critics consider a political postmodernist, worries that if the ironic work is not "derived from a process of politicization, although it claims a politics," it will simply end up in the art-critical establishment, where even feminist work— which *has* been affiliated with a politics—may become no more than "just a competing style of the sixties and seventies . . . outdated by fashion."[34] I recognize in Rosler's worry the outlines of two old but apparently inexhaustible arguments: can art which claims an oppositional edge take the risk of entering a museum? Can it afford to be negative and individualistic, rather than offering a positive, collective "alternative vision" of "how things might be different"? (p. 72).

Related to these arguments is the question of the symbolic versus the real. Meaghan Morris recently criticized the facile uses that apologists for postmodernism have made of the verb "appropriate": "It outrages humanist commitments, adds a little *frisson* of impropriety and risk by romanticizing as violation the intertextual *sine qua non* of all cultural activity, and semantically guarantees a politics to practitioners by installing predation as the universal rule of cultural exchange . . . All energies become seizures and we all get a piece of the action."[35] Morris's critique is both humorous and apt: it *is* too easy to endow metaphorical appropriation with the power of real takeovers, and one *should* look for connections between "the politics of culture and the politics of politics" (p. 125). One should also, however, not belittle the value of symbolic interventions in the field of the real. Is it necessary to belabor the fact that language is part of the world (the "real world") and plays a non-negligible part in shaping both our perceptions of it and our actions in it?

And then there are those who believe only a certain kind of "real" can be political. Laura Kipnis, who identifies herself as a video artist and critic, dismisses all "first-world" writing that is not concerned with immediate political action—for example, French feminist theory—as an elitist luxury. "Real shifts in world power and economic distribution have little to do with *jouissance,* the pre-Oedipal, or fluids," she notes sarcastically.[36] (Sarcasm, as we know, is not to be confused with "blank" postmodern pastiche.) For Kipnis, if I read her right, the true postmodernist critique is an act of international terrorism in which "retaliation is taken, as has been announced, for 'American arrogance'"; and a truly new form of political struggle, which the West in its blindness has not recognized, is one "in which civilian tourists are held responsible for the actions of their governments" (p. 163).

This position, for all its hard-nosed charm, strikes me as too close for comfort to the murderous anti-intellectualism of commissars and other ayatollahs—or, since Kipnis is neither, to the traditional self-hatred of intellectuals who dream of getting their hands dirty.

Jeanette Winterson's *Boating for Beginners* is an outrageously blasphemous rewriting of the flood story from *Genesis.* It is also very funny. Has it escaped the censorious eyes of those who picket Scorsese's *Last Temptation of Christ* because it is "only a novel," by an author who is not a household name? Or because it is not "serious"? And yet, what could be more serious than the realization (if indeed it is true) that "there is no such thing as a true story"?

Postmodernism for postmodernism, politics for politics, I'd rather be an ironist than a terrorist.

To Market, to Market: Oppositional Art in Mass Culture

> The whole world is constrained to pass through the filter of the culture industry.
>
> —MAX HORKHEIMER AND THEODOR ADORNO, *DIALECTIC OF ENLIGHTENMENT*

Horkheimer and Adorno's pessimistic analysis of the power of the culture industry has become so much a part of contemporary intellectual discourse (to the point that it is almost itself a cliché, part of an anonymous "general wisdom") that one may wonder whether there is any new way to conceptualize the relation between authentic art and degraded entertainment, or between genuine thought and the manipulated thought-control of advertising and the mass media.[37] It is not that their argument hasn't been criticized for its elitism—it has been, by Andreas Huyssen among others. Furthermore, it can be criticized as a "grand narrative," explaining all of contemporary culture in terms of a single paradigm: the culture industry, in their analysis, appears to be a monolithic mechanism whose effects are omnipresent and inescapable.

Yet, the argument still has power; it is hard to get around. One possible conclusion to which their analysis leads has been stated by Thomas Crow, concerning the deep logic of innovative art since the mid-nineteenth century: "the avant-garde serves as a kind of research and development arm of the culture industry."[38] According to Crow (whose rich and complex argument would be worth following in detail), there exists a predictable pattern from Impressionism on, in which the avant-garde "appropriates" certain dynamic oppositional practices from "below," from marginal groups or subcultures (here Crow differs significantly from Horkheimer and Adorno); these practices, transformed into avant-garde invention, become, after a moment of productive tension between the "high" and the "low" (or between the oppositional and the institutional), simply a part of high art, but are eventually "recuperated" by the culture industry and returned to the lower zone of mass culture—in a form, however, where the avant-garde invention is "drained of its original force and integrity" (p. 258). This cycle, alternating between "moments of negation and an ultimately overwhelming recuperative inertia" (p. 259), accounts for the chronically problematic status of avant-garde art movements, which claim to want to have a real effect in the world but are always, in the end, "domesticated."

What hope is there for postmodernism, and specifically for feminist postmodernism, as an oppositional avant-garde practice? Quite possibly, not much—or not more than for previous avant-gardes. But that does not mean that the attempt is not worth making. Rozsika Parker and Griselda Pollock suggest that "feminism explores the pleasures of resistance, of deconstruction, of discovery, of defining, of fragmenting, of redefining."[39] Is it possible that such pleasures can be experienced by more than a privileged few and still maintain their critical charge? I think it is significant that a number of politically motivated experimental women artists working today have found some unexpected ways to *use* technologies associated with the culture industry.[40] Jenny Holzer's use of electronic signs in airports and other public places—such as the Spectacolor Board in Times Square, which flashed her message in huge letters (part of a series titled "Truisms"): PRIVATE PROPERTY CREATED CRIME—is one well-known example (fig. 11). Barbara Kruger, who has used billboards to display (and occasionally to transform into political posters) some of her photographs, usually shown in galleries and museums (figs. 12–15), has also used the Spectacolor Board, to display the message: I AM NOT TRYING TO SELL YOU ANYTHING.[41]

In an interview in 1985, Holzer explained: "My work has been designed to be stumbled across in the course of a person's daily life. I think it has the most impact when someone is just walking along, not thinking about anything in particular, and then finds these unusual statements either on a poster or on a sign."[42] In the same interview, Holzer mentioned her discovery that "television is not prohibitively expensive . . . You can buy 30 seconds in the middle of *Laverne & Shirley* for about seventy-five dollars, or you can enhance the *CBS Morning News* for a few hundred dollars. The audience is all of Connecticut and a little bit of New York and Massachusetts, which is enough people" (p. 297). Barbara Kruger, in turn, has stated that she works "with pictures and words because they have the ability to determine who we are, what we want to be, what we become."[43] While harboring no illusions about the alienating effects of television ("TV is an industry that manufactures blind eyes"), Kruger, like Holzer, seeks new ways to *use* it: for her, it is in the very "site of the stereotype," characteristic of TV representations, that "the rules of the game can be changed and subtle reformations can be enacted" (p. 304).

The hope expressed in such statements is that it is possible to find openings even in the monolithic mechanism of the culture industry; that it is possible for innovative, critical work to reach a large audience without passing through the "upward and downward" cycle analyzed by Crow, where what reaches the mass public is always already "evacuated cultural goods," deprived of force and integrity.

I am sure there must exist arguments to deflate this hope. But I will not look for them here.

11. Jenny Holzer, selection from *Truisms* ("Private property created crime"), Spectacolor Board, Times Square, N.Y., 1982

12. Barbara Kruger, *Untitled* ("We don't need another hero"), billboard, Queens, N.Y., 1989

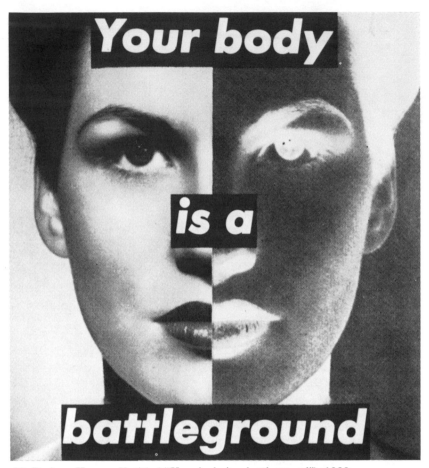

13. Barbara Kruger, *Untitled* ("Your body is a battleground"), 1989

Of Cyborgs and (Other) "Women": The Political Status of Decentered Subjects

> What kind of politics could embrace partial, contradictory, permanently unclosed constructions of personal and collective selves and still be faithful, effective—and, ironically, socialist feminist?
>
> —DONNA HARAWAY, "A MANIFESTO FOR CYBORGS"

The question asked by Donna Haraway sums up, as well as any could, what is at stake in the feminist embrace, but also in the feminist sus-

14. Barbara Kruger, *Untitled* ("Your body is a battleground"), poster, 1989

picion, of postmodernism.[44] Haraway, proposing the technological cyborg as an "ironic political myth" to take the place of earlier, naturalistic
myths of the goddess, celebrates the postmodernist model of "identity
out of otherness and difference"; she proclaims herself antiessentialist,
antinaturalist, antidualist, antimaternal, utopically "for a monstrous
world without gender" (p. 100). All of this ironically, and politically to
boot.

Next to such inventiveness, those feminists who want to hang on to

15. Barbara Kruger, *Untitled* ("Your body is a battleground"), series of posters on a wall, New York City, 1989

a notion of feminine specificity may look (in Naomi Schor's ironic self-characterization) like "wallflowers at the carnival of plural sexualities."[45] But the differences between worshipers of the goddess and celebrants of the cyborg may themselves need to be put into question.

"If authenticity is relational, there can be no essence except as a political, cultural invention, a local tactic," writes James Clifford.[46] Which makes me think that sometimes it is politic to "be" a goddess, at other times a cyborg—and at still other times, a laughing mother or an "alone-standing woman"[47] who sweeps the detritus of civilization.

Julia Kristeva's latest book, an exploration of what it means to be "foreign," recently reached the bestseller list in France—a country, Kristeva writes, which is both the best and the worst place to be an *étranger*. It is the worst, because the French consider everything that is not French "an unpardonable offense to universal taste";[48] it is the best, because (as Kristeva, being herself one, knows) in France a foreigner is a constant object of fascination, loved or hated, never ignored.

Of course it makes a difference (nor would Kristeva suggest otherwise) whether one feels loved or hated. It also makes a difference if one is actively persecuted for being "different." Still, for yet another ironic myth, I feel much drawn to her evocation of the "happy cosmopolitan," foreign not only to others but to him- or herself, harboring not an essence but a "pulverized origin." Such a person "transmutes into games what for some is a misfortune and for others an untouchable void" (p. 57). Which may not be a bad description of a feminist postmodernist.

As for politics, I don't hesitate to make my own ("appropriate" is the word) a message I recently found on a card sold at the Centre Georges Pompidou. The card is by Jamie Reid, the British artist whose work appeared on posters and jacket covers for the short-lived punk rock group the Sex Pistols. I bought it at the Paris opening of the exhibition on Situationism, a revolutionary movement of the 1960s that spurned museums (their chief spokesman was Guy Debord—he was not at the opening). Some of Reid's other work, ironic and anti-Thatcher, is shown in the exhibit.

The card is quite expensive, as cards go, and comes wrapped in cellophane; it is sold only in the museum. The picture on the cover shows Delacroix's *Liberty Leading the People,* against a background formed by four tilted modernist skyscrapers. The message reads (not exactly in this order): "Live in the Present. Learn from the Past. Look to the Future."

Notes

Introduction

1. "Editorial," *L'Infini*, 1 (1983), 3, 5. Here and throughout, translations from the French are my own, unless otherwise indicated.
2. Philippe Sollers, "Réponses," *Tel Quel*, 43 (1970), 76; A. Breton, *Manifestoes of Surrealism*, trans. Richard Seaver and Helen R. Lane (Ann Arbor: University of Michigan Press, 1969), p. 241. I discuss in some detail the complicated relations between *Tel Quel* and Surrealism in my essay "As Is," in *A New History of French Literature*, ed. Denis Hollier (Cambridge, Mass.: Harvard University Press, 1989).
3. P. Sollers, "Pourquoi j'ai été chinois" (interview with Shuhsi Kao), *Tel Quel*, 88 (1981), 13.
4. P. Sollers, "On n'a encore rien vu" (interview with Chowki Abdelamir), *Tel Quel*, 85 (1980), 20–21.
5. Sollers, "Pourquoi j'ai été chinois," p. 16.
6. Not by chance, that book dealt with a "closed" genre, whose distinguishing feature is the attempt to impose a single, unambiguous meaning on a given story, as its title indicates: *Authoritarian Fictions: The Ideological Novel as a Literary Genre* (New York: Columbia University Press, 1983).
7. Marcelin Pleynet, "Les problèmes de l'avant-garde," *Tel Quel*, 25 (1966), 82.
8. I find compelling, however, Sara Ruddick's argument that the *social category* of the "maternal" (which can be occupied by men as well as women, although in fact it is mostly occupied by women) carries with it certain specific, largely beneficial ways of thinking. See her essay "Maternal Thinking," *Feminist Studies*, 6, no. 2 (1980), 342–367; this essay forms the basis of Ruddick's recent book, *Maternal Thinking: Toward a Politics of Peace* (Boston: Beacon Press, 1989).

Prologue

1. Ludwig Wittgenstein, *Philosophical Investigations*, trans. G. E. M. Anscombe, 3d ed. (Oxford: Blackwell, 1972), paragraphs 66–70.
2. Gregory Bateson, *Steps to an Ecology of Mind* (San Francisco: Chandler Publishing Company, 1972), p. 1. Bateson's metalogues are on pp. 3–58.

3. Bruce Morrissette, "Games and Game Structures in Robbe-Grillet," *Yale French Studies*, 41 (1968), 159–167.
4. Warren F. Motte, Jr., *The Poetics of Experiment: A Study of the Work of Georges Perec* (Lexington, Ky.: French Forum Publishers, 1984). See also Claude Burgelin's recent study, *Georges Perec* (Paris: Editious du Seuil, 1989).
5. Samuel Beckett, *Malone Dies,* in *Three Novels by Samuel Beckett* (New York: Grove Press, Evergreen Black Cat edition, 1963), pp. 180, 182, 189.
6. Roger Caillois, *Les Jeux et les hommes* (Paris: Gallimard, 1967), p. 62 n.
7. Georges Bataille, "Sommes-nous là pour jouer ou pour être sérieux?" *Critique,* 51–52 (1951), 736, 740, 742–743.
8. D. W. Winnicott, *Playing and Reality* (New York: Basic Books, 1971), p. 64.
9. Jacques Derrida, "Structure, Sign, and Play in the Discourse of the Human Sciences," in *The Structuralist Controversy,* ed. Richard Macksey and Eugenio Donato (Baltimore: Johns Hopkins University Press, 1972), pp. 264–265 (name of translator not given).
10. Alain Robbe-Grillet, in discussion recorded in *Nouveau roman: Hier, aujourd'hui,* vol. 1, ed. Jean Ricardou and Françoise Van Rossum-Guyon (Paris: 10/18, 1972), p. 127.
11. Unnumbered foldout inserted as a separate text (*prière d'insérer*) in Robbe-Grillet, *Projet pour une révolution à New York* (Paris: Editions de Minuit, 1970). The passage quoted is on the last page.
12. Roland Barthes, *Le Plaisir du texte* (Paris: Editions du Seuil, 1973), pp. 60–61.
13. Roland Barthes, *Leçon* (Paris: Editions du Seuil, 1978), pp. 42–43.

1. A Double Margin

1. Theodor Adorno, *Aesthetic Theory,* trans. C. Lenhardt (London and New York: Routledge and Kegan Paul, 1984), p. 36.
2. Peter Bürger, *Theory of the Avant-Garde,* trans. Michael Shaw (Minneapolis: University of Minnesota Press, 1984), p. 61, and more generally chaps. 3 and 4. Bürger's pessimism about the adversary possibilities of the "neoavant-garde" of the 1960s corresponds, with some variations, to Fredric Jameson's pessimistic appraisal of the political potential of postmodernism, which I discuss in some detail in Chapter 8.
3. Andreas Huyssen, "The Search for Tradition: Avantgarde and Postmodernism in the 1970's," and "Mapping the Postmodern," in *After the Great Divide: Modernism, Mass Culture, Postmodernism* (Bloomington: Indiana University Press, 1986).
4. Rosalind Krauss, "The Originality of the Avant-Garde," in *The Originality of the Avant-Garde and Other Modernist Myths* (Cambridge, Mass.: MIT Press, 1985).
5. Charles Russell, *Poets, Prophets, and Revolutionaries: The Literary Avant-Garde from Rimbaud through Postmodernism* (New York: Oxford University Press, 1985); Renato Poggioli, *The Theory of the Avant-Garde,* trans.

Gerald Fitzgerald (Cambridge, Mass.: Harvard University Press, 1968).

6. The Situationist movement officially dissolved itself in 1972, after four-teen years of continuous existence culminating in their participation in the "events of May 1968." They are currently eliciting renewed interest among students of the avant-garde, however, and were the object of a recent exhibition in Paris, subsequently traveling to London and Boston. (For a frankly partial account of the movement's history, see J.-F. Martos, *Histoire de l'Internationale Situationniste* [Paris: G Lebovici, 1989]. For a sympa-thetic but detached overview, see Peter Wollen, "The Situationist Inter-national," *New Left Review,* 174 [March 1989], 67–95.) I discussed the demise of *Tel Quel* in the Introduction. The French women's movement, although showing some signs of an attempted revival (there was an im-pressive gathering of women scholars and activists in the Grand Amphi-théâtre de la Sorbonne, under the banner of "Etats Généraux des Femmes," on March 8, 1989), is generally considered to be over—and seems certainly to be over as a broadly based intellectual and artistic movement.

7. Alice A. Jardine, *Gynesis: Configurations of Woman and Modernity* (Ithaca: Cornell University Press, 1985), pp. 33–34; hereafter, page numbers are given in parentheses in the text.

8. Nancy K. Miller, "The Text's Heroine: A Feminist Critic and Her Fictions," *Diacritics,* 12, no. 2 (1982), 53. Reprinted in Miller, *Subject to Change: Reading Feminist Writing* (New York: Columbia University Press, 1988), p. 76.

9. Denis Hollier, "Collage," foreword to *The College of Sociology, 1937–1939,* ed. Hollier, trans. Betsy Wing (Minneapolis: University of Minnesota Press, 1988), p. xv.

10. Marguerite Duras and Xavière Gauthier, *Les Parleuses* (Paris: Editions de Minuit, 1974), p. 61; hereafter, page numbers are given in parentheses in the text. *Les Parleuses* has been published in English as *Woman to Woman* (Lincoln: University of Nebraska Press, 1987).

11. Interestingly, Duras continues to see herself as the object of misogyny and even, somehow, as in danger of not being recognized *in France,* despite her worldwide fame. See her interview with Alice Jardine and Anne Menke, excerpted in *Yale French Studies,* 75 (1988), pp. 238–240. Duras states: "The only thing that reassures me is the fact that I've become a bit of an international phenomenon now, and even a pretty big one. And what France won't do, other countries will. So I'm safe. But I have to speak in those terms. I am not safe in France. There my position is still shaky" (p. 239).

12. Rosalind Krauss, "Corpus Delicti," in R. Krauss and Jane Livingston, *L'A-mour Fou: Photography and Surrealism* (New York: Abbeville Press, 1985), p. 95; hereafter, page numbers are given in parentheses in the text.

13. It is true that the English language is partly responsible for this slippage, since "subject" can mean subject matter, a synonym for object of represen-tation. Krauss obviously knows the other, more "Gallic" meaning of "sub-ject" as agent of action, but she does not take it into account in this essay.

14. Hélène Cixous, "Le Rire de la Méduse," *L'Arc,* 61 (1975), 49; "The Laugh of the Medusa," trans. Keith Cohen and Paula Cohen, in *New French Feminisms,* ed. Elaine Marks and Isabelle de Courtivron (New York:

Schocken Books, 1981), p. 258; hereafter, page numbers are given in parentheses in the text. For further discussion of this essay, see Chapters 6 and 7.

15. The phrase "écriture à venir," "writing to come," is Maurice Blanchot's; its application to avant-garde writing (specifically, to Surrealist writing) was pointed out in a lecture by Denis Hollier at the 1987 Harvard Summer Institute on the Study of Avant-Gardes, which I codirected with Alice Jardine. For an excellent discussion of the manifesto as genre, see Marjorie Perloff, *The Futurist Moment,* chap. 3.

16. Julia Kristeva, *Des Chinoises* (Paris: Editions des Femmes, 1974), p. 47; and "Unes Femmes," *Cahiers du GRIF,* 12 (1975), 26. Kristeva's theory of the (male) avant-garde subject is most systematically laid out in *La Révolution du langage poétique* (Paris: Editions du Seuil, 1974); see also "Le Sujet en procès" (on Artaud), "L'Expérience et la pratique" (on Bataille), and "Polylogue" (on Sollers) in Kristeva, *Polylogue* (Paris: Editions du Seuil, 1977).

17. Kristeva, "Unes Femmes," p. 24.

18. This sense is confirmed by the large number of recent publications in France, emphasizing (usually in a celebratory perspective) the "return of the individual" and the end of the collective. This seems to be part of the general French turn away from "ideology," including the various ideological currents of the post-1968 decade. For a useful overview and sampling of current positions, see the special double issue of *Le Magazine Littéraire,* "L'Individualisme: Le grand retour," no. 264, April 1989.

19. Xavière Gauthier, prefatory remarks to "Le Surréalisme et la sexualité" (an excerpt from her book), in *La Femme Surréaliste,* special issue of *Obliques,* 14–15 (1977), 42. See Gauthier's *Surréalisme et sexualité* (Paris: Editions Gallimard, 1971).

20. See, for example, Mary Ann Caws, "Ladies Shot and Painted: Female Embodiment in Surrealist Art," in *The Female Body in Western Culture: Contemporary Perspectives,* ed. Susan Rubin Suleiman (Cambridge, Mass.: Harvard University Press, 1986), pp. 262–287; and Susan Gubar, "Representing Pornography: Feminism, Criticism, and Depictions of Female Violation," *Critical Inquiry,* 13, no. 4 (1987), 712–741.

21. See Whitney Chadwick, *Women Artists and the Surrealist Movement* (Boston: Little, Brown, 1985), the first comprehensive study of Surrealist women artists, lavishly illustrated; Jacqueline Chénieux, *Le Surréalisme et le roman* (Lausanne: L'Age d'Homme, 1983), which includes serious discussion of work by Surrealist women writers; and Gloria Feman Orenstein, "Reclaiming the Great Mother: A Feminist Journey to Madness and Back in Search of a Goddess Heritage," *Symposium,* 36, no. 1 (1982), 45–69, which discusses work by both women writers and artists. Chénieux and Orenstein contributed to the *Obliques* issue *La Femme Surréaliste.* Despite all this valuable work, no one has attempted until now a systematic reflection on the historical relation of women to the Surrealist movement and on implications of this relation for French literary and cultural history, as well as for a possible theory of the avant-garde.

22. Quoted in Maurice Nadeau, *Histoire du Surréalisme* (Paris: Editions du

Seuil, 1964), pp. 61–62, Aragon's emphasis; in English, *The History of Surrealism,* trans. Richard Howard (Cambridge, Mass.: Harvard University Press, 1989), p. 92. I have modified the translation somewhat—notably, I have put verbs in the present tense as they were in the original, published in 1924 and explicitly referring to the "here and now."

23. Robert Short, "Dada and Surrealism," in *Modernism, 1890–1930,* ed. Malcolm Bradbury and James McFarlane (Harmondsworth, Middlesex: Penguin Books, 1976), p. 303.

24. See Luce Irigaray, *This Sex Which Is Not One,* trans. Catherine Porter with Carolyn Burke (Ithaca: Cornell University Press, 1985), p. 84. The concept of "womanliness as masquerade" was proposed by Joan Rivière in 1929.

25. This painting should be compared with Magritte's famous 1926 painting, *Ceci n'est pas une pipe,* which shows a pipe accompanied by the inscription ("This is not a pipe") that gives the work its title. Although both paintings are playing with representation, they do so in diametrically opposed ways: the "reality" of the painted pipe is negated by the inscription, which highlights the difference between image and word, image and thing. The painted woman, on the contrary, is so "real" that she can *replace* the word that would be used to designate her. In the first instance, the differences between visual representation, language, and reality are emphasized; in the second, these differences are blurred—as if, where woman was concerned, the real, the imaginary, and the symbolic were interchangeable (for a male subject?).

26. Note that the cast of main characters has changed somewhat since 1924, owing to various exclusions and new arrivals to the movement. Clockwise from Breton (top center), the men are: Luis Bunuel, Jean Caupenne, Paul Eluard, Marcel Fourrier, René Magritte, Albert Valentin, André Thirion, Yves Tanguy, Georges Sadoul, Paul Nougé, Camille Goemans, Max Ernst, Salvador Dali, Maxime Alexandre, Louis Aragon.

27. Luce Irigaray, "Une lacune natale (pour Unica Zürn)," *Le Nouveau Commerce,* 62–63 (1985), 42. Irigaray's cryptic remark about "not leaving her *ulè* to maternity" would need to be explained and qualified, given that for so many contemporary women writers—including Irigaray herself—the maternal body has provided a fertile source of imagery and inspiration; one of the major texts by a woman Surrealist, Leonore Carrington's *The Hearing Trumpet,* is based on a complicated playing with and valorization of the mother's body and the mother's *voice,* as I argue in Chapter 7.

28. Carrington was the only woman included in the original version of Breton's *Anthologie de l'humour noir* (1939). Her works currently in print include *The Hearing Trumpet* (San Francisco: City Lights Books, 1985), which I discuss at length in Chapter 7, and two recent volumes that bring together her shorter works from the 1930s through the 1970s: *The House of Fear: Notes from Down Below* (New York: E. P. Dutton, 1988) and *The Seventh Horse and Other Tales* (New York: E. P. Dutton, 1988). Carrington is particularly interesting in that she wrote both in French and English (and even a few stories in Spanish). By Unica Zürn, see *L'Homme-Jasmin* (Paris: Editions Gallimard, 1971) and *Sombre printemps* (Paris: Belfond, 1985), with a biographical postface by Ruth Henry. For an interesting discussion of Zürn's work and its relation to Hans Bellmer's see Renée Riese-Hubert,

"Portrait d'Unica Zürn en anagramme," *Pleine Marge*, 7 (June 1988), 61–73.

29. Neither Mansour nor Prassinos is included in Michael Benedikt's supposedly comprehensive anthology in English, *The Poetry of Surrealism: An Anthology* (Boston: Little, Brown, 1974); nor do they appear in Paul Auster's more recent bilingual anthology, *The Random House Book of Twentieth-Century French Poetry* (New York: Vintage Books, 1984). Benedikt's anthology, covering two generations of Surrealists, includes no work by women; Auster's, covering the whole century, includes one woman: Anne-Marie Albiach. In France Gisèle Prassinos's *Les Mots endormis* (Flammarion, 1967) and *Trouver sans chercher* (Flammarion, 1976), containing selections from her poetry of the 1930s as well as some later work, are in print; she also has a number of novels and collections of stories written in a "post-Surrealist" mode. The first book-length study on her work appeared in 1988: Madeleine Cottenet-Hage, *Gisèle Prassinos, ou, Le Désir du lieu intime* (Paris: Jean-Michel Place). As of January 1989, all of Mansour's numerous books are out of print (though some can still be found in specialized bookstores). They include: *Cris* (Paris: Seghers, 1953); *Les Gisants satisfaits* (Paris: J.-J. Pauvert, 1958); *Rapaces* (Paris: Seghers, 1960), and *Carré blanc* (Paris: Le Soleil Noir, 1965). *Rapaces* is available in a shortened bilingual edition in the United States: *Birds of Prey*, trans. Albert Herzing (Perivale Press, 1979).

30. Belen's comic, erotic novel, *Mémoires d'une liseuse de draps* (Paris: J.-J. Pauvert, 1974) is currently available; her shorter fiction has recently been collected in a single volume, under her own name: Nelly Kaplan, *Le Réservoir des sens* (Paris: J.-J. Pauvert, 1988).

31. See Irigaray, *This Sex Which Is Not One*, p. 76. As Irigaray suggests, mimicry may be only an "initial phase," a first strategy adopted traditionally by the oppressed. This raises the question of how one might go beyond mimicry, to other possible strategies not based on an ironic relation to a preexisting situation.

32. See M. M. Bakhtin, *The Dialogic Imagination*, ed. Michael Holquist, trans. Caryl Emerson and Michael Holquist (Austin: University of Texas Press, 1981), pp. 282ff.

33. Gloria Feman Orenstein, "Towards a Bifocal Vision in Surrealist Aesthetics," *Trivia*, 3 (Fall 1983), 72. The quoted phrase is actually from Elaine Showalter's essay "Feminist Criticism in the Wilderness," in *Writing and Sexual Difference*, ed. Elizabeth Abel (Chicago: University of Chicago Press, 1980).

34. Just how invisible the Surrealist women were twenty years ago is demonstrated by William Rubin's otherwise still very useful book (the catalogue of a major exhibition at the Museum of Modern Art) *Dada, Surrealism, and Their Heritage* (New York: Museum of Modern Art, 1968). Among the dozens of artists mentioned by Rubin, the only woman is Méret Oppenheim, whose fur-covered teacup (1936) is perhaps the best-known Surrealist object. It has also been, almost invariably, the *only* work by Oppenheim mentioned or displayed in books or exhibits on Surrealism.

35. See Sandra Gilbert and Susan Gubar, "Tradition and the Female Talent" in *The Poetics of Gender,* ed. Nancy K. Miller (New York: Columbia University Press, 1986), pp. 183–207, as well as their book *No Man's Land,* vol. 1, *The War of the Words* (New Haven: Yale University Press, 1987). For an informative historical study, devoted chiefly to English and American women modernists in exile, see Shari Benstock, *Women of the Left Bank: Paris, 1900–1940* (Austin: University of Texas Press, 1986).

36. For a very useful, complete listing of Surrealist journals published in France between 1948 and 1972, see Marguerite Bonnet and Jacqueline Chénieux-Gendron, *Revues surréalistes françaises autour d'André Breton, 1948–1972* (Millwood, N.Y.: Kraus International Publications, 1982). For an account of the political evolution of Surrealism, more detailed than Nadeau's though not contradicting any of his analyses, see Helena Lewis, *The Politics of Surrealism* (New York: Paragon House, 1988). It is almost touching to note that there exists, in the late 1980s, a Surrealist group in Chicago that publishes collective declarations. A leader of the group, Franklin Rosemont, has edited a selection of Breton's writings in English, with a book-length introduction which, although adulatory toward Breton and truculent toward almost everyone else, provides a good indication of a certain American strain of Surrealism. See André Breton, *What Is Surrealism? Selected Writings,* ed. and introduced by Franklin Rosemont (Chicago: Monad Press, 1978).

37. Reproduced in Maurice Nadeau, *Histoire du Surréalisme* (Paris: Editions du Seuil, 1964), pp. 422–432. A 1934 declaration, opposing the Fascist demonstrations of February 6 and calling for a united front of workers and intellectuals against Fascism, contained three women's signatures (Nadeau, pp. 381–386). However, this was not a specifically Surrealist declaration like "Du temps que les surréalistes avaient raison." I did not find women's signatures on any document, prior to 1934, reproduced in Nadeau's book. The English translation of *Histoire du surréalisme* includes many fewer documents than the original French edition.

38. On the role of women editors, see Benstock, *Women of the Left Bank,* chap. 10. Interestingly, there *were* women artists and performers participating in the early days of various Dada movements (even though they were generally ignored by later historians): Sophie Tauber and Emmy Hennings in Zurich, Hanna Höch in Berlin, among others. Could we then see French Surrealism as already a defensive reaction to the rise of "avant-garde women"? Alternatively, given the heavily literary orientation of the French movement in its early years, the relevant category here is that of writing and "literary women" in France, which I discuss below.

39. Prassinos's first volume of poetry and prose texts, *La Sauterelle arthritique,* was published in 1935, when she was fifteen years old, with a preface by Paul Eluard. J. H. Matthews, in his long and interesting study *The Imagery of Surrealism* (Syracuse: Syracuse University Press, 1977), quotes Eluard's preface but has nothing to say about Prassinos. He does devote half a page to Mansour, however; and he subsequently published a short monograph on her work: *Joyce Mansour* (Amsterdam: Rodopi, 1985).

40. Mary Blume, "Portrait of a Surrealist," *International Herald Tribune,* August 17, 1987, p. 14.

41. Most of the first generation male Surrealists were born around the turn of the century: Breton in 1896, Aragon in 1897, Eluard in 1895, Desnos in 1900, Ernst in 1891, Man Ray in 1890, Bellmer in 1902. Of the women, only Valentine Hugo was older (born in 1887); Toyen (1902) and Agar (1904) were around the same age. The other women who came to Surrealism before 1945 were at least a decade younger: Maar was born in 1909, Tanning in 1912, Oppenheim in 1913, Carrington in 1917, Fini in 1918, Prassinos in 1920.

42. There were, to be sure, some young male disciples—notably Jean Schuster, who became Breton's literary executor (Schuster's writings are collected in *Archives 57/68* [Paris: Eric Losfeld, 1969]), and José Pierre, who now codirects (with Jacqueline Chénieux-Gendron) a research group on Surrealism at the Centre National de la Recherche Scientifique and is a leading member of ACTUAL, an association devoted to collecting, preserving, and gradually publishing the archives of Surrealism. In general, the work of postwar male Surrealists (in contrast to the women's work) strikes me as oriented more toward preservation of the "archive" than toward making a major contribution to it, or better still, transforming it.

43. Christine Brooke-Rose, "Illiterations," in *Breaking the Sequence: Women's Experimental Fiction,* ed. Ellen G. Friedman and Miriam Fuchs (Princeton: Princeton University Press, 1989), p. 65.

44. In this respect, the contrast with Situationism (whose dynamic years were 1958–1968) is quite striking, for the Situationists appear to have been even more of a "men's club" than the Surrealists. Whereas the Surrealists, even in their early years, privileged women as intermediaries in their quest for self (like Nadja for Breton—see Chapter 5) or as partners, even if not fully equal partners, in the adventure of *amour fou,* the Situationists seem to have ignored women altogether—except perhaps as sex objects in the most banal sense. A full exploration of the differences between Surrealism and Situationism as avant-garde movements, including (but not restricted to) the place they accorded to women would be extremely interesting.

45. Annie Le Brun expresses outrage and anger at the feminist critique in her collections of essays *Lâchez tout* (Paris: Le Sagittaire, 1977) and *A Distance* (Paris: Pauvert/Carrère, 1984). Dorothea Tanning is represented only by a letter of refusal in Vergine's *L'Autre Moitié de l'avant-garde* and is absent altogether from the *Obliques* special issue *La Femme Surréaliste.*

2. Aggressions and Counteraggressions

1. Poggioli, *The Theory of the Avant-Garde,* p. 30.

2. *Tel Quel* was always critical of Surrealism—but as I have argued elsewhere, its very criticism may be read as a symptom of its "repetition" of Surrealism's political and aesthetic trajectory. See my essay "As Is," in *A New History of French Literature,* ed. Denis Hollier.

3. "Programme" first appeared in *Tel Quel,* 31 (Fall 1967), and was reprinted

as the opening essay in Sollers's *Logiques* (Paris: Editions du Seuil, 1968). The sentences I quote are on p. 12.

4. See Jean Ricardou, *Problèmes du nouveau roman* (Paris: Editions du Seuil, 1967), and *Pour une théorie du nouveau roman* (Paris: Editions du Seuil, 1971), for his most polemical statements. Two later books published by Editions du Seuil (*Le Nouveau Roman*, 1973, and *Nouveaux problèmes du roman*, 1978) emphasize the analytical rather than the polemical. In recent years, Ricardou's influence as an explicator of the *nouveaux romanciers* has waned; indeed, several among them (Pinget, Simon, Robbe-Grillet) have publicly distanced themselves from his interpretations.

5. See, for example, Roland Barthes, *S/Z* (Paris: Editions du Seuil, 1970); Gérard Genette, "Vraisemblance et motivation," in *Figures II* (Paris: Editions du Seuil, 1969); Susan Rubin Suleiman, *Authoritarian Fictions: The Ideological Novel as a Literary Genre* (New York: Columbia University Press, 1983); Philippe Hamon, "Qu'est-ce qu'une description?" *Poétique*, 18 (1974), 215–235; Henri Mitterand, *Le Discours du roman* (Paris: Presses Universitaires de France, 1980); and *Poétique*, 16, a special issue devoted to "le discours réaliste."

6. Denis Ferraris, "Quaestio de legibilibus aut legendis scriptis: Sur la notion de lisibilité en littérature," *Poétique*, 43 (September 1980), 283; hereafter, page numbers are given in parentheses in the text.

7. Roland Barthes, *Sollers écrivain* (Paris: Editions du Seuil, 1979), p. 69. To call *H* a novel may seem to be stretching the term beyond recognition; yet, the subtitle *Roman* appears conspicuously on the cover of the book. Sollers, like other practitioners of *le scriptible*, seems to take delight in precisely the kind of stretching-beyond-recognition that is involved here. For a rigorous analysis of transgressive narrative procedures in Robbe-Grillet, Sollers, and Roche, see Christine Brooke-Rose, "Transgressions: An Essay-say on the Novel Novel Novel," *Contemporary Literature*, 19, no. 3 (Summer 1978), 378–407.

8. Barthes, *Sollers écrivain*, p. 69.

9. Roland Barthes, *S/Z*, trans. Richard Miller (New York: Hill and Wang, 1974), p. 4. Here and in subsequent quotations from *S/Z*, I have modified Miller's translation; in particular, I have translated *lisible* and *scriptible* as "readable" and "writable," whereas Miller renders them as "readerly" and "writerly." I prefer the more literal translations for both theoretical and linguistic reasons. Subsequent page references to *S/Z* are given in parentheses in the text.

10. Tzvetan Todorov, "La réflexion sur la littérature dans la France contemporaine," *Poétique*, 38 (April 1979), 131–148.

11. Interestingly enough, David Lodge concludes that Barthes's "plural" reading of Balzac is a "triumphant vindication of the classic text," since it can support such a reading. See Lodge, *The Modes of Modern Writing: Metaphor, Metonymy, and the Typology of Literature* (Ithaca: Cornell University Press, 1977), p. 68.

12. Quoted in Naomi Schor, *Reading in Detail: Aesthetics and the Feminine* (New York and London: Methuen, 1987), p. 43. Schor's observation that

in classical aesthetics details and decadence are associated with femininity is on p. 22.

13. It may appear that I am overstating the case here, for Barthes nowhere explicitly associates the "writable" text with masculinity or maleness, whereas he does associate the "readable" text with femaleness. In the essay on Sollers I have quoted, he speaks positively about the predominance of the word over the sentence in Sollers's text (an indication of his preference for the "decadent" style) and associates the sentence with the Law. My own sense is that for Barthes the "writable" text, and even more clearly its later avatar, the text of *jouissance,* is associated with a perverse son who defies the Father's law. Such a text is therefore coded as "male" not in the paternal (repressive) sense, but in the filial, (polymorphously?) perverse sense. For an extended discussion of perversion as a figure in male avant-garde practice, see Chapter 7, especially the section "Parody, Perversion, Collage: Surrealists at Play."

14. Roland Barthes, *The Pleasure of the Text,* trans. Richard Miller (New York: Hill and Wang, 1975), p. 37; *Le Plaisir du texte* (Paris: Editions du Seuil, 1973), p. 60. As my reader will notice, this is a passage I have found crucial to my thinking throughout this book. I will quote part of it again, though in a different context, in the next chapter—and will allude to it yet again in Chapter 7.

15. Roland Barthes, in discussion with Alain Robbe-Grillet and others, in *Pré-texte: Roland Barthes,* proceedings of a *décade de Cerisy* held in 1977, ed. Antoine Compagnon (Paris: 10/18, 1978), p. 266.

16. Barthes, *The Pleasure of the Text,* p. 3 (*Le Plaisir du texte,* pp. 9–10).

17. Alain Robbe-Grillet, *Le Miroir qui revient* (Paris: Editions de Minuit, 1984), and *Angélique ou l'enchantement* (Paris: Editions de Minuit, 1987). Robbe-Grillet calls these works "Romanesques," not quite novels but not straight autobiography either. Nevertheless, they correspond to the auto-biographical genre at least in the minimal sense defined by Philippe Le-jeune: the narrator who says "I" has the same name as the author whose name appears on the cover (see Lejeune, *Le Pacte autobiographique* [Paris: Editions du Seuil, 1975]).

18. The distinction between *nouveau roman* and *nouveau nouveau roman,* first proposed by Jean Ricardou and others at the 1971 *décade de Cerisy,* is a slender one. According to Ricardou the *nouveau roman,* or "first phase" *nouveau roman,* "contests" traditional narrative, whereas the *nouveau nou-veau roman* goes further and "subverts" it. In the former, one can manage to reconstruct a certain unity of the story; in the latter, such reconstruction is no longer possible (see J. Ricardou, *Le Nouveau Roman,* p. 139). By that definition, Robbe-Grillet's early novels (especially *Les Gommes* and *Le Voyeur*) belong to the first category, whereas his later novels (beginning with *La Maison de rendez-vous*) belong to the second. The distinction can also be seen, if one adopts Brian McHale's categories, as one between "modernist" and "postmodernist" fiction. According to McHale, modernist fiction is "dominated by epistemological issues" (there is a story, it's a matter of knowing how to reconstruct it), whereas postmodernist fiction is "domi-

nated by ontological issues" (there is no coherent story to reconstruct, only a collision of multiple "possible worlds") (see McHale, *Postmodernist Fiction* [New York and London: Methuen, 1987]). Despite some local disagreements, I find McHale's distinction quite persuasive.

19. See Bruce Morrissette, *Les Romans de Robbe-Grillet* (Paris: Editions de Minuit, 1963). It should be said that Morrissette's readings of Robbe-Grillet have evolved considerably since that early study. See his *Novels of Robbe-Grillet* (Ithaca: Cornell University Press, 1975), a revised, updated, and expanded vesion of the earlier work.

20. Robbe-Grillet, "Order and Disorder in Film and Fiction," *Critical Inquiry,* 4, no. 1 (Autumn 1977), 17.

21. This view, although never stated as such, is implicit in Jean Ricardou's book, *Le Nouveau Roman* (Paris: Seuil, 1973), in which he deals with the work of seven "new novelists" including Robbe-Grillet. See also Vicki Mistacco, "The Theory and Practice of Reading *Nouveaux Romans:* Robbe-Grillet's *Topologie pour une cité fantôme,*" in *The Reader in the Text: Essays on Audience and Interpretation,* ed. S. Suleiman and I. Crosman (Princeton: Princeton University Press, 1980), pp. 371–400.

22. See, for example, Morrissette, *Les Romans de Robbe-Grillet; Robbe-Grillet: Colloque de Cerisy,* ed. Jean Ricardou, 2 vols. (Paris: 10/18, 1976); Mistacco, "The Theory and Practice of Reading *Nouveaux Romans*"; the chapters devoted to Robbe-Grillet in Stephen Heath, *The Nouveau-Roman: A Study in the Practice of Writing* (Philadelphia: Temple University Press, 1972); Leon Roudiez, *French Fiction Today* (New Brunswick: Rutgers University Press, 1972); *Nouveau roman: Hier, aujourd'hui,* ed. J. Ricardou and F. Van Rossum-Guyon, 2 vols. (Paris: 10/18, 1972); Ricardou, *Le Nouveau Roman;* Inge Crosman Wimmers, *Poetics of Reading: Approaches to the Novel* (Princeton: Princeton University Press, 1988). And so on.

23. Poggioli, *The Theory of the Avant-Garde,* p. 56.

24. *Boston Globe,* January 19, 1989, p. 82.

25. *Prétexte: Roland Barthes,* p. 253.

26. Roche's commentary on *Codex,* made in an interview with David Hayman, is instructive: "In *Codex* there is a sort of *cantus firmus* more or less hidden by literary objects which would seem to be foreign to it" (interview in *SubStance,* 17 [1977], 9). Although I do not consider this an invitation to unearth the hidden melody by throwing out the pile of "foreign" objects among which it is hidden, it does seem to be an invitation to notice *both* the melody and the "noises" that surround it.

27. Maurice Roche, *Compact* (Paris: Seuil, 1966), p. 156; hereafter page numbers are given in parentheses in the text.

28. Laurent Jenny, "La Stratégie de la forme," *Poétique,* 27 (1976), 270.

29. The term "isotopy," first proposed by the structural semantician A. J. Greimas, designates a redundant semantic category within a text; it is because of such redundancies that texts have semantic coherence.

30. Jenny, "La Stratégie de la forme," p. 271.

31. Actually, that is exactly what one finds in the publisher's "blurb" advertising the English translation of *Compact* (by Mark Polizzotti): after noting that

the work is "composed—as if a musical score—of six intertwining narratives (each distinguished by its own voice, tense, and typeface)," the blurb moves into a straight narrative mode: "It is the story of a blind man living in a city of his own imagining. Confined to his deathbed . . ." As publishers know, stories sell books more effectively than "musical scores." (Advertising flyer for *Compact,* by The Dalkey Archive Press, October 1988.)

32. In fact, I do make this argument at some length in my reading of Robbe-Grillet's *Projet pour une révolution à New York,* in the next chapter.

3. Reading Robbe-Grillet

1. Jean Ricardou, "La fiction flamboyante," in *Pour une théorie du nouveau roman* (Paris: Editions du Seuil, 1971), pp. 211–233. Ricardou's dismissal of the journalist Pierre Bourgeade is on p. 227. Subsequent page references to Ricardou's essay are given in parentheses in the text. All page references to *Projet pour une révolution à New York* (Paris: Editions de Minuit, 1970) are given in the text, as are page numbers for the English translation: *Project for a Revolution in New York,* trans. Richard Howard (London: Calder and Boyers, 1972). I have occasionally modified Howard's translation.

2. See Bruce Morrisette's pioneering study, *Les Romans de Robbe-Grillet* (Paris: Editions de Minuit, 1963); J. Ricardou, *Le Nouveau Roman* (Paris: Editions du Seuil, 1973); L. Roudiez, *French Fiction Today* (New Brunswick: Rutgers University Press, 1972); Heath, *The Nouveau Roman: A Study in the Practice of Writing.* For Robbe-Grillet's own comments on his works, see *Pour un nouveau roman* (Paris: Editions de Minuit, 1963), as well as his numerous interventions at the 1971 *décade de Cerisy* devoted to the *nouveau roman,* published as *Nouveau roman: Hier, aujourd'hui,* 2 vols. (Paris: 10/18, 1972).

3. Morrissette, *Les Romans de Robbe-Grillet,* new ed. (Paris: Editions de Minuit, 1971), p. 284.

4. Ricardou's book *Le Nouveau Roman* appeared in the popular "Ecrivains de toujours" ("Writers for always") series of the Editions du Seuil.

5. Heath, *The Nouveau Roman,* p. 134.

6. For the Freudian definition of fantasy, see J. Laplanche and J.-B. Pontalis, *Vocabulaire de la psychanalyse* (Paris: Presses Universitaires de France, 1973), p. 153: "Imaginary scenario in which the subject is present and which figures, with more or less distortion due to defensive processes, the realization of a desire, in the last instance of an unconscious desire." See also Catherine Clément, "De la méconnaissance: Fantasme, texte, scène," *Langages,* 31 (1974), 36–52. Clément defines fantasy as a "fixed form whose elements change"—in other words, as a *structure.*

7. The notion of intertextuality, first elaborated (though not named as such) by the Russian critic Mikhail Bakhtin (see esp. *Rabelais and His World,* trans. Helen Iswolsky [Cambridge: MIT Press, 1968]), was introduced into contemporary critical theory by Julia Kristeva (see *Séméiotikè: Recherches pour une sémanalyse* [Paris: Editions du Seuil, 1969], pp. 115,

133–137, 255–257, and *passim*). "Intertextuality" may be defined as the presence, either explicit (as in direct quotation, identified as such) or implicit (as in allusion, parody, imitation) of one text in another. In the case of an implicit intertext, the perception of the intertext depends on the literary experience and competence of the reader; in *Projet*, the Sadean intertext is implicit.

8. Ricardou, *Pour une théorie du nouveau roman*, pp. 20–22.

9. When I speak of avoidance, I am not suggesting that no one until now has mentioned the presence of sado-erotic elements in *Projet*, and in Robbe-Grillet's work in general. That is emphatically not the case. What I mean is that Robbe-Grillet's most sympathetic and most knowledgeable critics (we excluded the category of "naive" and simply moralizing critics at the outset) have tended either to gloss over the sado-erotic material as a personal "quirk" on Robbe-Grillet's part, or else to rationalize it in various ways. In psychoanalytic terms, the phenomenon is that of negation: the presence of sado-erotic material is acknowledged, but its importance and significance in the text are denied.

10. Alain Robbe-Grillet, "Sur le choix des générateurs," in *Nouveau roman: Hier, aujourd'hui*, vol. 2 (Paris: 10/18, 1972), pp. 157–162. Robbe-Grillet did not mention Ricardou's name in connection with *vocables producteurs*, but the examples he gave—*rouge, rogue,* orgue (p. 157)—clearly point to Ricardou's essay, published shortly before the Cerisy *décade*.

11. Robbe-Grillet, "Sur le choix," p. 159.

12. See "Le Sadisme contre la peur," interview with Robbe-Grillet published in *Le Nouvel Observateur*, October 19, 1970. A revised version of the interview in essay form was inserted separately into the first edition of *Projet pour une révolution à New York*.

13. In his recent autobiographical works, Robbe-Grillet has stated unambiguously (indeed, with a touch of humorous defiance) that the sado-erotic fantasies in his works are his own. But he also maintains his argument that their effect is cathartic, both for himself and for the reader. See *Angélique ou l'enchantement* (Paris: Editions de Minuit, 1987), pp. 189–215. In these pages Robbe-Grillet is quite ironic toward his feminist critics, but he tends to confuse all feminist criticism with a narrow-minded moralizing—as if he knew it more by hearsay (in terms of negative stereotypes especially prevalent in France) than through first-hand acquaintance.

14. For a useful discussion of the term *mise en abyme*, or internal reduplication, see Bruce Morrissette, "Un Héritage d'André Gide: La Duplication intérieure," *Comparative Literature Studies*, 8, no. 2 (1970), 125–142. For detailed analyses of the *nouveaux romanciers*' use of the *mise en abyme* and its variants, see Jean Ricardou, *Le Nouveau Roman*, pp. 47–75. For a whole book devoted to this device, see Lucien Dällenbach, *Le Récit spéculaire: Essais sur la mise en abyme* (Paris: Editions du Seuil, 1977).

15. If I have dwelt at such length on Ricardou's essay, it is not only because he is among the most intelligent analysts of Robbe-Grillet's novels, but also because, a practicing novelist in his own right, Ricardou has become the foremost theoretician and codifier of the aesthetics of the *nouveau roman*.

His influence on other critics is, justifiably, enormous—all the more reason why any "revisionist" reading must begin with a critique of Ricardou.

16. Sigmund Freud, "The Relation of the Poet to Day-Dreaming" (1908), reprinted in *On Creativity and the Unconscious* (Harper Torchbooks, 1958), pp. 44–54.

17. Norman Holland, *The Dynamics of Literary Response* (New York: Oxford University Press, 1969), p. 189.

18. In some instances the scene presents the state of the victim *after* the aggression has been completed (e.g., the blond Claudia lying in a pool of blood: Fr. pp. 142–143; Eng. p. 118), rather than the act of aggression itself. This is simply a variant, however, and in no way alters the basic structure of the fantasy. The description of the victim is always couched in terms that make clear what has been done to her, thus maintaining the aggressive act but putting it into the (recent) past.

19. In a much earlier scene, in which the Narrator rapes the blond adolescent Laura, the victim's reaction is described in similarly ambiguous terms: she whimpers, but not only out of fear, according to the Narrator. At the end, her "shining curls" move back and forth on the pillow more and more rapidly, "until long successive spasms run through her entire body . . . Her flesh was warm and sweet, her limbs were quite limp, the joints obedient" (p. 11)—"jusqu'à ce que de longs spasmes successifs lui traversent tout le corps . . . Sa chair était tiède et douce, ses membres avaient leurs articulations toutes molles, complaisantes" (p. 19).

20. Roland Barthes, *Sade, Fourier, Loyola* (Paris: Editions du Seuil, 1971), pp. 27, 28, 127–128.

21. D. A. F. de Sade, *Juliette, ou, Les Prospérités du vice* (Paris: 10/18, 1969), pp. 174–177.

22. Gilles Deleuze, *Présentation de Sacher-Masoch* (Paris: 10/18, 1967), p. 58.

23. Sade, *Juliette*, pp. 92–93.

24. Nancy Miller, "*Juliette* and the Posterity of Prosperity," *L'Esprit Créateur*, Winter 1975, 416.

25. Apollinaire, in an often-cited statement, claimed that Sade was a liberator of women (see F. Laugaa-Traut, *Lectures de Sade* [Paris: Armand Colin, 1973], p. 180). This view has been persuasively contested of late, however, chiefly by women critics. See Miller, "*Juliette* and the Posterity of Prosperity"; and C. Claude, "Une lecture de femme," *Europe*, October 1972, 64–70.

26. Barthes, *Sade, Fourier, Loyola*, p. 36.

27. Catherine Clément, "De la méconnaissance: Fantasme, texte, scène," *Langages*, 31 (1974), 37.

28. Barthes, *Sade, Fourier, Loyola*, p. 37.

29. One finds the same structure in Sade's *120 Jours de Sodome*, where the "historiennes" address their stories to the four "maîtres," to whom they are totally subordinated; the express purpose of the stories is to "feed" the sexual imagination of the masters. And then there is Scheherazade . . .

30. Barthes, *Le Plaisir du texte*, p. 60; *The Pleasure of the Text*, p. 37.

31. My discussion in this and the following paragraph is based on the excellent

article by J. Laplanche and J.-B. Pontalis, "Fantasme originaire, fantasme des origines, origine du fantasme," *Les Temps Modernes,* April 1964, 1833–68.

32. Freud, *Gesammelte Werke,* X, 242. Quoted in French by Laplanche and Pontalis, "Fantasme originaire," pp. 1850–51.

33. This possibility is not raised by Laplanche and Pontalis, and Freud's own writings do not deal with it either. The area is sufficiently unexplored, however, to allow for such a hypothesis.

34. Deleuze, *Présentation de Sacher-Masoch,* pp. 58–59; my emphasis.

35. Sade, *Les Infortunes de la vertu* (Paris: 10/18, 1968), p. 67.

36. Jane Gallop, "Sade, Mothers, and Other Women," paper discussed at the MLA Seminar "Sade and Women," San Francisco, 1975. Gallop, who today is known as more than "a Sade specialist," has included this paper in her recent book of essays *Thinking through the Body* (New York: Columbia University Press, 1988).

37. See "The Most Prevalent Form of Degradation in Erotic Life" (1912), reprinted in Freud, *Sexuality and the Psychology of Love,* ed. Philip Rieff (New York: Collier Books, 1963), pp. 58–70.

38. The "historiennes" of *120 Journées de Sodome* do, it is true, tell invented tales. But they are only second-level narrators, and their role within the fiction is precisely to tell tales. The frame-story, told by the omniscient narrator, is presented as "real."

39. Serge Doubrovsky, *La Place de la Madeleine* (Paris: Mercure de France, 1974), p. 157.

40. Ibid., p. 158.

41. Harold Bloom, *The Anxiety of Influence* (New York: Oxford University Press, 1973), p. 5.

42. For a recent explicative essay that tries to take into account feminist readings like mine, see Inge Crosman Wimmers, "Toward a Reflexive Act of Reading: Robbe-Grillet's *Projet pour une révolution à New York,*" in *Poetics of Reading* (Princeton: Princeton University Press, 1988), pp. 121–153. My only reservations about Wimmers's detailed and intelligent reading is that it is perhaps a bit too "respectful" toward the text, a bit too carefully "balanced." I believe that women critics can learn from women poets and novelists about the virtues of irreverence (see Chapter 7).

4. Transgression and the Avant-Garde

1. The works by Georges Bataille referred to in this paragraph are: "La morale de Miller," *Critique,* 1, no. 1 (1946), 3–17; *L'Erotisme* (Paris: Editions de Minuit, 1957); *La Littérature et le mal* (Paris: Editions Gallimard, 1957); *L'Expérience intérieure* (Paris: Editions Gallimard, 1943). Sartre's essay, "Un nouveau mystique," is reprinted in his *Situations,* vol. 1 (Paris: Editions Gallimard, 1947), pp. 143–188.

2. Actually, it was preceded by an even earlier publication, never mentioned by Bataille: a pious pamphlet published in 1918, celebrating the cathedral of Reims, which had been bombed by the Germans. This essay, *Notre-*

Dame de Reims, discovered only after Bataille's death, appears as an appendix to Bataille's *Oeuvres complétes,* vol. 1 (Paris: Editions Gallimard, 1970). It is reprinted and commented on in detail by Denis Hollier in his *La Prise de la Concorde: Essai sur Georges Bataille* (Paris: Editions Gallimard, 1974). *Histoire de l'oeil* is in *Oeuvres complètes,* I, 13–78; *Madame Edwarda* is in *Oeuvres complètes,* vol. 3 (Paris: Editions Gallimard, 1971).

3. *Histoire de l'oeil* was first published in a private edition (134 copies) in 1928, under the pseudonym "Lord Auch." New, equally limited editions appeared in 1940 and 1941; although all three editions were published in Paris, the second and third gave Burgos and Seville as places of publication, respectively. The work appeared for the first time under Bataille's name in 1967, five years after his death (published by Editions J.-J. Pauvert). *Madame Edwarda* has a similar publishing history, and two other well-known works, *Ma mère* and *Le Mort,* were published only posthumously (in 1966 and 1967, respectively). The only two novels Bataille himself published under his own name are *Le Bleu du ciel* and *L'Abbé C.*

4. For a transcription of the trial, see *L'Affaire Sade* (Paris: J.-J. Pauvert, 1957). Bataille was one of those testifying, unsuccessfully, on behalf of the publisher and in defense of Sade as a significant writer.

5. Paradoxically, Bataille remained virtually unknown to English-speaking readers until very recently, despite his enormous influence on French theorists who have had a wide and long-standing audience in England and in the United States. Over the past few years, however, Bataille's works have entered the American intellectual scene. See, in particular, the important volume of his selected writings in English, *Notions of Excess: Selected Writings, 1927–1939,* ed. Allan Stoekl, trans. A. Stoekl with Carl R. Lovitt and Donald M. Leslie, Jr. (Minneapolis: University of Minnesota Press, 1985). See also Michele H. Richman, *Reading Georges Bataille: Beyond the Gift* (Baltimore: John Hopkins University Press, 1982), the first book on Bataille to be published in English; and Allan Stoekl's *Politics, Writing, Mutilation: The Cases of Bataille, Blanchot, Roussel, Leiris, and Ponge* (Minneapolis: University of Minnesota Press, 1985). Denis Hollier's excellent book, *La Prise de la Concorde,* has recently been translated into English (University of Minnesota Press, 1990).

6. Michel Foucault, "Présentation," in Bataille, *Oeuvres complètes,* I, 5.

7. Philippe Sollers, "Pourquoi Artaud, pourquoi Bataille," in *Artaud,* ed. P. Sollers (Paris: 10/18, 1973), pp. 9–12.

8. Susan Sontag, "The Pornographic Imagination," in *Styles of Radical Will* (New York: Delta, 1981), p. 44; hereafter, page numbers are given in parentheses in the text.

9. Philippe Sollers, "Le Toit," in *L'Ecriture et l'expérience des limites* (Paris: Editions du Seuil, 1968), p. 122.

10. Jacques Derrida, "De l'économie restreinte à l'économie générale," in *L'Ecriture et la différence* (Paris: Editions du Seuil, 1967), p. 404.

11. Roland Barthes, "La métaphore de l'Oeil," in *Essais critiques* (Paris: Editions du Seuil, 1964), p. 244. This essay was first published in *Critique,* August–September 1963, in the commemorative issue devoted to Bataille after his death.

12. See Derrida, "De l'économie restreinte à l'économie générale," pp. 404–405: "The greatest force is that of a writing [*écriture*] which, in the most audacious transgression, continues to maintain and to recognize the necessity of the system of prohibitions (knowledge, science, philosophy, work, history, etc.). Writing is always traced between these two sides of the limit." I will return to the implications of this paradoxically conservative view at the end of this essay.

13. Derrida, "De l'économie restreinte à l'économie générale," pp. 373–384.

14. Ibid., pp. 392, 383–384.

15. Kristeva, "L'expérience et la pratique," in *Polylogue*, p. 123. This essay was first published in the proceedings of the 1972 *décade de Cerisy*.

16. Maurice Blanchot, "L'expérience limite," in *L'Entretien infini* (Paris: Editions Gallimard, 1969), p. 301.

17. Andrea Dworkin, *Pornography: Men Possessing Women* (New York: Perigee, 1981); Anne-Marie Dardigna, *Les Châteaux d'Eros, ou, Les Infortunes du sexe des femmes* (Paris: Maspero, 1981).

18. The essay on *L'Erotisme*, "Le Toit," was first published in *Tel Quel* (1967), then collected in *Logiques* (Paris: Editions du Seuil, 1968), and reprinted in *L'Ecriture et l'expérience des limites*. The essay on *Ma mère*, "Le Récit impossible," appeared in *Logiques* but was not reprinted in *L'Ecriture et l'expérience des limites*.

19. The only sustained commentary on one of Bataille's pornographic works by a well-known textual critic is Lucette Finas's book on *Madame Edwarda*, *La Crue* (Paris: Editions Gallimard, 1972). Finas's line-by-line reading, based on a principle of dictionary-inspired free associations to Bataille's text, is extremely interesting and takes greater account of the representational content of the work than does Barthes's reading of *Histoire de l'oeil*. Finas's main emphasis, however, remains textual; what interests her chiefly is the way "*Madame Edwarda* [as] narrative is constituted by this effort, always disappointed, to envelop Her by him" (p. 219).

In a somewhat different vein, one might also mention Brian Fitch's monograph, *Monde à l'envers, texte réversible: La Fiction de Georges Bataille* (Paris: Lettres Modernes, 1982), devoted exclusively to Bataille's novels. Fitch's elegant readings analyze the various forms of self-reflexive doubling in Bataille's fiction; but Fitch specifically excludes the question of eroticism and erotic representation, on the grounds that "Bataillian eroticism" is an experience to be understood only by reading the theoretical essays, not the novels! (p. 48). Here then is yet another reading of Bataille, a "strictly literary," formalist reading that manages to exclude even the metaphoric notion of transgression central to the textual reading. Bataille is shown to be a highly inventive, self-conscious writer—but one is tempted to say, "So what?"

20. This display was visual as well as verbal in the first (1928) edition of *Histoire de l'oeil*, which contained—printed on heavy paper in large format—eight original lithographs by André Masson, illustrating some of the more "scandalous" scenes. (I saw this edition at the Houghton rare book library at Harvard University.) It is only a small step, after this, to associate the textual critics' "averting of the gaze" with the aversion traditionally inspired

by the Medusa's head, which, the myth tells us, had the power to turn men to stone—and which, Freud has told us, is a symbolic representation of the female genitals. I shall argue later that the son's problematic seeing of the mother's genitals is centrally inscribed in *Histoire de l'oeil*, which may then turn out to be a *mise en abyme* of the problematic "seeing" practiced by its critics. In a different perspective, Teresa de Lauretis has related Medusa to the question of female subjectivity and female seeing/spectatorship; see her *Alice Doesn't: Feminism, Semiotics, Cinema* (Bloomington: Indiana University Press, 1984), pp. 109–111, 136, and *passim*. My thanks to Nancy Miller for calling this work to my attention, and for reminding me about the beautiful Gorgon.

21. Derrida, "De l'économie restreinte à l'économie générale," p. 372.

22. Dworkin, *Pornography,* p. 167; hereafter page numbers are given in parentheses in the text.

23. Gérard Genette, *Introduction à l'architexte* (Paris: Editions du Seuil, 1979); also *Palimpsestes: La Littérature au second degré* (Paris: Editions du Seuil, 1982).

24. *Histoire de l'oeil,* in *Oeuvres complètes,* I, 13–14: "Je restai quelque temps devant elle, immobile, le sang à la tête et tremblant pendant qu'elle regardait ma verge raide tendre ma culotte. Alors je me couchai à ses pieds sans qu'elle bougeât et, pour la première fois, je vis sa chair 'rose et noire' qui se rafraîchissait dans le lait blanc." This is the text of the 1928 edition, which Bataille revised extensively in 1940. The English translation, by Joachim Neugroschel (New York: Berkley Books, 1982) follows the original version. The translations here are my own.

25. During the discussion that followed the delivery of an earlier version of this essay at the International Poetics Conference at Columbia University (November 1984), Michael Riffaterre suggested that Simone's dipping her genitals in the plate of milk (which the text says was there for the cat, *le chat*) is already inscribed in the word *chat,* which, similar to the English "pussy," has an obscene slang meaning in French. This would therefore, he concluded, be simply an example of Bataille's play with language, for "what she does, after all, is put her *chat* in its natural place, in the milk." The interpretation is ingenious, but whether the shock value or pornographic force of Simone's action is thereby diminished is highly debatable.

26. Sollers made a somewhat similar remark apropos of a sentence in *Ma mère,* noting that the result of such incongruous juxtapositions "will be all the more effective, the greater the spread between the noble aspect (thought) and the inavowable (excrement, sex)" ("Le récit impossible," in *Logiques,* p. 160). In fact, this may be a particular variation on the Surrealist theory of metaphor, founded on the idea of incongruous juxtaposition; for a discussion of the link between this aesthetic theory and what I call the "figure of perversion" (Bataille being a case in point), see Chapter 7, "Parody, Perversion, Collage: Surrealists at Play."

27. It is unfortunate that the English translation by Joachim Neugroschel mitigates Bataille's stylistic transgression by rendering "rose et noire" as "pink and dark." There are some other problems with the translation as well (e.g.,

"cunt" for the less specific term "cul"). Dworkin's reading is based on the English version—but even so, it is reductive. For another discussion of "the pink and the black" in Bataille, see Denis Hollier, "Bataille's Tomb: A Halloween Story," *October,* 33 (Summer 1985), 80ff.

28. The violence of such a metaphoric equation is made explicit in René Magritte's painting, *Le Viol* (*The Rape,* 1934), which represents a woman's face, the eyes being her breasts, the nose her navel, and the mouth her pubis. The shock provoked by a first viewing of the painting is considerable. It is reproduced in color in Robert Hughes, *The Shock of the New* (New York: Knopf, 1982), p. 150. Here again, Bataille's affinity with Surrealist aesthetics is evident.

29. The fact that both of the main characters are adolescents is significant, since adolescence is that period when experimentation with sexual roles is part of a more general search for the self. In both cases, the search is intimately bound up with an awareness of the (parental) Law and the possibilities of its infraction. This is repeatedly emphasized in *Histoire de l'oeil.* I consider the Oedipal implications of the fiction later in this chapter.

30. Dardigna, *Les Châteaux d'Eros,* pp. 312–313. Dardigna's book was published several years after my essay on Robbe-Grillet. The fact that we arrived at our somewhat similar conclusions independently adds to their weight, I believe.

31. See Georges Bataille, "Kafka," in *La Littérature et le mal* (Paris: Editions Gallimard, 1957), pp. 173–196; also Simone de Beauvoir, *Faut-il brûler Sade?* (Paris: Editions Gallimard, 1955). One sometimes hears (or even reads) people who have not read Beauvoir's book, but know her as a feminist, scoffing at her "inquisitorial" stance. It is therefore worth emphasizing that Beauvoir did not ask the question about burning seriously (to ask it seriously is already to show who one is) and indeed recognized fully Sade's importance as a thinker, representing a kind of absolute noncompromise that Beauvoir admired.

32. In *Les Châteaux d'Eros,* Dardigna devotes several interesting chapters to detailed readings of Pierre Klossowski's trilogy, *Les Lois de l'hospitalité.* But in her latest book, a full-length study of Klossowski's oeuvre, Dardigna has virtually abandoned the feminist perspective that gave an edge to her earlier work. (See Dardigna, *Pierre Klossowski: L'Homme aux simulacres*). Are respect for and "total immersion" in a writer's work somehow incompatible with critical distance and judgment? A question worth pondering, especially by feminist critics.

33. Bataille, *Oeuvres complètes,* I, 77; Bataille's emphasis. This passage, as well as the whole second part of *Histoire de l'oeil,* has generally been read as straight autobiography, testifying to Bataille's tormented childhood. (See, for example, Michel Surya, *Bataille: La Mort à l'oeuvre* [Paris: Librairie Séguier, 1987]—a biography which bases most of its account of Bataille's early years on this text.) Whether Bataille is speaking here in his own name or not, the fact is that part 2 (titled "Coincidences") has the same textual status as part 1 (titled "Récit"): it is set in the same type and is in no way marked as being "different" in truth value from the first part. Although the

reference, in the sentence I quote, to the title of the work as a whole suggests that its *author* (rather than an invented character) is speaking, this indication is complicated by the fact that the work was signed with a pseudonym—its author was therefore also "invented." At any rate, there is at least as much justification for reading part 2 as part of the fiction as there is for reading it as straight autobiography.

34. See Sigmund Freud, "The Case of the Wolf-Man," in *The Wolf-Man by the Wolf-Man*, ed. Muriel Gardiner (New York: Basic Books, 1971), pp. 181–191, 214–230.

35. Denis Hollier, in a rich analysis of the father-son relation in Bataille and of its political and psychological implications, has suggested that the son's deepest desire may be a "glorious castration," at once violent and incestuous, at the hands of the father (Hollier, "La Tombe de Bataille," unpublished manuscript). In that case, the mother becomes superfluous, and indeed Hollier suggests as much. Is the elimination of the mother, and *a fortiori* of female subjectivity, the "real" logic of Oedipus? For a far-ranging feminist critique of the Oedipal narrative, viewed as the single most powerful narrative model in patriarchal culture, see De Lauretis, *Alice Doesn't*, chap. 5. For an analysis of the Oedipal logic that leads to the male child's violent repudiation of the mother, see Jessica Benjamin, "The Bonds of Love: Rational Violence and Erotic Domination," *Feminist Studies*, 6, no. 1 (Spring 1980), 144–174.

36. Kristeva, "L'expérience et la pratique," p. 121.

37. See, for example, the passage I quoted from Derrida, in n. 12. The question of whether, and to what extent, the theory of *écriture* is "revolutionary," or even genuinely subversive, is part of the general current debate regarding the politics of the "posts": postmodernism, poststructuralism, deconstruction. I discuss some aspects of the debate in Chapter 8.

38. Harold Bloom, *A Map of Misreading* (New York: Oxford University Press, 1975), p. 33.

5. Love Stories

1. Shoshana Felman, "Women and Madness: The Critical Phallacy," *Diacritics*, 5, no. 4 (1975), 2–10; hereafter, page numbers are given in parentheses in the text.

2. Michel Beaujour, "Qu'est-ce que *Nadja?*" *La Nouvelle Revue Française*, 172 (1967), 794.

3. Breton, *Nadja*, rev. ed. (Paris: Editions Gallimard, Folio edition, 1964); Breton's preface is dated "Noël 1962." Hereafter, page references to this French text are given in parentheses in the text. The translations are my own, but I have consulted with profit Richard Howard's translation of the 1928 edition (New York: Grove Press, 1960). One of Breton's more extended commentaries on *Nadja* is in his volume of interviews, *Entretiens* (Paris: Editions Gallimard, 1969).

4. See, for example, Marguerite Duras and Michelle Porte, *Les Lieux de Marguerite Duras* (Paris: Editions de Minuit, 1979), p. 90. Duras mentions *Lol V. Stein* in just about all of her autobiographical writings, including

L'Amant (Paris: Editions de Minuit, 1984), La Vie matérielle (Paris: P.O.L., 1987), and other recent works.

5. See Chapter 1, where I discussed Duras's identification of her writing as at once "feminine" (in the sense of écriture féminine as that term was used in the mid-1970s) and "totally revolutionary, totally avant-garde."

6. There is at least one important feature that differentiates Dora from the other two texts: it is a factual, clinical case history, whereas Nadja and Le Ravissement de Lol V. Stein are "literature"; and between these two texts there is a difference too, for Le Ravissement clearly presents itself as fiction (the author is a woman, the narrator is a man), whereas Nadja explicitly rejects the fictional mode and claims to tell "nothing but the truth" (although not all the truth) about Breton's life. These generic distinctions, although not insignificant, are not relevant to my present argument. For a good sampling of commentaries and a detailed bibliography on Dora, see Charles Bernheimer and Claire Kahane, eds., In Dora's Case: Freud—Hysteria—Feminism (New York: Columbia University Press, 1985). Hélène Cixous wrote a play based on Freud's case history, Portrait de Dora (Paris: Editions des Femmes, 1976), which has been staged by the avant-garde feminist director Simone Benmussa. (English translation by Anita Barrows, "Portrait of Dora," in Diacritics, Spring 1983, 2–32.) The experimental film Sigmund Freud's Dora (1979), by Tyndall, McCall, Pajaczkowska, and Weinstein, is discussed by E. Ann Kaplan in Women and Film: Both Sides of the Camera (New York and London: Methuen, 1983), chap. 11.

7. See, for example, Jean-Louis Houdebine, "Méconnaissance de la psychanalyse dans le discours surréaliste," Tel Quel, 46 (1971), 67–82. In its effort to distinguish itself from Surrealism, Tel Quel came down heavily on what it perceived to be the Surrealists' (especially Breton's) misunderstanding of Freud and Marx. Although much of their criticism is persuasive, one should also read it (as I suggest in my essay "As Is") with an eye to the context in which it was elaborated. Jean Starobinski has argued that Breton was in fact closer to the French psychiatrist Charcot (with whom Freud studied) than to Freud (see Starobinski, "Freud, Breton, Myers," in La Relation Critique [Paris: Editions Gallimard, 1970], pp. 320–341). My reading of Nadja will bear out that point.

8. Shoshana Felman, "Turning the Screw of Interpretation," Yale French Studies, 55–56 (1977), 94–207.

9. Peter Brooks, "Constructions psychanalytiques et narratives," Poétique 61 (1985), 63–74; hereafter, page numbers are given in parentheses in the text.

10. Annie Reich, Psychoanalytic Contributions (New York: International University Press, 1973); quoted in Donald P. Spence, Narrative Truth and Historical Truth: Meaning and Interpretation in Psychoanalysis (New York: Norton, 1982), p. 188.

11. Spence, Narrative Truth and Historical Truth, p. 284; hereafter, page numbers are given in parentheses in the text.

12. Jacques Lacan, Le Séminaire, XI: Les Quatre Concepts fondamentaux de la psychanalyse (Paris: Editions du Seuil, 1973), p. 210.

13. Sigmund Freud, Dora: An Analysis of a Case of Hysteria (New York: Collier

Books, 1963), p. 32; hereafter, page numbers are given in parentheses in the text. In *The Standard Edition of the Complete Psychological Works of Sigmund Freud,* ed. James Strachey et al., 24 vols. (London: Hogarth Press, 1953–1974), the Dora case appears in vol. 7 under the title "Fragment of an Analysis of a Case of Hysteria."

14. Steven Marcus, "Freud and Dora: Story, History, Case History," in his *Representations: Essays on Literature and Society* (New York: Random House, 1975), p. 278. A shortened version of this essay is reprinted in *In Dora's Case,* ed. Bernheimer and Kahane.

15. Freud, "The Case of the Wolf-Man," esp. pp. 191–203. For an excellent discussion, see Peter Brooks, "Fictions of the Wolf-Man: Freud and Narrative Understanding," in his *Reading for the Plot: Design and Intention in Narrative* (New York: Knopf, 1984), pp. 264–285.

16. Sigmund Freud, "The Dynamics of Transference," in *Therapy and Technique,* ed. Philip Rieff (New York: Collier, 1963), p. 114.

17. Jacques Lacan, "Intervention on Transference," trans. Jacqueline Rose, in *In Dora's Case,* ed. Bernheimer and Kahane, pp. 92–104.

18. Herr K., much older than Dora, was the husband of Dora's father's mistress. In the "scene by the lake," which occurred when Dora was sixteen, he openly propositioned her, and she slapped him. He, his wife, and Dora's father all denied the truthfulness of her account of the scene by the lake. Dora's anger stemmed partly from her sense that she was being used as a pawn by the three adults. Although Freud refused to cooperate with Dora's father, who asked him to "bring her to reason," his insistence that she loved Herr K. could have been interpreted by Dora in that light.

19. Marcus, "Freud and Dora," p. 307.

20. An even simpler, although not altogether implausible explanation would be that Freud was aware all along of "the other story" but chose consciously not to pursue it with Dora, either because of a cultural prejudice against lesbianism (he didn't want to give her ideas) or for aesthetic reasons: he didn't want to confuse things by offering her "alternative stories" that might, in addition, delay the cure. The problem with this explanation is that Freud would then have to have been less than honest in his encounters with Dora, a conclusion I do not wish to draw.

21. Jerre Collins et al., "Questioning the Unconscious: The Dora Archive," in *In Dora's Case,* ed. Bernheimer and Kahane, p. 248.

22. *The Complete Letters of Sigmund Freud to Wilhelm Fliess, 1887–1904,* ed. and trans. Jeffrey Moussaieff Masson (Cambridge, Mass.: Harvard University Press, 1985), p. 434; my emphasis. Freud mentions finishing the manuscript "yesterday" in his letter of January 25, 1901 (p. 433).

23. Neil Hertz, "Dora's Secrets, Freud's Techniques," in *In Dora's Case,* ed. Bernheimer and Kahane, p. 234; hereafter, page numbers given in parentheses in the text.

24. Freud, *Complete Letters,* p. 374.

25. Freud, *Dora,* pp. 119–120; I have modified the translation somewhat to conform more closely to the original German.

26. I thank Dorrit Cohn for helping me to analyze this passage in German and

for providing me with the original text. See Freud, "Bruchstück einer Hysterie-Analysie," *Studienausgabe*, vol. 6 (Frankfurt: S. Fischer, 1971), pp. 166–167.

27. This slip has been noted, in a different context of argumentation, by Madelon Sprengnether; see her "Enforcing Oedipus: Freud and Dora," in *In Dora's Case*, ed. Bernheimer and Kahane, 66.

28. Breton, *Entretiens*, p. 139.

29. See P. L. Palau, *Les Détraquées*, in *Le Surréalisme, Même*, 1 (1956), 73–120; the passages quoted are on pp. 116 and 109–110. The postface by Palau gives the original date of the play's production as 1921. In his original text, Breton refers to its "authors," in the plural, but he evidently knew only about Thiéry, not about Babinsky. I discuss Babinsky below.

30. See Elizabeth Roudinesco, *La Bataille de cent ans: Histoire de la psychanalyse in France*, vol. 1 (Paris: Ramsay, 1982), pp. 68–69. For this and other information about the history of French psychoanalysis, Roudinesco's work (including the second volume, chiefly on Lacan, which was published in 1986) is invaluable.

31. André Breton and Louis Aragon, "Le Cinquantenaire de l'hystérie," *La Révolution Surréaliste*, 11 (1928), 20.

32. Sigmund Freud, "Further Recommendations in the Technique of Psychoanalysis: Observations on Transference-Love" (1915), in Freud, *Therapy and Technique*, ed. Philip Rieff (New York: Collier Books, 1963), pp. 167–180.

33. For recent selections from the *Leçons*, see J. B. Charcot, *L'Hystérie: Textes choisis et présentés par E. Trillat* (Toulouse: Privat, 1971), and *Leçons de mardi à la Salpêtrière* (Paris: Centre d'étude et de promotion de la lecture, 1975). The *présentation de cas* has remained a central teaching procedure in French psychiatry down to our own day and was used by Lacan as well. Lacan, however, did not address remarks to his public about the patient in the latter's presence. For an example of a Lacanian case presentation, see "A Lacanian Psychosis: Interview by Jacques Lacan," in *Returning to Freud: Clinical Psychoanalysis in the School of Lacan*, ed. Stuart Schneiderman (New Haven: Yale University Press, 1980), pp. 19–41.

34. Marguerite Bonnet, *André Breton: Naissance de l'aventure surréaliste* (Paris: J. Corti, 1975), p. 375.

35. Anna Balakian, *André Breton: Magus of Surrealism* (New York: Oxford University Press, 1971), p. 114.

36. Bonnet, *André Breton*, p. 401.

37. Roger Shattuck, "The Nadja File," *Cahiers Dada/Surréalisme*, 1 (1966), 55.

38. Gloria Orenstein, "*Nadja* Revisited: A Feminist Approach," *Dada/Surrealism*, 8 (1978), 94.

39. In saying this, I do not mean to endorse the view (expressed, for example, by Anna Balakian) that Nadja may never have existed, may have been simply invented by Breton—or that if she did exist, it was still likely that "the poetization of the irrational world of Nadja is Breton's rather than that of the little, uneducated waif he met by chance" (Balakian, *André Breton*,

p. 112). My own bracketing of the "real Nadja" means to suggest, rather, that the interesting subject is the *couple* of "the poet and the madwoman," even if only as seen and reported by the former.

40. Breton, *Entretiens*, pp. 141–142. Interestingly, Breton goes on to compare his relation to Nadja to the one that existed between the late nineteenth-century hypnotist Théodore Flournoy and the medium Hélène Smith, whom Flournoy observed and wrote about. Here again, as in the 1962 preface to *Nadja*, Breton is placing himself in the position of scientific observer.

41. She was also poor, and a prostitute on occasion. This introduces the important element of class and social respectability into her relations with Breton, who, despite his ideological hatred of the bourgeoisie, was unmistakably a member of that class and lived as such. Jean-Louis Houdebine remarks that Breton "missed" not only Freud's epistemological revolution but that of Marx as well. (See n. 7 above.)

42. Marguerite Duras, *Le Ravissement de Lol V. Stein* (Paris: Editions Gallimard, Folio edition, 1964); hereafter, page numbers are given in parentheses in the text.

43. Jacques Lacan, "Hommage fait à Marguerite Duras, du *Ravissement de Lol V. Stein*," in M. Duras, et al., *Marguerite Duras* (Paris: Editions Albatros, 1979), p. 133; hereafter, page numbers are given in parentheses in the text.

44. Interestingly, one thing Lacan nowhere mentions is that Jacques Hold is a doctor. Could this have been Lacan's own avoidance of the entanglements of transference?

45. It seems to me that some of the recent feminist readings of this novel fall into the trap of the too easy summary, treating Jacques Hold as a "macho villain" who destroys Lol by violating her privacy. Martha Noel Evans (in *Masks of Tradition: Women and the Politics of Writing in Twentieth-Century France* [Ithaca: Cornell University Press, 1988]) goes so far as to speak of literal rape: according to her, Jacques rapes Lol on the night of their lovemaking at T. Beach (p. 140). For Evans, "Jacques Hold's narrative embodies the principles and values of male literary tradition, [which] includes a territorial, if not proprietary, notion of language, an authoritarian concept of authorship" (p. 140). Not only do I think that Jacques Hold does not fit this description, but I also do not believe that there exists a single, monolithic "male tradition" characterized by an "authoritarian concept of authorship." The whole project of male avant-garde writing, as I have discussed it in earlier chapters, can be said to contest and complicate the "authoritarian concept of authorship"—which does not mean that male avant-garde writers have not been sexist in their ideology. Complicated, indeed—and for that very reason, requiring more subtle treatment than a simply hostile feminist indictment.

46. Marcelle Marini, *Territoires du féminin: Avec Marguerite Duras* (Paris: Editions de Minuit, 1977), p. 31.

47. See, in this regard, Duras's conversations with Xaviére Gauthier, *Les Parleuses*, which I discussed briefly in Chapter 1.

48. This view comes close to the one expressed by Michèle Montrelay, at the end of her essay on *Le Ravissement*. Montrelay suggests that what Duras "wants for the men who inhabit her books" is to "bring them back to a 'feminine' kind of *jouissance*, from which they have been exiled" (Montrelay, *L'Ombre et le nom: Sur la féminité* [Paris: Editions de Minuit, 1977], p. 21). Montrelay's reading, generally cited as "Lacanian," does not insist on the feminist implications of "what Duras wants," but they are implicit in her analysis.

49. J. Lacan, *Le Séminaire, XX: Encore* (Paris: Editions du Seuil, 1975), p. 132. The sentences quoted at the beginning of this paragraph, about "le rapport sexuel," are on pp. 17, 36.

50. I have been asked, by some who read an earlier version of this essay in manuscript, whether I am "advocating a Laingian approach where the therapist 'shares' in the patient's madness." In fact, I am in no position to advocate any approach at all *for* psychoanalysis or psychoanalysts; I can only suggest, speaking as an outsider, what aspects of psychoanalytic discourse strike me as more or less appealing, more or less relevant to feminist thinking about sexual difference and about narrative. My reading of Lacan is itself unorthodox, tending to "feminize" Lacan's discourse as Duras feminizes Jacques Hold's. But Lacan, like Duras's narrator/lover, lends himself quite readily to such takeovers. After finishing this essay, I was pleased to see this view of Lacan confirmed and developed by Jane Gallop, in her *Reading Lacan* (Ithaca: Cornell University Press, 1985).

6. The Politics and Poetics of Female Eroticism

1. The recent decisions of the United States Supreme Court, eroding those laws, confirm the fact that much more is at stake in the abortion issue than the specific question (itself already highly political) of who controls a woman's body. That question, as has once again been made clear, is implicated with larger social, political, and ethical questions concerning the nature of the family, the responsibility for the welfare of children, and the role of women in the active population, among others.

2. Shere Hite, *The Hite Report: A Nationwide Study of Female Sexuality*, new revised edition (New York: Dell, 1981), p. 60.

3. See Kate Millett, *Sexual Politics* (New York: Avon Books, 1971), pp. 3–8.

4. Erica Jong, *Fear of Flying* (New York: Signet, 1974), p. 30; hereafter, page references to this edition are given in parentheses in the text.

5. Patricia Meyer Spacks, "Fiction Chronicle" (review of *Fear of Flying*), *Hudson Review*, 27, no. 2 (1974), 284.

6. Millicent Dillon, "Literature and the New Bawd," *Nation*, February 22, 1975, p. 220.

7. Claudine Herrmann, *Les Voleuses de langue* (Paris: Editions des Femmes, 1976).

8. Anonymous review of *Fear of Flying*, London Observer, March 28, 1976, p. 29.

9. Rita Mae Brown, *Rubyfruit Jungle* (New York: Bantam Books, 1977), p. 199.

10. Nancy Huston, *Mosaique de la pornographie* (Paris: Denoel/Gonthier, 1982), p. 87. See also Robert Scholes, "Uncoding Mama: The Female Body as Text," in Scholes, *Semiotics and Interpretation* (New Haven: Yale University Press, 1982), pp. 127–142.

11. For an excellent general discussion of the lesbian novel in English, see Catharine R. Stimpson, "Zero Degree Deviancy: The Lesbian Novel in English," *Critical Inquiry*, 8, no. 2 (1981), 363–379. Stimpson discusses two major patterns in lesbian fiction: "the narrative of damnation" or guilty lesbianism, whose prototype is Radclyffe Hall's *The Well of Loneliness;* and the narrative of "the lesbian's rebellion against social stigma and self-contempt," a more recent trend of which *Rubyfruit Jungle* may be considered an example. I find it interesting, however, that Brown's heroine never has to "rebel against self-contempt," for she is self-assured and non-guilt-ridden from the beginning. This is in marked contrast to the more predictable "guilt–self-acceptance" pattern of a somewhat more recent lesbian novel, Noretta Koertge's *Who Was That Masked Woman?* (New York: St. Martin's Press, 1981).

12. In a just-published essay, Larry McCaffery contrasts *Fear of Flying* and other popular novels of the early 1970s with Kathy Acker's fiction—noting that 1973 was also the year Acker published her first novel, *The Childlike Life of the Black Tarantula,* which went almost completely unnoticed (McCaffery, "Kathy Acker and 'Punk' Aesthetics," in *Breaking the Sequence: Women's Experimental Fiction,* ed. Ellen G. Friedman and Miriam Fuchs [Princeton: Princeton University Press, 1989], pp. 215–230). The "avant-garde vs. mass market" distinction is pertinent; still, as I have tried to suggest, the assimilation by the mass market of potentially (or "momentarily") subversive gestures is itself culturally significant. And besides, if Kathy Acker's work can be considered as part of the "punk" aesthetic, that aesthetic itself has strong links to the market—as is obvious in the case of music (Patti Smith, Jim Morrison, the Sex Pistols), if less so in that of literature.

13. This term became popular after the publication of the important anthology edited by Elaine Marks and Isabelle de Courtivron, *New French Feminisms: An Anthology* (New York: Schocken Books, 1981).

14. Luce Irigaray, *Ce Sexe qui n'en est pas un* (Paris: Editions de Minuit, 1977), p. 28; hereafter, page numbers are given in parentheses in the text.

15. For detailed commentaries on this text, see Carolyn Burke, "Introduction to Luce Irigaray's 'When Our Lips Speak Together,'" *Signs*, 6, no. 1 (1980), 66–68; and Jane Gallop, "*Quand Nos Lèvres S'écrivent:* Irigaray's Body Politic," *Romanic Review*, 74, no. 1 (1983), 77–83.

16. Carolyn Burke, "Irigaray through the Looking Glass," *Feminist Studies*, 7, no. 2 (1981), 288–306. Jane Gallop has emphasized the potentially revolutionary, or at least revisionary, role of metaphor, especially the metaphor (actually, as she points out, a catachresis) of the lips, in Irigaray's conception of both "feminine writing" and female sexuality (see Gallop, "*Quand Nos Lèvres S'écrivent*").

17. See Jane Gallop, *The Daughter's Seduction: Feminism and Psychoanalysis* (Ithaca: Cornell University Press, 1982), p. 74. In an even more recent book, *Ethique de la différence sexuelle* (Paris: Editions de Minuit, 1984), Irigaray reaffirms the necessity of women's actively creating a "world for women" [*monde pour elles*], in opposition to the existence "for the other" which has been women's traditional place and role (p. 106). Such an affirmation of self-love, or love for "the same" (essentially, a woman's love for her mother) is the necessary precondition for any love for the other, or love between women and men.

18. See, for example, Diane Griffin Crowder, "Amazons and Mothers? Monique Wittig, Hélène Cixous, and Theories of Women's Writing," *Contemporary Literature*, 24, no. 2 (1983), 114–144; and Hélène Vivienne Wenzel, "The Text as Body Politics: An Appreciation of Monique Wittig's Writings in Context," *Feminist Studies*, 7, no. 2 (1981), 264–287.

19. Hélène Cixous, *L'Exil de James Joyce, ou, L'Art de remplacement* (Paris: Grasset, 1968).

20. See Hélène Cixous, "Sorties," in H. Cixous and C. Clément, *La Jeune Née* (Paris: 10/18), pp. 114–245; and "Le Sexe ou la tête?" *Cahiers du GRIF*, 3 (1976), 5–15.

21. Cixous, "Sorties," p. 179.

22. Hélène Cixous, *Ou l'art de l'innocence* (Paris: Editions des Femmes, 1981), p. 53.

23. Hélène Cixous, "Entretien avec Françoise van Rossum-Guyon," *Revue des Sciences Humaines*, 44 (1977), 485.

24. For a number of years, Cixous has devoted her seminar at the University of Paris VIII to a study of the great Brasilian woman writer Clarice Lispector, about whose work she published several articles and a book (*Vivre l'orange*, 1979). At the same time, she has continued in some of her texts to celebrate a certain kind of bisexuality or an undecidable merging of genders. (See, for example, "Tancrède continue," from which I quote in the last section of this essay.) In the mid-1980s, her work took still another turn as she became more involved with writing for the theater, on historical subjects of epic scope. See her plays *L'Indiade, ou, L'Inde de leurs rêves* (1987) and *L'Histoire terrible mais inachevée de Norodom Sihanouk, roi du Cambodge* (1985), written for Ariane Mnouchkine's Théâtre du Soleil. In her most recent book as of this writing, *Manne: Au Mandelstams aux Mandelas* (Paris: Editions des Femmes, 1988), she is concerned with ethical and political issues not specifically in terms of gender politics.

25. Monique Wittig, "The Straight Mind," *Feminist Issues*, 1, no. 1 (1980), 108; hereafter, page numbers are given in parentheses in the text.

26. Two of Wittig's most recent works, the novel *Virgile, non* (1985) and the play *Le Voyage sans fin* (1985), based on *Don Quixote*, rewrite classic works of Western literature by transforming the male protagonist into a woman. I discuss *Virgile, non* briefly in Chapter 7.

27. I discuss the Medusa figure in greater detail in Chapter 7, in the section "Daughters Playing."

28. Such a politics seems to me equally implicit in some of Cixous's works, especially in *Ou l'art de l'innocence*. But it is most clear in Wittig's. I should

say that in personal conversations, both Wittig and Cixous have insisted that they are not separatists. Here is one place where "real life" politics diverges from what I see as a "poetic politics." Possibly, my notion of a politics implicit in a poetics needs to be revised, or refined. For now, I shall stick to it.

29. Helene Wenzel, "The Text as Body Politics: An Appraisal of Monique Wittig's Writings in Context," *Feminist Studies,* 7, no. 2 (1981), 279.

30. Diane Griffin Crowder, "Amazons and Mothers? Monique Wittig, Hélène Cixous, and Theories of Women's Writing," *Contemporary Literature,* 24, no. 2 (1983), 128.

31. This is what Wittig herself suggested, in a conversation at Harvard University (March 1983). Although I understand the theoretical argument, I have trouble superimposing it on my reading of Wittig's texts. On the question of the "mothers vs. Amazons" opposition, which I find quite problematic, Wittig stated that she now has some regrets and that if she and Zeig ever redid *Brouillon,* she would want to deemphasize that conflict. (See my discussion of *Virgile, non* in Chapter 7 for more on this opposition.)

32. Beverly Brown and Parveen Adams, "The Feminine Body and Feminist Politics," *m/f,* 3 (1979), 44.

33. Parveen Adams, "The Distinction between Sexual Division and Sexual Difference," *m/f,* 3 (1979), 57.

34. Jacques Derrida and Christie V. McDonald, "Choreographies," *Diacritics,* 12, no. 2 (1982), 75–76.

35. Hélène Cixous, "Trancrède continue," *Etudes Freudiennes,* 21–22 (March 1983), 118.

36. Angela Carter, *The Passion of New Eve* (London: Virago, 1982); page references to this edition are given in parentheses in the text.

37. The source for this chase is Desnos's *La Liberté ou l'amour* (1927). See Chapter 7, the section "Parody, Perversion, Collage," and n. 47.

38. Lest all this seem intolerably racist/sexist, let me jump ahead a bit: much later, Eve will meet a very different Leilah and discover that Evelyn's earlier perception of her was an illusion—either due to his own blindness or to her conscious deception. (Leilah, now called Lilith, turns out to be the daughter of a female plastic surgeon, the graduate of an East Coast university, a black feminist militant, etc. This is one of the many accumulated plot twists in the novel.)

39. I must report, somewhat ruefully, that when I have discussed this novel with students in various courses over the past few years, their reactions to this scene have been much more skeptical and ironic than mine, regardless of their gender. Indeed, a recent group of women students, in a highly theoretical course on women and the avant-garde, almost convinced me that the whole novel must be read as an extreme version of feminist postmodernist parody, sparing nothing and no one, not even its own "positive" moments. So much for the dream . . . A generation gap, perhaps?

40. For the sake of some literal-minded readers, I want to emphasize that I do *not* consider castration or sex-change operations as solutions, political or other! My reading of *The Passion of New Eve* is not referential but, in a

particular way, allegorical: the allegory residing not in the specific narrative content but in the possibilities of sexual role-playing and fluid gender boundaries that the narrative suggests.

7. Feminist Intertextuality and the Laugh of the Mother

1. Osip Mandelstam, "Literary Moscow," in *Critical Prose and Letters,* trans. Jane Gary Harris and Constance Link (Ann Arbor, Mich.: Ardis Press, 1979); quoted in Svetlana Boym, "Life and Death in Quotation Marks: Cultural Myths of the Modern Poet" (Ph.D. diss., Harvard University, 1988), p. 318; forthcoming from Harvard University Press. Translation slightly modified by Boym.
2. Boym, "Life and Death in Quotation Marks," pp. 318–319.
3. Jacques Lacan, "God and the *Jouissance* of The Woman: A Love Letter," trans. Jacqueline Rose, in *Feminine Sexuality: Jacques Lacan and the Ecole Freudienne* (London: Macmillan, 1982), p. 144. In French, see Lacan, *Le Séminaire, XX: Encore* (Paris: Editions du Seuil, 1975), p. 68.
4. Sandra Gilbert and Susan Gubar, *The Madwoman in the Attic: The Woman Writer and the Nineteenth-Century Literary Imagination* (New Haven: Yale University Press, 1979), p. 80.
5. Alicia Ostriker, *Stealing the Language: The Emergence of Women's Poetry in America* (Boston: Beacon Press, 1986), p. 7.
6. Patricia Yaeger, *Honey-Mad Women: Emancipatory Strategies in Women's Writing* (New York: Columbia University Press, 1988), p. 18; see also Chaps. 7 and 8. Mary Russo, "Female Grotesques: Carnival and Theory," in *Feminist Studies/Critical Studies,* ed. Teresa de Lauretis (Bloomington: Indiana University Press, 1986), pp. 213–229.
7. See, among other works, Bakhtin's *Rabelais and His World,* trans. Helene Iswolsky (Cambridge, Mass.: MIT Press, 1968), and *The Dialogic Imagination,* trans. Caryl Emerson and Michael Holquist (Austin: University of Texas Press, 1981). Although Bakhtin maintained that lyric poetry was essentially "monological," not participating in the heteroglossia of the novel, contemporary theorists of intertextuality, starting with Julia Kristeva who coined that term, have seen no need to uphold that distinction.
8. One of Kristeva's first published works was a long essay on Bakhtin in 1966, "Le mot, le dialogue, et le roman," reprinted in *Séméiotikè: Recherches pour une sémanalyse* (Paris: Editions du Seuil, 1969), pp. 143–173. The essay in which she coined the term "intertextuality," "Poésie et négativité," is in the same volume, pp. 246–277.
9. Bakhtin, *The Dialogic Imagination,* p. 60; hereafter, page numbers are given in parentheses in the text.
10. The power of stories in shaping people's perceptions and behavior in the world has been recognized for some time, notably by analysts of myth. It is remarkable that the "rewriting of old stories" has not only given impetus to recent fiction and poetry by women but has also fueled the work of feminist scholars across a whole range of disciplines. Among literary critics, the currently influential notion of revising the canon revolves around the

question of how to tell the story of a given literature or literary movement; feminist historians, starting with the pioneering work of Sheila Rowbotham and Joan Kelly Gadol, have obliged us to look again at the story of Western civilization; feminist psychologists like Carol Gilligan and Jessica Benjamin are significantly rewriting the psychoanalytic story of human development. Gilligan's current work on the myth of Psyche, which she proposes as a more benign alternative to the founding myth of psychoanalysis, Oedipus, seems to me especially relevant, for it specifically makes the link between changes in psychoanalytic paradigms and the real lives of adolescent girls. (See her "Oedipus and Psyche: Two Stories about Love," unpublished ms.)

11. Peter Stallybrass and Allon White, *The Politics and Poetics of Transgression* (Ithaca: Cornell University Press, 1986), p. 6; hereafter, page numbers are given in parentheses in the text.

12. Terry Eagleton, *Walter Benjamin: Towards a Revolutionary Criticism* (London: Verso, 1981), p. 148; quoted in Stallybrass and White, *Politics and Poetics*, p. 13. Other similar critiques cited by Stallybrass and White have been formulated in an anthropological perspective by Max Gluckman and Georges Balandier, and in a literary historical perspective by Roger Sales (pp. 12–14).

13. One of the first arguments presenting such a contextual interpretation of carnival is in Natalie Zemon Davis's often-cited essay "Women on Top," in Davis, *Society and Culture in Early Modern France* (Stanford: Stanford University Press, 1965), chap. 5. As a historian, Davis shows that the typically carnivalesque "image of the disorderly woman did not always function to keep women in their place. On the contrary, it was a multivalent image that operated . . . to widen behavioral options for women . . . and to sanction riot and political disobedience for both men and women in a society that allowed the lower orders few formal means of protest" (p. 131). A similarly nuanced view, relating specifically to parody as an artistic genre, is expressed by Linda Hutcheon in her book *A Theory of Parody* (New York: Methuen, 1985). Hutcheon argues that parody has a "potentially conservative impulse," since it necessarily affirms the tradition even while parodying it; at the same time, "parody can, like the carnival, also challenge norms in order to renovate, to renew" (p. 76). In her most recent book, *A Poetics of Postmodernism* (New York and London: Routledge, 1988), Hutcheon has emphasized the critical and radical aspect of parody, especially in the work of contemporary feminists, blacks, and other minorities. I discuss Hutcheon's view of postmodernism, along with others, in Chapter 8.

14. For a brief but up-to-date biographical essay on Carrington, see Marina Warner's Introduction to Carrington's recently published collection of stories, *The House of Fear: Notes from Down Below* (New York: E. P. Dutton, 1988). Carrington's life and work figure prominently in Whitney Chadwick's *Women Artists and the Surrealist Movement*.

15. For a detailed account of the friendship between Carrington and Varo (which has its comic fictional counterpart in *The Hearing Trumpet*), see

Janet Kaplan's recent biography, *Unexpected Journeys: The Art and Life of Remedios Varo* (New York: Abbeville Press, 1988).

16. Among the more intelligent reviews were those by Gabriele Annan, *Times Literary Supplement*, May 27, 1977, p. 644, and Bettina Knapp, *World Literature Today*, Winter 1978, pp. 80–81. My own interest in this novel was sparked by Gloria Orenstein's essay "Reclaiming the Great Mother," which discusses it along with other works by women Surrealists.

17. Angela Carter and Christine Brooke-Rose are among those who had started publishing earlier but gained special prominence only in the 1970s or later. The younger writers, who did not begin publishing until the late 1970s or early 1980s, include Jeanette Winterson and Kathy Acker.

18. The two volumes are *The House of Fear: Notes from Down Below* and *The Seventh Horse and Other Tales* (New York: Dutton, 1988). In addition to these stories, Carrington has published two novels: *The Stone Door* (New York: St. Martin's Press, 1977), written a few years before *The Hearing Trumpet;* and *The Hearing Trumpet,* currently published by City Lights Books (San Francisco, 1985). Subsequent page references are to this edition of the novel and are given in parentheses in the text.

19. See Bürger, *Theory of the Avant-Garde,* pp. 73–82. Bürger calls such techniques of juxtaposition montage rather than collage, and maintains that "a theory of the avant-garde must begin with the concept of montage" (p. 77).

20. For an excellent brief discussion of Aragon's "transposition" (in Gérard Genette's terminology) of Fénelon's text, see Genette, *Palimpsestes: La Littérature au second degré* (Paris: Editions du Seuil, 1982), pp. 410–413. Genette's book is a veritable catalogue and treasure trove of rewritings, parodic and otherwise; he shows that although extended, playful transpositions like Aragon's *Télémaque* (or Joyce's *Ulysses*) are particularly frequent in modern times and have been particularly favored by experimental or avant-garde writers, the practice of "hypertextuality" (Genette's term for one text's rewriting of a previous text) in all its varied forms has a long history.

21. The name, as it happens, is the name of the nymph Eucharis, whom Aragon's (but not Fénelon's) Telemachus weds and beds on Calypso's island—and who is also mentioned in one of Rimbaud's most famous poems, "Après le déluge." Rimbaud was the other poet, besides Lautréamont, whom the Surrealists venerated, especially in their early years. The whole last section of *Télémaque* is, in fact, a nonparodic rewriting of the Rimbaud poem. Such a thick texture of allusions and intertextual references characterizes the best Surrealist work, and we will find it again in *The Hearing Trumpet*. Aragon wrote about the importance of Rimbaud for the Surrealists in his 1943 memoir, which remained unpublished until 1989: *Pour expliquer ce que j'étais* (Paris: Editions Gallimard).

22. For a fine detailed discussion of *La Liberté ou l'amour!* including its publication history, see Marie-Claire Dumas, *Robert Desnos, ou, L'Exploration des limites* (Paris: Klincksieck, 1980).

23. See Benjamin Péret, *Oeuvres complètes,* vol. 4 (Paris: José Corti, 1987), p. 255.

24. Louis Aragon, *Le Libertinage* (Paris: Editions Gallimard, 1924; reprinted in the collection "L'Imaginaire," 1983), pp. 274, 271; hereafter, page references to this edition are given in parentheses in the text.

25. Rosalind Krauss, "Corpus Delicti," in *L'Amour Fou: Photography and Surrealism,* pp. 91–95; the phrase "fetishization of reality" is on p. 91.

26. Janine Chasseguet-Smirgel, "Perversion and the Universal Law," *International Review of Psycho-Analysis,* 10 (1983), 299, 293; hereafter, page numbers are given in parentheses in the text.

27. See, for example, Ernst's *Une Semaine de bonté* (New York: Dover Publications, 1976), which has all of the elements I've just mentioned.

28. The quotations in this paragraph are from Freud's *Three Essays on the Theory of Sexuality* (1905), which discusses perversion as a regression to (or, more exactly, as an "inhibition in development" from) infantile sexuality. See *The Standard Edition,* VII, 123–245.

29. Sigmund Freud, "Fetishism" (1927), in *Sexuality and the Psychology of Love,* ed. Philip Rieff (New York: Collier Books, 1963), p. 216.

30. This version is reproduced in Sarane Alexandrian, *Surrealist Art,* trans. Gordon Clough (London: Thames and Hudson, 1970), p. 32.

31. For a color reproduction and a succinct summary of the current wisdom regarding this work, see Hughes, *The Shock of the New,* pp. 66, 67. For a juxtaposition of *L.H.O.O.Q.* with a photograph by Man Ray of Duchamp dressed as Rrose Sélavy, see William S. Rubin, *Dada, Surrealism, and Their Heritage,* p. 17.

32. Hughes, *The Shock of the New,* p. 66.

33. The word "Dada," of course, also has an infantile connotation often exploited by Dada artists (notably Tristan Tzara). The primary French meaning of the word, given in the *Petit Robert* dictionary, is: "(langage enfantin) cheval," "horse (in child's language)."

34. Ernst refers to this painting as a picture-manifesto, "painted after an idea of André Breton," in a footnote to his essay "Beyond Painting" (1934), in Max Ernst, *Beyond Painting and Other Essays by the Artist and His Friends* (New York: Wittenborn, Schulz, 1948), p. 9.

35. Margot Norris, *Beasts of the Modern Imagination: Darwin, Nietzsche, Kafka, Ernst, and Lawrence* (Baltimore: Johns Hopkins University Press, 1985), p. 150; subsequent page references are given in parentheses in the text. I wish to thank Paul Panadero for calling Norris's book to my attention.

36. Barbara Babcock, *The Reversible World: Symbolic Inversion in Art and Society* (Ithaca: Cornell University Press, 1978); quoted in Stallybrass and White, *Politics and Poetics,* p. 17.

37. Freud, *Sexuality and the Psychology of Love,* p. 107; hereafter, page numbers are given in parentheses in the text.

38. This is also, ultimately, what the unconscious fantasy means for the girl, according to Freud's interpretation; but in her case, he claims, the unconscious masochistic fantasy is preceded by a conscious sadistic one of seeing her father beat another child—which means, "My father does not love this

other child, he loves only me." The masochistic fantasy then intervenes as a sexually charged "punishment" for this incestuous desire. In the case of boys, by contrast, Freud sees no sadistic precursor to the masochistic fantasy: for the boy, he claims, "I am being beaten by my father" *means* "I am loved by my father"—whence his conclusion that "the boy's beating-phantasy is . . . passive from the very beginning, and is derived from a feminine attitude towards his father" (p. 127).

39. I should note that Freud himself does not make this rapprochement between fetishism and male masochism. His essay on fetishism (1927) appeared eight years after the "child is being beaten" essay. Reading the two essays together, I find the rapprochement unavoidable.

For a very different reading of the "child is being beaten" essay, which concludes that the male masochist, by identifying with a feminine role, tends "ultimately . . . to exclude the father," see Kaja Silverman, "Masochism and Male Subjectivity," *Camera Obscura,* 17 (1988), 31–68. Silverman's interpretation of male masochism (and of Freud's essay) is greatly influenced, as she herself states, by what she sees as Gilles Deleuze's "radical reconfiguration" of male masochism. Spinning out the implications of Deleuze's analysis, Silverman writes: "In inviting the mother to beat and/or dominate him, [the male masochist] transfers power and authority from the father to her, remakes the symbolic order, and 'ruins' his own paternal legacy" (p. 57). This is an ingeniously "antipatriarchal" interpretation, consonant with the view that the son's perversion is directed against the father's law. I believe that it does not sufficiently take into account, however, the deep complicity between the son and the father, which Freud's account of the male beating fantasy clearly recognizes; my own interpretation, as will be evident shortly if it is not already so, emphasizes the exclusion not of the father but (once again) of the mother, even by the perverse son. I wish to thank Mary Russo for reminding me about Kaja Silverman's very interesting essay—and more generally for her perceptive and helpful comments on this chapter.

40. Evan M. Maurer, "Images of Dream and Desire: The Prints and Collage Novels of Max Ernst," in *Max Ernst: Beyond Surrealism,* ed. Robert Rainwater (New York: The New York Public Library and Oxford University Press, 1986), p. 68.

41. Ernst, *Beyond Painting and Other Writings,* pp. 27–28.

42. The painting is reproduced, in black and white, in Uwe M. Schneede, *The Essential Max Ernst,* trans. R. W. Last (London: Thames and Hudson, 1972), p. 9.

43. This painting can be seen in only one book, to my knowledge, and there only in a small black and white reproduction. The original was destroyed by the artist. For the reproduction, see William S. Rubin, *Dada and Surrealist Art* (New York: Harry N. Abrams, 1968), p. 143, fig. 127.

44. See n. 34 above. Adding yet another Oedipal twist to the tale, Ernst's own son, Jimmy Ernst, reports in his autobiography that "he [Max] told me that he got the idea from watching Maja [Jimmy's nurse] disciplining me in Tyrol," when Jimmy was two or three years old. The autobiographical

associations of the painting are thus both to Max Ernst as a son and to Max Ernst as a father watching *his* son "being beaten"—Oedipus upon Oedipus, as it were. (See Jimmy Ernst, *A Not-So-Still Life* [New York: St. Martin's/ Marek, 1984], p. 52. I wish to thank Whitney Chadwick for calling this reference to my attention.)

45. Julia Kristeva, *La Révolution du langage poétique* (Paris: Editions du Seuil, 1974), p. 469; hereafter, page numbers are given in parentheses in the text.

46. Gayatri Chakravorty Spivak, "French Feminism in an International Frame," *Yale French Studies,* 62 (1981), 167; Spivak's emphasis.

47. I am thinking specifically of the spectacular chase scene in Carter's *The Passion of New Eve,* where the protagonist (still Evelyn, a cocky male) follows a beautiful black woman who, wrapped in her fur coat, sheds her dress and panties as she goes; exactly the same configuration occurs in Desnos's *La Liberté ou l'amour!* (chap. 2), where the narrating "I" follows the beautiful Louise Lame, who is wearing a fur coat and drops her panties and dress for him to pick up. Carter's obvious borrowing here does not make her work "derivative," it simply shows that like all good artists she knows how to make use of the tricks of predecessors with whom she feels an affinity. Carter's affinities with Surrealism are quite clear and would be interesting to explore in detail. In the meantime, another example. In her novel *Nights at the Circus,* Carter attributes to an illiterate Siberian shaman one of the more famous ideas of the first Surrealist Manifesto, for which Breton himself cites the poet Saint-Pol-Roux as the source: the idea that a poet, while sleeping, is a "man at work," since dreams are both the source and the matter of poetry. Saint-Pol-Roux, Breton recounts, would hang a sign on his door every evening before he went to sleep: POET AT WORK. Carter's version, for which no source is acknowledged, is as follows: "When he slept, which he did much of the time, he would, could he have written it, put a sign on his door: 'Man at work'" (Carter, *Nights at the Circus* [London: Chatto and Windus, 1984], p. 253).

48. Angela Carter, *Nothing Sacred: Selected Writings* (London: Virago Press, 1982).

49. Among the writers one could cite here, besides Carter, are Rikki Ducornet, whose graphic work and short narrative texts were published in Surrealist-affiliated journals of the 1960s and 1970s in France and the United States, and whose recent novels (*The Stain* and *Entering Fire*) are clearly Surrealist in inspiration; Kathy Acker, who besides her numerous intertextual allusions to European male avant-garde writers (in *Blood and Guts in High School* and *Great Expectations,* among other works), is currently writing a novel about Rimbaud; and Jeanette Winterson, whose three novels published so far (I discuss one in the next section) all have Surrealist echoes. Among other artists, one thinks of Cindy Sherman, whose recent photographs allude quite explicitly to the work of Hans Bellmer; Barbara Kruger, whose photocollages and combinations of word and image clearly harken back to the work of John Heartfield and other Dada initiators of photomontage (including a woman artist, Hanna Höch, who was for a long time "suppressed" by art historians); the dancer and choreographer Lucinda Childs, who refers her work to Duchamp; and the filmmakers Yvonne Rainer and Chantal

Akerman, whose works are in obvious dialogue with those of Godard and his male avant-garde predecessors, including Surrealists.

50. Jeanette Winterson, *Oranges Are Not the Only Fruit* (New York: Atlantic Monthly Press, (1985); page numbers to this edition will be given in parentheses in the text.

51. The fact that the mother is not the biological but an adoptive mother has little to do with the story, other than to underline the mother's repressive attitude toward sex. After a first fling in Paris when she was a girl, and despite the fact that she is married, she seems to have had no sexual activity: the child, we are told, is "her flesh now, sprung from her head" (p. 10)—that is, not from her sex.

52. Robin Lydenberg, *Word Cultures: Radical Theory and Practice in William Burroughs' Fiction* (Urbana and Chicago: University of Illinois Press, 1987), p. 168.

53. "Hands Off Love!" first published in *La Révolution Surréaliste,* 9–10 (1927), is reprinted in its entirety in Maurice Nadeau, *Histoire du Surréalisme* (Paris: Editions du Seuil, 1964), pp. 252–260; the phrase "la fabrication des mioches" is on p. 256. The original title of the French text is in English.

54. Whitney Chadwick has noted that very few women Surrealist artists became mothers, and that most had quite negative feelings about motherhood (see Chadwick, *Women Artists and the Surrealist Movement,* pp. 129–135). Although their attitude can be seen as part of their revolt against conventional female roles, the male Surrealists' image of woman as erotic partner (in *l'amour fou*) or as "free spirit" (*la femme enfant*) also militated against women Surrealists' self-image as mothers. In Surrealist writing by women, mothers are generally either absent or negative figures, this being also true of Carrington's short stories of the 1930s. Carrington (whose two sons were born in the late 1940s) may be the only Surrealist woman writer who has represented a mother (albeit a rather untypical one) as a heroine—not only a positive figure but a self-consciously playful one as well. Nelly Kaplan, my other favorite Surrealist woman writer, has written extremely funny parodies of sacred texts, including the Gospels (see, for example, her "Aimez-vous les uns sur les autres," a rewriting of Christ's betrayal by Judas as a story of homosexual jealousy, in *Le Réservoir des sens*)—but Kaplan writes exclusively as a daughter, and indeed the father's daughter; her attitude toward mothers, as well as toward motherhood, is unambiguously negative. See, in particular, her comic novel (under the pen name Belen), *Mémoires d'une liseuse de draps.*

55. Monique Wittig, *Virgile, non* (Paris: Editions de Minuit, 1985), p. 51.

56. Nancy K. Miller, *Subject to Change: Reading Feminist Writing* (New York: Columbia University Press, 1988), p. 10.

57. Cixous, "The Laugh of the Medusa," trans. Keith Cohen and Paula Cohen, in *New French Feminisms,* ed. Elaine Marks and Isabelle de Courtivron, pp. 251, 257; in French, "Le rire de la Méduse," *L'Arc,* 61 (1975), 44, 48–49; hereafter page references to both versions are given in parentheses in the text.

58. Domna Stanton, "Difference on Trial: A Critique of the Maternal Metaphor

in Cixous, Irigaray, and Kristeva," in *The Poetics of Gender,* ed. Miller, p. 174.

59. Ovid, *Metamorphoses,* trans. Rolfe Humphries (Bloomington: Indiana University Press, 1955), p. 106.

60. Does this refusal make of such a woman a female version of the fetishist? Cixous, I think, would say no, for it is not a matter of endowing the woman with a (fantasized) penis—which in Freudian terms would correspond to a "masculinity complex"—but rather of seeing the female (mother's) genitals themselves as a positive term. Naomi Schor has suggested that "female fetishism" might be a term for describing not the "masculinity complex" but rather a strategy of undecidability, "a refusal firmly to anchor woman— but also man—on either side of the axis of castration" ("Female Fetishism: The Case of George Sand," in *The Female Body in Western Culture: Contemporary Perspectives,* ed. Susan Rubin Suleiman, p. 369). Although Cixous would probably fit in general under this description (her theory of bisexuality is just such a refusal of sexual binarism, as I suggested in Chapter 6), in this particular passage I believe that undecidability is not what is at stake; rather, it is the decidability (and desirability) of the traditionally denied, repressed, feared, etc. female genitals.

61. Sigmund Freud, "Medusa's Head" (1922), in *Sexuality and the Psychology of Love,* p. 212.

62. See, for example, Annie Leclerc, *Parole de femme* (Paris: Livre de Poche, 1974); Chantal Chawaf, *Maternité* (Paris: Stock, 1979); Julia Kristeva, "Stabat Mater," in *Histoires d'amour* (Paris: Denoel, 1983), pp. 225–250 (English translation in *The Female Body in Western Culture: Contemporary Perspectives,* ed. Susan Rubin Suleiman, pp. 99–118).

63. In his short essay of 1927, "Humor" (which immediately follows the essay on fetishism in *The Standard Edition*), Freud emphasizes the "liberating" function of humor and contrasts it to mere jokes—humor possessing, according to him, "grandeur" and "dignity" whereas jokes (which, as he analyzes them in *Jokes and Their Relation to the Unconscious,* are always at someone else's expense) do not. Even more interestingly in the present context, Freud suggests that the origin of humor is in the superego, not in the unconscious as is the case with jokes. Given that in Freud's system the superego usually has a repressive rather than a rebellious or liberating function, I find this ascription of the origin of humor to the "parental agency" extremely suggestive. (See "Humor," in *The Standard Edition,* xxi, 159–166.)

64. Interview with John Engstrom, *Boston Globe,* October 28, 1988, p. 62. Carter was referring here to Martin Scorsese's film *The Last Temptation of Christ,* which she said she would not go to see because it is "not blasphemous." "I mean, this is 1988, you know!" she added.

65. After being published separately (Chicago: Black Swan Press, 1983), *Down Below* is now included, with a 1987 Postscript and a Note on the Text, in *The House of Fear: Notes from Down Below* (New York: Dutton, 1988), pp. 160–214; hereafter, page references to this edition are given in parentheses in the text.

66. Interestingly enough, scholars of the Grail legend seem to agree that the Grail tradition is pre-Christian, probably of Celtic origin. Roger Sherman Loomis suggests that the Grail was originally a miraculous dish or "vessel of the Gods," whose Christianization (starting in the twelfth century with Chrétien de Troyes's *Perceval*) was largely the result of a misreading: since the grail (Old French, *sains graaus*) was often associated with a similarly blessed drinking horn (*cors beneiz*), and since *cors* could also mean "body," the Grail became associated with Christ's body and blood "in an era when all Christendom was obsessed by the cult of relics, particularly those of the Passion" (Loomis, *The Grail: From Celtic Myth to Christian Symbol* [New York: Columbia University Press, 1963], p. 274). Carrington's "blasphemous" paganization of the Grail thus appears to be a reappropriation rather than a theft.

67. I say sly because a 92-year-old bearded lady, with a grown son who drops out of her story—and out of the novel—after the first twenty pages is not the most obvious stereotype of the mother; however, in a rewriting of the Grail quest whose heroine is a woman with a son named Galahad, an indentification of the heroine with a (the) mother strikes me as unavoidable. It is also significant, as I note below, that Carrington's association of the Grail with Venus emphasizes her role as mother, rather than exclusively as the goddess of erotic love.

68. Gloria Feman Orenstein, "Reclaiming the Great Mother: A Feminist Journey to Madness and Back in Search of a Goddess Heritage," *Symposium*, Spring 1982, 65. In all fairness to Orenstein, I should note that her essay does not claim to give a complete or even "interesting" reading of any single work; rather, she introduces the reader to a number of works by women associated with Surrealism. As such, it was an extremely timely essay when it was published and remains a very useful introduction.

69. Spivak, "French Feminism in an International Frame," p. 167.

70. For an analysis of postmodernist fiction in such terms, see Brian McHale, *Postmodernist Fiction* (New York: Methuen, 1987).

71. On the association of Aphrodite with Ishtar, see Edward Tripp, *The Meridian Handbook of Classical Mythology* (New York: New American Library, 1970), p. 60. For a more detailed analysis, see Paul Friedrich, *The Meaning of Aphrodite* (Chicago: University of Chicago Press, 1978). Sandra Gilbert, in a provocative reading of Kate Chopin's novel *The Awakening*, has suggested that Chopin proposes "a feminist and matriarchal myth of Aphrodite/Venus as an alternative to the masculinist and patriarchal myth of Jesus." This interpretation is not at all obvious as far as *The Awakening* is concerned, but it applies very nicely to *The Hearing Trumpet*. I note, however, that Gilbert too considers Venus exclusively as erotic rather than maternal, "a radiant symbol of the erotic liberation that turn-of-the-century women had begun to allow themselves to desire." (See Gilbert, "The Second Coming of Aphrodite," *The Kenyon Review*, 5 [1983], 42–65.)

72. Whitney Chadwick suggested to me, after reading this essay in manuscript, that Marian's beard might be usefully put into relation with my earlier discussion of the bearded Mona Lisa. I find the association suggestive but

am not prepared to explore it at the moment. Marina Warner, in turn, has written to me that "the bearded virgin martyr, Wilgefortis, also known as Liberata, or Saint Uncumber, is the patron saint of women who want to get rid of their husbands—a carnival saint, if you like." Like Santa Barbara, Wilgefortis was killed by her father when she refused to marry the man he had picked for her—whence Marina Warner's suggestion that this may be another female version of the "filial" transgression against the father, which I analyzed in the case of Surrealist parody. Clearly, Carrington's intertextual allusions are not exhausted by a single reading. I thank Whitney Chadwick and Marina Warner for their rich associations to my own text.

73. For a brief discussion of the importance of alchemy in Surrealism, see Inez Hedges, *Languages of Revolt: Dada and Surrealist Literature and Film* (Durham, N.C.: Duke University Press, 1983), chap. 1; her discussion of the serpent biting its own tail is on p. 4.

74. Carrington is multiplying her Goddess lore here, since both Hecate and the Queen Bee have ancient associations with matriarchal cults. But her allusions to the Goddess always have an element of humor and self-irony, as I suggest below.

75. Orenstein, "Reclaiming the Great Mother," p. 65.

76. There is a good reproduction of Seligmann's *Ultra-Furniture* in Susan Gubar, "Representing Pornography," *Critical Inquiry*, 13, no. 4 (Summer 1987), 716. For a discussion of the praying mantis as an object of fascination for the Surrealists, see Rosalind Krauss, "No More Play," in *The Originality of the Avant-Garde and Other Modernist Myths*, pp. 69–72.

77. There are a few indications, at the end of the novel (pp. 145, 146), that the earthquake, ice age, and general upheaval are taking place after an atomic war. *The Hearing Trumpet* was written at the height of the Cold War, at a time of particular anxiety about a nuclear apocalypse. (I remember serious talk, among schoolchildren in the United States in the early 1950s, about building bomb shelters in backyards.)

78. Barthes, *Roland Barthes par lui-même*, p. 137.

79. D. W. Winnicott, *Playing and Reality* (New York: Basic Books, 1971), pp. 55, 64.

80. Nancy K. Miller, "The Text's Heroine," in Miller, *Subject to Change*, p. 75; Naomi Schor, "Dreaming Dissymetry," in *Men in Feminism*, ed. Jardine and Smith (New York: Methuen, 1987), p. 109.

81. This idea has gained a lot from my recent conversations with Carol Gilligan, whose research and reflection on adolescent girls and their relation to their mothers intersects in many interesting ways with my thinking about the importance of the mother's play. See also n. 10.

82. Jessica Benjamin, *The Bonds of Love: Psychoanalysis, Feminism, and the Problem of Domination* (New York: Pantheon Books, 1988).

83. The metaphor of the mother as a "peaceful center" which makes possible the child's (actually, the son's) freedom to play is Roland Barthes's (*Leçon*, pp. 42–43), and I already quoted it in my "Metapolylogue" in the Prologue. The image of the fixed mother and mobile child is common in psychoanalytic thought—Winnicott's notion of the child playing "alone in the presence

of the mother" is one version of it. However, Winnicott also envisages the mother playing with the child, "playing together in a relationship" (*Playing and Reality*, p. 48), which I find a lot more appealing.

84. Thomas O'Connor, "Tracey Ullman: She's a Real Character," *New York Times*, Arts and Entertainment section, September 25, 1988, p. 34.

85. Yaeger, *Honey-Mad Women*, p. 228.

8. Feminism and Postmodernism

1. Fredric Jameson, "Postmodernism, or the Cultural Logic of Late Capitalism," *New Left Review*, July–August 1984, 56; hereafter, page numbers are given in parentheses in the text.

2. *Libération*, March 2, 1989, p. 37.

3. This interpretation seems actually to have been proposed by the Soviet Union in its first official pronouncement on the affair, as reported by the *International Herald Tribune* of March 3, 1989. According to the Soviet news agency Tass, "one cannot fail to notice that the world press has been presenting the conflict in black and white terms, as Iran having thrown down a gauntlet to the West. But perhaps Imam Khomeini, the supreme religious authority in Iran, had no choice proceeding from Koran teachings, other than denouncing a man who has insulted Islam" (p. 2). In other words, everybody says what his job requires, and nobody's words should be taken too seriously . . . or, the poetics of postmodernism according to Tass.

4. *International Herald Tribune*, March 1, 1989, p. 2. The same page carries a boxed headline: "2 Sellers of Rushdie Book Firebombed in California," reporting the bombing of Cody's and of Waldenbooks in Berkeley.

5. Jean-François Lyotard, *La Condition postmoderne: Rapport sur le savior* (Paris: Editions de Minuit, 1979). English translation: *The Postmodern Condition: A Report on Knowledge*, trans. Geoff Bennington and Brian Massumi (Minneapolis: University of Minnesota Press, 1981); hereafter, page numbers are given in parentheses in the text.

6. Suleiman, "Naming and Difference: Reflections on 'Modernism *versus* Postmodernism' in Literature," in *Approaching Postmodernism*, ed. Douwe Fokkema and Hans Bertens (Amsterdam and Philadelphia: John Benjamins, 1986), p. 255. As I note in that essay, the first footnote in Lyotard's book cites Hassan's *The Dismemberment of Orpheus: Toward a Post Modern Literature* (New York: Oxford University Press, 1971) as a source for his use of the term "postmodern"; in the introduction, Lyotard justifies his choice of "postmodern" to characterize "the condition of knowledge in the most highly developed societies" by noting that "the word is in current use on the American continent among sociologists and critics" (*The Postmodern Condition*, p. xxiii).

Recent works on postmodernism that use Lyotard as an obligatory reference and make virtually no mention of any work before his on the subject include: *Universal Abandon? The Politics of Postmodernism*, ed. Andrew Ross (Minneapolis: University of Minnesota Press, 1988); *Postmodernism and Its Discontents*, ed. E. Ann Kaplan (London: Verso, 1988); "Modernity and Modernism, Postmodernity and Postmodernism," special issue of *Cultural Critique*, no. 5 (Winter 1986–87); "Postmodernism," special issue of *Social Text*, no. 18 (Winter 1987–88). This may be a specifically American, or Anglo-American, phenomenon; Richard Martin informs me that in Germany, where he teaches, Lyotard's book is known but Hassan's work remains the starting reference. I wish to thank Richard Martin, as well as Bernard Gendron, Ingeborg Hoesterey, and Mary Russo, for their careful reading and useful criticisms of this essay.

7. Lyotard situates himself explicitly in opposition to Baudrillard early on in *The Postmodern Condition,* when he notes that the "breaking up of the grand Narratives . . . leads to what some authors analyze in terms of the dissolution of the social bond and the disintegration of social aggregates into a mass of individual atoms thrown into the absurdity of Brownian motion. Nothing of the kind is happening: this point of view, it seems to me, is haunted by the paradisaic representation of a lost 'organic' society" (p. 15). Although he does not name Baudrillard in the text, Lyotard footnotes Baudrillard's 1978 book, *A l'ombre des majorités silencieuses,* as the one example of the analyses he is contesting here. Baudrillard's theory of the simulacrum, to which I referred, dates from 1975: *L'Echange symbolique et la mort* (Paris: Editions Gallimard). This theory is much indebted to Debord's theory of the "society of the spectacle," which dates from just before 1968 (Guy Debord, *La Société du spectacle* [Paris: Buchet-Chastel, 1967]). In 1988 Debord published a short commentary on his earlier book, which reiterates and reinforces his earlier pessimistic analyses. See his *Commentaries sur la société du spectacle* (Paris: Gérard Lebovici, 1988).

8. Habermas's contribution to the debate was the now famous essay, "Modernity—An Incomplete Project" (1981), reprinted in *The Anti-Aesthetic: Essays on Postmodern Culture,* ed. Hal Foster (Port Townsend, Wash.: Bay Press, 1983) pp. 3–15. Habermas criticized all those, including the French poststructuralists (whom he called "anti-modernist young conservatives"), who argued for a "break" with the "modernist" project of the Enlightenment. Habermas does not seem to have been responding here to Lyotard's book (the essay does not mention Lyotard), and he did not link postmodernism to poststructuralism. Lyotard, however, responded to Habermas in his 1982 essay "Réponse à la question: Qu'est-ce que le postmoderne?" which appears in English as an appendix to *The Postmodern Condition.* It was after that essay that the version of the "modernism-postmodernism" debate associated with the names of Lyotard and Habermas reached full swing. There are other versions of the debate as well. For an American response specifically to this debate, see Richard Rorty, "Habermas and Lyotard on Postmodernity," in *Habermas and Modernity,* ed. Richard J. Bernstein (Cambridge, Mass.: MIT Press, 1985), pp. 161–175.

9. For a somewhat useful historical overview (as of about 1985), see Hans Bertens, "The Postmodern *Weltanschauung* and Its Relation with Modernism: An Introductory Survey," in *Approaching Postmodernism,* ed. Fokkema and Bertens, pp. 9–51. My essay in the same volume, "Naming and Difference," distinguishes various discourses on the postmodern in terms of their founding impulse: ideological, diagnostic, or classificatory.

10. Irving Howe, "Mass Society and Postmodern Fiction," in *The Decline of the New* (New York: Harcourt, Brace and World, 1970); first published in *Partisan Review* in 1959. The term "postmodernismo" was, it appears, already used in Spain by Federico de Onis in 1934; however, its meaning was quite different. See John Barth, "Postmodernism Revisited," *The Review of Contemporary Fiction*, 8, no. 3 (Fall 1988), 18.

11. Leslie Fiedler, "The New Mutants" (1965), reprinted in *Collected Essays*, vol. 2 (New York: Stein and Day, 1971), pp. 379–400; Robert Venturi, Denise Scott Brown, and Steven Izenour, *Learning from Las Vegas: The Forgotten Symbolism of Architectural Form*, revised edition (Cambridge, Mass.: MIT Press, 1988 [original ed. 1977]). In the Preface to the First Edition, Brown and Venturi cite their 1968 article "A Significance for A&P Parking Lots, or, Learning from Las Vegas," as the basis for the book.

12. Suleiman, "Naming and Difference."

13. The most successful effort of this kind so far is, I believe, Brian McHale's *Postmodernist Fiction* (New York and London: Methuen, 1987). Describing his work as an example of "descriptive poetics," McHale makes no attempt to link postmodernist fiction to contemporary cultural issues—indeed, he concludes that postmodernist fiction, like all significant literature, treats the "eternal themes" of love and death. Within its self-imposed formalist parameters, I find McHale's criterion for distinguishing modernist from postmodernist fiction (the former being dominated by epistemological issues, the latter by ontological ones) extremely interesting, and his detailed readings of postmodernist works in terms of the ontological criterion suggestive and persuasive.

14. Rosalind Krauss, "The Originality of the Avant-Garde: A Postmodernist Repetition," *October*, 18 (Fall 1981), 47–66; Douglas Crimp, "Pictures," *October*, 8 (Spring 1979), 75–88, both reprinted in *Art after Modernism: Rethinking Representation*, ed. Brian Wallis (New York and Boston: The New Museum of Contemporary Art and David R. Godine, 1984). Among literary critics, Brian McHale has included some discussion of the work of women, notably Angela Carter and Christine Brooke-Rose, in his *Postmodernist Fiction*, without, however, raising the question of sexual difference. Ihab Hassan, in the new Postface to the second edition of *The Dismemberment of Orpheus*, cites Brooke-Rose's name in some of his postmodernist lists (she was not cited in the first edition, 1971). The only general study of postmodernist writing to date that discusses women's work (along with that of other marginal groups) and also makes some attempt to take into account its political specificity is Linda Hutcheon's *A Poetics of Postmodernism: History, Theory, Fiction* (New York and London: Routledge, 1988).

15. Poggioli, *The Theory of the Avant-Garde*, chaps. 5 and 8.

16. Craig Owens, "The Discourse of Others: Feminists and Postmodernism," in *The Anti-Aesthetic: Essays on Postmodern Culture*, ed. Hal Foster, (Port Townsend, Wash.: Bay Press, 1983), p. 59; hereafter, page numbers are given in parentheses in the text.

17. See n. 8 above. The most explicit linking of postmodernism and poststructuralism in the debate was made by Terry Eagleton, in his highly negative

Marxist critique, "Capitalism, Modernism, and Postmodernism," *New Left Review,* 152 (1985), 60–73.

18. Hal Foster, "(Post)Modern Polemics," in *Recodings: Art, Spectacle, Cultural Politics* (Seattle: Bay Press, 1985), p. 136.

19. Andreas Huyssen, "Mapping the Postmodern," in *After the Great Divide: Modernism, Mass Culture, Postmodernism* (Bloomington: Indiana University Press, 1986), pp. 219–221.

20. Hutcheon, *A Poetics of Postmodernism,* chap. 4.

21. It is true, as Richard Martin reminds me, that some feminists are critical of this "high theoretical" discourse (or of any theoretical discourse closely associated with a male tradition) and would just as soon not participate in it. That raises a whole number of other questions regarding alliances and dialogue between men and women, which I will not attempt to deal with here. My own position on these questions should be clear enough by now; my favoring of dialogue and "complication" over separatist and binarist positions is explicitly argued in Chapters 4, 6, and 7.

22. The same argument can be made (as Linda Hutcheon's grouping together of "ex-centrics" and Huyssen's and Foster's use of the concept "Others" shows) for the alliance between postmodernism and "Third World" minorities or Afro-American writers, male and female. Many black American critics (Henry Louis Gates comes especially to mind) have recognized the similarity of concerns and of analytic concepts between feminist criticism and Afro-American criticism. The links between Afro-American writing and postmodernism have also been recognized, notably in the novels of Ishmael Reed. Black women writers, however, have rarely been called postmodernists, and even less feminist postmodernists. A case can be made for considering Toni Morrison and Ntozake Shange (among others) "black women feminist postmodernists." But the question of priorities (race or gender?) remains.

23. To be sure, there were a number of important women writers and artists associated with Anglo-American modernism and other earlier movements who were ignored or belittled by male critics, as recent feminist scholarship has shown. And as I argued in Chapter 1, there are significant historical and national differences that must be taken into account when discussing the participation of women in avant-garde movements. My sense is, however, that none of the early movements had the *critical mass of outstanding, innovative work by women, both in the visual arts and in literature* (the phrase is worth restating and underlining) that exists today.

Is naming names necessary? Here, for the doubtful, is a partial list of outstanding English and American women artists working today, who can be (and at some time or other have been) called feminist postmodernists: In performance, Joanne Akalaitis, Laurie Anderson, Karen Finley, Suzanne Lacy, Meredith Monk, Carolee Schneemann; in film and video, Lizzie Borden, Cecilia Condit, Laura Mulvey, Sally Potter, Yvonne Rainer, Martha Rosler; in photography and visual arts, Jenny Holzer, Mary Kelly, Barbara Kruger, Sherrie Levine, Cindy Sherman, Nancy Spero; in fiction, Kathy Acker, Christine Brooke-Rose, Angela Carter, Rikki Ducornet, Emily Prager, Jeanette Winterson. (See also n. 22.) I thank Elinor Fuchs, Heidi

Gilpin, and Judith Piper for sharing their expertise with me about women in postmodern performance. For more on contemporary women performers and visual artists, see the exhibition catalogue (which bears out my point about critical mass) *Making Their Mark: Women Artists Move into the Mainstream, 1970–1985* (New York: Abbeville Press, 1989).

24. Christine Brooke-Rose, "Illiterations," in *Breaking the Sequence: Women's Experimental Fiction*, ed. Ellen G. Friedman and Miriam Fuchs (Princeton: Princeton University Press, 1989), p. 59.

25. For an excellent collection of responses to "Guernica" and a clear exposition of its history as a "political" painting, see Ellen C. Oppler, ed., *Picasso's Guernica: Illustrations, Introductory Essay, Documents, Poetry, Criticism, Analysis* (New York: Norton, 1988).

26. Stanley Fish, *Is There a Text in This Class? The Authority of Interpretive Communities* (Cambridge, Mass.: Harvard University Press, 1980). For an overview of theories of reading, see my introductory essay, "Varieties of Audience-Oriented Criticism," in *The Reader in the Text*, ed. Suleiman and Crosman, pp. 3–45.

27. Mary Kelly, "Beyond the Purloined Image" (essay on a 1983 London exhibition with the same title, curated by Kelly), quoted in Rozsika Parker and Griselda Pollock, "Fifteen Years of Feminist Action: From Practical Strategies to Strategic Practices," in *Framing Feminism: Art and the Women's Movement, 1970–85* (London and New York: Pandora Press, 1987), p. 53. Aside from the excellent introductory essays by Parker and Pollock, this book offers a rich selection of written and visual work by women involved in various British feminist avant-garde art movements of the seventies and early eighties.

28. See Anders Stephanson, "Regarding Postmodernism—A Conversation with Fredric Jameson," in *Universal Abandon? The Politics of Postmodernism*, ed. Andrew Ross, pp. 3–30. Jameson suggests that Doctorow's works offer the possibility "to undo postmodernism homeopathically by the methods of postmodernism: to work at dissolving the pastiche by using all the instruments of pastiche itself, to reconquer some genuine historical sense by using the instruments of what I have called substitutes for history" (p. 17). The question Jameson does not answer (or raise) is: How does one tell the "fake" (homeopathic) postmodernist pastiche from the "real" one—which is itself a "fake," a substitute for history? The play of mirrors here may strike one as quite postmodernist . . .

29. Jean-François Lyotard, "Answering the Question: What Is Postmodernism?" trans. Régis Durand, in *The Postmodern Condition*, p. 77. Huyssen picks up the distinction in *Mapping the Postmodern*, p. 220. See also Foster, "(Post)Modern Polemics," in *Recodings*.

30. See Sherman's interview with Jeanne Siegel, in *Artwords 2: Discourse on the Early 80's*, ed. Siegel (Ann Arbor and London: UMI Research Press, 1988), p. 272.

31. Martha Rosler, "Notes on Quotes," *Wedge*, 2 (Fall 1982), 71. Rosler does not refer to anyone by name, but her critique appears clearly to be directed at the work of Kruger, Levine, and Sherman.

32. Hutcheon, *A Poetics of Postmodernism*, p. xiii and passim.

33. Craig Owens, "The Allegorical Impulse: Toward a Theory of Postmodernism," in *Art after Modernism,* ed. Brian Wallis, p. 235.

34. Rosler, "Notes on Quotes," pp. 72, 73; hereafter, page numbers are given in parentheses in the text. Rosler's characterization of her work as didactic but not hortatory is in an interview with Jane Weinstock, *October,* 17 (Summer 1981), 78.

35. Meaghan Morris, "Tooth and Claw: Tales of Survival and *Crocodile Dundee*," in *Universal Abandon?* ed. Andrew Ross, p. 123; hereafter, page numbers are given in parentheses in the text.

36. Laura Kipnis, "Feminism: The Political Conscience of Postmodernism?" in *Universal Abandon?* ed. Ross, p. 162; hereafter, page numbers are given in parentheses in the text.

37. Max Horkheimer and Theodor W. Adorno, "The Culture Industry: Enlightenment as Mass Deception," in *Dialectic of Enlightenment,* trans. John Cumming (New York: Continuum, 1982), pp. 120–167.

38. Thomas Crow, "Modernism and Mass Culture in the Visual Arts," in *Pollock and After,* ed. Francis Frascina (New York: Harper and Row, 1985), p. 257; hereafter, page numbers are given in parentheses in the text. I wish to thank Bernard Gendron for bringing this essay, in particular the remark I have quoted about the avant-garde and the culture industry, to my attention.

39. Rozsika Parker and Griselda Pollock, "Fifteen Years of Feminist Action: From Practical Strategies to Strategic Practices," in *Framing Feminism,* ed. Parker and Pollock, p. 54.

40. Women postmodernists are not the only ones to have practiced a kind of public intervention, of course; among men doing comparable things, Hans Haacke and Daniel Buren come to mind (though Buren's work questions more the politics of museums than the "politics of politics"). Nor is all of the political work by women exclusively feminist. These considerations do not invalidate my general point; rather, they enlarge it. For an interesting recent reflection on the critical possibilities of postmodernist art, which on several points intersects my own argument, see Abigail Solomon-Godeau, "Living with Contradictions: Critical Practices in the Age of Supply-Side Aesthetics," in *Universal Abandon?* ed. Ross, pp. 191–213.

41. Kruger refers to her use of billboards and the Times Square Spectacolor Board in her interview with Jeanne Siegel, "Barbara Kruger: Pictures and Words," in *Artwords 2,* ed. Siegel, pp. 299–311. In personal conversation with me, Kruger explained that she herself pays for all of the billboard and poster work; the abortion-march poster ("Your Body Is a Battleground," fig. 14) is being made into postcards and T-shirts, with proceeds going to Planned Parenthood. As Kruger is the first to point out, it is *because* she has a "name" in the artworld (she is represented by the highly visible, high-priced Mary Boone Gallery) that she is able to put up her billboards and posters. The idea that art should try to remain "pure," outside the circuits of the market, is, she stated, quite foreign to her—as, for that matter, is the idea of belonging to "the avant-garde," which she associates with elitism. I pointed out that the desire to bypass the elitist connotations of art and to

intervene with her work in the real world is precisely what makes her work, in *my* terms, "avant-garde." She, I must report, remained skeptical. But then, she is also skeptical about being called "postmodernist." We finally agreed that if it is the artist's prerogative to reject all critical labels, it is the critic's or theorist's prerogative to invent them.

42. Holzer, interview with Jeanne Siegel, "Jenny Holzer's Language Games," in *Artwords 2,* ed. Siegel, p. 286; hereafter, page numbers are given in parentheses in the text.

43. Kruger, interview in *Artwords 2,* ed. Siegel, p. 303; hereafter, page numbers are given in parentheses in the text.

44. Donna Haraway, "A Manifesto for Cyborgs: Science, Technology, and Socialist Feminism in the 1980's," *Socialist Review,* 50 (1984), 75; hereafter, page numbers are given in parentheses in the text.

45. Naomi Schor, "Dreaming Dissymetry," in *Men in Feminism,* ed. Jardine and Smith, p. 109.

46. James Clifford, *The Predicament of Culture* (Cambridge, Mass.: Harvard University Press, 1988), p. 12.

47. On the figure of the "alone-standing woman"—a fictional creation of Christine Brooke-Rose's—as an emblem of postmodernity, see my essay on Brooke-Rose's novel *Between:* "Living Between, or the Lone(love)liness of the *alleinstehende Frau*," *Review of Contemporary Fiction,* Fall 1989, 124–127.

48. Julia Kristeva, *Etrangers à nous-mêmes* (Paris: Fayard, 1988), p. 58; hereafter, page numbers are given in parentheses in the text.

Selected Bibliography

The following listing contains works cited or referred to in the text and only a few additional, immediately relevant works. For some of the best-known French titles, I have also included the English edition. For articles in collective volumes, usually only a short citation to the volume is given; the full citation is under the name of the editor.

Acker, Kathy. *Blood and Guts in High School.* New York: Grove Press, 1978.
———— *Great Expectations.* New York, Grove Press, 1983.
Adams, Parveen. "A Note on Sexual Division and Sexual Differences." *m/f*, 3 (1979): 51–58.
Adorno, Theodor. *Aesthetic Theory,* trans. C. Lenhardt. London and New York: Routledge and Kegan Paul, 1984.
Adorno, Theodor, and Max Horkheimer. "The Culture Industry: Enlightenment as Mass Deception." In *Dialectic of Enlightenment,* trans. John Cummings. New York: Continuum, 1982. Pp. 120–167.
Alexandrian, Sarane. *Surrealist Art,* trans. Gordon Clough. London: Thames and Hudson, 1970.
Annan, Gabriele. Review of Leonora Currington's *The Hearing Trumpet. Times Literary Supplement,* May 27, 1977, p. 644.
Aragon, Louis. *Les Aventures de Télémaque.* Paris: NRF, 1922.
———— *Le Libertinage.* Paris: Gallimard, 1983. (Original edition, 1924).
———— *Pour expliquer ce que j'étais.* Paris: Gallimard, 1989.
Auster, Paul, ed., *The Random House Book of Twentieth-Century French Poetry.* New York: Vintage Books, 1984.
Bakhtin, W. M. *The Dialogic Imagination,* trans. Caryl Emerson and Michael Holquist, ed. Michael Holquist. Austin: University of Texas Press, 1981.
———— *Rabelais and His World,* trans. Helen Iswolsky. Cambridge, Mass.: MIT Press, 1968.
Balakian, Anna. *André Breton: Magus of Surrealism.* New York: Oxford University Press, 1971.
Barth, John. "Postmodernism Revisited." *The Review of Contemporary Fiction,* 8:3 (Fall 1988): 16–24.
Barthes, Roland. *Essais Critiques.* Paris: Editions du Seuil, 1964.
———— *Leçon.* Paris: Editions du Seuil, 1978.

—— *Le Plaisir du texte*. Paris: Editions du Seuil, 1973. English translation: *The Pleasure of the Text*, trans. Richard Miller. New York: Hill and Wang, 1975.

—— Discussion with Alain Robbe-Grillet in *Prétexte: Roland Barthes*, ed. Antoine Compagnon. Paris: 10/18, 1978.

—— *Roland Barthes par Roland Barthes*. Paris: Editions du Seuil, 1975.

—— *Sade, Fourier, Loyola*. Paris: Editions du Seuil, 1971.

—— *Sollers écrivain*. Paris: Editions du Seuil, 1979.

—— *S/Z*. Paris: Editions du Seuil, 1970. English translation: *S/Z*, trans. Richard Miller. New York: Hill and Wang, 1974.

Bataille, Georges. *L'Abbé C*. Paris: Editions de Minuit, 1950.

—— *Le Bleu du ciel*. Paris: Jean-Jacques Pauvert, 1957.

—— *L'Erotisme*. Paris: Editions de Minuit, 1957.

—— *L'Expérience intérieure*. Paris: Gallimard, 1943.

—— *Histoire de l'oeil*. In *Oeuvres complètes*, vol. 1. Paris: Gallimard, 1970. English translation: *The Story of the Eye*, trans. Joachim Neugroschel. New York: Berkley Books, 1982.

—— *La Littérature et le mal*. Paris: Gallimard, 1957.

—— *Ma mère*. Paris: Jean-Jacques Pauvert, 1966.

—— *Madame Edwarda*. In *Oeuvres complètes*, vol. 3. Paris: Gallimard, 1971.

—— "La morale de Miller." *Critique*, 1 (1946): 3–17.

—— *Notions of Excess: Selected Writings, 1927–1939*, trans. Allan Stoekl with Carl R. Lovitt and Donald M. Leslie, Jr., ed. Allan Stoekl. Minneapolis: University of Minnesota Press, 1982.

—— "Sommes-nous là pour jouer ou pour être sérieux?" Article in two parts. *Critique*, 49 (1951): 512–522, and 51–52 (1951): 736–743.

Bataille, Georges, et al. *L'Affaire Sade*. Paris: Jean-Jacques Pauvert, 1957.

Bateson, Gregory. *Steps to an Ecology of Mind*. San Francisco: Chandler Publishing Company, 1972.

Baudrillard, Jean. *A l'ombre des majorités silencieuses*. Paris: UTOPIE, 1978.

—— *L'échange symbolique et la mort*. Paris: Gallimard, 1975.

—— "The Precession of Simulacra." In Wallis, ed., *Art after Modernism*, pp. 253–282.

Beaujour, Michel. "Qu'est-ce que *Nadja*?" *La Nouvelle Revue Française*, 172 (1967): 780–799.

Beauvoir, Simone. *Le Deuxième Sexe*. Paris: Gallimard, 1954. English translation: *The Second Sex*, trans. and ed. H. M. Parshley. New York: Bantam Books, 1961.

—— *Faut-t-il brûler Sade?* Paris: Gallimard, 1955.

Beckett, Samuel. *Malone Dies*. In *Three Novels by Samuel Beckett*. New York: Grove Press, Evergreen Black Cat Edition, 1963.

Belen. See Nelly Kaplan.

Benjamin, Jessica. *The Bonds of Love: Psychoanalysis, Feminism, and the Problem of Domination*. New York: Pantheon Books, 1988.

—— "The Bonds of Love: Rational Violence and Erotic Domination." *Feminist Studies*, 6:1 (Spring 1980): 144–174.

Benedikt, Michael, ed. *The Poetry of Surrealism: An Anthology*. Boston: Little, Brown and Co., 1974.

Benstock, Shari. *Women of the Left Bank: Paris, 1900–1940*. Austin: University of Texas Press, 1986.

Bernheimer, Charles, and Claire Kahane, eds. *In Dora's Case: Freud—Hysteria—Feminism*. New York: Columbia University Press, 1985.

Bertens, Hans. "The Post-modern *Weltanschauung* and Its Relation with Modernism: An Introductory Survey." In Fokkema and Bertens, eds., *Approaching Postmodernism*, pp. 9–52.

Blanchot, Maurice. *L'Entretien infini*. Paris: Gallimard, 1969.

Bloom, Harold. *The Anxiety of Influence*. New York: Oxford University Press, 1973.

——— *A Map of Misreading*. New York: Oxford University Press, 1975.

Blume, Mary. "Portrait of a Surrealist." *The International Herald Tribune*, August 17, 1987, p. 14.

Bonnet, Marguerite. *André Breton: Naissance de l'aventure surréaliste*. Paris: J. Corti, 1975.

Bonnet, Marguerite, and Jacqueline Chénieux-Gendron. *Revues surréalistes françaises autour d'André Breton, 1948–1972*. Millwood, N.Y.: Kraus International Publications, 1982.

Boston Women's Collective. *Our Bodies Ourselves*. New York: Simon and Schuster, 1973.

Boym, Svetlana. "Life and Death in Quotation Marks: Cultural Myths of the Modern Poet." Ph.D. diss., Harvard University, 1988.

Breton, André, *L'Amour fou*. Paris: Gallimard, 1937.

——— *Anthologie de l'humor noir,* revised edition. Paris: Jean-Jacques Pauvert, 1966. (Original edition, 1939.)

——— *Arcane 17*. Paris: Jean-Jacques Pauvert, 1971. (Original edition, 1947.)

——— *Entretiens*. Paris: Gallimard, 1969.

——— *Manifestoes of Surrealism,* trans. Richard Seaver and Helen R. Lane. Ann Arbor: University of Michigan Press, 1969.

——— *Nadja,* revised edition. Paris: Gallimard, "Folio," 1964. English translation: *Nadja,* trans. Richard Howard. New York: Grove Press, 1960.

——— *Les Vases communicants*. Paris: Gallimard, 1955. (Original edition, 1933.)

——— *What Is Surrealism? Selected Writings,* ed. F. Rosemont. Chicago: Monad Press, 1978.

Breton, André, and Louis Aragon. "Le Cinquantenaire de l'hystérie (1878–1928)." *La Révolution Surréaliste*, 11 (1928): 20–22.

Brooke-Rose, Christine. *Amalgamemnon*. London: Carcanet, 1986.

——— "Illiterations." In Friedman and Fuchs, eds., *Breaking the Sequence: Women's Experimental Fiction*, pp. 55–71.

——— "Transgressions: An Essay-say on the Novel Novel Novel." *Contemporary Literature*, 19:3 (Summer 1978): 378–407.

Brooks, Peter. "Constructions psychanalytiques et narratives." *Poétique*, 61 (1985): 63–74.

——— *Reading for the Plot: Design and Intention in Narrative*. New York: Alfred A. Knopf, 1984.

Brown, Beverly, and Parveen Adams. "The Feminine Body and Feminist Politics." *m/f*, 3 (1979): 3–50.

Brown, Rita Mae. *Rubyfruit Jungle*. New York: Bantam Books, 1977. (Original edition, 1973.)

Burgelin, Claude. *Georges Perec*. Paris: Editions du Seuil, 1989.

Bürger, Peter. *Theory of the Avant-Garde*, trans. Michael Shaw. Minneapolis: University of Minnesota Press, 1984.

Burke, Carolyn. "Irigaray through the Looking Glass." *Feminist Studies*, 6 (1981): 288–306.

Caillois, Roger. *Les Jeux et les hommes*. Paris: Gallimard, 1967.

Carrington, Leonora. *The Hearing Trumpet*. San Francisco: City Lights Books, 1985. (Original edition, 1976.)

—————— *The House of Fear: Notes from Down Below*. New York: E. P. Dutton, 1988.

—————— *The Seventh Horse and Other Tales*. New York: E. P. Dutton, 1988.

—————— *The Stone Door*. New York: St. Martin's Press, 1977.

Carter, Angela. Interview with John Engstrom. *Boston Globe*, October 28, 1988, p. 62.

—————— *Nights at the Circus*. London: Chatto and Windus, 1984.

—————— *Nothing Sacred: Selected Writings*. London: Virago Press, 1982.

—————— *The Passion of New Eve*. London: Virago Press, 1982. (Original edition, 1977.)

Caws, Mary Ann. "Ladies Shot and Painted: Female Embodiment in Surrealist Art." In Suleiman, ed., *The Female Body in Western Culture: Contemporary Perspectives*, pp. 262–287.

Chadwick, Whitney. *Women Artists and the Surrealist Movement*. Boston: Little, Brown and Co., 1985.

Charcot, J. B. *Leçons de mardi à la Salpêtrière*. Paris: Centre d'étude et de promotion de la lecture, 1975.

—————— *L'Hystérie: Textes choisis et présentes par E. Trillat*. Toulouse: Privat, 1971.

Chasseguet-Smirgel, Janine. "Perversion and the Universal Law." *International Review of Psychoanalysis*, 10 (1983): 293–301.

Chawaf, Chantal. *Maternité*. Paris: Stock, 1979.

—————— "Deux ou trois idées pour la survie de notre héros." *Roman*, 23 (June 1988): 26–45.

Chénieux, Jacqueline. *Le Surréalisme et le roman*. Lausanne: L'Age d'Homme, 1983.

Cixous, Hélène. "Entretien avec Françoise van Rossum-Guyon." *Revues des Sciences Humaines*, 44 (1977): 479–493.

—————— *L'Exil de James Joyce, ou, L'Art de remplacement*. Paris: Grasset, 1968.

—————— *L'Histoire terrible mais inachevée de Norodom Sihanouk, roi du Cambodge*. Paris: Théâtre du Soleil, 1985.

—————— *Illa*. Paris: Editions des Femmes, 1980.

—————— *L'Indiade, ou, L'Inde de leurs rêves*. Paris: Théâtre du Soleil, 1987.

—————— *Le Livre de Promethea*. Paris: Gallimard, 1983.

—————— *Manne: Aux Mandelstams aux Mandelas*. Paris: Editions des Femmes, 1988.

—————— *Ou L'art de l'innocence*. Paris: Editions des Femmes, 1981.

———— *Portrait de Dora.* Paris: Editions de Femmes, 1976. English translation: *Portrait of Dora,* trans. Sarah Burd. *Diacritics,* Spring 1983, 2–32.

———— "Le Rire de la Méduse." *L'Arc,* 61 (1975): 39–54. English Translation: "The Laugh of the Medusa," trans. Keith Cohen and Paula Cohen. In Marks and Courtivron, eds., *New French Feminisms,* pp. 245–264.

———— *Souffles.* Paris: Editions des Femmes, 1975.

———— "Tancrède continue." *Etudes Freudiennes,* 21–22 (March 1983): 115–132.

———— *Vivre l'orange.* Paris: Editions des Femmes, 1979.

Cixous, Hélène, and Catherine Clément. *La Jeune Née.* Paris: 10/18, 1975.

Cixous, Hélène, Madeleine Gagnon, and Annie Leclerc. *La Venue à l'écriture.* Paris: 10/18, 1977.

Claude, C. "Une lecture de femme." *Europe,* October 1972, 64–70.

Clément, Catherine. "De la méconnaissance: Fantasme, texte, scène." *Langages,* 31 (1974): 36–52.

Clifford, James. *The Predicament of Culture.* Cambridge, Mass.: Harvard University Press, 1988.

Collins, Jerre, et al. "Questioning the Unconscious: The Dora Archive." In Bernheimer and Kahane, eds., *In Dora's Case,* pp. 243–253.

Coover, Robert. *Pricksongs and Descants.* New York: New American Library, 1970.

Cottenet-Hage, Madeleine. *Gisèle Prassions, ou, Le Désir du lieu intime.* Paris: Jean-Michel Place, 1988.

Crimp, Douglas. "Pictures." *October,* 8 (Spring 1979): 75–88.

Crow, Thomas. "Modernism and Mass Culture in the Visual Arts." In Francis Frascina, ed., *Pollock and After.* New York: Harper and Row, 1985. Pp. 233–265.

Crowder, Dane Griffin. "Amazons and Mothers? Monique Wittig, Hélène Cixous, and Theories of Women's Writing." *Contemporary Literature,* 24:2 (1983): 117–144.

Dallenbach, Lucien. *Le Récit spéculaire: Essais sur la mise en abyme.* Paris: Editions du Seuil, 1977.

Dardigna, Anne-Marie. *Les Châteaux d'Eros ou les infortunes du sexe des femmes.* Paris: Maspero, 1981.

———— *Pierre Klossowski: L'Homme aux simulacres.* Paris: Navarin, 1986.

Davis, Natalie Zemon. "Women on Top." In *Society and Culture in Early Modern France.* Stanford: Stanford University Press, 1965. Pp. 124–152.

Debord, Guy. *Commentaires sur la société du spectacle.* Paris: Lebovici, 1988.

———— *La Société du spectacle.* Paris: Buchet-Chastel, 1967.

DeLauretis, Teresa. *Alice Doesn't: Feminism, Semiotics, Cinema.* Bloomington: Indiana University Press, 1984.

DeLauretis, Teresa, ed. *Feminist Studies/Critical Studies.* Bloomington: Indiana University Press, 1986.

Deleuze, Gilles. *Présentation de Sacher Masoch.* Paris: 10/18, 1967.

Derrida, Jacques. *L'Ecriture et la différence.* Paris: Editions du Seuil, 1967. English translation: *Writing and Difference,* trans. Alan Bass. Chicago: University of Chicago Press, 1978.

—— "Living On: Border Lines." In Harold Bloom et al., *Deconstruction and Criticism*. New York: Continuum, 1979.

—— "Structure, Sign, and Play in the Discourse of the Human Sciences." In Richard Macksey and Eugenio Donato, eds., *The Structuralist Controversy: A Discourse on the Human Sciences*. Baltimore: Johns Hopkins University Press, 1972.

Derrida, Jacques, and Christie V. McDonald. "Choreographies." *Diacritics,* 12:2, 66–76.

Desnos, Robert. *La Liberté ou l'amour!* Paris: Gallimard, 1962. (Original edition, 1927.)

Dillon, Millicent. "Literature and the New Bawd." *The Nation,* February 22, 1975, pp. 219–221.

Ducornet, Rikki. *Entering Fire.* San Francisco: City Lights Books, 1986.

—— *The Stain.* London: Chatto and Windus, 1984.

Dumas, Marie-Claire. *Robert Desnos, ou, L'Exploration des limites.* Paris: Klincksieck, 1980.

Duras, Marguerite. *L'Amant.* Paris: Editions de Minuit, 1984.

—— *L'Amour.* Paris: Gallimard, 1971.

—— *Le Ravissement de Lol V. Stein.* Paris: Gallimard, "Folio," 1964.

—— *Le Vice-Consul.* Paris: Gallimard, 1966.

—— *La Vie matérielle.* Paris: P.O.L., 1987.

Duras, Marguerite, et al. *Marguerite Duras.* Paris: Albatros, 1979.

Duras, Marguerite, and Xavière Gauthier. *Les Parleuses.* Paris: Editions de Minuit, 1974. English translation: *Woman to Woman,* trans. Katharine A. Jensen. Lincoln: University of Nebraska Press, 1987.

Duras, Marguerite, and Michelle Porte. *Les Lieux de Marguerite Duras.* Paris: Editions de Minuit, 1979.

Dworkin, Andrea. *Pornography: Men Possessing Women.* New York: Perigee, 1981.

Eagleton, Terry. "Capitalism, Modernism, and Postmodernism." *New Left Review,* 152 (1985): 60–73.

Eco, Umberto. Interview with J. J. Brochier and Mario Fusco. *Le Magazine Littéraire,* 262 (February 1989): 18–27.

Ernst, Jimmy. *A Not-So-Still-Life.* New York: St. Martin's/Marek, 1984.

Ernst, Max. *Beyond Painting and Other Essays by the Artist and His Friends.* New York: Wittenborn, Schultz, 1948.

—— *Une Semaine de bonté.* New York: Dover Publications, 1976. (Original edition, 1934.)

Evans, Martha Noel. *Masks of Tradition: Women and the Politics of Writing in Twentieth-Century France.* Ithaca: Cornell University Press, 1988.

Felman, Shoshana. "Turning the Screw of Interpretation." *Yale French Studies,* 55–56 (1977): 94–207.

—— "Women and Madness: The Critical Phallacy." *Diacritics,* 5:4 (1975): 2–10.

La Femme Surréaliste. Special Issue of *Obliques,* 14–15 (1977).

Ferraris, Denis. "Quaestio de legibilibus aut legendis scriptis: Sur la notion de lisibilité en littérature." *Poétique,* 43 (1980): 282–292.

Fiedler, Leslie. "The New Mutants" (1965) and "Cross the Border, Close the Gap" (1970). In *Collected Essays,* vol. 2. New York: Stein and Day, 1971.

Finas, Lucette. *La Crue.* Paris: Gallimard, 1972.

Fish, Stanley. *Is There a Text in this Class? The Authority of Interpretive Communities.* Cambridge, Mass.: Harvard University Press, 1980.

Fitch, Brian. *Monde à l'envers, texte réversible: La Fiction de Georges Bataille.* Paris: Lettres Modernes, 1982.

Fokkema, Douwe, and Hans Bertens, eds. *Approaching Postmodernism.* Amsterdam and Philadelphia: John Benjamins, 1986.

Foster, Hal. *Recodings: Art, Spectacle, Cultural Politics.* Port Townsend, Wash.: Bay Press, 1985.

Foster, Hal, ed. *The Anti-Aesthetic: Essays on Postmodern Culture.* Port Townsend, Wash.: Bay Press, 1983.

Foucault, Michel. "Preface to Transgression." In *Language, Countermemory, Practice: Selected Essays and Interviews,* ed. Donald F. Bouchard. Ithaca: Cornell University Press, 1977. Pp. 29–52.

——— "Présentation." In Bataille, Georges, *Oeuvres Complètes,* vol. 1. Paris: Gallimard, 1970.

Freud, Sigmund. "Bruchstück einer Hysterie-Analyse." In *Studienausgabe,* vol. 6. Frankfurt: S. Fischer, 1971.

——— *The Complete Letters of Sigmund Freud to Wilhelm Fliess, 1887–1904,* ed. and trans. Jeffrey Moussaieff Masson. Cambridge, Mass.: Harvard University Press, 1985.

——— *Dora: An Analysis of a Case of Hysteria.* New York: Collier Books, 1963.

——— "The Relation of the Poet to Day-Dreaming" (1908). In *On Creativity and the Unconscious.* New York: Harper Torchbooks, 1958.

——— "The Most Prevalent Form of Degradation in Erotic Life" (1912), "Medusa's Head" (1922), and "Fetishism" (1927). In *Sexuality and the Psychology of Love,* ed. Philip Rieff. New York: Collier Books, 1963.

——— "Humor" (1927). In *The Standard Edition of the Complete Psychological Works of Sigmund Freud,* ed. James Strachey et al., vol. 21. London: Hogarth Press, 1971.

——— "Three Essays on the Theory of Sexuality" (1905). In *Standard Edition,* vol. 7. London: Hogarth Press, 1963.

——— "The Dynamics of Transference" (1912) and "Further Recommendations in the Technique of Psychoanalysis: Observations on Transference-Love" (1915). In *Therapy and Technique,* ed. Philip Rieff. New York: Collier Books, 1963.

——— "The Case of the Wolf-Man: From the History of an Infantile Neurosis." In *The Wolf-Man by the Wolf-Man,* ed. Muriel Gardiner. New York: Basic Books, 1971.

Friedman, Ellen G., and Miriam Fuchs, eds. *Breaking the Sequence: Women's Experimental Fiction.* Princeton: Princeton University Press, 1989.

Friedrich, Paul. *The Meaning of Aphrodite.* Chicago: Chicago University Press, 1978.

Gallop, Jane. *The Daughter's Seduction: Feminism and Psychoanalysis.* Ithaca: Cornell University Press, 1982.
—— "Quand Nos Lèvres S'Ecrivent: Irigaray's Body Politic." *Romanic Review,* 74:1 (1983): 77–83.
—— *Reading Lacan.* Ithaca: Cornell University Press, 1985.
—— *Thinking through the Body.* New York: Columbia University Press, 1988.
Gauthier, Xavière. *Surréalisme et sexualité.* Paris: Gallimard, 1971.
—— "Le Surréalisme et la sexualité." In *Obliques* (special issue, *La Femme Surréaliste*), 14–15 (1977): 42–44.
Genette, Gérard. *Figures II.* Paris: Editions du Seuil, 1969.
—— *Introduction à l'architexte.* Paris: Editions du Seuil, 1979.
—— *Palimpsestes: La Littérature au second degré.* Paris: Editions du Seuil, 1982.
Gilbert, Sandra. "The Second Coming of Aphrodite." *Kenyon Review,* 5 (1983): 42–65.
Gilbert, Sandra, and Susan Gubar. *The Madwoman in the Attic: The Woman Writer and the Nineteenth-Century Literary Imagination.* New Haven: Yale University Press, 1979.
—— *No Man's Land,* vol. 1, *The War of the Words.* New Haven: Yale University Press, 1987.
—— "Tradition and the Female Talent." In Miller, ed., *The Poetics of Gender,* pp. 183–207.
Gilman, Charlotte Perkins. *Herland.* New York: Pantheon Books, 1979. (Original edition, 1915.)
Gubar, Susan. "Representing Pornography: Feminism, Criticism, and Depictions of Female Violation." *Critical Inquiry,* 13:4 (1987): 712–741.
Habermas, Jürgen. "Modernity—An Incomplete Project." In Foster, ed., *The Anti-Aesthetic,* pp. 3–15.
Hamon, Philippe. "Qu'est-ce qu'une description?" *Poétique,* 18 (1974): 215–235.
Haraway, Donna. "A Manifesto for Cyborgs: Science, Technology, and Socialist Feminism in the 1980's." *Socialist Review,* 50 (1984): 65–107.
Hassan, Ihab. *The Dismemberment of Orpheus: Toward a Postmodern Literature.* New York: Oxford University Press, 1971. (Updated second edition, 1982.)
Heath, Stephen. *The Nouveau Roman: A Study in the Practice of Writing.* Philadelphia: Temple University Press, 1972.
Hedges, Inez. *Languages and Revolt: Dada and Surrealist Literature and Film.* Durham, N.C.: Duke University Press, 1983.
Hertz, Neil. "Dora's Secrets, Freud's Techniques." In Bernheimer and Kahane, eds., *In Dora's Case* pp. 221–242.
Hite, Shere. *The Hite Report: A Nationwide Study of Female Sexuality.* New York: Dell, 1981.
—— *Sexual Honesty by Women for Women.* New York: Warner Paperback Library, 1974.
Holland, Norman. *The Dynamics of Literary Response.* New York: Oxford

University Press, 1969.

Hollier, Denis. "Bataille's Tomb: A Halloween Story." *October*, 33 (Summer 1985): 73–102.

——— "Collage." Introduction to *The College of Sociology*, ed. Denis Hollier, trans. Betsy Wing. Minneapolis: University of Minnesota Press, 1988.

———*La Prisc dc la Concorde: Essais sur Georges Bataille.* Paris: Gallimard, 1974.

Hollier, Denis, ed. *A New History of French Literature.* Cambridge, Mass.: Harvard University Press, 1989.

Holzer, Jenny. Interview with Jeanne Siegel. In Siegel, ed., *Artwords 2,* pp. 285–298.

Houdebine, Jean-Louis. "Méconaissance de la psychanalyse dans le discours surréaliste." *Tel Quel,* 46 (1971): 67–82.

Howe, Irving. "Mass Society and Postmodern Fiction." In *The Decline of the New.* New York: Harcourt, Brace and World, 1970.

Hubert, Renée Riese. "Portrait d'Unica Zürn en anagramme." *Pleine Marge,* 7 (1988): 61–73.

Hughes, Robert. *The Shock of the New.* New York: Alfred A. Knopf, 1982.

Huston, Nancy. *Mosaique de la pornographie.* Paris: Denöel/Gonthier, 1982.

Hutcheon, Linda. *A Poetics of Postmodernism: History, Theory, Fiction.* New York and London: Routledge, 1988.

——— *A Theory of Parody.* New York: Methuen, 1985.

Huyssen, Andreas. *After the Great Divide: Modernism, Mass Culture, Postmodernism.* Bloomington: Indiana University Press, 1986.

Irigaray, Luce. *Amante marine: De Friedrich Nietzsche.* Paris: Editions de Minuit, 1980.

——— "Une Lacune natale (pour Unica Zürn)." *Le Nouveau Commerce,* 62–63 (1985): 41–47.

——— *Passions elementaires.* Paris: Editions de Minuit, 1982.

——— *Ce Sexe qui n'en est pas un.* Paris: Editions de Minuit, 1977. English translation: *This Sex Which Is Not One,* trans. Catherine Porter with Carolyn Burke. Ithaca: Cornell University Press, 1985.

——— *Speculum de l'autre femme.* Paris: Editions de Minuit, 1974. English translation: *Speculum of the Other Woman,* trans. Gillian C. Gill. Ithaca: Cornell University Press, 1985.

Jameson, Fredric. "Postmodernism, or, The Cultural Logic of Late Capitalism." *New Left Review,* July–August 1984, 53–92.

——— Interview with Anders Stephanson. In Ross, ed., *Universal Abandon?* pp. 3–30.

Jardine, Alice A. *Gynesis: Configurations of Woman and Modernity.* Ithaca: Cornell University Press, 1985.

Jardine, Alice, and Paul Smith, eds. *Men in Feminism.* New York: Methuen, 1987.

Jenny, Laurent. "La Stratégie de la forme." *Poétique,* 27 (1976): 257–281.

Jong, Erica. *Fear of Flying.* New York: Signet, 1974. (Original edition, 1973.)

Johnson, Barbara. *A World of Difference.* Baltimore: Johns Hopkins University Press, 1987.

Kaplan, E. Ann. *Women and Film: Both Sides of the Camera.* New York and London: Methuen, 1983.

Kaplan, E. Ann, ed. *Postmodernism and Its Discontents.* London: Verso, 1988.

Kaplan, Janet. *Unexpected Journeys: The Art and Life of Remedios Varo.* New York: Abbeville Press, 1988.

Kaplan, Nelly [pseud. Belen]. *Mémoires d'une liseuse de draps.* Paris: J. J. Pauvert, 1974.

———— *Le Réservoir des sens.* Paris: J. J. Pauvert, 1988.

Kipnis, Laura. "Feminism: The Political Conscience of Postmodernism?" In Ross, ed., *Universal Abandon?* pp. 149–166.

Knapp, Bettina. Review of Leonora Carrington's *The Hearing Trumpet. World Literature Today,* Winter 1978, 80–81.

Koertge, Noretta. *Who Was That Masked Woman?* New York: St. Martin's Press, 1981.

Krauss, Rosalind. *The Originality of the Avant-Garde and Other Modernist Myths.* Cambridge, Mass.: MIT Press, 1985.

———— "The Originality of the Avant-Garde: A Post-Modernist Repetition." *October,* 18 (Fall 1981): 47–66.

Krauss, Rosalind, and Jane Livingston. *L'Amour Fou: Photography and Surrealism.* New York: Abbeville Press, 1985.

Kristeva, Julia. *Des Chinoises.* Paris: Editions des Femmes, 1974.

———— *Etrangers à nous-mêmes.* Paris: Fayard, 1988.

———— *Histoires d'amour.* Paris: Denöel, 1983. (English translation of the essay "Stabat Mater" in Suleiman, ed., *The Female Body in Western Culture,* pp. 99–118.)

———— *Polylogue.* Paris: Seuil, 1977.

———— *La Révolution du langage poétique.* Paris: Seuil, 1974. (Partial English translation: *Revolution in Poetic Language,* trans. Margaret Waller. New York: Columbia University Press, 1984.)

———— *Séméiotiké: Recherches pour une sémanalyse.* Paris: Editions du Seuil, 1969.

———— "Unes Femmes." *Cahiers du GRIF,* 12 (1975): 22–27.

Kruger, Barbara. Interview with Jeanne Siegel. In Siegel, ed., *Artwords 2,* pp. 299–312.

———— *We Won't Play Nature to Your Culture.* Exhibition Catalogue. Institute of Contemporary Art, London, 1983.

Lacan, J. "God and the *Jouissance* of The Woman." In *Feminine Sexuality: Jacques Lacan and the Ecole Freudienne,* ed. Juliet Mitchell and Jacqueline Rose, trans. Jacqueline Rose. London: Macmillan, 1982.

———— "Hommage fait à Marguerite Duras, du *Ravissement de Lol V. Stein.*" In Marguerite Duras et al., *Marguerite Duras.* Paris: Albatros, 1979. Pp. 131–138.

———— "Intervention on Transference," trans. Jacqueline Rose. In Bernheimer and Kahane, eds., *In Dora's Case,* pp. 92–104.

———— *Le Séminaire, XX: Encore.* Paris: Editions du Seuil, 1975.

Laplanche, J., and J. B. Pontalis. "Fantasme originaire, fantasme des origines, origine du fantasme." *Les Temps Modernes,* April 1964, 1833–1868.

—— *Vocabulaire de la psychanalyse*. Paris: PUF, 1973.

Laugaa-Traut, F. *Lectures de Sade*. Paris: Armand Colin, 1973.

Lebrun, Annie. *A Distance*. Paris: Pauvert/Carrère, 1984.

—— *Lâchez tout*. Paris: Le Sagittaire, 1977.

Leclerc, Annie. *Parole de femme*. Paris: Livre de Poche, 1974.

Lejeune, Philippe. *Le Pacte autobiographique*. Paris: Editions du Seuil, 1975.

Lewis, Helena. *The Politics of Surrealism*. New York: Paragon House, 1988.

Lodge, David. *The Modes of Modern Writing: Metaphor, Metonymy, and the Typology of Literature*. Ithaca: Cornell University Press, 1977.

Loomis, Roger Sherman. *The Grail: From Celtic Myth to Christian Symbol*. New York: Columbia University Press, 1963.

Lydenberg, Robin. *Word Cultures: Radical Theory and Practice in William Burroughs' Fiction*. Urbana and Chicago: University of Illinois Press, 1987.

Lyotard, Jean-François. *La Condition postmoderne: Rapport sur le savior*. Paris: Editions de Minuit, 1979. English translation: *The Postmodern Condition: A Report on Knowledge*, trans. Geoff Bennington and Brian Massumi. Minneapolis: University of Minnesota Press, 1981.

—— "Réponse à la question: Qu'est-ce que le postmoderne?" *Critique*, 419 (1982): 357–367.

Mansour, Joyce. *Birds of Prey*, trans. Albert Herzing. Van Nuys, Calif.: Perivale Press, 1979.

—— *Carré Blanc*. Paris: Soleil Noir, 1965.

—— *Cris*. Paris: Seghers, 1953.

—— *Les Gisants satisfaits*. Paris: J. J. Pauvert, 1958.

—— *Rapaces*. Paris: Seghers, 1960.

Marcus, Steven. "Freud and Dora: Story, History, Case History." In *Representations: Essays on Literature and Society*. New York: Random House, 1975. Pp. 247–310.

Marini, Marcelle. *Territoires du féminin: Avec Marguerite Duras*. Paris: Editions de Minuit, 1977.

Marks, Elaine, and Isabelle de Courtivron, eds. *New French Feminisms*. New York: Schocken Books, 1981.

Martos, J.-F. *Histoire de l'Internationale Situationniste*. Paris: G. Lebovici, 1989.

Matthews, J. H. *The Imagery of Surrealism*. Syracuse: Syracuse University Press, 1977.

—— *Joyce Mansour*. Amsterdam: Rodopi, 1985.

Maurer, Evan M. "Images of Dream and Desire: The Prints and Collage Novels of Max Ernst." *In Max Ernst: Beyond Surrealism*, ed. Robert Rainwater. New York: The New York Public Library and Oxford University Press, 1986.

McHale, Brian. *Postmodernist Fiction*. New York and London: Methuen, 1987.

Miller, Nancy K. *Subject to Change: Reading Feminist Writing*. New York: Columbia University Press, 1988.

—— "The Text's Heroine: A Feminist Critic and Her Fictions." *Diacritics*, 12:2 (1982): 48–53.

Miller, Nancy K., ed. *The Poetics of Gender.* New York: Columbia University Press, 1986.

Millett, Kate. *Sexual Politics.* New York: Avon Books, 1971.

Mistacco, Vicki. "The Theory and Practice of Reading *Nouveaux Romans:* Robbe-Grillet's *Topologie D'Une Cité Fantôme.*" In Suleiman and Crosman, eds., *The Reader in the Text,* pp. 371–400.

Mitterand, Henri. *Le Discours du roman.* Paris: PUF, 1980.

Modernity and Modernism, Postmodernity and Postmodernism. Special Issue of *Cultural Critique,* 5 (Winter 1986–87).

Montrelay, Michèle. *L'Ombre et le nom: Sur la féminité.* Paris: Editions de Minuit, 1977.

Morris, Meaghan. "Tooth and Claw: Tales of Survival in *Crocodile Dundee.*" In Ross, ed. *Universal Abandon?* pp. 105–127.

Morrison, Toni. *Beloved.* New York: Alfred A. Knopf, 1987.

Morrissette, Bruce. "Games and Game Structures in Robbe-Grillet." *Yale French Studies,* 41 (1968): 159–167.

――― "Un Héritage d'Andre Gide: La Duplication intérieure." *Comparative Literature Studies,* 8:2 (1970): 125–142.

――― *Les Romans de Robbe-Grillet,* new enlarged edition. Paris: Editions de Minuit, 1971. English translation: *The Novels of Robbe-Grillet.* Ithaca: Cornell University Press, 1975.

Motte, Warren F., Jr. *The Poetics of Experiment: A Study of the Work of Georges Perec.* Lexington, Ky.: French Forum Publishers, 1984.

Nadeau, Maurice, *Histoire du Surréalisme.* Paris: Editions du Seuil, 1964. English translation: *The History of Surrealism,* trans. Richard Howard. Cambridge, Mass.: Harvard University Press, 1989.

Norris, Margot. *Beasts of the Modern Imagination: Darwin, Nietzsche, Kafka, Ernst and Lawrence.* Baltimore: Johns Hopkins University Press, 1985.

O'Connor, Thomas. "Tracy Ullman: She's a Real Character." *The New York Times,* Arts and Entertainment Section, Sept. 25, 1988.

Oppler, Ellen C., ed. *Picasso's Guernica: Illustrations, Introductory Essay, Documents, Poetry, Criticism, Analysis.* New York: W. W. Norton, 1988.

Orenstein, Gloria Feman. "*Nadja* Revisited: A Feminist Approach." *Dada/Surrealism,* 8 (1978): 91–106.

――― "Reclaiming the Great Mother: A Feminist Journey to Madness and Back in Search of a Goddess Heritage." *Symposium,* 36: 1 (1982): 45–70.

――― "Towards a Bifocal Vision in Surrealist Aesthetics." *Trivia,* 3 (Fall 1983): 70–87.

Ostriker, Alicia. *Stealing the Language: The Emergence of Women's Poetry in America.* Boston: Beacon Press, 1986.

Ovid. *Metamorphoses,* trans. Rolfe Humphries. Bloomington: Indiana University Press, 1955.

Owens, Craig. "The Discourse of Others: Feminists and Post-Modernism." In Foster, ed., *The Anti-Aesthetic,* pp. 57–82.

――― "The Allegorical Impulse: Toward a Theory of Postmodernism." In Wallis, ed., *Art after Modernism,* pp. 203–236.

Palau, P. L. "Les Détraquées." *Le Surréalisme, Même,* 1 (1956): 73–120.

Parker, Rozsika, and Griselda Pollock, eds. *Framing Feminism: Art and the Wom-*

en's Movement, 1970–1985. London and New York: Pandora Press, 1987.

Péret, Benjamin, and Paul Eluard. "152 Proverbes mis au goût du jour." In Péret, Oeuvres complètes, vol. 4. Paris: Jose Corti: 1987. Pp. 251–265.

Perloff, Marjorie. The Futurist Moment: Avant-Garde, Avant-Guerre, and the Language of Rupture. Chicago: University of Chicago Press, 1986.

Pleynet, Marcelin. "Les Problèmes de l'avant-garde." Tel Quel, 25 (1966): 77–86.

Poggioli, Renato. The Theory of the Avant-Garde, trans. Gerald Fitzgerald. Cambridge, Mass.: Harvard University Press, 1968.

Postmodernism. Special Issue of Social Text, 18 (Winter 1987–88).

Prassinos, Gisèle. Les Mots endormis. Paris: Flammarion, 1967.

——— Trouver sans chercher. Paris: Flammarion, 1976.

Ricardou, Jean. Le Nouveau Roman. Paris: Editions du Seuil, 1973.

——— Nouveaux problèmes du roman. Paris: Editions du Seuil, 1978.

——— Pour une théorie du nouveau roman. Paris: Editions du Seuil, 1971.

——— Problèmes du nouveau roman. Paris: Editions du Seuil, 1967.

Prassinos, Gisèle, ed. Robbe-Grillet: Colloque de Cerisy. Paris: 10/18, 1976.

Ricardou, Jean, and Françoise van Rossum-Guyon, eds. Nouveau roman: Hier, aujourd'hui, 2 vols. Paris: 10/18, 1972.

Richman, Michele H. Reading Georges Bataille: Beyond the Gift. Baltimore: Johns Hopkins University Press, 1982.

Robbe-Grillet, Alain. Angélique, ou, L'Enchantement. Paris: Editions de Minuit, 1987.

——— Le Miroir qui revient. Paris: Editions de Minuit, 1984.

——— "Order and Disorder in Film and Fiction." Critical Inquiry, 4:1 (Autumn 1977): 1–20.

——— Projet pour une révolution à New York. Paris: Editions de Minuit, 1970. English translation: Project for a Revolution in New York, trans. Richard Howard. London. Calder and Boyers, 1972.

——— "Le Sadisme contre la peur." Interview. Le Nouvel Observateur, October 19, 1970.

Roche, Maurice. Codex. Paris: Editions du Seuil, 1974.

——— Compact. Paris: Editions du Seuil, 1966. English translation: Compact, trans. Mark Polizzotti. Elmwood Park, Ill.: Dalkey Archive Press, 1988.

——— Interview with David Hayman. Substance, 17 (1977): 5–11.

Rorty, Richard. "Habermas and Lyotard on Postmodernity." In Habermas and Modernity, ed. Richard J. Bernstein. Cambridge, Mass.: MIT Press, 1985. Pp. 161–175.

Rosen, Randy, et al. Making Their Mark: Women Artists Move into the Mainstream. New York: Abbeville Press, 1989.

Rosler, Martha. Interview with Jane Weinstock. October, 17 (Summer 1981): 77–98.

——— "Notes on Quotes." Wedge, 2 (Fall 1982): 68–73.

Roudiez, Leon. French Fiction Today. New Brunswick: Rutgers University Press, 1972.

Roudinesco, Elizabeth. La Bataille de cent ans: Histoire de la psychanalyse en France, 2 vols. Paris: Ramsay, 1980, 1982.

Rubin, William. Dada and Surrealist Art. New York: Harry N. Abrams, 1968.

——— *Dada, Surrealism, and Their Heritage*. New York: Museum of Modern Art, 1968.

Ruddick, Sara. "Maternal Thinking." *Feminist Studies*, 6:2 (1980), 342–367.

——— *Maternal Thinking: Toward a Politics of Peace*. Boston: Beacon Press, 1989.

Russell, Charles. *Poets, Prophets, and Revolutionaries: The Literary Avant-Garde from Rimbaud through Postmodernism*. New York: Oxford University Press, 1985.

Russo, Mary. "Female Grotesques: Carnival and Theory." In DeLauretis, ed., *Feminist Studies/Critical Studies*, pp. 213–229.

Sade, D. A. F. de. *Les Infortunes de la vertu*. Paris: 10/18, 1968.

——— *Juliette, ou, Les Prospérités du vice*. Paris: 10/18, 1969.

——— *Les 120 journées de Sodome*, 2 vols. Paris: 10/18, 1975.

Sartre, Jean-Paul. *Situations I*. Paris: Gallimard, 1947.

Schneede, Uwe, M. *The Essential Max Ernst*, trans. R. W. Last. London: Thames and Hudson, 1972.

Schneiderman, Stuart, ed. *Returning to Freud: Clinical Psychoanalysis in the School of Lacan*. New Haven: Yale University Press, 1980.

Scholes, Robert. *Semiotics and Interpretation*. New Haven: Yale University Press, 1982.

Schor, Naomi. "Dreaming Dissymetry: Barthes, Foucault, and Sexual Difference." In Jardine and Smith, eds., *Men in Feminism*, pp. 98–110.

——— "Female Fetishism: The Case of George Sand." In Suleiman, ed., *The Female Body in Western Culture*, pp. 363–372.

——— *Reading in Detail: Aesthetics and the Feminine*. New York and London: Methuen, 1987.

Schuster, Jean. *Archives 57/68*. Paris: Eric Losfeld, 1969.

Shattuck, Roger. "The Nadja File." *Cahiers Dada/Surréalisme*, 1 (1966): 49–56.

Sherman, Cindy. Interview with Jeanne Siegel. In Siegel, ed., *Artwords 2*, pp. 269–284.

Short, Robert. "Dada and Surrealism." In Malcolm Bradbury and James McFarlane, eds., *Modernism, 1890–1930*. Harmondsworth: Middlesex: Penguin Books, 1976.

Showalter, Elaine. "Feminist Criticism in the Wilderness." In Elizabeth Abel, ed., *Writing and Sexual Difference*. Chicago: Chicago University Press, 1980.

Siegel, Jeanne, ed. *Artwords 2: Discourse on the Early Eighties*. Ann Arbor and London: UMI Research Press, 1988.

Sigmund Freud's Dora. Film. Dir. McCall, Pajaczkowska, Tyndall and Weinstein, New York, 1979.

Silverman, Kaja. "Masochism and Male Subjectivity." *Camera Obscura*, 17 (1988): 31–68.

Sollers, Philippe. *L'Ecriture et l'expérience des limites*. Paris: Editions du Seuil, 1968.

——— "Editorial." *L'Infini*, 1 (Winter 1983): 3–6.

——— *Femmes*. Paris: Gallimard, 1983.

—— *Logiques*. Paris: Editions du Seuil, 1968.

—— "On n'a encore rien vu." *Tel Quel*, 85 (1980): 9–31.

—— *Paradis*. Paris: Editions du Seuil, 1981.

—— "Pourquoi j'ai été chinois." *Tel Quel*, 88 (1981): 11–30.

—— "Programme." *Tel Quel*, 31 (Fall 1967): 3–7.

—— "Réponses." *Tel Quel*, 43 (1970): 71–76.

—— *Vision à New York*. Interviews with David Hayman. Paris: Grasset, 1981.

Sollers, Philippe, ed. *Artaud*. Paris: 10/18, 1973.

—— *Bataille*. Paris: 10/18, 1973.

Solomon-Godeaut, Abigail. "Living with Contradictions: Critical Practices in the Age of Supply-Side Aesthetics." In Ross, ed., *Universal Abandon?* pp. 191–213.

Sontag, Susan. *Styles of Radical Will*. New York: Delta, 1981.

Spacks, Patricia Meyer. "The Fiction Chronicle." *Hudson Review*, 27:2, 283–295.

Spence, Donald P. *Narrative Truth and Historical Truth: Meaning and Interpretation in Psychoanalysis*. New York: W. W. Norton, 1982.

Spivak, Gayatri Chakravorty. "French Feminism in an International Frame." *Yale French Studies*, 62 (1981): 154–184.

Sprengnether, Madelon. "Enforcing Oedipus: Freud and Dora." In Bernheimer and Kahane, eds., *In Dora's Case*, pp. 254–276.

Stallybrass, Peter, and Allon White. *The Politics and Poetics of Transgression*. Ithaca: Cornell University Press, 1986.

Stanton, Domna. "Difference on Trial: A Critique of the Maternal Metaphor in Cixous, Irigaray, and Kristeva." In Miller, ed., *The Poetics of Gender*, pp. 157–182.

Starobinski, Jean. *La Relation critique*. Paris: Gallimard, 1970.

Stephanson, Anders. "Regarding Postmodernism: A Conversation with Fredric Jameson." In Ross, ed., *Universal Abandon?* pp. 3–30.

Stimpson, Catherine R. "Zero Degree Deviance: The Lesbian Novel in English." *Critical Inquiry*, 8:2 (1981): 363–379.

Stoekl, Allan. *Politics, Writing, Mutilation; The Cases of Bataille, Blanchot, Roussel, Leiris, and Ponge*. Minneapolis: University of Minnesota Press, 1985.

Suleiman, Susan Rubin. "As Is." In Hollier, ed., *A New History of French Literature*, pp. 1011–1018.

—— *Authoritarian Fictions: The Ideological Novel as a Literary Genre*. New York: Columbia University Press, 1983.

—— "Living Between, or, The Lone(love)liness of the *Alleinstehende Frau*." *Review of Contemporary Fiction*, Fall 1989, 124–127.

—— "Naming and Difference: Reflections on 'Modernism *versus* Postmodernism' in Literature." In Fokkema and Bertens, eds., *Approaching Postmodernism*, pp. 255–270.

Suleiman, Susan Rubin, ed. *The Female Body in Western Culture: Contemporary Perspectives*. Cambridge, Mass.: Harvard University Press, 1986.

Suleiman, Susan R., and Inge K. Crosman, eds., *The Reader in the Text: Essays on Audience and Interpretation.* Princeton: Princeton University Press, 1980.

Surya, Michel. *Bataille: La Mort à l'oeuvre.* Paris: Librairie Séguier, 1987.

Tanner, Tony. *Adultery in the Novel: Contract and Transgression.* Baltimore: Johns Hopkins University Press, 1980.

Tripp, Edward. *The Meridian Handbook of Classical Mythology.* New York: New American Library, 1970.

Venturi, Robert. *Complexity and Contradiction in Architecture.* New York: Museum of Modern Art and Doubleday, 1966.

Venturi, Robert, Denise Scott Brown, and Steven Izenour. *Learning from Las Vegas: The Forgotten Symbolism of Architectural Form,* revised edition. Cambridge, Mass.: MIT Press, 1988.

Vergine, Lea. *L'Autre Moitié de l'avant-garde, 1910–1940.* Paris: Editions des Femmes, 1982.

Vidal, Gore. *Myra Breckenridge.* New York: Bantam Books, 1968.

Wallis, Brian, ed. *Art after Modernism: Rethinking Representation.* New York and Boston: The New Museum of Contemporary Art and David R. Godine, 1984.

Wenzel, Helene. "The Text as Body Politics: An Appraisal of Monique Wittig's Writings in Context." *Feminist Studies,* 7:2 (1981): 264–287.

Wimmers, Inge Crosman. *Poetics of Reading: Approaches to the Novel.* Princeton: Princeton University Press, 1988.

Winnicott, D. W. *Playing and Reality.* New York: Basic Books, 1971.

Winterson, Jeanette. *Boating for Beginners.* London: Methuen, 1985.

—— *Oranges Are Not the Only Fruit.* New York: Atlantic Monthly Press, 1987. (Original edition, 1985.)

—— *The Passion.* New York: Atlantic Monthly Press, 1988.

Wittgenstein, Ludwig. *Philosophical Investigations,* trans. G. E. M. Anscombe. Oxford: Blackwell, 1972.

Wittig, Monique. *Le Corps lesbien.* Paris: Editions de Minuit, 1973. English translation: *The Lesbian Body,* trans. David LeVay. Boston: Beacon Press, 1986.

—— *Les Guérillères.* Paris: Editions de Minuit, 1969. English translation: *Les Guérillères,* trans. David LeVay. Boston: Beacon Press, 1985.

—— *Virgile, non.* Paris: Editions de Minuit, 1985.

—— *Le Voyage sans fin.* Paris: VLASTA, 1985.

Wittig, Monique, and Sande Zeig. *Brouillon pour un dictionnaire des amantes.* Paris: Grasset, 1976.

Wollen, Peter. "The Situationist International." *New Left Review,* 174 (March 1989): 67–95.

Yaeger, Patricia. *Honey-Mad Women: Emancipatory Strategies in Women's Writing.* New York: Columbia University Press, 1988.

Zürn, Unica. *L'Homme-Jasmin.* Paris: Gallimard, 1971.

—— *Sombre Printemps.* Paris: Belfond, 1985.

Index